# THE LAST SHIFT

# THE LAST SHIFT

## THE DECLINE OF HANDLOOM WEAVING IN NINETEENTH-CENTURY LANCASHIRE

*Geoffrey Timmins*

**Manchester University Press**
Manchester and New York

*Distributed exclusively in the USA and Canada by St. Martin's Press*

Copyright © Geoffrey Timmins 1993

*Published by* Manchester University Press
Oxford Road, Manchester M13 9PL, UK
*and* Room 400, 175 Fifth Avenue, New York, NY10010, USA

*Distributed exclusively in the USA and Canada*
*by* St. Martin's Press, Inc., 175 Fifth Avenue, New York,
NY 10010, USA

*British Library Cataloguing-in-Publication Data*
A catalogue record for this book is available from the British Library

*Library of Congress Cataloging-in-Publication Data*
Timmins, Geoffrey.
    The last shift: the decline of handloom weaving in nineteenth
-century Lancashire / Geoffrey Timmins.
      p.   cm.
    Includes bibliographical references and index.
    ISBN 0 7190-3725-5
    1. Handloom industry—England—Lancashire—History—19th century,
I. Title.
HD9861.7, L35T48   1993
338.4′767702822′094276—dc20                          92-26876

ISBN 0 7190 3725 5 *hardback*

Typeset in Hong Kong
by Graphicraft Typesetters Ltd., Hong Kong
Printed in Great Britain
by Biddles Ltd., Guildford and King's Lynn

# CONTENTS

|   | | page | |
|---|---|---|---|
| | Preface | page | vii |
| | List of abbreviations | | viii |
| | List of tables, maps, figures and plates | | ix |
| | Introduction | | 1 |
| | *Technological change during British industrialisation* | | |
| | *Sectoral studies of domestic outwork* | | |
| | *The cotton industry and outwork* | | |
| 1 | The changing balance in weaving technology: an overview | | 17 |
| | *The rise of the powerloom* | | |
| | *The demise of hand weaving* | | |
| 2 | The economic importance of hand weaving in the early nineteenth century | | 35 |
| | *Numbers of handloom weavers* | | |
| | *Geographical variation* | | |
| | *Impact on settlement formation* | | |
| 3 | The nature of the hand weaving labour force | | 71 |
| | *The emergence of the specialist weaver* | | |
| | *The change to cotton weaving* | | |
| 4 | The onset of decline in cotton hand weaving | | 91 |
| | *The impact of the mid-1830s trade upturn* | | |
| | *Intra-regional variation* | | |
| 5 | The survival of hand weaving in the mid-Victorian period | | 107 |
| | *Overall numbers and dependency* | | |
| | *Age/sex distribution* | | |

| | | |
|---|---|---|
| 6 | The means of survival | 128 |
| | *Hand weavers and family income* | |
| | *Type of fabric* | |
| 7 | Mid-Victorian hand weavers: reasons for survival | 146 |
| | *Historiographical issues* | |
| | *New perspectives* | |
| | Conclusion | 184 |
| | Bibliography | 189 |
| | Appendices | |
| | A1. *Computing hand weaver numbers in early nineteenth century Lancashire* | 200 |
| | A2. *Computing hand weaver numbers in mid-Victorian Lancashire* | 224 |
| | A3. *Statistical techniques* | 241 |
| | Index | 245 |

# PREFACE

In preparing this book, and the thesis upon which it is based, I am indebted to many people. Not least amongst them are the staffs of numerous libraries in the north-west and of the Lancashire County Record Office. They have provided most of the source material I have used and have invariably offered constructive and informed advice. The Brandwood illustrations are reproduced by courtesy of Turton Tower Museum.

I have benefited greatly from help given by Mary Rose, Maurice Kirby and John Walton of Lancaster University; by John Lyons of the University of Miami; and by Mike Rothwell. Hilary Glendinning and Carol Angarad have both assisted in the transcription of census material, whilst my wife, Carol, has provided support and help in so many ways, but especially in proof-reading and script collating. Profound thanks are also due to Ralph Peace, Peter van Dyke and John Payne for help with statistical techniques and to Avril Griffiths for drawing the maps and figures.

I was particularly fortunate to have Douglas Farnie of Manchester University as external examiner for my thesis. His perceptive and authoritative advice has been invaluable, especially in pointing to further lines of research. Despite the unremitting pressures of higher education lecturing, these are being actively pursued as opportunity arises.

My heaviest debt is to my thesis supervisor, Oliver Westall of Lancaster University. Throughout a period which must at times have seemed interminable, he provided constant advice and encouragement, as well as posing formidable challenges. I have learned a great deal from him and have enjoyed the experience.

# LIST OF ABBREVIATIONS

| | |
|---|---|
| BAS | Bolton Archive Service |
| *BC* | *Bolton Chronicle* |
| *BH* | *Business History* |
| BlMu | Blackburn Museum |
| *BM* | *Blackburn Mail* |
| BRL | Blackburn Reference Library |
| *BS* | *Blackburn Standard* |
| CRL | Chorley Reference Library |
| *EcHR* | *Economic History Review* |
| *EEH* | *Explorations in Economic History* |
| ED | Enumeration District |
| *HWJ* | *History Workshop Journal* |
| *JEH* | *Journal of Economic History* |
| *LPS* | *Local Population Studies* |
| LRO | Lancashire Record Office |
| MCLA | Manchester Central Library Archives |
| *MSA* | *Manchester and Salford Advertiser* |
| *P & P* | *Past and Present* |
| *PC* | *Preston Chronicle* |
| *PG* | *Preston Guardian* |
| PP | Parliamentary Papers |
| *PrP* | *Preston Pilot* |
| RRL | Rawtenstall Reference Library |
| *TL & CAS* | *Transactions of the Lancashire and Cheshire Antiquarian Society* |
| *THSL & C* | *Transactions of the Historic Society of Lancashire and Cheshire* |
| TTM | Turton Tower Museum |

# LIST OF TABLES, MAPS, FIGURES AND PLATES

### Tables

| | | |
|---|---|---|
| 1.1 | Growth of powerloom use in Great Britain, 1835–50 | 20 |
| 1.2 | Pre-Victorian estimates of the number of hand weavers in the British cotton industry | 25 |
| 1.3 | Hand weavers in the British cotton industry: Ellison's estimates | 27 |
| 1.4 | Numbers of cotton handloom weavers in Britain, 1806–62: Wood's estimates | 28 |
| 2.1 | Handloom weaver totals in Lancashire, 1821 | 37 |
| 2.2 | Rankings of bridegroom weaver proportions in Lancashire parishes, groups of parishes and parish districts, 1818–22 | 44 |
| 2.3 | Hand weaver concentrations in Lancashire rural districts, 1818–22 | 46 |
| 2.4 | Proportions of dwellings in rural areas occupied by hand weavers in 1851 | 63 |
| 4.1 | Handloom weaver totals in south Lancashire towns, 1834–36 | 98 |
| 5.1 | Estimates of handloom weavers in Lancashire, 1851–71 | 109 |
| 5.2 | Hand weaver numbers, 1821 and 1851 | 112 |
| 5.3 | Hand and power weavers in central Lancashire, 1851 and 1861 | 114 |
| 5.4 | Proportions of hand and power weavers in Lancashire's major textile towns, 1851 and 1861 | 116 |
| 5.5 | Female and child handloom weavers in selected districts, 1851 and 1861 | 119 |
| 5.6 | Handloom weavers by age group and gender in selected districts, 1851 and 1861 | 120 |
| 5.7 | Proportions of male and female hand weavers in districts with power weaving sheds, 1861 | 122 |

| | | |
|---|---|---|
| 6.1 | Weekly earnings in Manchester trades, 1832 | 131 |
| 6.2 | Hand weavers by fabric type, 1851–71 | 136 |
| 7.1 | Mid-Victorian handloom weaving manufacturers | 171 |
| A1.1 | Number of bridegroom weavers recorded in Lancashire Anglican registers, 1813–17 | 204 |
| A1.2 | Number of bridegroom weavers recorded in Lancashire Anglican registers, 1818–22 | 205 |
| A1.3 | Frequency of monthly gaps in Lancashire marriage registers, 1813–22 | 207 |
| A1.4 | Father and bridegroom weaver numbers, 1813–22 | 212 |
| A1.5 | Rankings of bridegroom weaver proportions in Lancashire parishes, groups of parishes and parish districts, 1813–17 | 216 |
| A1.6 | Anglican and non-Anglican church sittings in Lancashire, 1851 | 217 |
| A1.7 | Male weavers in Lancashire, 1821 | 218 |
| A1.8 | Handloom weavers recorded in selected census enumerations | 221 |
| A2.1 | Handloom weavers in Blackburn parish, 1851 | 226 |
| A2.2 | Handloom weavers in smaller Lancashire towns, 1851 | 226 |
| A2.3 | Age distribution of powerloom weavers in selected districts, 1851 and 1871 | 231 |

## Maps

| | | |
|---|---|---|
| 1 | Hand weaver proportions in the Lancashire textile districts, 1818–22 | 45 |
| 2 | Club Houses, Horwich in the mid-1840s | 61 |
| 3 | Hand weavers' cottages at Chorley, *c.* 1845 | 64 |
| 4 | Lancashire parishes, 1822 | 206 |
| 5 | Parish groups and parish divisions in the early 1820s | 208 |
| 6 | The Whitefield area in the mid-1840s | 234 |

## Figures

| | | |
|---|---|---|
| A1.1 | Relationship of father and bridegroom weaver numbers in selected Lancashire districts, 1813–22 | 214 |
| A1.2 | Relationship of father and bridegroom weaver proportions in selected Lancashire districts, 1813–22 | 215 |

## Plates

| | | |
|---|---|---|
| 1 | Armygreaves House, Turton, near Bolton, Brandwood Account Book | 54 |
| 2 | West View Place, Blackburn | 55 |
| 3 | Plan of cellar loomshops, Brandwood Account Book | 56 |

*List of tables, maps, figures and plates*

| | | |
|---|---|---|
| 4 | Club Houses weavers' cottages, Horwich | 62 |
| 5 | Urban hand weavers' colony, Limbrick, Blackburn | 65 |
| 6 | Former hand weavers' cottages, Top o'th Lane, Brindle | 83 |
| 7 | Rear loomshop weavers' cottages, Lower Darwen | 84 |
| 8 | Plan of rear loomshop weavers' cottages, Brandwood Account Book | 85 |
| 9 | Cottages built with upper-storey loomshops, Blacko, near Colne | 87 |

# INTRODUCTION

## 1 Technological change during British industrialisation

A recurring theme in the literature on early and mid-nineteenth century economic history is that, for the most part, British industrialisation was achieved with relatively low levels of technology. The theme has become commonplace in general accounts of the Industrial Revolution era, stress being laid on the finding that, at mid-century, steam-powered mechanisation was confined to only a few economic sectors and that relatively small numbers were employed in factory industry.[1] It is a theme of much interest to those taking an international perspective on industrial development and has been seen to have implications for Britain's relative economic decline in the late nineteenth century and beyond. Essentially, its proponents have sought to correct an overemphasis on the degree of technological advance achieved during Britain's Industrial Revolution.

Prominent amongst recent contributors to the theme is N. F. R. Crafts. In his major reassessment of the nature and course of British Industrialisation, he highlights the low levels of productivity associated with the persistence of traditional manufacturing activity. He writes:

> As a useful crude approximation, it can be said that the triumph of the industrial revolution lay in getting a lot of workers into industry rather than obtaining high productivity from them once there.[2]

Taking the economy overall, he argues that productivity only improved slowly until the second quarter of the nineteenth century, attaining around 0.2 per cent between 1760 and 1800; 0.3 per cent between 1800 and 1830; and 0.8 per cent from 1830 to 1860. Just a few sectors dominated this growth, cotton accounting for perhaps half the total.[3]

Such low productivity levels do not surprise Crafts, since much of British manufacturing remained traditional. As late as 1841, no more than one in five workers could be counted amongst those in 'revolutionised industry'. In few parts of the country would this figure have reached 30 per cent, whilst in most of southern England it would have been well under 10 per cent. Even in Lancashire and the West Riding, probably the most advanced industrial areas, figures of under 40 per cent would have applied.[4] Crafts concedes that the extent of structural change in the British economy was far more advanced than in the rest of Europe, but points out that much industrial activity remained small-scale, being little affected by the use of steam power.[5] In short, a picture is drawn of an economy characterised by low productivity growth, with a good deal of manufacturing activity remaining traditional and innovation being far from pervasive.[6]

Other recent contributors to the discussion have also stressed Britain's low productivity levels. For example, Patrick O'Brien and Caglar Keyder have argued that, until the 1890s, the average productivity of labour employed in French industry remained above that of Britain.[7] Explanations, they feel, can be couched in labour supply terms.

In Britain the continuous influx of unskilled labour into the workshop and smaller-scale sector of industry kept average labour productivity from rising, either to the levels attained in the factory sector or up to the standards achieved in large areas of manufacturing in France.[8]

They argue that the supply of industrial labour in Britain grew faster than in France because population rose at about three times the French rate and because French agriculturalists absorbed a far higher proportion of additional labour supplies than their British counterparts. Crafts' estimates suggest that Britain actually had a small edge over France in terms of labour productivity throughout the Victorian years, though he accepts O'Brien and Keyder's contention that British labour productivity could not be regarded as being particularly high.[9] And it should be noted that domestic production remained important in the French economy during this period,[10] as was also the case elsewhere in Europe.[11]

The continuing use of hand technology in nineteenth-century Britain is equally evident in discussions on capital formation. In reviewing the estimates made by Phyllis Deane and C. H. Feinstein for this period, François Crouzet remarks on the 'astonishingly low' proportion of UK national product that was absorbed in fixed capital formation. Even taking Feinstein's estimates, which, Crouzet notes, are 'noticeably and consistently' higher than those of Deane, fixed capital expenditure still averaged only 7.5 per cent of GNP during the 1860s and did not attain a decennial average of 8 per cent until the early twentieth century.[12] These figures compare with between 20–25 per cent that advanced countries have experienced since World War II and scarcely suggest that a marked degree of mechanisation had been achieved in Britain during the conventional Industrial Revolution or that mechanisation proceeded with any rapidity thereafter. It is true that in commenting on the sectoral distribution of his figures, Feinstein draws attention to a sharp increase in fixed capital expenditure by trade and industry between 1820 and

## Introduction

1860 — especially on machines that 'symbolise the industrial revolution' — but he also cautions that the sums involved were small in proportion both to national income and to expenditure on industrial and other types of building.[13] G. N. von Tunzelmann has reached a similar conclusion.

Even where technical change did smite, its normally small-scale character meant that there was little demand for large capital expenditures.[14]

Such a view is favoured by others, including Crafts, though J. G. Williamson maintains that low investment in Britain during the Industrial Revolution was a function of an inelastic savings supply rather than of modest investment demands associated with limited technical progress. Scarce savings encouraged firms to keep their investment requirements low.[15]

In explaining the lack of technological advance associated with low productivity and limited capital formation in nineteenth century Britain, historians have frequently turned to labour supply arguments, as in the case of O'Brien and Keyder. In essence, these arguments hold that the availability of a cheap and plentiful labour force gave little incentive for manufacturers to switch from hand techniques to mechanical production. The ramifications of this approach have long engaged the interest of historians and remain to the fore in recent discussions on the nature of British industrialisation.

Perhaps the best-known statement of the argument is that of H. J. Habakkuk. His approach, as S. B. Saul observes, is one of expounding ideas rather than upon presenting the fruits of detailed research.[16] Habakkuk adopts a comparative stance, seeking to offer explanations as to why, in several economic sectors, technological change was less advanced in Britain during the nineteenth century than in the United States. The crux of his argument is that the differences can be largely explained in terms of relative labour and capital costs. Thus, the cost of labour relative to the cost of capital was higher in the United States than in Britain, a reflection of the availability of British labour and the scarcity of American. He recognises that this was not the sole determinant of the differences, but it did profoundly affect the nature of the industrialisation process. He writes:

It seems obvious — it certainly seemed so to contemporaries — that the dearness and inelasticity of American, compared with British labour, gave the American entrepreneur with a given capital a greater inducement than his British counterpart to replace labour by machines.[17]

The relative high cost of industrial labour in America arose from the competitive rates paid to agricultural workers there, whose marginal product was high. If labour was to be attracted to industry, employers had to offer high real wages comparable with those obtainable in agriculture. In Britain, by contrast, industrialists could

acquire labour from agriculture at a wage equal to the very low product of the marginal agricultural labourer plus an addition to cover costs of transport and of overcoming inertia.[18]

One refinement of Habakkuk's thesis concerns types of labour. He reasons that the highest differentials between Britain and the United States occurred with unskilled labour, wages in the latter country being between a third to a half higher for this group during the early nineteenth century. By contrast, the figure was only about 20 per cent for semi-skilled labour, performing tasks of 'the type undertaken by women in the textile industry'.[19] Habukkuk's argument, therefore, is less powerful with regard to some sectors in manufacturing industry than to others, though even a differential of 20 per cent would have been significant, especially given the high proportion that labour costs formed of total costs.

Foremost amongst the critics of Habakkuk's analysis is J. S. Field. He complains that those taking the Habakkuk line have been too easily swayed by comments of contemporary British observers, whose reports on American industry were far from representative. In fact, Field maintains, American technology was not only less machine-intensive than British technology, but, more generally, it was less capital-intensive. At the root of the issue lie the higher interest rates in America. These forced American industrialists to devise procedures which enabled them to reduce their stocks of fixed and working capital, including running their machinery faster and depreciating it more quickly.[20]

Field's observations emphasise the nature of American rather than British industry and do not negate the idea that, in general, British entrepreneurs still operated with low levels of technology during the mid-nineteenth century and beyond. Indeed, the persistence of hand techniques in mid-Victorian Britain has been comprehensively documented by Raphael Samuel. Not surprisingly, his Marxist perspective highlights the importance of labour rather than capital in promoting Britain's industrialisation. He thus argues that the balance of advantage between steam power and hand technology was then far from settled, labour often proving more attractive to entrepreneurs than machinery.[21] Several explanations are offered, including the notion of labour abundance. With this he strongly agrees, maintaining that, in striking contrast to the Industrial Revolution period, labour surpluses were usual. In workshop trades, as in labouring work, there existed a 'reserve army of labour', unable to find regular work and forced to travel in search of new opportunities.[22]

Further discussion on the link between abundant labour and lack of technological progress is found in the debate between O. E. Williamson and S. R. H. Jones on why the factory system developed in nineteenth century Britain. Their explanations centre on cost reductions arising through the stricter control of factory operatives compared with outworkers; on savings resulting from transferring a set of transaction costs (including those arising from transporting goods, theft of materials and maintenance of inventories) from the market into the firm; and on the opportunities offered by the factory environment to exploit technological change to the maximum extent. Of course, closer control of workers and transfer of outwork costs could be achieved in factories using only hand technology. Whether the economies arising would have been sufficient to induce entrepreneurs to abandon

*Introduction*

domestic production is debatable, however. Ultimately, their decision may have depended on whether significant economies could also be reaped from technological change. Unless and until this happened, their preference may have continued to lie strongly with hand techniques and outwork production,[23] as was normally the case in textile weaving.[24] That such a choice was available reflects Britain's early start in industrialisation. Entrepreneurs in countries industrialising later had little choice but to use new techniques if they were to compete effectively.

The issue is complicated, as Jones observes, by the fact that entrepreneurs had to take into account the economic advantages obtained from outwork. To the fore here were cheap labour costs. These arose because a large pool of labour existed, often rurally based and often comprising the elderly, housewives and children, which was unable or unwilling to take factory jobs. Such people were prepared to work for payment little above subsistence level. Indeed, as far as women are concerned, Sonya Rose argues that gender ideology reinforced payment of low wages by emphasising domestic responsibilities and dependency.[25] Moreover, low levels of investment in buildings and machinery under the putting-out system meant that employers were not averse to hiring and dimissing outworkers in line with trade cycle movements. From their standpoint, outwork was a convenient and flexible system of employment.

One other aspect of the relationship between labour supply and the nature of British industrialisation to emerge in recent writings concerns the manner in which large amounts of labour became available for industrial purposes. As far as Crafts is concerned, the explanation lies in a more rapid movement of labour from agriculture to industry than was usual elsewhere, the result of Britain's relatively high levels of agricultural productivity.[26] Here is the corollary of O'Brien and Keyder's finding that French agriculture absorbed a higher proportion of available labour than British. That British agriculture was as productive as Crafts maintains, however, is doubted by Joel Mokyr, largely from concern about the output and labour force data upon which Crafts' calculations are based. As far as the supply of factory labour is concerned, Mokyr prefers to emphasise the importance of rural labour drawn from households engaged in non-agricultural occupations, observing that, as late as 1850, hundreds of thousands of such workers were to be found in cottage industries and 'little one-family workshops'.[27] How far such people were welcomed by factory owners is debatable, though, especially the older ones amongst them. It is true that their children may often have been better placed, but, as Hugh Cunningham shows, it is easy to exaggerate the extent to which young children could find jobs in factories, or, indeed, in other occupations.[28] Yet for older children the opportunities were often there, whether their background was agricultural or not. And as Mary Rose has demonstrated, transfer of pauper children into industrial work was for long facilitated by positive attitudes of parishes and charitable institutions.[29]

Whilst historians have been especially concerned with labour supply issues in explaining the limited technological advance in nineteenth century Britain, other

5

considerations have not been ignored. They are conveniently, if rather graphically, summarised by Raphael Samuel. One concerns improvements in the productivity of traditional technology. These, Samuel asserts, arose partly from manufacturers 'screwing down piece rates' to the point where earnings only reached subsistence level by the use of unpaid family labour. How far employers could adopt this policy, and whether families were able to respond, is uncertain, though Samuel maintains that the practice was prevalent in the clothing and furniture trades and in nail- and chain-making. More convincing is the argument he raises concerning the technical shortcomings of new machinery. All too often, he suggests, claims made by inventors did not materialise and even when new machines could be applied, only modest improvements in productivity might result. Of substance, too, is the argument he advances concerning the difficulty firms experienced in raising the finance they required to mechanise. For small firms 'engaged in a week-by-week struggle for survival', the cost of mechanisation was unthinkable and even for large concerns it could be daunting. Yet this line of argument needs qualification, not least because small firms were often soundly based and might not mechanise for other reasons. Finally, Samuel turns to demand-side aspects. He mentions that consumers might still prefer hand-made wares, since these could be of high quality and superior finish. Moreover, from the manufacturer's point of view, the limited or irregular demand for a product could make the installation of machinery unprofitable.[30] Both are appealing arguments, but, because evidence is sparse, the extent to which they operated can be extremely difficult to judge.

In concluding his discussion, Samuel stresses the juxtaposition of hand and steam technology.

In mid-Victorian times, as earlier in the nineteenth century, they represented concurrent phases of capitalist growth, feeding on one another's achievements, endorsing one another's effects.[31]

That 'dualism' of this type was frequent in nineteenth century Britain has been noted by several scholars,[32] and David Landes mentions that some hand trades grew appreciably as mechanisation in related sectors led to marked reductions in costs and final product prices.[33] This was so, for example, in the clothing trades, which benefited greatly from technical advances in yarn and cloth production. Complementary relationships of this type, which arose between sequential stages of production, have also been remarked upon by John Lyons. He refines the concept by observing that modern and traditional sectors could equally well coexist at the same stage of production, as in textile weaving, thereby raising the question as to whether interaction between the two sectors was complementary, competitive, or a mixture of the two.[34]

Whilst the argument that technological advance had made comparatively little headway in Britain by the mid-nineteenth century has received much support in recent writing, it is by no means a new idea and can certainly be traced back to the writings of J. H. Clapham and the Hammonds. Thus, commenting on the period

*Introduction*

1820–50, Clapham states that, beyond the engineering, textile and metallurgical industries, the 'applications of novel machinery and of steam power were only tentative'.³⁵ And the Hammonds remark that for half a century after steam power was introduced, domestic trades continued to expand alongside factory industry.³⁶ These ideas are not explored in any depth, but they provide an early exposition of the gradualist viewpoint. They also contrast sharply with the ideas propounded in the 1950s and 1960s by Ashton and especially Rostow, which, in the Toynbee tradition, emphasise the dramatic nature of British industrialisation.³⁷ However, there now exists a considerable body of literature, which not only accepts a gradualist stance, but which has integrated it into a wider analytical framework, thereby enhancing understanding of British industrialisation, especially in relation to the experience of other countries.

## 2 Sectoral studies of domestic outwork

Much of the discussion about low productivity and lack of innovation in nineteenth century Britain has taken place at a macro-economic level. However, some historians have addressed these issues from the standpoint of particular industries or groups of related industries. This is true of Duncan Bythell and James Schmiechen. Bythell deals principally with outwork in textiles, shoes and clothing and in nail- and chain-making. In seeking to explain their durability during the nineteenth century, he sets the modest aim of 'introducing some of the pitfalls and possibilities'.³⁸ Nevertheless, his discussion is comprehensive, embracing both supply- and demand-side aspects. Schmiechen's work, which is concerned with the London clothing trades, examines the growth of sweated outwork as a substitute for factory work during the half century after 1860. His is a study which demonstrates that exceptions did exist to the long-term tendency in the British economy for production to become centralised.³⁹

With regard to the supply-side, Bythell points out that the potential amount of outwork labour in nineteenth century Britain was massive. This was because population growth was rapid; little training was normally required; barriers to entry were absent; and employees could be drawn from both sexes and from all working age groups. As a result, a high proportion of outworkers were women, children and elderly people. They regarded their work as part-time or casual, providing only a supplement to family income. They entered outwork because no other type of employment was available locally or because it was the only type of work they could conveniently undertake. The survival of outwork was helped by a measure of labour immobility, not least amongst elderly people convinced they were 'too old to change'. Such conservatism might be encouraged by out relief granted under Poor Law provisions and by positive attitudes amongst the labour force to domestic work.⁴⁰

As to whether capital shortages or the inadequacies of technology explain the long survival of industrial outwork, Bythell is sceptical. He argues that the costs of building and rents in urban centres might have deterred employers from sinking capital into large workshops or factories, though the point has less force when applied to sites on town outskirts, which industrialists increasingly occupied.[41] He also maintains that entrepreneurs would not have lacked the resources to purchase machines, since, in many cases, they were already providing them for outworkers. Sometimes, moreover, the equipment outworkers required was 'remarkably sophisticated and expensive'. He concludes that, despite defects in the nineteenth century capital market, investment funds could be made available when required. With regard to the inadequacies of technology, he suggests that early nineteenth century machines were often imperfect and that their adoption might not be justified because market size was limited. By the mid-nineteenth century, however, the establishment of a specialised machine-making industry allowed the technical shortcomings of machinery to be effectively tackled.[42]

Turning to assess how market considerations helped outwork to continue, Bythell draws a distinction between industries in which long-term demand grew steadily and those in which it rose in 'swift, sharp, but irregular bursts'. It was in the latter circumstances that mechanisation would have taken place more quickly, since periods would soon have arisen when the existing capacity of the outwork system would have been stretched beyond its limits. This was the more likely when overseas as well as home markets were being served and when semi-manufactured rather than final products were concerned. For these reasons, the textile trades became mechanised sooner than the clothing and boot and shoe trades.[43] It should be noted, though, that volatile markets would also have encouraged employers to keep a reserve of outwork labour, so they could cope with periods of abnormal demand.

Having assessed the economic influences on the survival of outwork, Bythell turns to consider how far political influences should be taken into account. In particular, he explores the impact of collective actions by the outworkers themselves, not least through trade unionism and radical politics, and by the state. Through neither means, however, were the outworkers he studied able to resolve the fundamental difficulties they faced concerning long hours of toil, inadequate wages and appalling working conditions.[44] And in terms of halting mechanisation, they achieved only short-term and localised success, as Church found in the case of the footwear trades.[45]

Turning briefly to Schmiechen, it is apparent that, in several respects, his research develops the views put forward by Bythell. He makes it clear, for example, that the growth of outwork in the clothing trades was helped by an abundant supply of cheap labour, especially female and alien Jew; by the ease with which machine sewing could be learned; by low entry costs in the trade; and by the high rents in London which prohibited factory development.[46] He shows, too, that demand-side aspects were important, as an insatiable requirement for ready-made, mass-produced clothing developed. Increasingly this came from the home market and was closely associated with the rise of middle-class purchasing power.[47]

*Introduction*

## 3  The cotton industry and outwork

It is apparent from the foregoing discussion that, across a wide section of British industry, hand techniques continued to prevail beyond the mid-nineteenth century; that differing views have been expressed as to why this was so; and that consideration of the theme has proved as durable as it has ubiquitous. Yet one industry which does not feature to any great extent in these debates is cotton textiles.

The conventional view of development in this industry offers two perspectives which appear contradictory and which have not been adequately integrated. On the one hand, the great expansion of domestic weaving during the late eighteenth and early nineteenth centuries is acknowledged. So, too, is its durability, factory weaving not becoming dominant until perhaps the 1830s. On the other, maybe as a residual idea from the 1960s, the industry is still seen as a leading sector, exhibiting dramatic technological and industrial change. Indeed, in textbooks at least, the contributions made by that redoubtable trio of textile luminaries, Hargreaves, Arkwright and Crompton, continue to receive particular, and perhaps undue, attention.

But how appropriate is such an interpretation? After all, it is easy to overstate the degree of innovation in the cotton trade from the late eighteenth century onwards. Not only was technical change more pronounced in spinning than in weaving and finishing, but the degree of mechanisation it brought was far from complete. Thus, the jenny remained a hand machine and the mule was not made 'self-acting' until the late 1820s.[48] Nor would the hand mule have been superseded without some delay. This is not to deny that improved textile machinery helped greatly to expand output of cotton thread and to create a vast demand for handloom weavers. Indeed, by the early nineteenth century, before the powerloom had made any appreciable advances, cotton hand weaving gave direct employment to as many as a quarter of a million people.[49] Technological change in cotton spinning created the most significant expansion of traditional, handicraft industry that was ever achieved in the British economy.

Given the massive size attained by the cotton hand weaving trade and the interest of historians in the lack of innovation in nineteenth century British industry, it is surprising that the two issues have not been considered in relation to one another. Interest has centred on the rate at which handloom weaving declined, so that its importance has inevitably been seen in rather negative terms. Hand weavers have been viewed more as the victims of economic change than as a group which continued to make a significant, albeit a diminishing, contribution to output and employment in the textile industry, even into the mid-Victorian period.

It is evident, then, that a reinterpretation of the way in which the British cotton industry developed during the nineteenth century is needed, taking account of recent findings about the nature and pace of industrialisation in the economy as a whole. This revision recognises that outwork based on intermediate technology continued to play a central role in promoting economic growth well beyond the early decades of the century and that, in consequence, productivity levels remained low. It differs from other interpretations, however, in arguing that, to a much greater extent than has been recognised, this was also the case with cotton textiles, usually seen as the most advanced sector of the economy and one in which innovation and relatively high productivity prevailed. Taking the weaving branch of the trade as its focus, it argues that mechanisation took place extremely gradually and hand techniques remained surprisingly durable. It demonstrates that significant decline in hand weaving began later, and took far longer to complete, than has been generally recognised. To appreciate this, and to understand why it was so, provides important new insights into the manner in which Britain's industrialisation was achieved.

In propounding this viewpoint, it is necessary to enter into a long-standing controversy amongst historians as to the rate at which the decline in cotton handloom weaving took place. At one extreme, and at variance with the interpretation given in this book, is the view of Duncan Bythell. He maintains that the trade was quickly replaced by power weaving, beginning its decline in the mid-1820s and having virtually disappeared by mid-century. 'Thus', he remarks,

the speed with which the handloom weavers disappeared, rather than the protraction of their agony, is the really notable feature of their history — although since Lancashire was at the time the world's most advanced industrial region we should hardly be surprised to find that labour there redeployed itself so easily.[50]

Written in the 1960s, Bythell's is very much a revisionist view, tying in well with current ideas on the dramatic nature of industrial change, but differing sharply from that of earlier historians. For instance, S. J. Chapman, writing in the early years of this century, argues that cotton hand weaving was carried on to an appreciable extent, in some places and in some goods, well into the second half of the nineteenth century.[51] According to J. H. Clapham, perhaps 40,000 to 50,000 people were still employed in cotton weaving at mid-century. However, he thought this figure to have been only around 20 per cent of the early 1830s total.[52] Numbers of this order, in fact, have often been quoted, though little attempt has been made to assess their accuracy.

In considering the observations of these and other historians, it becomes apparent that heavy reliance has been placed on fragmentary and often impressionistic evidence, especially that derived from the opinions of contemporaries. This raises the question as to whether more authoritative estimates of cotton hand weaver numbers might be prepared, drawing on sources that have as yet been little exploited. Amongst them, mid-Victorian census schedules stand out. Several local studies have pointed to the insights that can be obtained from using this source to assess occupational distributions, as well as to the type of difficulties that might be encountered.[53] Yet they strongly suggest that census material can be used to analyse the changing importance of cotton hand weaving during the mid-Victorian years with a very high degree of precision.

To confine attention largely to the 1850s and 1860s, however, produces a limited picture of this change. In particular, it does not enable any judgement to be made of how far, in employment terms, the trade had diminished from the peak years of the early nineteenth century, without relying on other contemporary estimates, equally untested. Nor does it allow much to be said about any geographical variation in the rate of change, since no appraisal has been made of the extent to which the trade became localised during the peak years. Further, by omitting the long-term perspective, the explanatory potential of the study is limited; it would not be possible, for example, to see how far the survival of hand weaving was a rural rather than an urban phenomenon.

It is necessary, therefore, to take the study back into the early decades of the nineteenth century. Occupational data are available for this period in parish register entries — a neglected but valuable source for this purpose as A. E. Wrigley and M. T. Wild have shown — and these may be used to assess the extent of dependency on hand weaving from district to district.[54] Moreover, by comparing the census detail with that obtained from parish registers, a numerical assessment can be made of the long-term changes in employment opportunities offered by handloom weaving.

This approach allows a new perspective to be taken. Emphasis has usually been placed on changes in the textile industry rather than on continuities. As a result, the contribution of the new technology has been assessed at the expense of the traditional. Yet, as has been shown in other industries, the latter often remained significant well into the mid-Victorian era. Preliminary research indicated this would also be the case in cotton weaving. Accordingly, new insights might be obtained by taking a stance concentrating on developments within the traditional technology rather than on its abandonment.

To make as full an examination as possible of the extent to which hand weaving survived in the mid-Victorian period, the scope of the research has been extended beyond the cotton industry. It is commonplace for historians to state that redundant cotton hand weavers turned to weaving silk and other fabrics as competition from the powerloom intensified. Census schedule evidence suggests that this happened in a few districts, though its overall importance should not be exaggerated. Even so, that numerous handloom weavers were willing to adapt to changing circumstances, including moving into fine or fancy cottons, or into non-cottons, and were able to do so, suggest key reasons for their survival, notwithstanding the relentless advance of the powerloom.

The geographical coverage of the study is restricted to Lancashire, wherein resided the bulk of Britain's cotton handloom weavers. Thus, a reasonably full analysis of the trade is undertaken, as well as one which allows general ideas about outwork to be tested at a regional level. Besides, useful data are available on the cotton hand weaving trade of Scotland, the other major centre, in Norman Murray's recent study.[55] Parish register and census material for the whole of the Lancashire textile districts is examined, thereby enabling the nature and changing importance of the trade to be assessed in detail. Such an approach inevitably entails a formidable task of numerical collation, about which any scholar might have serious misgivings. Yet, in the absence of suitable alternative evidence and because the issues involved are crucial in obtaining a full appreciation of Britain's industrial development, the work is seen as essential.

The book takes the following form. In Chapter 1, a reassessment is made of the pace at which the powerloom was introduced, arguing this was much slower than has been appreciated. It is also noted that, prior to the Victorian era, the powerloom had little impact in rural areas. Additionally, a critical review is undertaken of historians' ideas about how quickly cotton hand weaving was abandoned, highlighting the disagreement between them and stressing the need for neglected evidence from censuses and parish registers to be utilised.

In Chapter 2, new estimates of hand weaver numbers in early nineteenth century Lancashire are presented. Based on baptism and marriage register data, they show the fundamental importance of hand weaving in the Lancashire economy when the trade was at, or near to, its height. Additionally, they allow geographical variation in the importance of hand weaving to be considered. This links the study with the debate on proto-industrialisation, since the new estimates allow analysis of one of the central concepts in the debate, namely the extent to which early handicraft industry became concentrated in upland pastoral districts, where advantage could be taken of cheap and plentiful labour supplies. It is argued that the notion accords well with the Lancashire experience, but that it needs qualification, since the association between upland areas and textile production does not always hold and factors other than labour availability influenced the localisation of textile production in the upland districts. Lastly, the impact of colonisation by hand weavers on the formation of rural and urban settlement is examined. It is argued that this was profound, not only extending existing settlement to a substantial degree, but also giving rise to numerous new settlements, mostly comprising short terraces of up to twenty or so dwellings.

Unfortunately, the parish register data yield little information about the nature of the hand weaving labour force. In assessing the economic importance of the trade, though, it is necessary to investigate the extent to which hand weavers became specialist workers, rather than, as they had often been during the proto-industrial era, workers who derived income from both farming and weaving. Also, since hand technology gave way to mechanisation at differing rates according to the type of fabric woven, the extent to which cotton weaving grew to prominence in Lancashire must be assessed. Unless this is done, it is not possible to determine how common it was for districts to maintain an interest in hand weaving by switching from one type of fabric to another. Chapter 3 addresses both of these

*Introduction*

issues, stressing that, by the early nineteenth century, most hand weavers were specialists, reflecting their growing concentration in urban areas, and that they worked with cotton rather than the traditional fustians.

The fourth chapter provides a fresh interpretation of the onset of decline in the Lancashire handloom weaving trades. From an analysis of the impact of the major trade upturn during the mid-1830s and a reinterpretation of contemporary estimates of changes in hand weaver numbers, it is argued that no significant reduction took place in the size of the Lancashire hand weaving labour force before the late 1830s, a decade or more later than is usually thought.

Chapter 5 presents new estimates of hand weaver numbers derived from mid-Victorian census schedule counts. These enable the continuing importance of the handloom weaving trades in the Lancashire economy to be assessed, along with the structure and nature of the hand weaving labour force. It is shown that, in rural districts especially, hand weaving continued to provide a great many jobs, despite having declined considerably in overall terms since the peak years. And it is suggested that, whilst most mid-Victorian hand weavers were women and children, a significant minority were adult males.

In Chapter 6, an analysis is undertaken into the means by which handloom weavers continued to ply their trade. Attention is centred on the crucial part played by family income, often still derived solely from hand weaving, and on the switch from the plainer and coarser cottons, which the powerloom had taken over.

Drawing on the findings of previous chapters, and making use of a range of neglected primary evidence, the final chapter explains the continuing importance of hand weaving in Lancashire during the mid-Victorian years. The reasons offered by historians for the survival of textile outwork during this period provide context for the discussion. It is argued that, despite major technical progress during the early 1840s, the powerloom did not prove economic in the manufacture of certain grades and types of cloth until further improvements were made during the mid-Victorian years. Additionally, as census evidence makes clear, the supply of hand weaving labour remained extensive beyond mid-century, providing entrepreneurs with the option of persevering with hand techniques if they so wished. The continuing supply of hand weavers strongly reflects the favourable attitudes they held towards domestic work, even though alternatives were often available to them, especially if they were young and if they lived in urban areas.

What emerges is an interpretation suggesting that, despite the substantial inroads made by mechanisation, the Lancashire textile weaving trades continued to use traditional technology during the mid-Victorian years to a surprising degree. It is suggested, indeed, that they comprised a major instance of those trades characterised by 'technological dualism', and that, in certain parts of the county, this was so to a greater extent, and for a good deal longer, than has hitherto been recognised. Indeed, it is clear that the cotton textile industry is much less of an exception to the general pattern of British industrialisation than has been thought.

## Notes

1 See, for example, F. Crouzet, *The Victorian Economy* (1982), p. 11 and A. E. Musson, 'The British Industrial Revolution', *History*, 67 (1982), pp. 252–3.

2 N. F. R. Crafts, *British Economic Growth During the Industrial Revolution* (1985), p. 156.

3 *Ibid.*, pp. 84–5.

4 *Ibid.*, p. 8. McCloskey suggests a somewhat higher figure for the country as a whole. Using census data, he calculates that, by 1860, about 30 per cent of the labour force was employed in 'activities that had been radically transformed in technique since 1780 ...' (D. N. McCloskey, 'The Industrial Revolution 1780–1860: a survey', in J. Mokyr (ed.), *The Economics of the Industrial Revolution*, 1985, p. 58.

5 Crafts, *op. cit.*, p. 69.

6 *Ibid.*, p. 87.

7 P. O'Brien and C. Keyder, *Economic Growth in Britain and France, 1780–1914* (1978), ch. 4.

8 *Ibid.*, p. 173.

9 Crafts, *op. cit.*, p. 88 and 'Economic growth in France and Britain, 1830–1910: a review of the evidence', *JEH*, XLIV (1984), pp. 49–67.

10 A. Milward and S. B. Saul, *The Development of the Economies of Continental Europe, 1850–1914* (1977), pp. 100–2.

11 D. Landes, *The Unbound Prometheus* (1969), p. 330; K. Bruland, '*The transformation of work in European industrialization*' in P. Mathias and S. A. Davis (eds), *The First Industrial Revolutions* (1989), pp. 157–8.

12 Crouzet, *op. cit.*, pp. 129–38.

13 C. H. Feinstein, 'Capital accumulation in the industrial revolution', in R. Floud and D. McCloskey (eds), *The Economic History of Britain since 1700*, 1 (1981), p. 133.

14 G. N. von Tunzelmann, 'Technical progress during the Industrial Revolution', in Floud and McCloskey, *op. cit.*, p. 160.

15 J. G. Williamson, 'Debating the Industrial Revolution', *EEH*, 24 (1987), p. 286.

16 S. B. Saul, *Technological Change: The United States and Britain in the 19th Century* (1970), pp. 1–3.

17 H. J. Habakkuk, *American and British Technology in the 19th Century* (1967), p. 17.

18 *Ibid.*, p. 14.

19 *Ibid.*, p. 22.

20 A. J. Field, 'On the unimportance of machinery', *EEH*, 22 (1985), esp. pp. 386–90. See also his article 'Land abundance, interest/profit rates, and nineteenth century British and American technology', *JEH*, 43 (1983), pp. 405–31 and M. Berg, *The Age of Manufactures, 1700–1820* (1985), pp. 181–7.

21 R. Samuel, 'Workshop of the world: steam power and hand technology in mid-Victorian Britain', *HWJ*, 3 (1977), pp. 12 and 58.

22 *Ibid.*, p. 47.

23 For a discussion of these issues see O. E. Williamson, 'The organisation of work', *Journal of Economic Behavior and Organisation*, 1 (1980), pp. 5–38 and S. R. H. Jones, 'Technology, transaction costs, and the transition to factory production in the British silk industry', *JEH*, XLVII (1987), pp. 71–96.

24 See pp. 147–50 and 157–60.

*Introduction*

25 S. Rose, 'Gender at work: sex, class and industrial capitalism', *HWJ*, 23 (1986), p. 115.
26 N. F. R. Crafts, 'British economic growth during the Industrial Revolution: some difficulties of interpretation', *EEH*, 24 (1987), p. 259; and 'The new economic history and the Industrial Revolution', in Mathias and Davis, *op. cit.*, pp. 37–8.
27 J. Mokyr, 'Has the Industrial Revolution been crowded out? Some reflections on Crafts and Williamson', *EEH*, 24 (1987), p. 315.
28 H. Cunningham, 'The employment and unemployment of children in England, c. 1680–1851', *P&P*, 126 (1987), pp. 115–50.
29 M. B. Rose, 'Social policy and business: parish apprenticeship and the early factory system, 1750–1834', *BH*, (1989), pp. 5–29.
30 Samuel, *op. cit.*, pp. 49 and 51–7.
31 *Ibid.*, p. 60.
32 See, for example, M. Berg, *Technology and Toil in Nineteenth Century Britain* (1979), p. 9 and Mokyr, *op. cit.*, p. 314. And in his seminal article on proto-industrialisation, Mendels observed that handicrafts could survive the proto-industrial phase, adapting themselves to new industry. See F. F. Mendels, 'Proto-industrialisation: the first phase of the industrialisation process', *JEH*, 32 (1972), pp. 246–7.
33 Landes, *op. cit.*, p. 119.
34 J. S. Lyons, 'Technological dualism, rivalry and complementarity: handicrafts in the transition to modern industry' (forthcoming). I am most grateful to the author for providing a copy of the article prior to publication.
35 J. H. Clapham, *An Economic History of Modern Britain*, vol. 1 (1967 reprint of 1926 edition), p. 156.
36 J. and B. L. Hammond, *The Town Labourer* (1917), p. 9. See, also, J. D. Chambers, *The Workshop of the World* (1961), pp. 14–15.
37 T. S. Ashton, *An Economic History of England: The 18th Century* (1955), p. 125; W. W. Rostow, *The Stages of Economic Growth* (1960).
38 D. Bythell, *The Sweated Trades* (1978), p. 158.
39 J. A. Schmiechen, *Sweated Industries and Sweated Labour* (1984), p. 2.
40 Bythell, *op. cit.*, pp. 158–80.
41 *Ibid.*, pp. 181–4.
42 *Ibid.*, p. 182.
43 *Ibid.*, pp. 189–98.
44 *Ibid.*, ch. 5.
45 R. Church, 'Labour supply and innovation, 1800–1860: the boot and shoe industry', *BH*, XII, (1970), pp. 29–43.
46 Schmiechen, *op. cit.*, pp. 16–17 and 32–6.
47 *Ibid.*, pp. 12–15.
48 Samuel, *op. cit.*, p. 19; A. E. Musson, *The Growth of British Industry* (1978), pp. 80 and 82; C. Aspin and S. D. Chapman, *James Hargreaves and the Spinning Jenny* (1964), p. 36.
49 See pp. 27–8.
50 D. Bythell, *The Handloom Weavers* (1969), p. 268.
51 S. J. Chapman, *The Lancashire Cotton Industry* (1904), p. 29.
52 Clapham, *op. cit.*, p. 554.
53 See, for example, J. A. Williams, 'A local population study at a college of education', *LPS*, 11 (1977), pp. 23–39; M. Anderson, *Family Structure in Nineteenth Century Lancashire*

(1971), ch. 4; and P. Horn, 'Victorian villages from census returns', *The Local Historian*, 15 (1982), pp. 25–32.

54  A. Wrigley, 'The changing occupational structure of Colyton over two centuries', *LPS*, 18 (1977), pp. 9–21 and M. T. Wild, 'The Saddleworth parish register', *Textile History*, 1 (1969), pp. 214–32.

55  N. Murray, *The Scottish Handloom Weavers, 1790–1850* (1978).

# Chapter 1

# THE CHANGING BALANCE IN WEAVING TECHNOLOGY: AN OVERVIEW

This chapter examines critically the views expounded by historians regarding the rate at which hand techniques in the Lancashire weaving trades gave way to mechanisation. It identifies key issues about the economic relationship between the emergence of the new technology and the supersession of the traditional, each of which is addressed in subsequent chapters.

The first section deals with the rise of the powerloom. It is argued that although the slow adoption of the powerloom during the early decades of the nineteenth century has been acknowledged, it has not been sufficiently emphasised. This is partly because attention has been focused too strongly on the cotton trade. More importantly, the large-scale adoption of the powerloom has been viewed as taking place at rather too early a date. A reassessment of the available figures suggests that this occurred in the early Victorian years rather than during the 1820s and early 1830s. The implication is that the hand weaving trade did not show any significant decline until the Victorian era. These conclusions reopen the discussion on why the early powerloom was introduced so slowly, taking into account its concentration in urban areas and the types of cloth it could profitably weave.

The second section investigates the growth and demise of handloom weaving. In particular, it considers the debate amongst historians regarding the rate at which the decline took place and the opposing views as to which parts of Lancashire were the slowest to abandon the handloom. Major reservations are expressed about the conclusions drawn on these issues, mainly because they are based on very inadequate evidence. This sets the scene for discussion in later chapters, where the argument is advanced that the decline set in later, and was a far more protracted affair, than has been conceded.

In drawing the two discussions together, it becomes apparent that historians have failed to consider adequately the economic relationship between the development of power weaving and the demise of hand weaving. Important questions remain unresolved as to the impact that the powerloom had on local hand weaving communities and the ways in which their inhabitants responded. For example, how far were these communities able to protect themselves by turning to alternative fabrics or by diversifying family income? It is only through the exploration of such issues that more revealing insights may be obtained into how and why handloom weavers continued to pursue their trade once the powerloom became a major threat.

## 1   The rise of the powerloom

Although attempts were made to mechanise weaving during the eighteenth century, all proved either unsuccessful or peripheral and were completely overshadowed by the impact of the fly shuttle. This device, patented by John Kay in 1733, appreciably improved hand weaver productivity — some contemporaries claimed twofold — and, in consequence, reduced the need to develop a mechanised loom.[1]

Kay was, nevertheless, interested in progressing the powerloom and was amongst the earliest to attempt mechanised textile weaving commercially. In 1745, he took out a patent concerning the application of water power to the so-called Dutch loom. In association with his business partner, Joseph Stell, Kay took advantage of this patent by setting up a weaving factory at Keighley in Yorkshire around 1750.[2] Unfortunately, no details have been unearthed as to the outcome of their venture.

It was not until the following decade that mention is made of a similar development taking place in Lancashire. The initiator, one Gartside, owned water-powered premises near Garrett Hall in Manchester. It appears, however, that the enterprise did not prove successful. Weavers were not able to operate more than a single loom at once and the risk of damage to the cloth was appreciable.[3]

The Dutch looms were a specialised type of machine used to manufacture smallwares — narrow goods, such as tapes and ribbons. They could weave several of these items simultaneously and their moving parts — healds, reeds and shuttles — could be fairly easily harnessed to operate from a single power source.[4] For looms weaving wider cloths, however, the technical difficulties of combining the moving parts proved much more intractable. In consequence, the innovations employed by Kay were probably of little value to the weaving trades in general.[5]

These early attempts to introduce the powerloom pre-dated the advent of the major technological advances in textile spinning brought by the jenny, the waterframe and the mule and by improved carding machinery. Probably, therefore, the pressure to innovate in weaving remained limited. The argument is strengthened because weaver productivity slowly improved during the mid-eighteenth century with the increasing use of the fly-shuttle, though many weavers still preferred to throw the shuttle by hand.[6] It was not until the final decades of the century that the productivity of weaving gave cause for concern. By then, the fly-shuttle was used widely,[7] if not universally,[8] but the impact of mechanised spinning had become only too apparent. Not only were vast numbers of additional hand weavers required, but large-scale exports of cotton yarn developed, much to the dismay of such contemporaries as William Radcliffe, who feared this would encourage foreigners to make their own cloth rather than import from Britain.[9]

Given these circumstances, it is remarkable enough that the powerloom continued to make slow progress. It is the more so because, as early as the mid-1770s, Robert and Thomas Barber patented a powerloom that seemed capable of being developed into a commercially viable machine. In the event, nothing seems to have come of it.[10] Further, the machine which was to be used commercially during the late eighteenth century — that invented by Edmund Cartwright — was the product of intellectual curiosity rather than of a desire to redress the technological imbalance that arose between the spinning and weaving branches of the cotton industry as the former mechanised and the latter did not.[11]

All the available evidence indicates that the Cartwright loom, along with those of other pioneers, was little used.[12] Cartwright's own powerloom factory at Doncaster, established in 1787, lasted no more than a few years, whilst Grimshaw's factory at Manchester, opened in 1790 and containing twenty-four Cartwright looms, was burnt down by irate hand weavers after only two years of operation.[13] W. English has suggested several reasons for Cartwright's apparent failure, mentioning the crude construction of his looms; his inexperience in business affairs; and the lack of machinery in his mills to undertake the preparatory processes of dressing the warp (applying a starch paste to strengthen it) and of winding the warp on to a beam ready for the loom. Without such machinery, the warps had to be dressed in the loom, allowing time for the warp threads to dry before weaving could recommence.[14] Consequently, the productivity advances that the powerloom could achieve remained fairly limited. Indeed, it was the introduction of dressing machinery in 1803, which is associated with the name of William Radcliffe, that marked an important step in the successful development of the powerloom.[15]

The loom which came into general use during the early nineteenth century was that devised by William Horrocks, a cotton manufacturer from Stockport. He secured several patents concerning the development of his machine, one of the most important being an improved means of taking up the cloth on to the beam once it was woven. This loom was described by Edward Baines as being neat and compact, occupying so little space that hundreds could be at work in the single room of a large factory.[16]

Whether rooms with hundreds of powerlooms occurred frequently during the early decades of the nineteenth century is extremely doubtful, however. According to estimates quoted by Baines, only 2,400 had been installed in British factories by 1813, 14,150 by 1820 and 55,500 by 1829.[17] No doubt the sharp trade upturn during the mid-1820s was influential in this advance.[18] Even so, during the late 1820s, handlooms in cotton weaving alone may still have outnumbered powerlooms by as many as four to one.[19] Almost half a century had elapsed since a supposedly commercial powerloom had become available, yet textile weaving still depended largely on traditional technology. In part, this may reflect a general shortage of investment funds during the Napoleonic era. But it was also a consequence of the

Table 1.1  Growth of powerloom use in Great Britain, 1835–50

| Area | Year | Fabric type | | | | |
| --- | --- | --- | --- | --- | --- | --- |
| | | cotton | wool | worsted | silk | other |
| Lancashire | 1835 | 61,176 | 1,142 | – | 365 | – |
| | 1850 | 176,947 | 4,839 | 13,770 | 1,977 | – |
| Elsewhere | 1835 | 47,013 | 1,188 | 2,864 | 1,348 | 456 |
| | 1850 | 72,680 | 4,600 | 18,847 | 4,115 | 3,412 |
| Total | 1835 | 108,189 | 2,330 | 2,864 | 1,713 | 456 |
| | 1850 | 249,627 | 9,439 | 32,617 | 6,092 | 3,412 |

technical inadequacy of the powerloom, which still required fundamental improvement.

It was not until the mid-1830s that the first official figures on the number of powerlooms in Britain were compiled[20] and this was followed by a second set in 1850.[21] Both sets were derived from factory inspectors' returns and, on the inspectors' own admission, neither is entirely complete.[22] As to the accuracy of the figures, no comment was passed though there is no particularly strong reason to suppose that the manufacturers who did respond made false returns.[23] The figures cannot be regarded as being entirely satisfactory, therefore, but they are, none the less, useful in helping to gauge the long-term growth in the use of the powerloom, as well as the pace of its introduction during the early Victorian era. Figures from both sets of returns are summarised in Table 1.1.

There is some concern as to how strictly the figures on cotton powerlooms may be compared. Those of 1835 refer to both cotton and fustian looms, whereas it is not clear that the latter are included in the 1850 cotton estimates.[24] It is doubtful, though, that any substantial adjustment would be required even if they have been omitted, since, in Lancashire at least, the weaving of fustians had been largely replaced with all cotton cloths by the early nineteenth century.[25]

Assuming the 1829 figure is reasonably correct, the number of powerlooms in use virtually doubled during the first half of the 1830s, mainly during the trade cycle upswing at mid-decade. Notable progress had thus been made. Even so, the impact on the hand weaving trade was still limited, at least in employment terms. This point will be developed more fully in the following section, where it will be argued that no substantial diminution in overall hand weaver numbers occurred prior to the late 1830s. Here it may be noted that, whilst cotton hand weavers in Britain are estimated to have exceeded 200,000 in the mid-1830s,[26] power weavers in the cotton trade numbered only around 50,000.[27] The productivity of the former, of course, would have been inferior to that of the latter, perhaps appreciably, so that, in output terms, the impact of the powerloom was stronger than these figures indicate.[28] Yet, because of their numerical supremacy and because they continued to produce the higher quality cloths, the total value added achieved by the hand weavers represented a significant proportion of the industry total and may still have exceeded that of power weavers.

It should also be noted from Table 1.1 that the powerloom was still largely confined to cotton weaving. As yet, only a small percentage of the nation's powerlooms wove silk, wool or flax and in Lancashire they numbered no more than 1,500. Technical difficulties of applying powerlooms economically to non-cottons were largely responsible for this difference, the motion of the powerloom being too harsh at this stage to cope satisfactorily with anything but the coarsest cottons.[29]

As Table 1.1 shows, it was only during the early Victorian years that the growth of the powerloom reached proportions that had a profound effect on the cotton hand weaving trade. Between 1835 and 1850, 140,000 additional powerlooms were installed, comfortably more than the total number in the previous fifty years. Given, as Bythell points out, that comparatively little investment would have taken place during the mainly depressed years of the late 1830s and early 1840s, the bulk of this expansion must have been the product of the major economic upturn of the mid-1840s.[30] And there is ample evidence in the writings of Leonard Horner, the factory inspector, to show this was probably the case. During 1843 alone, he noted 117 instances of 'new investments of capital' in his district, which covered the four northern counties, Lancashire and part of Yorkshire. Amongst the extensions he cited (he did not identify them by name) was an entirely new mill with 800 looms; a new loom shed with a capacity of between 400 and 500 looms; and a loom shed extension from 440 to 1,600 looms.[31] During the next sixteen months, Horner's returns showed a further 8,542 powerlooms were installed, though he thought this to be much below the actual number.[32] Plainly, the powerloom was progressing rapidly and the balance between hand and power weaving was at last swinging decisively in favour of the new technology. From then, rather than before, vast numbers of cotton hand weavers deserted their trade. Some may have done so in response to wage reductions and falling work opportunities in the depressed years, though alternative jobs would have been hard to find. Others remained as hand weavers, perhaps working at a much reduced level, until the general economic upsurge brought new, more lucrative jobs. And they continued to leave as powerlooms were installed at a relentless pace, a further 150,000 being utilised in the cotton trade during the 1850s.[33]

A second important issue arising from the factory inspectors' returns also needs fuller consideration. It concerns the location of early power weaving sheds. For the most part, this is given in some detail in 1835, though not in 1850, and has led Bythell to remark that the last places to take up the powerloom were the 'straggling manufacturing villages or market towns' which had grown to some importance as hand weaving centres.[34] The idea is incorporated into a more general argument about the location of early powerlooms, the 1835 returns showing a pronounced bias towards the south of the county.[35]

Whilst there is much substance in Bythell's view, the argument can be usefully restated to enable a clearer distinction to be drawn between the growth of powerloom weaving in urban and rural locations, irrespective of whether these were in the south of the county or not. The figures given in the 1835 returns are for parishes and for settlements within parishes and they reveal that the vast majority of powerlooms were located in the major urban centres, especially in the Manchester, Blackburn and Bury areas. For instance, in Blackburn parish, where over 4,000 powerlooms were operated, only one mill was in a village location and it contained as few as 96 looms. In the rural districts surrounding the town, including large tracts of that hand weaving stronghold, the Ribble Valley, no powerlooms at all were recorded. Again, in Bolton parish, just two powerloom mills were situated outside the town and they contained only 273 powerlooms out of the parish total of 1,699.[36] In the factory villages around the town, including Egerton and New Eagley, the base of Henry and Edmund Ashworth, powerlooms were thinly represented; indeed, the Ashworths did not install any until 1839.[37] Without doubt, the early power weaving industry was largely urban based and had made little headway throughout the rural districts.

The importance of this finding lies in the insights it provides into why the emergence of power weaving was so long delayed and why the abandonment of hand weaving was so protracted. The issue is addressed more fully in Chapter 7, but it may be proposed here that one key explanation centres on the notion that rural cotton entrepreneurs were more reluctant to invest in powerlooms than were their urban counterparts. Several reasons may account for this, including the inadequacy of reserves at their disposal for investment purposes; the limitations of water-powered sites in generating additional power and providing space for expansion; and the continued availability of cheap handloom labour in rural districts. That the structure of the cotton industry during this period was characterised by small firms, many of which may have become increasingly marginal as the competition from the larger urban producers intensified, suggests that the limited reserves argument may have much to commend it. Indeed, taking evidence from the 1833 Factory Commissioners' Report, A. J. Taylor concludes that in country districts only the owners of the larger mills could afford to install powerlooms.[38] Amongst them, no doubt, he would have grouped the Gregs of Styal as well as the Ashworths of Egerton. The former concern entered power weaving as early as 1824 and by the mid-1830s operated almost 1,000 looms at mills in Lancaster and Bury.[39]

Yet it is not certain that the lack of powerloom investment in rural areas was as much the function of restricted investment funds available to local manufacturers as it was of the desire amongst larger, urban-based firms, either specialist manufacturers or combined weavers and spinners to retain an interest in putting out to rural hand weavers in their locality. That they should wish to do so reflects the economic advantages they were able to derive from persisting with traditional technology, including the high degree of responsiveness that outwork labour showed towards changing market conditions; the relative cheapness of outworkers; and the savings on fixed capital expenditure. Nor would such advantages have been ignored by rural textile manufacturers.

Other explanations for the delay in transforming weaving technology also need revision. In particular, the development of powerloom technology must be linked more firmly with the great surge of investment in powerlooms during the mid-1840s. The importance of the technical advances achieved at this time by Kenworthy and Bullough is widely acknowledged. It was their weft stop motion (a way of halting the loom automatically when the weft broke or the shuttle emptied), roller temple (an improved means of keeping woven cloth at its proper width), and loose reed (a facility allowing the reed to back away when it encountered a shuttle trapped in the warps) which greatly improved the speed and efficiency of the powerloom.[40] However, these developments have not been explicitly viewed in relation to the factory inspectors' powerloom returns. Again, census schedule data allow new insights into the debate on how far the introduction of powerlooms was retarded by the presence of a plentiful and cheap supply of hand weavers, a view advanced by Habakkuk but criticised by Bythell.[41] Bythell maintains the argument cannot be taken too far, since cotton handloom weavers were quickly superseded.[42] If, because of the slow adoption of the powerloom, this was not so, Habakkuk's reasoning may have much validity after all, especially in explaining the durability of the rural hand weaver. What is plain is that key issues of this type have not been fully explored and that fresh evidence is needed to advance the debate.

Discussion on the pace and extent of technological change in weaving also gives rise to considerations about the size and nature of the hand weaving labour force during the early decades of the nineteenth century, when hand weaving was at its height. As Lloyd-Jones and Lewis have observed, the intensive growth of factory cotton spinning, which vastly expanded the volume of yarn production as well as sharply reducing its price, had a profound impact on the development of the weaving trade. Yet, because the powerloom had made little progress at this stage, weaving developed on an extensive (outwork) basis, organised through a warehouse system which assumed major significance.[43] For the most part, the warehouses were located in urban centres, especially Manchester; indeed, it was not uncommon to find manufacturers in Lancashire's major towns occupying a Manchester warehouse as well as their local premises.[44]

The question remains unanswered, however, as to how important handloom weaving actually became. In all probability, local communities often assumed a very high degree of dependence on the trade, but the extent of this has not been spelled out in any detail. Nor has much consideration been given as to the ways in which hand weavers responded to the challenges brought by the powerloom, however belated its arrival, and how effective these responses proved. For instance, were they able to find ways of adapting which enabled them to continue with domestic outwork for an appreciable period, or were they absorbed quickly into alternative jobs? How far indeed were the employment opportunities provided by the powerloom sector available to them? Questions of this type have been addressed by historians, but little of the available evidence has been adduced in seeking convincing answers.

A further important aspect of the development of power weaving must also be addressed. It concerns the type of cloth to which the powerloom could be applied. On this matter there is a measure of agreement amongst historians, at least regarding the early use of the powerloom during the 1820s and 1830s. Thus, D. A. Farnie neatly summarises the prevailing view by remarking that the

> powerloom ramained imperfect and confined to the production of three types of plain goods in printers, domestics and shirtings, so that it did not compete with the hand weaving of superior and fancy goods.[45]

Historians have noted, too, the delay in applying power to weaving certain types of specialist cotton and non-cotton cloths, which were of considerable importance in several districts.[46] Thus, W. P. Crankshaw maintains that handlooms were still largely used at mid-century in the Bolton quilt trade,[47] and G. Greathead that patterned and figured muslins were not threatened by the powerloom until the late 1850s, when the dobby was introduced.[48] In the woollen trade, meanwhile, the main period of transition to powerlooms was as late as the 1850s or 1860s.[49]

Two main conclusions arise from these considerations. One is that much uncertainty exists amongst historians as to precisely when particular types and grades of fabric were taken over by the powerloom. Most of the evidence they have adduced relates to the pre-1840 period and is drawn from the various official enquiries into the hand weaving trades; little has been written about the position in subsequent decades. Secondly, even when the powerloom did become commercially viable in the production of any particular type of cloth, it would not necessarily have been adopted for the purpose on a widespread basis without a time lag. Indeed, an interval may often have occurred during which a particular grade of cloth was woven on both hand and power looms. What is important here is that any delays of this type may have provided further opportunity for hand weavers to remain at their trade. Once more, an issue concerning the rise of the powerloom requires deeper investigation.

It is clear from a review of the literature on the growth of power weaving that a number of major questions arise regarding developments in hand weaving. Such issues as the size and distribution of the handloom weaving force during the period before mechanised weaving set in, and the rate at which hand weaving gave way to the powerloom, readily present themselves. Before new evidence can be introduced, however, it is necessary to consider the existing state of knowledge on these matters.

## 2  The demise of hand weaving

The population growth engendered in Lancashire's textile districts during the late eighteenth and early nineteenth centuries, largely the product of a sustained increase

Table 1.2  *Pre-Victorian estimates of the number of hand weavers in the British cotton industry*

| Year | Compiler | Estimate |
|------|----------|----------|
| 1819 | John Kennedy | 240,000 |
| 1820 | Richard Guest | at least 360,000 |
| 1833 | Edward Baines | at least 250,000 |
| 1833 | James Grimshaw | about 250,000 |
| 1833 | George Smith | 200,000 |

in birth rate, was both a rural and an urban phenomenon.[50] In the country districts, the numbers involved were often quite small — perhaps a few score per decade — whilst in urban areas, some impressive growth rates were recorded as several major textile towns grew to national prominence.[51] For the emerging textile industry, this growth of population was of considerable importance, since it helped to ensure that an adequate labour supply became available, especially to meet the growing needs of a largely unmechanised weaving sector.

Of course, it was not solely as a result of population expansion that the number of cotton handloom weavers was able to grow. As Bythell points out, labour was drawn into the trade from other sectors. He suggests that the nucleus came from the traditional fustian weavers and that they were joined by weavers of wool, linen and sailcloth, who found the new fabric more profitable. There was also a 'great influx' of displaced domestic spinners, the casualties of growing mechanisation in the textile industry, though they were less numerous than those drawn into the trade from other occupations, amongst whom agricultural labourers were strongly represented. Other groups Bythell mentions who swelled the hand weavers' ranks during the early nineteenth century were returning servicemen and Irish immigrants, though he remarks that neither group would have provided a vast number of recruits.[52] The attractions of hand weaving embraced a high earning potential (perhaps twice that in agriculture); low entry costs (a handloom cost only a few pounds and, for the most part, training was neither lengthy nor expensive); not having to move house (perhaps avoiding the drawbacks of a less congenial environment); and the attractions of family-based work (thereby maintaining a traditional way of life).[53]

How numerous a body of cotton hand weavers arose during this period and how important an element they became in the labour force, are issues that have only been partially explored by historians. Moreover, all have depended on a relatively small number of estimates left by contemporaries, the reliability of which gives much cause for concern. Some of these relate to the country as a whole and are summarised in Table 1.2.[54]

## The last shift

Taken at face value, the figures indicate that cotton hand weavers became a major occupational group prior to the large-scale adoption of the powerloom. However, there is some reservation about their accuracy. No details are known of the sources used by John Kennedy and Richard Guest, though it seems that Baines relied on the figures provided by two contemporary cotton entrepreneurs, James Grimshaw and George Smith. Baines gives no reason for favouring those of the former to those of the latter. Since both Grimshaw and Smith were intimately connected with the cotton trade, a reasonable degree of accuracy may be anticipated in the estimates they gave. However, both estimates must be treated with caution. When asked to give the number of handloom weavers in the country, Grimshaw admitted: 'there is no data that I can come upon which I can form a calculation: but my impression has been about 250,000 cotton weavers on handlooms'. It is true that George Smith made his estimate following a more painstaking analysis than James Grimshaw, declaring: 'I form my calculation partly upon the quantity of yarn spun in the year, deducting the quantity which goes abroad in the thread'. Even so, he tells nothing about the problems he encountered. How was he able to compute an average output per weaver, especially when allowance had to be made for those who regarded hand weaving as by-employment? What allowance did he make for wasted thread and for thread that was knitted rather than woven? Could he be sure that figures of yarn spun were accurate? That the figures supplied by Grimshaw and Smith differ by 50,000, giving, on their estimates, a possible 20 to 25 per cent error, hardly gives ground for optimism. Without data from other sources by which to judge the accuracy of these statistics, uncertainty remains as to their reliability and hence their usefulness. Their value is further limited because numbers employed indicate loom capacity rather than cloth output, the gap between the two fluctuating appreciably over time, especially under the influence of trade cycle movements.

Similar concerns arise regarding more local estimates of hand weaver numbers. It might be argued that contemporaries would have had closer insights into the circumstances of their own districts than they would into those of the country as a whole and that the task of calculating the number of handloom weavers over limited areas would have been much less formidable. This may be so, but it is plain that some local estimates, including that appearing in a letter to the *Liverpool Commercial Chronicle* early in 1827, were largely conjectural:

Cotton weavers principally reside in the neighbourhood of Bolton, Chorley, Wigan, Blackburn Haslingden, Padiham, Burnley, Colne and Todmorden. Number of cotton weavers in these places must exceed 60,000 and may be nearer 100,000.[55]

Other local estimates were claimed to be the products of more careful surveying, but, as with the national estimates, there is little or no discussion of the techniques employed. For instance, in telling the 1833 Select Committee that there were no less than 23,500 handloom weavers in the division of Bolton in 1817, Richard Needham, a local handloom weaver, confined himself to the remark that he and

Table 1.3 *Hand weavers in the British cotton industry: Ellison's estimates*

| Years | Estimates |
| --- | --- |
| 1819–21 | 240,000 |
| 1829–31 | 225,000 |
| 1844–46 | 60,000 |
| 1859–61 | 5–10,000 |

another person had undertaken the survey.[56] Unfortunately, committee members did not press him to reveal his methods. Again, a survey of several townships in the Padiham area taken during 1826 claimed that 1,801 hand weavers were to be found, but the only comment on the means used to obtain this information was that it resulted from 'strict enquiry'.[57]

The uncertainties surrounding the size of the hand weaving labour force prior to the powerloom era become no less acute thereafter. Nevertheless, comparison of these with later estimates has been made so as to chart the declining numbers of cotton hand weavers in Britain. The figures have been conveniently summarised by Thomas Ellison. They are reproduced as Table 1.3.[58]

The 1819–21 figure is the familiar Kennedy estimate, whilst that for 1829–31 seems to have been calculated by taking the halfway point between the Grimshaw and Smith computations. No explanation is given of how the later figures were derived. Nevertheless, Ellison is prepared to argue that, by the late 1850s, hand weaving had 'nearly ceased to form an item in the manufacture of cotton goods'.

Ellison's figures imply that the overall decline in the cotton hand weaving labour force had already set in by the 1820s. Yet, given the inadequacies of his figures, such an argument is difficult to sustain. Had Ellison selected Grimshaw's figure of 250,000, quite a different conclusion would have been drawn. In fact, by failing to state why he felt Smith's estimate to be too low and that of Grimshaw to be too high, he merely adds to the uncertainty. Consequently, it is hard to have any more faith in his estimates than in those of his predecessors.

The interpretation of such figures brings further difficulties. One concerns the distinction between hand weavers in work and others who were unemployed, but who still regarded themselves as part of the hand weaving labour force. Arguably, the latter group became more common as the hand weaving trade declined, though the proportion they would have formed of the whole is impossible to determine. None the less, the point should be made that figures of hand weaver numbers for the 1840s and beyond may overstate the actual size of the active hand weaving labour force, thereby implying a somewhat less rapid decline that actually occurred.

That figures of only cotton handloom weavers are available for the early and mid-Victorian era poses a further problem. It has been noted that the powerloom was applied more quickly to cotton than to non-cotton cloths.[59] Accordingly, the

Table 1.4  *Numbers of cotton handloom weavers in Britain, 1806–62: Wood's estimates (000s)*

| Year | Total | Year | Total | Year | Total |
| --- | --- | --- | --- | --- | --- |
| 1806 | 184 | 1825 | 240 | 1844 | 72 |
| 1807 | 188 | 1826 | 240 | 1845 | 60 |
| 1808 | 192 | 1827 | 240 | 1846 | 57 |
| 1809 | 196 | 1828 | 240 | 1847 | 53 |
| 1810 | 200 | 1829 | 240 | 1848 | 50 |
| 1811 | 204 | 1830 | 240 | 1849 | 47 |
| 1812 | 208 | 1831 | 240 | 1850 | 43 |
| 1813 | 212 | 1832 | 227 | 1851 | 40 |
| 1814 | 216 | 1833 | 213 | 1852 | 37 |
| 1815 | 220 | 1834 | 200 | 1853 | 33 |
| 1816 | 224 | 1835 | 188 | 1854 | 30 |
| 1817 | 228 | 1836 | 174 | 1855 | 27 |
| 1818 | 232 | 1837 | 160 | 1856 | 23 |
| 1819 | 236 | 1838 | 147 | 1857 | 20 |
| 1820 | 240 | 1839 | 135 | 1858 | 17 |
| 1821 | 240 | 1840 | 123 | 1859 | 13 |
| 1822 | 240 | 1841 | 110 | 1860 | 10 |
| 1823 | 240 | 1842 | 97 | 1861 | 7 |
| 1824 | 240 | 1843 | 85 | 1862 | 3 |

question arises as to how many non-cotton hand weavers were to be found in Lancashire once the powerloom gained ascendancy. If the numbers were appreciable, say in tens of thousands, Ellison's figures give a misleading impression of the continuing importance of outwork in the textile trades. As well, a valuable insight into how hand weavers were able to continue at their trade is overlooked. There is evidently scope for further research here, drawing particularly on census schedule evidence.

Despite the strong reservation that must be voiced about Ellison's figures, subsequent writers have not hesitated to quote them with little in the way of critical comment. Indeed, they provide the basis for the most detailed of all the calculations made to estimate the numbers of cotton handloom weavers, that prepared by G. H. Wood and published in 1910. Wood summarised the nineteenth century figures — with the exception of that provided by Richard Guest in 1820 — and noted a 'general consensus' of opinion amongst contemporary observers that no diminution had occurred by 1833.[60] Notwithstanding his cautionary note that the contemporary figures were conjectural and that at best they allow nothing more than approximation, he felt able to use them to compute a series of annual totals of cotton handloom weavers for the years 1806–62.[61] These are reproduced as Table 1.4.

In fairness to Wood, it should be pointed out that he did not mean his estimates to be taken too literally, their purpose being no more than to gauge the relative importance of factory workers and hand weavers.[62] Even so, given the shaky foundations on which they are based, it is hard to see what value the figures have for the purpose intended. Especially disturbing is the regularity with which the decline is perceived to have occurred, no explanation being offered as to why some twelve to fifteen thousand weavers abandoned their looms each year between the early 1830s and mid-1840s and why this figure fell dramatically to between three and seven thousand thereafter. The effect, for each period, is to assume an increasing percentage rate of decline, a notion that might be regarded with suspicion given the effects that the major upturns of the trade cycle would have had on employment levels during the mid-1840s and early 1850s. Similar concerns arise with regard to the steady increases of four thousand per annum between 1806–20. Whether, additionally, the series can be taken to its ultimate conclusion must be questioned, since no attempt has been made to resolve this point by reference to the 1861 and 1871 census schedules.

No subsequent historian has attempted to refine the contemporary estimates further. Some, including Mark Blaug and Neil Smelser, have quoted them with apparent approval[63] and an accolade of respectability has been conferred upon them by their inclusion in Mitchell and Deane's *Abstract of British Historical Statistics*.[64] Nor have these commentators been reluctant to draw conclusions based on Wood's figures. For instance, Smelser contends that while the cotton handloom weavers still numbered 23,000 in 1856 and 'while handloom weaving lasted much longer in scattered communities, the 1840s mark its effective demise'.[65] In the absence of guidance as to how the concept of 'effective demise' should be judged, the precise meaning of Smelser's statement remains obscure.

Other historians, amongst them Sir John Clapham and Professor A. J. Taylor, have preferred to go back to the original estimates in attempting to substantiate their ideas as to the numerical rate of decline amongst the cotton handloom weavers.[66] Whether, as a result, their conclusions carry any more weight than those arising from the use of Wood's estimates is extremely doubtful, as may be seen in the case of Taylor's analysis based on Ellison's figures. He writes:

The long and intense depression which began in 1838 proved critical for hand-loom weaving, and, by 1846, according to Thomas Ellison, there remained only 60,000 hand-looms engaged in cotton production in Great Britain. The contrast between this figure and the 225,000 of the previous decade is startling; but it probably does not exaggerate the rapid disappearance of a section of the working community who had for many years been forewarned ... of this final catastrophe. All the coarser cloths had been abandoned to the powerloom; it was only in the finer fabrics of Bolton and Paisley that the handloom retained any measure of supremacy.[67]

However startling the speed of decline revealed by these figures, their deficiencies must not be forgotten. It would be instructive to know, for example, why, for the early 1830s, Ellison's estimate of 225,000 is preferred to George Smith's figure of 200,000. The use of the latter would plainly have produced a somewhat less rapid rate of decline. Moreover, no case is made out as to why the figure for the mid-1840s should be accepted as even an approximation of the truth. The fact is that both sets of figures used by Taylor appear to be based on little more than guesswork, so they cannot be used convincingly to establish the rate at which the cotton handloom weavers abandoned their looms. Further, no detailed evidence is adduced to substantiate the claim that the Bolton and Paisley districts were the only ones in which the handloom retained a measure of supremacy during and beyond the 1840s. To test the truth of this notion, recourse must again be made to the mid-nineteenth century census schedules.

Turning to more recent historians, particular attention must be given to the work of Duncan Bythell. His research has greatly extended knowledge of the cotton hand weavers' living standards and of their attempts to maintain an adequate level of remuneration in the face of continually falling piece rates. He rightly points out that 'it would be misleading to attempt to infer too much from the defective evidence which now survives'.[68] Accordingly, his general conclusions are suitably qualified, except with regard to the rate of decline in the number of cotton handloom weavers.

After reviewing the contemporary figures put forward in the 1820s and 1830s, Bythell feels able to assert that the number of cotton handloom weavers probably reached its peak in the mid-1820s.[69] His view is entirely consistent with the conclusions obtained from a comparison of the 1819, 1820 and 1833 figures (Table 1.2). He believes, too, that the cotton handloom weavers did not fully recover from the slump of 1826 and that, thereafter, people continued to enter the trade only if they were shiftless, or if they found it impossible to get alternative work. It was from this time that the number of weavers began to decline, with new entrants to the trade drying up and old weavers finding new jobs or dying out.[70]

Having detected a relatively early beginning to the decline in the number of cotton handloom weavers, Bythell suggests that their disappearance was virtually complete within the next twenty years or so. It is true that he points to variations in the rate of decline, with the swiftest reductions occurring in the large towns and the slowest in the country districts.[71] Nevertheless, he is unequivocal in his view that, by the late 1840s,

the cotton handloom weaver had become a comparatively rare species. In a few isolated places, small groups of elderly ones might be found, but they had become a mere handful after the cotton famine of the 1860s.[72]

In his later work, Bythell has reiterated these views, having found supportive evidence amongst the 1851 census enumerators' schedules. He writes:

According to the census of 1851, cotton handloom weavers were to be found at this date only in small numbers here and there; in the towns, little groups of survivors carried on in the fancy lines, such as the counterpane weavers of Bolton; and in the countryside, odd family groups were still treadling away in the more isolated farmhouses and hamlets. By the time of the cotton famine in the early 1860s, the trade was to all intents and purposes extinct.[73]

He finds, too, that the cotton handloom weavers survived longest, and that they were most numerous in relation to the total population, in the upland valleys of north and east Lancashire — in the Rossendale and Bowland Forests and around Pendle Hill.[74] The evidence on which this view is based is not stated.

The opinions advanced by Bythell concerning the rate of decline in cotton hand weaving have met with a mixed response. Amongst those giving support are Sydney Pollard and François Crouzet. The former maintains that the cotton industry was entirely factory based by 1850,[75] whilst the latter agrees with Bythell that hand weaver numbers began to fall much earlier than had been thought. To bear out this contention, Crouzet selects figures from the contemporary estimates to show that the decline began during the 1820s. At the same time, he acknowledges that it was not until the 1830s that power weavers became more numerous than hand weavers and that 40,000 of the latter still survived in 1850, a rather more generous interpretation than that of Bythell. Thereafter, Crouzet sees a rapid demise of the remaining hand weavers, their disappearance being complete within a fifteen-year period.[76] This stance is shared by A. E. Musson, who believes that the 50,000 cotton hand weavers who were still at work in the late 1840s had shrunk to an insignificant few thousand by the early 1860s.[77]

Other recent commentators, however, are more critical of Bythell's suggestions. D. A. Farnie accepts that no fall in cotton hand weaver numbers occurred before the mid-1820s, but opts for a lengthier period of decline than Bythell, with the main reductions taking place between the 1830s and 1860s. He also suggests that the number of handlooms in cotton weaving was not exceeded by the number of powerlooms until the 1840s.[78] Further, whilst Farnie agrees that there was a less rapid reduction in rural areas than in towns, he singles out the Ribble Valley hand weavers as being particularly tenacious,[79] thus agreeing with the view of a nineteenth century cotton trade historian, Richard Marsden.[80] Another scholar, J. S. Lyons, maintains that the disappearance of plain cotton hand weaving was a protracted process 'lasting over forty years from the upsurge of powerlooms after the end of the Napoleonic Wars'. He takes the view that the hand weaving labour force had ceased to grow by the early 1820s; that it stayed constant for a decade thereafter; and that, by mid-century, it still numbered perhaps 50,000 in the Lancashire region alone.[81] Lyons also postulates that there arose a handloom weaving labour force of older adults, whose children were employed in other sectors, particularly cotton textile mills.[82] Sharing Lyons' less cataclysmic stance, Patrick Joyce avers that the demise of hand weaving was neither so rapid, nor the introduction of the powerloom so triumphant, as Bythell maintains,[83] and John Rule supports Musson's contention that 50,000 cotton hand weavers were still to be found in Britain at mid-century.[84]

It is plain from these comments that much uncertainty exists amongst historians about the onset and pace of decline in the cotton hand weaving trade; about which areas retained a hand weaving industry the longest; and about how important the non-cotton handloom weavers became. Some comments appear to be largely conjectural, whilst others are based on limited or defective evidence. Consequently, despite the insistence on careful qualification, little further advance can be expected without recourse to alternative sources of information. To echo S. D. Chapman, it is necessary to mount additional locally-based studies, especially those which make use of occupational details derived from parish registers and census enumerators' schedules.[85] Only from systematic investigation of these sources is it possible to obtain fresh insights into the extent to which traditional technology continued to be used in the textile trades as the powerloom increasingly took over. It is the results obtained from these enquiries which allow more informed discussions than have hitherto been possible as to how and why hand weavers were able to coexist with power weavers, once the latter had become a firmly-established and numerous group.

### Notes

1 A. P. Wadsworth and J. de Lacy Mann, *The Cotton Trade and Industrial Lancashire* (1931), pp. 450–1.
2 *Ibid.*, p. 301.
3 J. Aikin, *A Description of the County from Thirty to Forty Miles Around Manchester* (1968 reprint of 1795 edition), pp. 175–6; Wadsworth and Mann, *op. cit.*, pp. 301–2.
4 W. English, *The Textile Industry* (1969), p. 89.
5 Wadsworth and Mann, *op. cit.*, p. 302.
6 *Ibid.*, pp. 467–71.
7 D. Bythell, *The Handloom Weavers* (1969), p. 70.
8 This was so as late as the 1820s, especially in silk weaving (J. Murphy, *A Treatise of the Art of Weaving*, 1827, p. 84).
9 W. Radcliffe, *Origin of the New System of Manufacture* (1828), *passim*. For a discussion see Bythell, *op. cit.*, pp. 68–71.
10 English, *op. cit.*, p. 90.
11 Bythell, *op. cit.*, p. 68.
12 Bythell notes that the total number of powerlooms in use by 1815 was very small (*ibid.*, p. 74). The other pioneers seem to have been based in Glasgow. See English, *op. cit.*, pp. 94–5 and E. Baines, *History of the Cotton Manufacture in Great Britain* (1966 reprint of 1835 edition), p. 231.
13 Bythell, *op. cit.*, pp. 73–4; R. L. Hills, *Power in the Industrial Revolution* (1970), p. 219.
14 English, *op. cit.*, pp. 96–7 and 103.
15 *Ibid.*, p. 102; Hills, *op. cit.*, pp. 226–7.
16 Baines, *op. cit.*, p. 234.
17 *Ibid.*, p. 237.
18 Bythell, *op. cit.*, p. 89.

19  For hand weaver numbers at this time see p. 27.
20  *PP*, 1836 (24) XLV.
21  *PP*, 1850 (745) XLII, pp. 455–77.
22  But the shortfalls do not amount to much. For instance, only four sets of returns were refused to Leonard Horner in 1850.
23  However, J. Heathcote, one of the 1835 inspectors, complained of the 'carelessness and unwillingness of Manufacturers in making the returns'.
24  Fustian looms comprised about 19 per cent of the 1835 cotton looms total.
25  See pp. 78–88.
26  See p. 28.
27  This assumes two looms per weaver. See pp. 157–8.
28  For contemporary estimates of this difference, see pp. 147–8.
29  See p. 24.
30  Bythell, *op. cit.*, p. 90.
31  *PP*, 1844 (583) XXVIII, pp. 547–9.
32  *PP*, 1845 (639) XXV, p. 449. Quoted in Bythell, *op. cit.*, p. 90. It was during this period that the construction of the world's largest powerloom shed was announced at Preston. See J. E. King, *Richard Marsden and the Preston Chartists, 1837–1848* (1981), p. 32.
33  The figures are summarised in J. R. T. Hughes, *Fluctuations in Trade, Industry and Finance* (1960), pp. 97–8.
34  Bythell, *op. cit.*, p. 92.
35  Probably fewer than a quarter were to be found in north and mid-Lancashire.
36  *PP*, 1836 (24) XLV, p. 5.
37  R. Boyson, *The Ashworth Enterprise* (1970), pp. 59–60.
38  A. J. Taylor, 'Concentration and specialization in the Lancashire cotton industry, 1825–1850', *EcHR*, (1948–49), p. 120.
39  M. Rose, *The Gregs of Styal* (1978), pp. 10–11 and 14–15; *PP*, 1836 (24) XLV, p. 5.
40  For details, see J. S. Lyons, *The Lancashire Cotton Industry and the Introduction of the Powerloom, 1815–1850* (PhD dissertation, 1977), pp. 176–7; C. P. Brooks, *Cotton Manufacturing* (1982), pp. 63 and 67.
41  For Habakkuk's views, see pp. 265–7.
42  Bythell, *op. cit.*, p. 81.
43  R. Lloyd-Jones and M. J. Lewis, *Manchester and the Age of the Factory* (1988), p. 59.
44  Trade directory lists confirm this.
45  D. A. Farnie, *The English Cotton Industry and the World Market, 1815–1896* (1979), p. 281.
46  For the location of these districts, see pp. 137–42.
47  W. P. Crankshaw, 'Famous Bolton cotton fabrics', in *Industrial Bolton* (1927), p. 39.
48  G. Greathead, *A Study of Handloom Weaving Decline in the mid-Nineteenth Century* (unpublished MA dissertation, 1986), p. 34.
49  D. J. Jenkins and K. G. Ponting, *The British Wool Textile Industry, 1770–1914* (1982), p. 115.
50  J. K. Walton, *Lancashire, A Social History, 1558–1939* (1978), pp. 123–4.
51  This is evident from the tables of provincial town rankings given in W. G. Hoskins, *Local History in England* (1959), pp. 176–8.
52  Bythell, *op. cit.*, pp. 41–2, 45–8 and 63–5.

53 *Ibid.*, p. 44.
54 The 1819 figure is from T. Ellison, *The Cotton Trade of Great Britain* (1968 reprint of 1868 edition), p. 65; the 1820 figure from R. Guest, *A Compendious History of the Cotton Manufacture* (1968 reprint of 1823 edition), p. 33; and those of 1833 from Baines, *op. cit.*, p. 237 and *PP*, 1833 (690) VI, Q.10,171 and Q.9,449.
55 Quoted in *BC*, 24.2.1827.
56 *PP*, 1833 (690) VI, Q.11,783. The division of Bolton included Bolton borough and several of the surrounding townships.
57 LRO, Padiham Relief Committee Papers, 1824–27, PR 2863/4 (2).
58 Ellison, *op. cit.*, pp. 65–6.
59 See p. 24.
60 G. H. Wood, *The History of Wages in the Cotton Trade* (1910), p. 24.
61 *Ibid.*, pp. 127–8.
62 *Ibid.*, p. 125.
63 M. Blaug, 'The productivity of capital in the Lancashire cotton industry during the nineteenth century', *EcHR*, XIII (1961), p. 38; N. J. Smelser, *Social Change During the Industrial Revolution* (1959), p. 137.
64 B. R. Mitchell and P. Deane, *Abstract of British Historical Statistics* (1962), p. 187.
65 Smelser, *op. cit.*, p. 207.
66 J. H. Clapham, *An Economic History of Britain*, I (1967 reprint of 1926 edition), p. 554; Taylor, *op. cit.*, pp. 116–17.
67 *Ibid.*, p. 117.
68 Bythell, *op. cit.*, p. 96.
69 *Ibid.*, p. 54.
70 *Ibid.*, p. 53.
71 *Ibid.*, pp. 265–6.
72 *Ibid.*, p. 267.
73 D. Bythell, *The Sweated Trades* (1978), p. 46.
74 *Ibid.*, p. 38.
75 S. Pollard, 'Labour in Great Britain', in P. Mathias and M. M. Postan (eds), *The Cambridge Economic History of Europe*, vol. 2, pt. 1 (1978) p. 133.
76 F. Crouzet, *The Victorian Economy* (1982), pp. 198–202.
77 A. E. Musson, *The Growth of British Industry* (1978), p. 204.
78 D. A. Farnie, *The English Cotton Industry and the World Market, 1815–1896* (1979), p. 278.
79 *Ibid.*, p. 283.
80 R. Marsden, *Cotton Weaving: Its Development, Principles and Practice* (1895), p. 232.
81 Lyons, *op. cit.*, pp. 3 and 15–6; and 'Family response to economic decline: handloom weavers in early nineteenth century Lancashire', *Research in Economic History*, 12 (1989), p. 50.
82 *Ibid.*, p. 57 *et seq.*
83 P. Joyce, *Work, Society and Politics* (1980), p. 57.
84 J. Rule, *The Labouring Classes in Early Industrial England, 1750–1850* (1986), p. 10.
85 S. D. Chapman, *The Cotton Industry in the Industrial Revolution* (1972), p. 61.

# Chapter 2

# THE ECONOMIC INPORTANCE OF HAND WEAVING IN THE EARLY NINETEENTH CENTURY

That mechanised weaving was slow to develop during the early decades of the nineteenth century raises questions about how important the hand weaving sector became in the cotton trade. It is suggested in the previous chapter that the issue has only been superficially examined and that the evidence used has severe limitations. In this chapter, the matter is reopened, using new estimates of hand weaver numbers derived from parish register entries.

Discussion begins with a brief account of the techniques involved. They are considered in detail in Appendix A1. The new estimates are then presented and a comparison is made with those offered by contemporaries. It is argued that, despite doubts about his methods of compilation, Kennedy's estimate of 240,000 in 1819 is reasonably accurate.[1] This gives confirmation to the notion that domestic weaving provided a remarkably high proportion of the employment opportunities available in textile Lancashire, a consideration that has not been spelled out with any clarity. A further neglected point is also raised, namely that the highest concentrations of hand weavers were generally to be found in the more urbanised parts of the county. This has importance with regard to assessing how far the farmer/weaver of the eighteenth century had given way to a new generation of specialist hand weavers by the early nineteenth century. It also helps to explain why, once the powerloom gained a strong foothold in the cotton towns from the mid-1840s onwards, vast numbers of handloom weavers could no longer compete and were forced to seek alternative work. For the most part, these weavers produced plain, coarse goods for a mass market, precisely the wares which, at an early stage, the powerloom came to manufacture far more economically than the handloom.

The second section of the chapter extends analysis into the geographical distribution of the Lancashire hand weaving trade during its peak years. The analysis takes account of the debate on proto-industrialisation, a rather neglected topic as far as the Lancashire textile industry is concerned. It is argued that the new estimates lend strong support to the hypothesis commonly advanced in discussions on proto-industrialisation that early handicraft industry became heavily concentrated in upland pastoral districts, where advantage could be taken of cheap and plentiful labour.[2] In the case of Lancashire, however, the hypothesis needs qualification. This is partly because domestic textile production was by no means confined to upland areas of the county and, as in Scotland, not all upland areas developed a sizeable textile industry.[3] It is also because labour availability was not the sole reason for textile production becoming localised in the upland zone. Of importance, too, were the relatively high humidity levels prevailing on higher ground, a benefit in fustian and cotton production alike. Moreover, as the textile industry expanded in the upland areas, it acquired a much improved infrastructure, not least an extensive communications network, which served further to reinforce its localisation.

The final section assesses the impact that the massive number of hand weavers had on the formation of settlement in Lancashire during the late eighteenth and early nineteenth centuries. It is argued that numerous rural districts owed a large part of their development to the creation of hand weavers' colonies and that, even in urban areas, such colonies could add appreciably to the total housing stock.

## 1 Numbers of handloom weavers

Parish registers are the only available source upon which to base new estimates of handloom weaver numbers in Lancashire during the early nineteenth century. From 1813 onwards, following the passage of Rose's Act, all Anglican baptism registers were obliged to comply with a standardised format, which required details of fathers' occupations.[4] Marriage registers also frequently record bridegrooms' occupations during this period, though there was no legal requirement that they should.[5]

The use of these data to prepare estimates of handloom weaver numbers poses several difficulties, not least of interpretation. In particular, reliance on Anglican baptism registers may distort figures on occupational distributions, should some occupational groups have been strongly drawn towards Nonconformity. This is certainly suspected to have been the case as far as hand weavers were concerned. Again, the possibility has to be faced that some groups of workers, including hand weavers, raised larger than average families during early industrialisation, a consequence of the high wages they could obtain. Both issues are discussed in Appendix A1.

Other difficulties arise from the procedures involved. Essentially, three stages of analysis are undertaken. To begin with, numbers of bridgeroom and father weavers are calculated for each parish in Lancashire during the quinquennium 1818–22, as well as the proportions they comprised of the total numbers recorded in each parish. It is assumed that, in line with the discussion in the previous chapter, very few of these would have been power weavers. It is further assumed that the vast majority would have been in their twenties and thirties. Next, using data from the 1821 census returns, the numbers of males aged 20 to 39 in each parish are computed. These data are combined with those of the weaver proportions to give likely numbers of male hand weavers in each parish for the years 1818–22, the period when hand weaver numbers would have been at, or near to, their peak. Finally, using mid-nineteenth century census data, estimates are made for several districts as to the proportions that male hand weavers in their twenties and thirties formed of the total hand weaving labour force. Combining these data with 1818–22 parish register data produces a range of estimated weaver numbers for each district in Lancashire.

The procedures involved in these computations are considered fully in Appendix A1, along with the techniques used to overcome the shortcomings of the parish register data. It must be stressed that these procedures may well produce inaccuracies at each stage, thereby compounding error. Accordingly, for each district, an estimate is given, along with the range within which the actual figure for each district probably lies. The data are presented in Table 2.1.[6]

Using the data in columns (a) and (c), it is estimated that between 150,000 and 190,000 hand weavers were to be found in Lancashire during 1821. For reasons stated in Appendix A1, the data in column (b) provide a better basis for estimation than the other two, giving a total of about 168,000. If this figure is reasonably correct, then as many as one in every six Lancastrians were then employed in the trade.[7] In terms of the working population, the ratio would have been appreciably higher, perhaps as much as one in four.[8] Quite clearly, handloom weavers were of fundamental importance to the Lancashire economy and comprised one of the largest occupational groups in the county. Moreover, given that relatively few were to be found in Merseyside, where around 15 per cent of Lancastrians lived in 1821, some extremely high concentrations must have occurred in the county's textile zone. Indeed, the new figures lend support to the claims of contemporaries that, in parts of Lancashire, hand weaving came to absorb a large majority of the available labour.[9]

Table 2.1 *Handloom weaver totals in Lancashire, 1821*

| District | Weaver totals | | |
|---|---|---|---|
| | (a) | (b) | (c) |
| Accrington & Altham | 1,158 | 1,005 | 914 |
| Ashton-under-Lyne | 5,663 | 4,915 | 4,472 |
| Blackburn | 16,995 | 14,750 | 13,421 |
| Bolton | 16,848 | 14,623 | 13,305 |
| Burnley | 3,712 | 3,222 | 2,931 |
| Bury | 9,913 | 8,604 | 7,828 |
| Central Lancashire | 6,370 | 5,528 | 5,030 |

Table 2.1 (*cont.*)

| District | Weaver totals | | |
|---|---|---|---|
| | (a) | (b) | (c) |
| Church | 2,174 | 1,887 | 1,717 |
| Clitheroe | 457 | 396 | 361 |
| Colne | 8,234 | 7,146 | 6,502 |
| Deane | 4,989 | 4,330 | 3,940 |
| Downham | 310 | 269 | 245 |
| East Bolton | 978 | 849 | 773 |
| Eccles | 7,625 | 6,618 | 6,021 |
| Flixton | 799 | 693 | 631 |
| Garstang | 190 | 165 | 150 |
| Haslingden | 2,886 | 2,505 | 2,279 |
| Kirkham | 2,266 | 1,967 | 1,790 |
| Lancaster Area | 690 | 599 | 545 |
| Leigh | 7,109 | 6,170 | 5,614 |
| Lune Valley | 98 | 85 | 77 |
| Manchester | 23,962 | 20,797 | 18,923 |
| Middleton | 2,902 | 2,519 | 2,292 |
| Newchurch-in-Pendle | 1,386 | 1,203 | 1,094 |
| Newchurch-in-Rossendale | 2,886 | 2,505 | 2,279 |
| North Fylde | 326 | 283 | 258 |
| North Meols | 418 | 363 | 330 |
| Oldham | 13,212 | 11,467 | 10,433 |
| Ormskirk | 772 | 670 | 609 |
| Padiham | 1,707 | 1,481 | 1,348 |
| Penwortham | 1,902 | 1,651 | 1,502 |
| Prescot | 755 | 656 | 597 |
| Preston | 4,505 | 3,910 | 3,558 |
| Prestwich | 4,837 | 4,198 | 3,820 |
| Ribchester | 1,136 | 986 | 897 |
| Rochdale | 12,337 | 10,708 | 9,742 |
| St Michael's-on-Wyre | 533 | 462 | 421 |
| Standish | 1,772 | 1,538 | 1,399 |
| Tarleton | 158 | 137 | 125 |
| Walton-le-Dale | 1,451 | 1,259 | 1,146 |
| Warrington | 1,587 | 1,377 | 1,253 |
| West Central Lancashire | 1,326 | 1,151 | 1,047 |
| West Fylde | 299 | 259 | 236 |
| West Lancashire Coast | 65 | 57 | 52 |
| Whalley | 473 | 410 | 373 |
| Wigan | 8,120 | 7,047 | 6,412 |
| Winwick | 4,592 | 3,986 | 3,627 |

## Economic importance of hand weaving in the early nineteenth century

Whether these totals comprised the highest attained in Lancashire's cotton hand weaving trade is uncertain. On the one hand, it has been shown that the powerloom had made little impact by the early 1820s and, given the continued expansion of the cotton industry, it is quite conceivable that more handloom weavers were still required, especially in producing the finer and fancier wares.[10] On the other, the two detailed studies that have been undertaken into the dating of handloom weavers' cottages, one relating to Blackburn and the other to Preston, conclude that little new building of such dwellings took place beyond 1820.[11] Moreover, some contemporaries were reporting that, except in the case of dandy looms, an improved type of handloom introduced in the early nineteenth century,[12] no new handlooms were built to weave cotton after the mid-1820s, though others disagreed.[13] Possibly, therefore, productive capacity was matched to market needs and a peak of production was being attained. Yet such evidence is scarcely adequate and does not confirm that expansion of cotton hand weaving had ceased. Nor does it show that hand weaver numbers were declining, a theme addressed in Chapter 4.

In comparing the new estimate of hand weaver numbers with those made by contemporaries, two major impediments arise. One is that contemporaries did not break down their estimates to give a total for Lancashire. The other is the marked difference that exists in the two national estimates available for comparison. Thus, Kennedy's 1819 total of 240,000 cotton weavers is only two-thirds that of Guest's for 1820 (Table 1.2).

In tackling these problems, some help is provided by Norman Murray's suggestion that approximately 78,000 handlooms could be found in Scotland during 1820, of which around 60 per cent would have been used to weave cotton.[14] Taking Lancashire and Scotland together, thereby encompassing the districts where the great majority of the nation's cotton weaving would have taken place, something in excess of 200,000 cotton hand weavers would have been at work in 1820. It will not be overlooked that this figure is not too far removed from that given by Kennedy (240,000), especially when the relatively small numbers of hand weavers that would have been found elsewhere in the country are also taken into account. There is good reason to suppose, then, that estimates of there having been upwards of a quarter of a million cotton hand weavers in Britain when the trade was at its height is by no means a fanciful idea, even if it is somewhat exaggerated. It is also evident that, as J. H. Clapham surmised, the Guest figure bears little semblance to reality.[15] This is an important conclusion because, as was shown in Chapter 1, comparison of the Guest estimate with those made by Grimshaw and Smith in the early 1830s indicates that the overall number of cotton handloom weavers fell dramatically during the 1820s.[16] If, however, a much lower weaver total occurred around 1820 than Guest believed, any reduction during the 1820s may have been quite marginal. Indeed, should the calculations of Smith and Grimshaw be tolerably accurate, then, given the major upturn in trade during the mid-1830s, the number employed as cotton hand weavers may not have shown any appreciable fall before the early years of Victoria's reign.

The emergence of such a vast force of handloom weavers in the early nineteenth century reflects a number of interrelated aspects of the manner in which the cotton textile industry developed. The first is the rapidity of its growth. In recent years, it has become fashionable to discount the importance of the cotton textile industry in terms of promoting Britain's early industrialisation. Yet its growth record is impressive. Between 1772–74, it is estimated that the industry's gross value of output attained £0.6 million, a figure which had risen to £5.4 million between 1798–1800 and to as much as £21.7 million between 1815–17. Even these figures may be underestimates, neglecting to include value added at the finishing stage. Throughout this period, moreover, it seems that the value added by the industry increased steadily as a proportion of national income, attaining as much as 7 or 8 per cent by the end of the Napoleonic Wars.[17] Without doubt, the expansion of the cotton textile industry had a pronounced impact on Britain's economic growth during the late eighteenth and early nineteenth centuries. It is also clear that the export element in this growth was of major importance to the hand weaving trade. Taking the years 1814–16, when virtually all cotton cloth was still produced on handlooms, the real value of cotton twist and yarn exports averaged £2.5 million, compared with a real value of total cotton exports of £16.5 million, calicoes and muslins predominating.[18] The difference between the two figures may be more a function of value than of quantity, but, none the less, overseas sales of cotton cloth reached considerable levels.

The second aspect is the massive increase in labour productivity in cotton spinning and, to a lesser extent, in cotton finishing. Catling's calculations, based on the concept of operative hours to process 100 lbs of cotton, reveal that the figure for an eighteenth century hand spinner was a minimum of 50,000 hours, whereas the early mules reduced this to 2,000 hours and the water frame to a few hundred.[19] In cotton finishing, it has been estimated that a powered printing machine fitted with engraved rollers and operated by a man and a boy could produce as much calico per hour, using four colours, as could 200 operatives using the traditional block prints.[20] Such impressive rises in productivity had significance for the weaving sector in that the labour requirements of the spinning and finishing branches were comparatively small. This may be exemplified by the figures of occupational distribution for the rapidly-expanding village of Over Darwen, near Blackburn. Here, Anglican baptism registers show that 55 per cent of fathers registered between 1813–15 were weavers, compared with 16 per cent in cloth finishing and 2 per cent in other types of textile processing.[21] Accordingly, over the long term, growth in the weaving sector was not constrained by strong competition for labour from within the industry. Further, the rapid growth in spinners' productivity helped ensure that the weaving trade benefited from adequate supplies of yarn at cheaper prices. That some of this enhanced supply was of high quality brought new opportunities in the fancy trades, as Lloyd-Jones and Lewis have observed.[22]

The final aspect is the failure to mechanise weaving. Given the rapid growth of the cotton industry and the remarkable increases in labour productivity in the spinning and finishing branches, this failure inevitably led to the recruitment of a veritable army of hand weavers to meet the rising demand for cotton cloth. That a high proportion of hand weavers were women and children, whose output may have been rather less than that of most adult men, would only have exacerbated the problem.[23] So, too, would the tendency amongst weavers to cling to a pre-industrial pattern of working whereby they sought to attain a given level of income rather than to maximise earnings. According to the disapproving teetotaller Joseph Livesey, this was certainly the case during the early nineteenth century at Walton-le-Dale, near Preston, where local weavers regularly crowded into public houses to keep 'St Monday'.[24] In such circumstances, it is hardly suprising that vast numbers were drawn into hand weaving, especially when briskness of trade enhanced wages to levels with which alternative occupations could not compete. As well, entry into hand weaving was not greatly hindered by barriers, either of skill or finance.[25]

Turning to the sub-regional level, new estimates of hand weaver numbers can be offered for individual parishes or groups of parishes, as Table 2.1 shows. It must again be stressed that these estimates are no more than approximations and that in parishes with high numbers of hand weavers, the range within which the actual figure lies can only be stated in broad terms. At the extreme, the range for the Manchester figure exceeds 5,000. Even so, some useful conclusions may be drawn.

The most striking point to emerge is the high concentrations of hand weavers in south Lancashire. In Manchester parish alone, around one in eight of the county's weavers were found and there were substantial numbers in the satellite parishes of Bolton, Rochdale, Oldham and Bury. Indeed, taken together, these five parishes may have accounted for almost 40 per cent of Lancashire weavers. Comparatively high totals were also recorded in the nearby parishes of Wigan, Eccles and Leigh. The only major exceptions to this southern dominance were in Blackburn and Preston parishes, the former being second only to Manchester parish in the size of its hand weaving labour force. Blackburn apart, the north-east Lancashire parishes did not contain very large hand weaver numbers, despite being heavily dependent on the trade.[26]

Such variation in the concentrations of hand weavers obviously reflects the general distribution of population and economic activity within Lancashire, since most of the major towns bordered Manchester. By contrast, most settlements in north-east Lancashire were relatively small, the next biggest town after Blackburn, Colne, having just 7,274 inhabitants in 1821, only a third of the Blackburn figure.[27] Moreover, not all the larger settlements in north-east Lancashire were strongly involved in hand weaving, Accrington with only about 800 of its 5,370 population in the trade being the prime example. This all casts doubt on Bythell's contention that the heaviest concentrations of handloom weavers occurred in north-east Lancashire.[28] Heavy concentrations certainly did arise there, but they were by no means absent elsewhere in the county, especially in the south.

## The last shift

The Accrington example serves as a reminder that the proportions of handloom weavers could show appreciable variations from district to district. Taking a regional perspective, this aspect is examined in the following section. It may be noted here, however, that local variations in the degree of participation in hand weaving reflected the extent to which particular areas could offer comparative site advantages for alternative activities. Thus, in the case of Accrington, it seems that the availability of abundant supplies of soft water proved a major stimulant to the growth of the finishing trades, an advantage which could not be matched in, say, the Preston area.[29] Generally, the hand weaving industry occupied a higher proportion of the working population when the range and extent of alternative work opportunities were limited.

One other implication of these findings may be noted. This is that because the highest weaver concentrations tended to occur in parishes with major urban centres, it seems likely that, by the early nineteenth century, hand weavers would frequently, if not mostly, have been urban workers. This is not to deny that rural communities often depended to a very great extent on hand weaving, nor that they comprised a numerous group. However, the urban hand weaving trades expanded rapidly during the early nineteenth century, giving rise to a labour force composed mainly of specialists. As a result, a marked swing away from the predominance of the farmer/weaver, so frequently mentioned by eighteenth century writers, took place, giving rise to a rather more productive force of handloom weavers.[30] Secondly, a body of hand weavers was emerging which would be particularly susceptible to competition from the powerloom. As Chapter 1 shows, it was in urban rather than country areas that the vast majority of powerlooms were installed during the second quarter of the nineteenth century, competing strongly with the hand weavers producing the cheaper grades of cotton cloth. Since these comprised the bulk of hand weavers in urban areas, except, perhaps, at Bolton, massive job losses resulted, especially once the improved powerloom was adopted from the early 1840s.

Even allowing for inaccuracy, it is clear from the new estimates that hand weaving was of fundamental importance at regional as well as at national level. Indeed, in Lancashire, it was probably by far the largest employer of labour during the early nineteenth century. It is evident, too, that in the face of a massive growth in demand for its services, the hand weaving labour force exhibited a marked shift in its locational emphasis, as well as in its composition. Increasingly, the Lancashire hand weaver was an urban dweller who specialised in his trade; the rural, non-specialist weaver of the proto-industrial era was being rapidly superseded.

## 2  Geographical variation

In preparing the new estimates of hand weaver numbers, it is necessary to compile proportions of bridegroom weavers for each parish in Lancashire. The resultant figures may be used to gauge dependency on hand weaving from district to district.

These figures are given in Table 2.2 and are also presented as Map 1. (The techniques used in their preparation are discussed in Appendix A1.)

The figures demonstrate the great reliance on handloom weaving throughout most of central Lancashire, especially in the parish of Blackburn and along the Ribble Valley, including Penwortham, Ribchester and Walton-le-Dale; in several south Lancashire parishes, most notably those to the north and west of Manchester, at Flixton, Leigh, Oldham, Prestwich, Bolton, Eccles and Middleton; and in eastern districts, principally in the Rochdale, Colne and Haslingden areas. In each of these places, parish registers commonly described between a third and a half of all bridegrooms and fathers as weavers, whilst in several cases, including the populous parishes of Rochdale and Blackburn, bridegroom and father weavers equalled, or outnumbered, those of all other occupational groups taken together. At Newchurch-in-Pendle, to take the extreme, bridegrooms did so in a ratio of four to one.

By comparing the data in Tables 2.1 and 2.2, it can be seen that not all the areas where high weaver concentrations were found contained large numbers of hand weavers. This was the case, for example, at Newchurch-in-Pendle and Flixton. As well, whilst the percentage of hand weavers was comparatively low in Manchester parish, it is clear from Table 2.1 that no other Lancashire parish could boast a greater number of hand weavers during the early nineteenth century. Such differences were the product both of the wide range of employment opportunities available in a major city, not least in the service sector, and of the narrow economic base in Lancashire's rural weaving districts.

The data on which Table 2.2 is based relate mainly to parishes or to groups of parishes. As such, they mask the extent of hand weaver concentrations that occurred more locally. These are revealed, however, in the baptism register entries from chapels of ease, as the figures in Table 2.3 demonstrate. It is evident from these figures that rural settlement in Lancashire could depend upon the handloom to a remarkable degree. Since, too, hand weaving was neither age- nor gender-specific,[31] it must often have provided far greater employment opportunities for country people than would any other occupation. Such dependency on a single trade helps to show why the impact of trade depressions, including that of 1826, could be so acute in Lancashire's rural communities and why, when hand weaving went into long-term decline, their continued existence could be so sorely threatened.[32]

Elsewhere in Lancashire, as Map 1 reveals, relatively little handloom weaving took place, though few parish registers fail to make at least some reference to the trade, even those from Merseyside and North Lancashire, where the lowest weaver proportions were recorded. In such districts, however, the handloom did not provide significant employment opportunities. Only occasionally were appreciable concentrations to be found, as at Kirkham parish, in the Fylde, where 28 per cent of bridegrooms were estimated to have been handloom weavers between 1818 and 1822; at North Meols, the present-day Southport area, where the estimate was 23 per cent; and at Warrington, where it was 15 per cent. As Table 2.1 shows, there

Table 2.2  *Rankings of bridegroom weaver proportions in Lancashire parishes, groups of parishes and parish districts, 1818–22*

| Parish, parish district or parish group | Bridegroom weaver proportion | Parish, parish district or parish group | Bridegroom weaver proportion |
|---|---|---|---|
| 1. Newchurch-in-Pendle | 82 | 28. Wigan parish* | 32 |
| 2. Colne* | 68 | 29. Kirkham parish* | 28 |
| 3. Penwortham parish | 58 | 30. West Central Lancashire | 25 |
| 4. Leigh parish | 57 | 31. North Meols* | 23 |
| 5. Blackburn parish | 55 | 32. Preston parish* | 23 |
| 6. Prestwich* | 55 | 33. Accrington* | 21 |
| 7. Flixton parish | 54 | 34. Altham* | 19 |
| 8. Rochdale parish | 50 | 35. Manchester parish+ | 18 |
| 9. Haslingden* | 49 | 36. St Michael's-on-Wyre parish* | 16 |
| 10. Bolton Parish | 47 | 37. Warrington parish* | 15 |
| 11. Oldham | 47 | 38. Tarleton parish | 14 |
| 12. Central Lancashire | 44 | 39. Clitheroe* | 12 |
| 13. Church* | 43 | 40. Ormskirk | 10 |
| 14. Eccles parish* | 43 | 41. North Fylde | 8 |
| 15. Winwick parish* | 43 | 42. West Fylde | 7 |
| 16. Middleton parish* | 42 | 43. Lancaster area | 5 |
| 17. Padiham* | 42 | 44. Garstang parish* | 5 |
| 18. Ribchester parish* | 41 | 45. Prescot parish | 5 |
| 19. Walton-le-Dale | 41 | 46. Aughton parish* | 3 |
| 20. Bury parish | 40 | 47. Rufford parish* | 3 |
| 21. Deane parish | 38 | 48. Lune Valley | 2 |
| 22. Downham* | 38 | 49. Heysham parish* | 1 |
| 23. Newchurch-in-Rossendale* | 37 | 50. Huyton parish* | 1 |
| 24. Burnley | 36 | 51. West Lancashire Coast | 1 |
| 25. East Bolton Area | 36 | 52. Central Liverpool+ | 0 |
| 26. Standish parish* | 34 | 53. Merseyside | 0 |
| 27. Whalley* | 33 | 54. Toxteth Park | 0 |

\* Indicates estimates based on baptism register data.
+ The Central Liverpool figure is derived by summing the entries taken from the Liverpool register totals listed in Table A1.2 and of Manchester parish by summing those of Central and West Manchester.

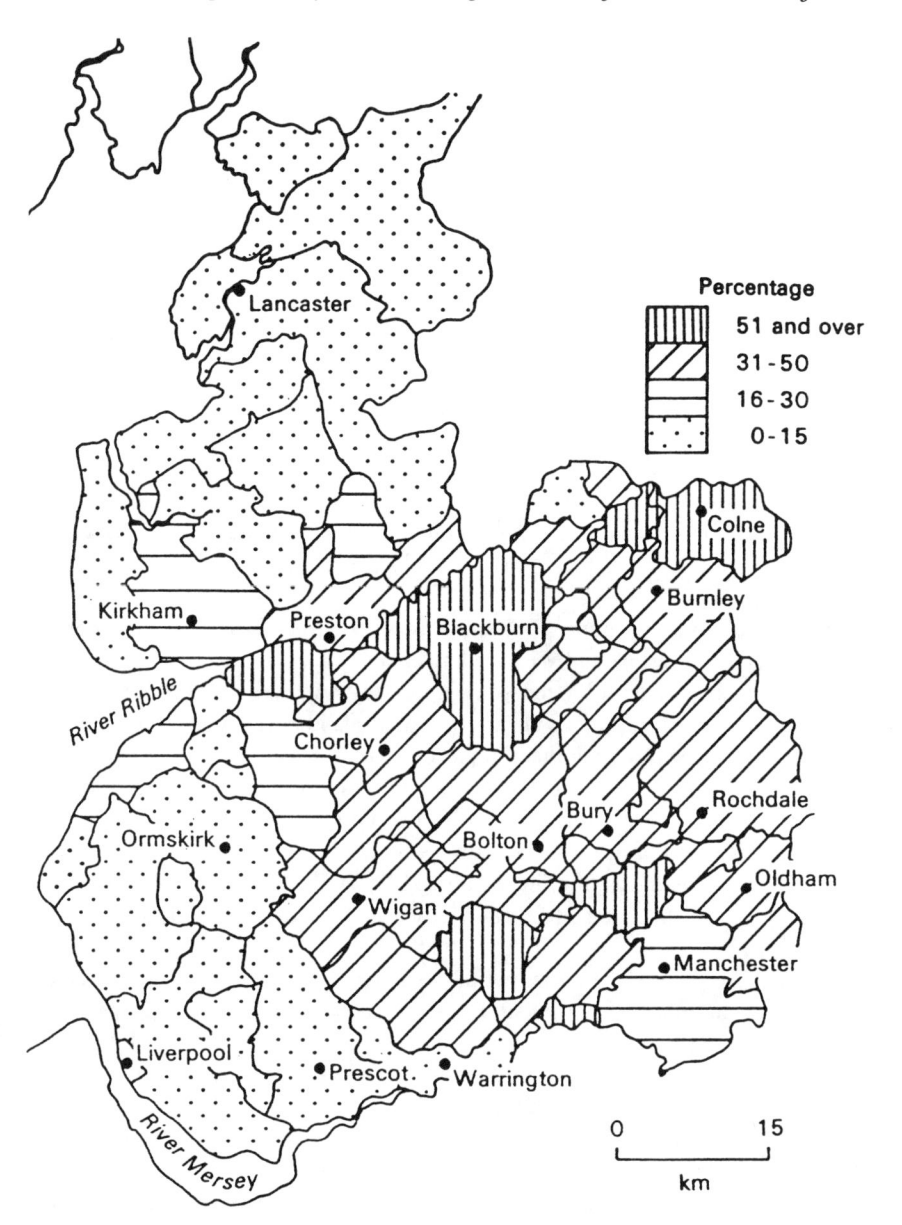

*Economic importance of hand weaving in the early nineteenth century*

*Map 1* Hand weaver proportions in the Lancashire textile districts, 1818–22

Table 2.3  *Hand weaver concentrations in Lancashire rural districts, 1818–22*

| District | Weaver numbers | Weaver % (all fathers) | Parish |
| --- | --- | --- | --- |
| Tockholes | 102 | 86 | Blackburn |
| Astley | 227 | 82 | Leigh |
| Brindle | 213 | 66 | Brindle |
| Milnrow | 260 | 65 | Rochdale |
| Tottington | 499 | 65 | Bury |
| Westhoughton | 403 | 65 | Deane |

may have been as many as 2,000 weavers in Kirkham parish and over 1,000 in Warrington parish. At North Meols, the total was no more than three or four hundred, but numbers may still have been rising (see Table 5.2). In the main, hand weavers were sparse in north and west Lancashire, non-manufacturing work usually remaining predominant.[33]

One approach to explaining the variations revealed in Map 1 is to consider the ways in which Lancashire's physical characteristics affected the nature of economic development. In line with the tenets of proto-industrialisation, most of the heaviest hand weaver concentrations occurred in the upland areas, where soils were too cold, damp and acidic, and the climate too harsh, to permit large-scale arable cultivation. Such districts included Rossendale in the east of the county and Pendle in the north-east. Of the former, G. H. Tupling remarks: 'the occupiers of land — small as well as great — had always been graziers rather than corngrowers because of the exigencies of climate and soil.'[34] Sarah Pearson, reaches a similar conclusion about the latter area, again observing that neither soil nor situation favoured arable cultivation. She finds that the amount of arable land here decreased during the early modern period — it averaged only about a third of the total during the mid-sixteenth century — and the pastoral nature of local farms become more pronounced.[35] Again, it was reported that there was little grain growing at Bury in 1800, whilst in the mid-1820s, land in the Blackburn area was principally put down to grass with 'very little ploughing'.[36] Such evidence helps to confirm T. W. Fletcher's view that farming was always limited in the east Lancashire textile districts.[37]

In considering how the prevalence of pastoral farming fostered domestic textile production and other types of proto-industry, emphasis has been placed on the notion of under-employed labour. It is held that pastoral farming, especially stock rearing, was relatively economical in terms of labour requirements. As a result, at least some labour in pastoral regions was available for alternative employment, perhaps in mining or in domestic textile production.[38] Such labour might also be comparatively inexpensive and hence attractive to those entrepreneurs engaged in industrial activities.[39] Nor would its supply have been restricted by guild regulations.[40] Moreover, because families in upland pastoral areas found it hard to make a living, they were keen to supplement their incomes through domestic industry.[41] Both employer and employed, therefore, had much to gain from industrial development.

Whilst this analysis may go some way to explaining the varying hand weaver concentrations that developed in Lancashire, it must be qualified in a number of respects. In the first place, a strong association between upland pastoral farming and handloom weaving did not always arise. Secondly, the argument that pastoral farming gave rise to surplus labour ignores other influences, particularly population growth and land inheritance customs. It also overlooks problems that could arise in lowland areas in attracting labour for industrial purposes. Lastly, the importance of labour availability, however it arose, in encouraging the concentration of handloom weaving must not be overemphasised. Other considerations were significant, too, especially climatic variations and the locational improvements that accompanied industrial expansion.

Turning to the first of these issues, it is apparent from parish register analysis that some upland pastoral areas, most notably the Forest of Bowland in the north of the county, did not develop textile production on any appreciable scale. Moreover, not every district in which hand weaving predominated was located in upland parts of the county. Several lowland parishes including Leigh and Flixton, to the west of Manchester, and Penwortham, Hoole, Croston and Leyland, all situated to the south of Preston, were highly dependent on the trade by the early nineteenth century. They provide yet other examples of the development of proto-industry in lowland zones, amongst which the East Anglian woollen industry stands out.[42]

One consideration which is important in explaining the Lancashire exceptions is accessibility. Each lowland parish with a high concentration of weavers in the early nineteenth century was adjacent to at least one major urban centre. From the manufacturers' point of view, this would have meant that any additional distribution and collection costs incurred by going further afield would have been kept within tolerable bounds. Some of these costs, if not all, might be passed on to the weavers. As a rule, though, weavers would have placed fairly strict limits on the distances they travelled in order to collect thread and return finished cloth. In exceptional circumstances, perhaps during a major upturn in trade, these arguments would have held less sway and relatively inaccessible labour would have been utilised, but remoteness from the main urban centres would normally have been a severe hindrance to the development of large-scale domestic weaving. Such considerations help to explain why handloom weaving never made much headway in the North Fylde and Bowland Forest areas. At a distance from the leading regional markets and from sources of raw materials and not easily accessible, these districts were at a fundamental disadvantage as far as industrial development was concerned, compared with the uplands in the vicinity of Manchester and the other major textile towns.[43]

A second point that arises in explaining the high concentrations of hand weavers in lowland districts is that the association with pastoral farming may still have occurred. Only limited areas of the Lancashire lowlands were devoted to arable farming during the early industrial period, as John Aikin observed. Writing in the 1790s, he noted that some wheat and a good deal of barley was grown in lowland Lancashire, but that it was supposed that county 'did not raise more than one quarter of the grain it consumes.' He continued:

The lands near the great towns are chiefly employed in pasturage; and at a greater distance, a large portion of the ground is in pasturage and meadow. A great number of cows are kept near the towns for the purpose of supplying them with milk and butter.[44]

Dairying would probably have been more labour-intensive than beef rearing, but may still have provided insufficient employment opportunities to fully absorb the available labour.

Whether all the major centres of hand weaving in lowland Lancashire concentrated on pastoral farming during the proto-industrial era is far from certain, however. Local detail is lacking and the position is complicated by the growing practice from the late eighteenth century of converting from arable to pasture.[45] On the other hand, there is not much evidence to suggest that a strong association existed in Lancashire between domestic textile production and arable farming, a link which scholars such as Gullickson and Clarkson have found elsewhere.[46] It is true that hand weaving was not unimportant in the Fylde, traditionally regarded as Lancashire's granary, but the area could scarcely be regarded as a major centre of textile production.[47]

It may be, then, that the connection between hand weaving and pastoral farming was important in both upland and lowland Lancashire. Even so, the prevalence of animal husbandry was not the sole, or even the major, reason why labour surpluses arose. Other explanations can be offered, including the impact of land inheritance customs. In particular, it has been argued that partible inheritance created small, uneconomic plots of land, which were insufficient in size to provide families with an adequate living. Accordingly, it became necessary for at least some family members to seek jobs outside agriculture, often, though by no means always, in domestic industry.[48]

As far as Lancashire is concerned, evidence has been adduced to demonstrate that partible inheritance was indeed practised in the textile districts. Thus, G. H. Tupling has shown that Rossendale parents often divided their estates amongst their children, with the result that the predominance of small land holdings was noticeably more pronounced in the nineteenth century than it had been during the seventeenth. He also notes that the subdivision of land in Rossendale had been taking place for centuries prior to the early industrial era and that industrialisation may have assisted the practice. He concludes that the continued fragmentation of land would have left families without sufficient means of subsistence, had they not been able to combine agrarian pursuits with domestic manufacturing.[49]

Whether similar practices were usual elsewhere in the Lancashire textile districts during the proto-industrial era is unclear. However, John Swain has discovered that primogeniture rather than partible inheritance dominated in the Colne area. Here younger sons only inherited when land was available in more than one place or on a temporary basis. Nevertheless, much subdivision of land still took place in the area, as both he and Mary Brigg have demonstrated.[50] Sometimes this was permanent, being achieved through the sale and mortgage of plots; through the establishment of subtenancies; and, to a limited extent, through partible inheritance.[51] Swain reasons that this subdivision could have arisen from severe financial problems arising when the eldest son inherited land, not least because of provision he had to make for his family. A widowed mother, for example, might expect to receive a quarter of her husband's land holdings, as well as a third of his personal estate.[52] Consequently, Swain argues, land holdings became fragmented to the point where supplementary income often became essential, both for those with land and those without.[53]

The subdivision of land holdings referred to by Brigg, Tupling and Swain took place in Lancashire's upland hand weaving districts. However, it also occurred, but for a different reason, in at least one lowland hand weaving centre. This was at Culcheth, near Leigh, where, G. N. Gandy found, thirty-five 'charterers' acquired small plots of land from an enclosure award made in 1751. None received as much as an acre and twenty-four were given areas equivalent, on average, to no more than twenty square yards. Such plots were plainly too small to constitute viable agricultural holdings. Even so, Gandy observes, they were 'entirely suited to supporting cottage industry'.[54] This indeed emerged strongly in the village, parish registers regularly listing over two-thirds of the fathers as hand weavers between 1813 and 1825.[55]

How far inheritance customs and enclosure awards created subdivisions of land elsewhere in Lancashire is uncertain, though Wadsworth and Mann point out the frequency with which small land holdings occurred in various parts of Lancashire by the late eighteenth century.[56] And Walton suggests that landless, or almost landless cottagers, dependent entirely on manufacturing, were increasing rapidly by the middle of the century.[57]

Further discussion as to why surplus labour arose in proto-industrial areas concerns the extent to which inmigration took place and the degree to which, at local level, the emergence of proto-industry stimulated birth rates. As far as the former aspect is concerned, the restrictions imposed on industrial development in 'closed' villages and the encouragement given in 'open' villages have been seen as crucial.[58] Regarding the latter, family reconstitution studies have indicated that, in some instances, early industrialisation was accompanied by a marked reduction in the age of first marriage and by an appreciable rise in fertility.[59] Whether this was because parents saw economic opportunities in having children is doubted, however, not least because any return would take many years to materialise and because demographic changes of this type also occurred outside proto-industrial areas, where child employment opportunities were limited.[60]

Detail relating to Lancashire on both these issues is sparse, though some evidence is available for Rossendale. Here, it is argued, abolition of the Forest Laws in 1507 removed a major impediment to in-migration. Accordingly, throughout the seventeenth and eighteenth centuries, migrants were attracted into the area from neighbouring lowlands, either establishing new colonies or creating offshoots to existing ones.[61] In Tupling's words:

Settlers were attracted not so much by the prospect of becoming well-to-do farmers, as by the mere facility with which land might be enclosed or acquired to set up a homestead.[62]

In the Colne area, too, squatters found that common land was plentiful; that entry fines could be avoided; and that rent from encroachments was seldom payable.[63]

As far as Rossendale's natural population increase is concerned, William King's research has shown that the birth rate there rose from under thirty per thousand in 1716 to almost forty-one per thousand in 1731. Thereafter it stabilised at around forty per thousand until the 1760s. Marriage rates also rose during the period, whilst the interval between births fell from an average of 27.8 months in the early 1720s to 22.3 months in the early 1780s.[64] Walton observes that this is very much as the proto-industrialists would expect, especially since population remained widely dispersed,[65] reflecting the development of a rurally-based labour force rather than an urban one. And, reasonably enough, he also expresses the view that similar changes almost certainly took place at some point in the early to mid-eighteenth century throughout the Lancashire textile districts.[66]

One part of upland Lancashire where eighteenth century population does not seem to have risen, however, is the Forest of Bowland. John Porter has shown that the number of families in the Forest — only around 150 — did not alter between the Hearth Tax year of 1664 and the national census year of 1801.[67] Probably, therefore, a lack of available labour as well as remoteness ensured that Bowland Forest did not move into proto-industry on any significant scale. In the absense of any dynamic interaction between industrial development and demographic change, the area tended to stagnate and remained heavily dependent on pastoral agriculture.[68]

Before leaving the labour supply issue, one more hypothesis must be examined. It concerns possible difficulties textile manufacturers could encounter in finding sufficient labour to establish themselves in lowland districts. Given the sustained development of the Lancashire economy during the late eighteenth and early nineteenth centuries, the labour market remained buoyant, not least for farm workers. This is reflected in John Marshall's finding that Lancashire's agricultural wage rates were amongst the highest in the kingdom at that time. Marshall also notes that they often tended to be higher on town outskirts than at a distance.[69] Accordingly, there was comparatively little opportunity for textile manufacturers to save on labour costs by seeking employees in lowland districts, except, perhaps, in more remote locations, with the attendant problems. In general, their ability to attract labour from established activities, including agriculture, would always have been difficult when comparative locational advantages operated strongly against them. This may help to explain the relatively low weaver proportions found in Manchester, where competition for labour from the commercial interests may have been powerful enough to curb the ability of handloom manufacturers to find the labour they required, even allowing for the rapidity of the town's population growth. Doubtless, too, lowland labour would often have lacked the skills and experience necessary to undertake certain types of textile work, including the finer and fancier grades of weaving, even if tempting piece rates had been offered.

There are strong indications, therefore, that the availability of labour for textile production in eighteenth century Lancashire arose for a variety of reasons, not just because of the limited demands on its services made by pastoral farming. To some extent, indeed, the opportunities for farmwork in pastoral areas must actually have grown as waste land was increasingly turned into pasture. However, this expansion was insufficient to absorb the growing body of landless labourers created by a rising population and the division of land holdings. It was from this group that much of the labour force required by the emerging textile industry was drawn.

It remains to discuss the third qualification concerning the association between hand weaving and upland pastoral areas. This is the need to avoid overstating the influence of labour availability on the localisation of hand weaving. As has been noted, other considerations are also important and their impact must be assessed. To begin with, the climatic variations that occurred between upland and lowland Lancashire are taken.

It has often been said that the main centres of cotton production in Lancashire were located where natural humidity was highest. As D. A. Farnie explains:

That humidity was maintained by the prevailing westerly winds which became saturated with moisture as they flowed unchecked across the warm waters of the Atlantic and were forced to shed their moisture only when they reached the windward slopes of the Pennines. The mountainous backbone of northern England served a dual function: it kept back to leeward the harmful dry easterly winds and it attracted to its western slopes the rain-bearing westerlies, whose prevalence raised the moisture-content of the air almost to saturation point . . .[70]

Not every scholar, however, has accepted this theory. In particular, it has been roundly challenged by W. H. Ogden who, in a closely-argued paper written in 1927, urged that the theory was 'much overrated'.[71] He based his criticisms on the humidity records collected at nine weather stations in various parts of the north-west. Most of the records were made over comparatively long periods in the late nineteenth and early twentieth centuries and comprised all that were available. Unexpectedly, they revealed that the highest humidity levels did not always occur in the major textile districts. In particular, the humidity levels for Southport proved to be somewhat higher than those for either Manchester or Bolton. This was also true of the Warrington and St Helens readings, though these had only been taken over four- and nine-year periods respectively. Ogden concluded that an area around Liverpool, stretching through St Helens to Warrington, appeared to have an atmosphere at least as humid as that of Manchester and Bolton. Accordingly, he urged

> a stronger control still must have been exercised to pull the manufacture through this belt to one with only the same or less humidity very much further from the seaboard.

This control, he continued, could perhaps be found by studying the rainfall map of Lancashire which, he maintained, showed a progressive increase in values from the Dee Valley to the Rossendale Anticline.

Ogden's ideas have been accepted by a number of more recent commentators, some of whom have taken them to more extreme lengths. For example, Freeman, Rogers and Kinvig, writing in 1960, observe that they can be summarily dismissed as a factor in explaining the restricted location of cotton production in Lancashire, since the available statistics show little difference between the east and west of the county.[72] However, D. A. Farnie has offered an altogether more searching appraisal of the Ogden thesis. He points out that it is based on statistics of 1893–1922 and is not corroborated by contemporary evidence. Additionally, he stresses the importance of humidity in the processing of cotton, pointing out that cotton fibres are hygroscopic, so that they become more pliable and less brittle as their moisture-content approaches its optimum level. He suggests, too, that adequate humidity was more important in weaving than in spinning cotton, having particular value in reducing the incidence of faults in the finished product and making possible the manufacture of fine cloths. He also emphasises the pains taken by cotton handloom weavers to create humid conditions in their workshops, which led them to prefer cellar rather than groundfloor locations and to make use of earth floors.[73]

Any assessment of these conflicting opinions must begin by confirming the vital importance of attaining adequate humidity levels in order to spin and weave cotton successfully. The essential point is that prior to weaving, the warps in the loom had to be strengthened by the application of size, a thin paste normally made by boiling together wheat flour and potatoes.[74] The size was brushed on to the warps and had to be dried before weaving could commence. However, it was necessary to ensure that the size did not dry too much. If it did, the warps became hard and brittle and difficult for the weaver to work.[75] Only by ensuring a high and constant level of humidity in the loomshop could the problem be overcome. It is for this reason that the great majority of handloom weavers' cottages in the Lancashire cotton districts were provided with cellar or groundfloor loomshops. At lower levels, damp conditions could be more readily obtained, not least by means of earth floors. As one contemporary explains, it was common for weavers to scoop out a hole in the floor beneath each loom and to fill them with water. The water could then evaporate up through the warps, helping to keep them pliable.[76]

The evidence both of contemporaries and of fieldwork observations lends overwhelming support to the idea that cellar and groundfloor loomshops prevailed in cotton weaving. As an example of the former, the authoritative comments of William Hickson, the assistant handloom weavers' commissioner, may be cited:

> The great majority of hand-loom cotton-weavers work in cellars sufficiently light to enable them to throw the shuttle, but cheerless because seldom visited by the sun. The reason cellars are chosen is, that cotton requires to be woven damp. The air, therefore, must be cool and moist, instead of warm and dry.

He added that the cellar floors were seldom boarded or paved; that access was via a step-ladder; and that, on occasions, he had seen the walls running with water. Some cellar loomshops, though, he found to be 'light and convenient apartments'. Nor, he observed, were they always situated in cellars, many being found in 'an unboarded room on the groundfloor'.[77]

Other contemporary evidence verifies Hickson's comments. Both Friedrich Engels and William Longson, a Manchester weaver, maintained that domestic weaving shops in Lancashire were usually in cellars.[78] Again, illustrations of eighteen domestic loomshops which James Brandwood of Turton built, or planned to build, were all situated in cellars or at groundfloor level. Brandwood also shows that cotton weavers' loomshops possessed design features for maintaining humidity other than earth floors (Plate 1). Most notable amongst them was the avoidance of direct outside access.[79] This could have been crucial on dry, sunny days, when the problem of maintaining the desired level of humidity would have been greatest. Whilst natural humidity was normally high in the Lancashire cotton districts, it was not always high enough, especially when the finest cottons and fancy goods were being woven.[80]

Investigation of surviving examples of former domestic loomshops adds further weight to the argument. Fieldwork carried out in the mid-1970s revealed several hundred examples, very few of which showed evidence of upper-storey weaving.[81] This is also the case with regard to more recent surveys in the Blackburn and Accrington area.[82] In fact, survivals are particularly numerous in Blackburn, and include such important colonies as Mile End, where over sixty cottages with groundfloor and cellar loomshops were built (Plate 2).[83] It has to be conceded that alterations to houses often make it difficult to recognise former loomshops. Also, rooms used for domestic weaving were not always equipped with the characteristic rows of windows (Plate 3).[84] Hence, upper-storey loomshops with single windows or, more likely, pairs of separated windows may have been constructed. This certainly appears to have been the case in the extreme north-east of Lancashire, around Burnley and Colne, a point that is dealt with in Chapter 3.[85] In general, however, it seems improbable that upper-storey loomshops were usual in the Lancashire cotton districts. The absence of numerous rows of cottages with long ranges of upper-storey windows, so characteristic of the woollen areas of the West Riding and east Lancashire, is striking.[86] Besides, the contemporary evidence that,

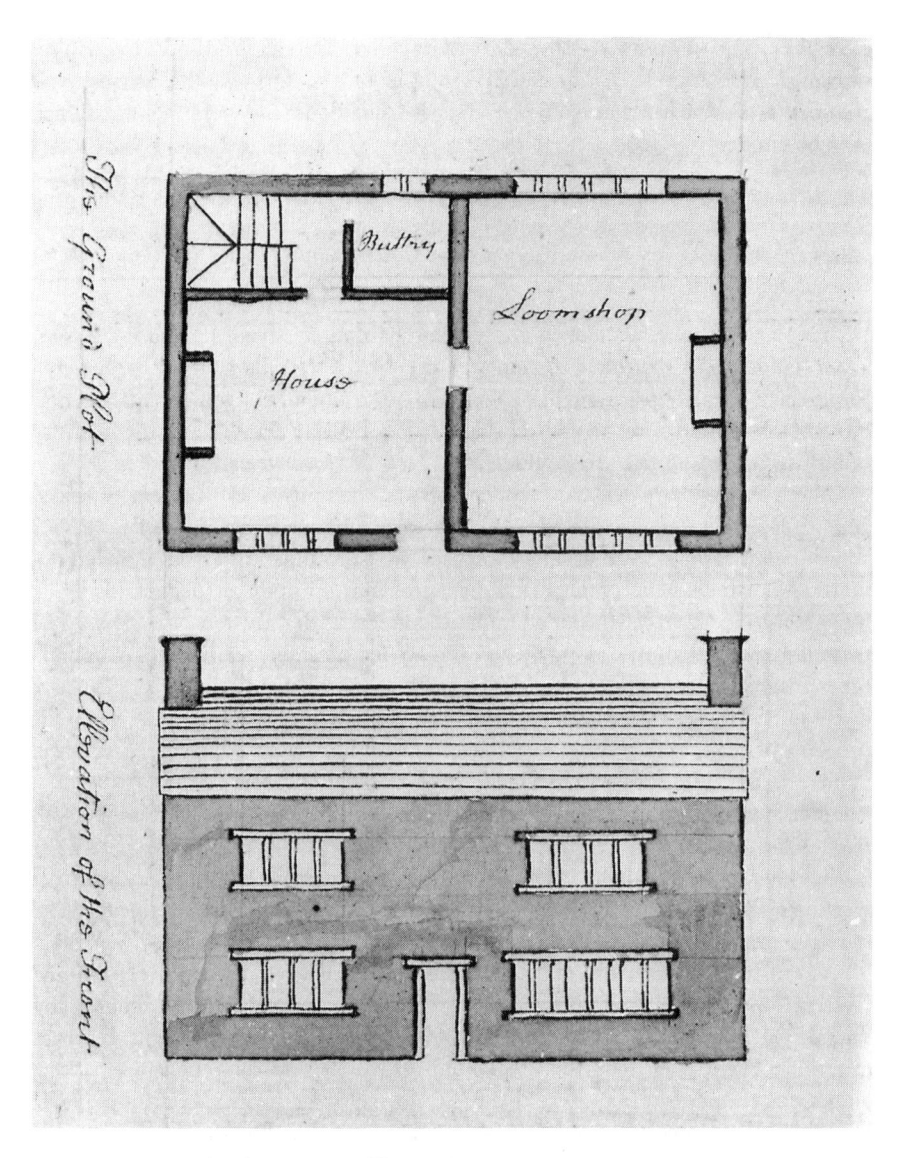

1  Armygreaves House, Turton, near Bolton, 1809

*Economic importance of hand weaving in the early nineteenth century*

2 West View Place, Blackburn. Good lighting was obtained by raising the cellar windows above ground-floor level and, perhaps, by providing a cellar-well in front of the windows.

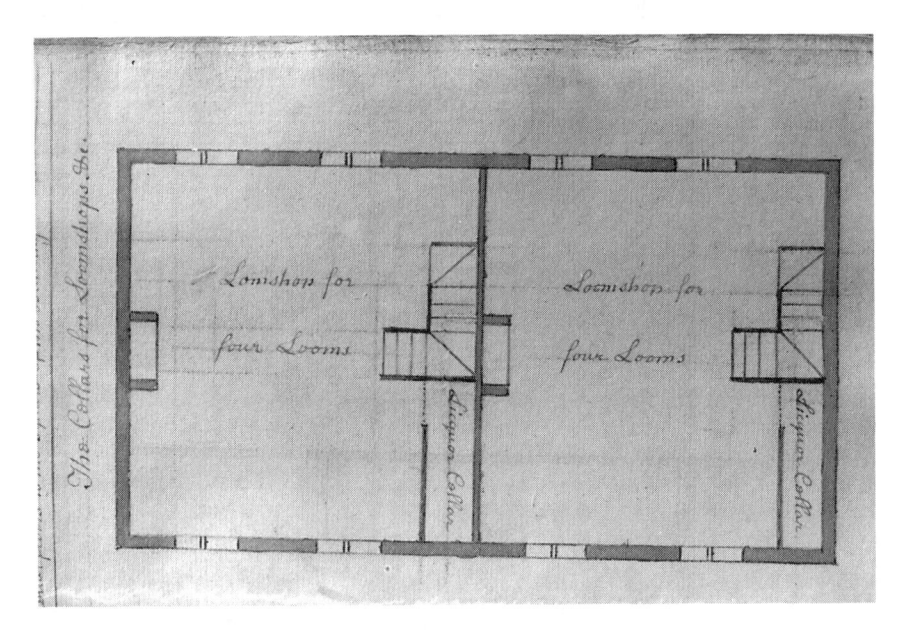

3 Plan of cellar loomshops drawn by James Brandwood, c. 1800. Instead of two rows of windows, four separated windows are shown.

for technical reasons, lower-storey loomshops were needed in cotton weaving is far too strong to dismiss.

Faced with this weight of evidence, it is hard to dispute that humidity levels were of crucial importance in the cotton hand weaving trade. The question remains, however, as to whether the areas in which hand weaving was highly concentrated, including the lowland areas, had significantly higher levels of humidity than those where the trade was only sparsely represented.

The greatest obstacle in seeking to decide the issue is the paucity of humidity statistics. None are available for the early nineteenth century, when hand weaving would have attained its maximum geographical spread, and those used by Ogden are drawn from a relatively small number of stations. Whether, as Ogden appears to believe, they give an accurate enough portrayal on which to base firm conclusions must be doubted. At first sight, three anomalies in nine readings might be seen as a telling point in his favour. However, it must be recalled that two of the figures relate to much shorter time periods than the others and are not, therefore, strictly comparable. If, in reality, only one of the statistics, that for Southport, was out of line, his argument loses much of its force. The absence of figures for other parts of lowland Lancashire, especially for settlements to the north of the Ribble, is also a serious weakness when attempting to generalise about the county as a whole.

## Economic importance of hand weaving in the early nineteenth century

Even if Ogden's figures are considered to be reliable indicators that humidity levels were likely to have been as high, or higher, in certain parts of lowland Lancashire than in the county's upland zone, the value of the humidity argument is little diminished as far as cotton hand weaving is concerned. In the first place, as Map 1 reveals, the trade was by no means confined to the upland zone. Indeed, there were noticeable concentrations of hand weavers in the Southport area, around a quarter of the North Meols fathers being engaged in the trade between 1818 and 1822, as well as at Warrington, where the corresponding figure was 15 per cent. Thus, Ogden's most reliable lowland humidity figure was obtained from a district where cotton handloom weaving was of some importance, perhaps providing more employment than any other occupation. Secondly, it is by no means certain that any differences in natural humidity between the upland and lowland areas were sufficient to exert a critical influence. For the most part, it seems that the Southport figures were only a few per cent more than those of Bolton or Manchester, though those from Warrington were notably higher than any others. What may have been more significant than the differentials was the attainment of a minimum degree of humidity, below which cotton processing would not have been economically worthwhile. Nor should it be overlooked that humidity levels could be improved artificially in the domestic loomshop, as has already been noted. In the absence of more conclusive evidence, it must remain an open question as to how far the expansion of cotton handloom weaving into lowland Lancashire was inhibited by inadequate levels of humidity.

Other influences on the geographical containment of the Lancashire handloom weaving trade were linked to the general locational advantages acquired by the cotton industry as it expanded rapidly during the late eighteenth and early nineteenth centuries. Foremost amongst them was the localisation of spinning and finishing in the upland districts, where abundant water was available to generate power and to meet processing requirements. As well, the terrain was hilly enough to allow the use of the more efficient overshot and backshot waterwheels, as field observation so often indicates.[87] William Yates' map of Lancashire, published in 1786, shows a marked concentration of water-power sites in the eastern half of the county,[88] a pattern repeated on later maps.[89] Indeed, water-powered spinning and finishing mills in upland rural areas were slow to decline, despite the growing importance of the steam-powered urban mill. One authority takes the view that waterwheels continued to provide most of the power used in the British cotton industry until after 1820.[90] Essentially, the relationship between the spinning, weaving and finishing trades was symbiotic and to have any one branch located at an appreciable distance from the others added to organisational problems and overall costs. To an extent, though, this happened because of the relative quickness with which the spinning branch of the industry became urbanised. And even when both spinning and weaving had become largely town based, the need for pure water ensured that cotton finishing remained firmly located in rural areas.[91]

The localisation of hand weaving in upland Lancashire was also reinforced by extensive improvements made to the transport system in the late eighteenth and early nineteenth centuries. Best known is the establishment of a canal network, which, despite difficulties brought by the steepness of slope, penetrated into every part of the textile zone, except Rossendale, by 1821.[92] Its importance is best illustrated, perhaps, by noting that no large town in textile Lancashire was without a canal link. Of equal significance, but less well appreciated, is the major programme of road improvement undertaken by turnpike trusts, the impressive scale of which can be seen from comparison of Lancashire's early county maps.[93] It involved the easing of gradients; the straightening and widening of carriageways; the reduction of summit heights; and, in some instances, route shortening. For example in 1824, the promoters of a new road between Preston and Blackburn claimed that traffic on the existing route (the present-day Preston Old Road) was hindered by 'five formidable hills', the gradients on which were as high as one in five.[94] Their new road, they maintained, would not exceed a slope of one in twenty and would shorten the route by two miles, a reduction of some 20 per cent. In the event, this seems to have been achieved, though, in order to accommodate the reduced distance, the summit height on the new road was increased, as map evidence reveals.[95] Similar improvements are evident throughout the upland textile area during this period, the road between Bolton and Blackburn, for instance, being re-routed to achieve a slope of no more than 1.5 inches to the yard (one in twenty-four).[96] Minor routes, too, were improved, James Brandwood, for example, amending the line of the road through the village of Edgworth, near Bolton to achieve a much easier gradient.[97]

Such improvements to transport facilities were of profound importance to an industry dependent on outwork, on imported raw materials and on export sales. Additionally, the need for textile entrepreneurs to attend the Manchester market had to be met. By the mid-1820s, more than a thousand were visiting the town regularly, a sizeable proportion of them engaged in hand weaving.[98] The expansion of coach traffic they helped to generate is typified by the case of Preston. In 1800, a dozen coaches plied daily to and from the town, a figure which had risen almost sixfold thirty years later.[99]

Finally, it should be noted that the concentration of cotton weaving in upland Lancashire was also facilitated by the availability of local finance. Of course, that needed to meet fixed capital cost per unit of production was comparatively small in an outwork compared with a factory industry. Nevertheless, given the size to which the domestic weaving trades developed in early nineteenth century Lancashire, the total investment required in warehouse buildings and equipment would have been far from insignificant. No doubt the cost to individual manufactures could, in some instances, be lessened by conversion of existing buildings and premises might be rented rather than bought. Moreover, the cost of loomshop provision was borne partly from sources outside the textile industry. Some manufacturers did own weavers' cottages,[100] but there is no doubt that many such dwellings were financed by terminating building societies, the funds for which came from local people in various walks of life. This was so in the case of weavers' cottages erected by the building society formed at Longridge, near Preston in 1793. Of the twenty original subscribers, only four were weavers, compared with nine yeomen and two stonemasons. The others were a cotton spinner, a shopkeeper, a carpenter, a clogger and a travelling dealer.[101] Most members, therefore, may have been motivated to join the society for investment purposes, or because they saw work opportunities in building the houses, rather than for reasons to do with self help. They were certainly permitted to rent their dwellings rather than to become owner occupiers.[102] But the wider point is that local finance was often available to help in the construction of domestic loomshops and that this could be drawn from beyond the textile sector.

With regard to working capital provision, examples provided by M. M. Edwards are instructive. These reveal that textile manufacturers could obtain short-term credit from various local sources during the late eighteenth and early nineteenth centuries. Thus, John Smalley, a Blackburn cotton manufacturer, frequently exchanged long-dated for short-dated bills of exchange drawn by him on his Manchester dealer.[103] Again, James Brierley, an Oldham cotton manufacturer, settled his account with Manchester merchants by assigning his house to them.[104] And instances are cited of cotton manufacturers engaging in banking activities for others in the trade, including Ephriam Maymon of Blackburn.[105] These examples testify to the importance of local business connections in securing working capital in the weaving trade, though, as is well known, more distant sources were also tapped, including London merchants.[106]

To summarise, parish register evidence reveals that handloom weaving in Lancashire became highly localised, mainly, but not entirely, in the upland zone, Bowland excepted. This was probably so throughout the proto-industrial era, with, if anything, some extension of the trade into lowland areas as upland labour became fully engaged in textile work.[107] In part, this localisation is explained by the availability of cheap and plentiful labour, a feature of handloom weaving throughout much of its history. This labour was the product of a growing population and of an emerging groups of landless workers, which could not be supported by pastoral farming and which, therefore, turned to textile work. As well, the upland weaving zone possessed, or acquired, other locational advantages for textile manufacture, which were absent, or less pronounced, in the lowland zone. These included the natural advantages of site associated with climate and relief; the growth of textile spinning and finishing; and the general improvements made to the ecomonic infrastructure of the area, especially in terms of transport and credit networks, as industry and commerce continued to expand.

## 3  Impact on settlement formation

Field surveys in rural Lancashire have revealed numerous extant examples of former handloom weavers' cottages.[108] In some instances they are single dwellings, or pairs, but short terraces are also common. Where several terraces occur in close proximity, they often gave rise to small settlements of around a dozen or twenty cottages. Occasionally, bigger hand weavers' colonies were created, including those at Mile End, Blackburn and Club Houses, Horwich, each of which consisted of around fifty dwellings (see Map 2 and Plate 4).[109] Thus, hand weavers' colonies could constitute quite sizeable rural settlements of a few hundred people, even though the population of most was far less than this.

Such settlements grew up on sites that were previously uninhabited. But hand weavers' terraces were also built in established hamlets and villages, as at Ribchester and Mellor, near Blackburn.[110] Here, as elsewhere, hand weavers' terraces added appreciably to existing settlement, perhaps to an unprecedented extent.

Precisely how much rural settlement was generated in textile Lancashire by hand weavers' colonies is difficult to judge, largely because cottages which may have been erected for handloom weaving have often been altered beyond recognition. However, useful insights may be obtained from mid-nineteenth century census schedule entries. For many rural settlements, these allow the number of houses containing hand weavers to be identified, so that the proportion they formed of the total number of houses can be computed. Examples drawn from rural settlements around Blackburn in 1851 are presented in Table 2.4.

In interpreting these figures, it must be borne in mind that, in each settlement, an indeterminate number of weavers' cottages may have been taken out of commission by 1851 and that, compared with the early nineteenth century, the total number of houses may have increased. Thus, when hand weaving was at its height, the proportion of weavers' cottages in these settlements may have been higher than those given in the table. On the other hand, it cannot be assumed that all cottages containing hand weavers were built for domestic weaving, nor that all domestic weavers worked in the house in which they lived. For both these reasons, the percentage figures in the table might be too high. Where the balance lies can only be conjectural, though it is unlikely that anything more than a small proportion of domestic loomshops were converted from existing premises or that the great majority of hand weavers did not work in their own residences. If anything, therefore, the proportionate figures given in the table would have been higher had they referred to the early rather than to the mid-nineteenth century.

This being so, it is plain that colonisation by hand weavers could have a profound effect on the development of rural settlement. This was by no means always the case, as the figures for Great Harwood and Rishton demonstrate. Yet it is quite evident that, even as late as mid-century, hand weavers' terraces could often form the majority of houses in rural areas, in some cases by a sizeable margin.

In urban areas, too, there are clear indications of the importance of hand weavers' colonies in settlement growth. Compared with rural areas, census data are less useful in judging this, mainly because hand weaving tended to decline relatively quickly in towns, so that conversion of domestic loomshops to other uses was already well advanced by mid-century. Even so, other sources from this period are available, some of which, including large-scale map surveys, do not extend to rural

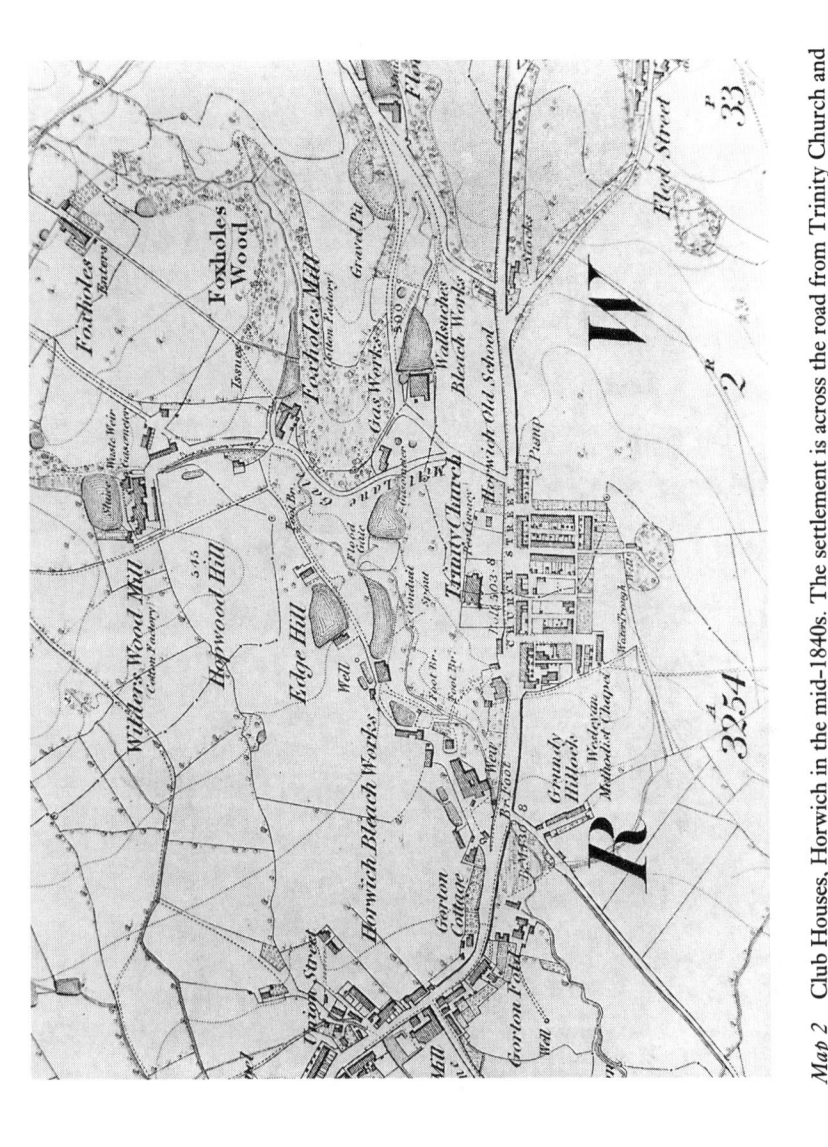

*Map 2* Club Houses, Horwich in the mid-1840s. The settlement is across the road from Trinity Church and its siting was strongly influenced by the proximity of finishing mills.

4 Most cottages in the settlement had cellar loomshops, though a number may have been equipped with small groundfloor loomshops.

*Economic importance of hand weaving in the early nineteenth century*

Table 2.4 *Proportions of dwellings in rural areas occupied by hand weavers in 1851*

| District | Total houses | Houses with hand weavers | % age of houses with hand weavers |
| --- | --- | --- | --- |
| Salesbury | 67 | 55 | 82 |
| Dinckley | 25 | 19 | 76 |
| Osbaldeston | 49 | 37 | 76 |
| Ramsgreave | 76 | 51 | 67 |
| Tockholes | 170 | 98 | 58 |
| Balderstone | 122 | 70 | 57 |
| Wilpshire | 49 | 27 | 55 |
| Samlesbury | 260 | 97 | 37 |
| Pleasington | 84 | 28 | 33 |
| Great Harwood | 490 | 126 | 26 |
| Rishton | 142 | 28 | 20 |

districts. Thus, at Blackburn, map evidence can be combined with newspaper sale notice data to show that hand weavers' cottages were to be found in a least one-third of the town's streets during the early nineteenth century.[111] Also at Blackburn, rate book evidence reveals that one leading textile manufacturer, Bannister and Eccles, owned no less than eighty-four houses with cellars during the early 1840s, presumably occupied by hand weaving families.[112] Even more striking are the results of a survey undertaken at Wigan in 1849. This counted 520 cellar weaving shops, which would have comprised around 15 per cent of the town's total housing stock during the early 1820s.[113]

It is evident, too, that colonies of urban hand weavers could be of substantial size. In Queen Street, Preston, for instance, forty-one cottages with loomshops were offered for sale in 1818. All but ten contained cellar loomshops, each holding four or five pairs of looms.[114] Another colony, situated off Oldham Road in Manchester, consisted of no fewer than 145 cottages with capacity for over 600 handlooms.[115] Other sizeable hand weavers' colonies are shown on the first edition O.S. maps, published in the 1840s. The extract below, taken from the sixty-inch map for Chorley (Map 3), reveals numerous dwellings with steps leading to front and rear doors, a strong indication that there were basement loomshops projecting above ground floor level. Indeed, an 1816 survey shows this part of Chorley to be where the town's hand weavers were most heavily concentrated.[116]

Evidence of this type has been drawn together by Nigel Morgan to provide a detailed analysis of the extent of hand weaver colonisation in Preston. He confesses his results are open to a margin of error, but concludes that the number of houses in the town equipped with cellar loomshops probably exceeded one thousand. This comprised over a quarter of the town's housing stock in 1821, by which time most handloom weavers' cottages had been built.[117] About half were located on the

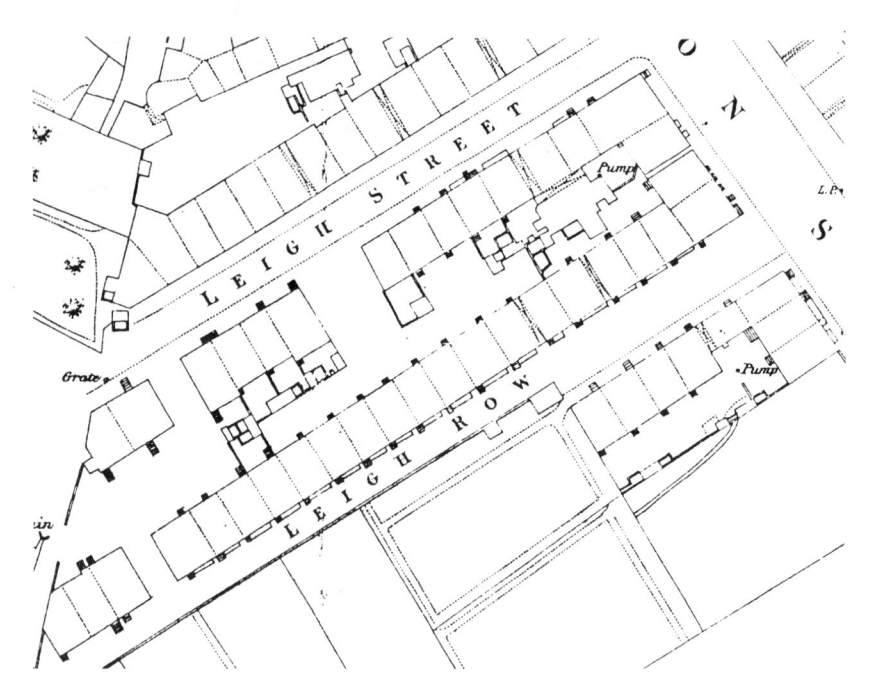

*Map 3* Hand weavers' cottages at Chorley, *c.* 1845.

eastern edge of the town around Horrocks' mill, the other major settlement being in the Friargate area, north-west of the town centre. Additionally, the Horrocks' concern built several hand weaving sheds adjoining their mill.[118]

The location of hand weaving cottages on the periphery of the central business district was a characteristic of other towns also (Plate 5). Commercial interests continued to dominate urban centres and sufficient building land was only available on the outskirts. Here, too, were the early spinning mills, the proprietors of which would no doubt have made use of nearby hand weavers. In so doing, they would certainly have reduced the transport costs incurred in outwork production and, compared with more distant workers, may also have been able to maintain closer supervision over quality and delivery dates. Indeed, other things being equal, the urban cotton manufacturer could well have achieved useful economies by employing urban rather than rural hand weavers.

There is no doubt that both rural and urban development in Lancashire during the late eighteenth and early nineteenth centuries was powerfully influenced by hand weavers' colonisation. In urban areas especially, it accompanied the development of early factory settlement, helping to generate new zones of growth, which reached well beyond traditional boundaries. In rural areas, meanwhile, the erection of hand weavers' cottages served to create new settlements, as well as to extend

5 Urban hand weavers' colony, Limbrick, Blackburn. The most easily recognised of the former weavers' cottages is that with the flight of steps to the front door. In most of the remainder, a loomshop would probably have been situated in the rear downstairs room.

existing ones. For the most part, these new settlements remained small, but because they were so numerous, their impact on the landscape was as marked as it was distinctive.

## Notes

1 See p. 25.
2 P. Kriedte et al., *Industrialization Before Industrialization* (1981), pp. 14–15; D. C. Coleman, 'Proto-industrialization: a concept too many', *EcHR*, 36 (1983), pp. 438–41; and P. Hudson, 'The regional perspective', in P. Hudson (ed.), *Industries and Regions* (1989), p. 25. For the specific case of the West Riding worsted trade, see P. Hudson, 'From manor to mill: the West Riding in transition', in M. Berg et al. (eds), *Manufacture in Town and Country Before the Factory* (1983), pp. 124–44.
3 I. Whyte, 'Proto-industrialisation in Scotland', in Hudson, *op. cit.*, pp. 229–39.
4 W. E. Tate, *The Parish Chest* (1946), p. 50.
5 Standard forms were used from 1754 onwards, but no heading was provided under which to record occupations.
6 These figures are obtained through multiplying the male weaver totals in Table A1.8 by 100 and then dividing by 18.4 (column a); 21.2 (column b); and 23.3 (column c).
7 The total population of Lancashire in 1821 was 1,052,948 (W. Farrer and J. Brownbill, *A History of the County of Lancaster*, 2 (1908), p. 332).
8 This figure is based on the supposition that the labour force comprised about two-thirds of the total population.
9 For example, a survey made in 1826 showed that in the townships of Padiham, Higham, Simonstone and Heyhouses (in the Burnley area) there were 4,499 inhabitants and 3,237 hand looms (LRO, Relief Committee Papers, 1824–27, PR 1863/4, 2).
10 See p. 19.
11 M. Rothwell, *Industrial Heritage: A Guide to the Industrial Archaeology of Blackburn*, 1 (1985), p. 6; N. Morgan, *Vanished Dwellings* (1988), p. 40.
12 This view was propounded by two cotton manufacturers, Robert Gardner and John Makin. See *PP*, 1834 (556) X, Q.5,037 and 1835 (341) XIII, Q.1,759–60.
13 In 1833, the cotton manufacturer, George Smith, thought that 500–600 had been built during the last ten years (*PP*, 1833, 690, VI, Q.9,459).
14 N. Murray, *The Scottish Handloom Weavers, 1790–1850* (1978), p. 21.
15 J. H. Clapham, *An Economic History of Modern Britain*, 1 (1967 reprint of 1926 edition), p. 143.
16 See p. 25.
17 S. D. Chapman, *The Cotton Industry in the Industrial Revolution* (1972), p. 64.
18 *PP*, 1819 (301) XVI, pp. 95 and 121.
19 H. Catling, *The Spinning Mule* (1970), p. 54. Quoted in Chapman, *op. cit.*, pp. 20–1.
20 B. Bracegirdle, 'Textile finishing in the north west' in J. H. Smith (ed.), *The Great Human Exploit* (1973), p. 37.
21 Darwen WEA, *The Darwen Area During the Industrial Revolution* (1987), p. 18.
22 R. Lloyd-Jones and M. J. Lewis, *Manchester and the Age of the Factory* (1988), p. 96.
23 See pp. 118–19.

24 J. Livesey, 'The editor's autobiography', *The Staunch Teetotaller*, 13 (1868), p. 200.
25 See pp. 25 and 154.
26 See Table 2.2, p. 44.
27 Farrer and Brownbill, *op. cit.*, p. 335.
28 D. Bythell, *The Handloom Weavers* (1969), p. 56.
29 In the mid-nineteenth century, three printing works at Accrington employed about 1,200 hands, marginally fewer than the town's twelve integrated cotton spinning and weaving mills. See W. Turner, 'Patterns of migration of textile workers into Accrington in the early nineteenth century', *LPS*, 30 (1983), p. 28. They are based on data provided in M. Rothwell, *Industrial Heritage: A Guide to the Industrial Archaeology of Accrington* (1978) and exclude employment figures for three bleachworks, which are unobtainable.
30 See pp. 71–8.
31 See pp. 118–24.
32 A graphic picture of the 1826 depression on hand weavers in the Westhoughton area is given by William Hulton, the landowner, coal proprietor and JP, in *PP*, 1826/7 (237) V, QQ.2,075–7.
33 Indeed, the town of Poulton-le-Fylde de-industrialised in the first half of the nineteenth century (D. Foster, 'Poulton-le-Fylde: a nineteenth century market town', *THSL&C*, 127, 1978), pp. 92–9.
34 G. H. Tupling, *The Economic History of Rossendale* (1927), p. 164.
35 S. Pearson, *Rural Houses of the Lancashire Pennines, 1560–1760* (1985), p. 3.
36 *PP*, 1826/7 (237) V, Q.1,959; J. P. Dodd, 'South Lancashire in transition; a study of the crop returns for 1795–1801', *THSL&C*, 117 (1966), p. 90.
37 T. W. Fletcher, 'The agrarian revolution in arable Lancashire', *TL&CAS*, 72 (1962), p. 94.
38 See, for example, J. Thirsk, *The Rural Economy of England* (1984), p. 219.
39 L. A. Clarkson, *Proto-Industrialization: The First Phase of Industrialization?* (1985), pp. 19–20.
40 *Ibid.*, p. 20.
41 R. K. Fleischman, Jr, *Conditions of Life Amongst the Cotton Workers of Southeastern Lancashire During the Industrial Revolution, 1780–1850* (unpublished PhD thesis, 1975), pp. 10–11.
42 R. Houston and K. D. M. Snell, 'Proto-industrialization? Cottage industry, social change, and the industrial revolution', *The Historical Journal*, 27 (1984), pp. 447–8.
43 Despite the establishment of numerous turnpike trusts in Lancashire during the late eighteenth and early nineteenth centuries, no turnpike road was built in Bowland. By contrast, Rossendale was well served with improved roads (T. W. Freeman *et al.*, *Lancashire, Cheshire and the Isle of Man*, 1966, p. 84).
44 J. Aikin, *A Description of the County from Thirty to Forty Miles Round Manchester* (1968 reprint of 1795 edition), p. 18.
45 J. Holt, *General View of the Agriculture of the County of Lancaster* (1969 reprint of 1795 edition), p. 71; J. K. Walton, *Lancashire, a Social History, 1558–1939* (1987), p. 122; Dodd, *op. cit.*, p. 89.
46 Clarkson, *op. cit.*, p. 21; G. L. Gullickson, 'Agriculture and cottage industry: redefining the causes of proto-industrialization', *JEH*, XLIII (1983), pp. 837–51.
47 Freeman *et al.*, *op. cit.*, p. 230.
48 Thirsk refers to mining being important in this context (Thirsk, *op. cit.*, p. 219).

**49** Tupling, *op. cit.*, pp. 227 and 161 *et seq.*
**50** J. Swain, *Industry before the Industrial Revolution* (1986), pp. 71–2 and 97; M. Brigg, 'The Forest of Pendle in the seventeenth century', *HSL&C*, 113 (1961), p. 72.
**51** Swain, *op. cit.*, pp. 76–7 and 200; Clarkson, *op. cit.*, p. 43.
**52** Swain, *op. cit.*, pp. 74–5.
**53** Swain, *op. cit.*, p. 70.
**54** G. N. Gandy, *Illegitimacy in a Handloom Weaving Community: Fertility Patterns in Culcheth, Lancashire, 1781–1860* (unpublished PhD thesis, 1978), pp. 16 and 40.
**55** *Ibid.*, p. 49.
**56** A. P. Wadsworth and J. de Lacy Mann, *The Cotton Trade and Industrial Lancashire* (1931), pp. 317–19.
**57** J. K. Walton, 'Proto-industrialization in Lancashire', in Hudson, *op. cit.*, p. 61.
**58** Thirsk, *op. cit.*, p. 222; Clarkson, *op. cit.*, p. 22.
**59** D. Levine, *Family Formation in an Age of Nascent Capitalism* (1977), pp. 60–5.
**60** Houston and Snell, *op. cit.*, p. 480; H. Cunningham, 'The employment and unemployment of children in England *c.* 1680–1851', *P&P*, 126 (1987), pp. 147–8.
**61** J. Porter, *The Making of the Central Pennines* (1980), pp. 30–1.
**62** Tupling, *op. cit.*, p. 167.
**63** Swain, *op. cit.*, pp. 91–3.
**64** W. King, *The Economic and Demographic Development of Rossendale, c. 1650–c. 1795* (unpublished PhD thesis, 1979), p. 147.
**65** Walton, *op. cit.*, p. 57.
**66** J. K. Walton, *Lancashire, a Social History, 1558–1939* (1987), p. 78.
**67** J. Porter, 'A forest in transition; Bowland, 1500–1650', *THSL&C*, 125 (1974), p. 45.
**68** Freeman *et al.*, *op. cit.*, pp. 103–4.
**69** J. D. Marshall, 'The Lancashire rural labourer in the early nineteenth century', *TL&CAS*, 71 (1961), pp. 97–9.
**70** D. A. Farnie, *The English Cotton Industry and the World Market, 1815–1896* (1979), pp. 47–8.
**71** H. W. Ogden, 'The geographical basis of the Lancashire cotton industry', *Journal of the Manchester Geographical Society* (1927), pp. 8–30.
**72** Freeman *et al.*, *op. cit.*, p. 98.
**73** Farnie, *op. cit.*, pp. 48–51.
**74** R. Marsden, *Cotton Weaving: Its Development, Principles and Practice* (1895), p. 321.
**75** J. Watson, *The Theory and Practice of the Art of Weaving by Hand and Power* (1873), p. 83.
**76** Marsden, *op. cit.*, p. 358. See also C. Aspin (ed.), *Manchester and the Textile Districts in 1849* (1972), p. 100.
**77** *PP*, 1840 (639) XXIV, p. 7.
**78** F. Engels, *The Condition of the Working-Class in England in 1845* (1971 reprint of 1845 edition), p. 140.
**79** TTM, Brandwood Account Book. A number of the Brandwood drawings are reproduced in W. J. Smith, 'The cost of building Lancashire loomhouses and weavers' workshops: the account book of James Brandwood of Turton, 1794–1814', *Textile History*, 8 (1977), pp. 56–76 and in J. G. Timmins, *Handloom Weavers' Cottages in Central Lancashire* (1977). Lack of direct outside access to domestic loomshops has received comment in

J. T. Jackson, *Housing and Social Structure in mid-Victorian Wigan and St. Helens* (unpublished PhD thesis, 1977), p. 61.

80   According to one hand weaver, fancy goods had to be 'wrought in damp situations, six or eight feet below the surface of the earth, with closed windows not to admit either the earth or the sun' (*PP*, 1834, X, p. 453).

81   Timmins, *op. cit.*, pp. 60–74.

82   Rothwell, *op. cit.*, pp. 6–18 (1985) and *Industrial Heritage: A Guide to the Industrial Archaeology of Oswaldtwistle* (1980), pp. 4–9.

83   Timmins, *op. cit.*, pp. 50–2.

84   For examples in the Mellor area, see R. F. Taylor, 'A type of handloom weaving cottage in mid-Lancashire', *Industrial Archaeology*, 3 (1966), pp. 251–5.

85   See pp. 86–7.

86   See, for example, W. J. Smith, 'The architecture of the domestic system in south-east Lancashire and the adjoining Pennines', in S. D. Chapman, *The History of Working-Class Housing* (1971), pp. 247–75. In silk areas, too, upper-storey loomshops were utilised, as Samuel Bamford found at Leek, for example (S. Bamford, *Passages in the Life of a Radical*, 2, 1967 reprint of 1844 edition, p. 110).

87   Excellent examples can be seen in the Cheesden Valley, between Bury and Rochdale.

88   J. B. Harley, *William Yates' Map of Lancashire, 1786* (1968), p. 16.

89   This is seen most clearly on the 1840s six-inch to the mile O.S. maps.

90   S. D. Chapman, *The Cotton Industry in the Industrial Revolution* (1972), p. 18.

91   O. Ashmore, *The Industrial Archaeology of Lancashire* (1969), pp. 58–9.

92   *Ibid.*, p. 168.

93   In particular, Yates' of 1786; Greenwood's of 1818; and Hennet's of 1828. See also, G. H. Tupling, 'The turnpike trusts of Lancashire', *Memoirs and Proceedings of the Manchester Literary and Philosophical Society*, 94 (1952–53), pp. 1–23.

94   LRO, Blackburn and Preston Turnpike Trust; Case for the Promoters, 1824 (TTJ).

95   The summit height on the old road is 450 feet (at Hoghton Church), 100 feet less than on the new road at Billinge.

96   *BM*, 16.5.1798.

97   Brandwood Account Book, pt.1, map of 1795.

98   E. Baines, *History, Directory, and Gazetteer of the County of Lancaster*, II (1968 reprint of 1825), pp. 379–90.

99   *PC*, 5.6.1830. Quoted in C. Aspin, *Lancashire, The First Industrial Society* (1969), p. 10.

100   See p. 63.

101   S. J. Price, *Building Societies, Their Origins and History* (1958), pp. 35–6.

102   For a discussion see J. G. Timmins, 'Early building societies in Lancashire', in S. Jackson (ed.), *Industrial Colonies and Communities* (1988), pp. 19–24.

103   M. M. Edwards, *The Growth of the British Cotton Trade, 1780–1815* (1967), p. 222.

104   *Ibid.*, p. 229.

105   *Ibid.*, p. 222.

106   Chapman, *op. cit.*, p. 40.

107   Thus, baptism register counts reveal that the proportion of father weavers at Croston rose from 6 per cent between 1753–55 (143 entries) to 19 per cent between 1818–22; at Penwortham from 19 per cent in 1725–28 (198 entries) to 50 per cent between 1818–22 and at Eccleston from 16 per cent between 1760–64 (125 entries)

to 28 per cent between 1818–22. The Penwortham figures are given in Wadsworth and Mann, *op. cit.*, p. 314.
108 See the Rothwell surveys cited in the bibliography.
109 See Timmins, *op. cit.*, pp. 50–6.
110 These are reported in M. Rothwell, *Industrial Heritage: A Guide to the Industrial Archaeology of the Ribble Valley* (1990), pp. 63–4 and 70.
111 J. G. Timmins, 'Handloom weavers' cottages in central Lancashire: some problems of recognition', *Post-Medieval Archaeology*, 13 (1979), p. 270.
112 BRL, Blackburn Rate Book, 1841–42, p. 351.
113 G. T. Clark, *Report to the General Board of Health on . . . the Borough of Wigan* (1849), p. 8.
114 *BM*, 22.4.1818.
115 *PP*, 1834 (556) X, pp. 607–9.
116 CRL, Chorley Town's Book, 1781–1818 (transcript), meeting held 26.8.1816.
117 N. Morgan, *Vanished Dwellings* (unpublished typescript, 1988), p. 40.
118 Sir C. Brown, *Origins and Progress of Horrocks and Company* (1925), p. 5.

# Chapter 3

# THE NATURE OF
# THE HAND WEAVING LABOUR FORCE

It is suggested in the previous chapter that, during the seventeenth and eighteenth centuries, upland pastoral farming in Lancashire was often associated with domestic textile production. Individuals who were unable to earn sufficient income from farming began to supplement their earnings by spinning and weaving, sometimes perhaps to a significant degree. Not only, therefore, must the growing importance of the textile industry be seen in terms of the expanding number of workers, but also in terms of the extent to which they specialised in textile production. The size of the handloom weaving labour force has been considered; in this chapter, the degree of specialisation that emerged in the trade is assessed. It is argued that, contrary to the views of some historians, dual occupations amongst hand weavers had become comparatively rare by the early nineteenth century. By then, the vast majority were specialist workers, reflecting both the extraordinarily rapid growth that had occurred in the hand weaving trade and its increasing urbanisation.

Another theme which relates to the changing nature of hand weaving in Lancashire is also addressed. It concerns the extent to which the production of traditional cloths, most notably fustians, gave way to cloths made solely of cotton. The commercial development of an all-cotton cloth became possible following the introduction of water twist (the product of Arkwright's water-frame) in 1769.[1] The line is taken that the transition to cotton had already taken place to an appreciable extent by the end of the eighteenth century and that cotton weaving had spread widely throughout the textile districts. By the early nineteenth century, then, the typical Lancashire hand weaver not only specialised in his or her trade, but also worked with cotton, often from an urban base. An assessment of the degree to which this changed in later decades is essential in explaining why domestic outwork remained important in Lancashire well into the Victorian era.

### 1 The emergence of the specialist weaver

Contemporaries tend to stress the frequency with which farming and hand weaving went together. John Aikin, for example, writing of Middleton parish in 1795, states that farms were generally from twenty to thirty acres in size and were mostly occupied by weavers, who 'alternately engage themselves in the pursuits of husbandry, and the more lucrative one of the shuttle'.[2] Another late eighteenth century writer, Sir Fredrick Morton Eden, gives a similar picture of the Bury area, where, he found, cotton manufacturing was 'carried on extensively in most of its branches'. He observes that the land was principally in grass and that local landowners divided their farms into small lots, so that the 'labouring manufacturers' could keep a cow or two.[3]

Dual occupations were also mentioned by William Radcliffe, cotton manufacturer of Mellor, near Stockport.

> In the year 1770, the land in our township was occupied by between fifty to sixty farmers ... and ... there were only six or seven who raised their rents directly from the produce of their farms; all the rest got their rent partly in some branch of trade, such as spinning or weaving woollen, linen or cotton.[4]

Radcliffe draws a distinction between the farmer/textile workers and a class of cottagers who were employed almost entirely in spinning or weaving 'except for a few weeks in the harvest.'

Other contemporaries report that weaving was still to be found in combination with farming well into the nineteenth century. In 1817, John Butterworth noted that, in the Oldham area, there were a considerable number of weavers working on their own account who also held small pieces of land.[5] A decade later, another writer observed that in Lancashire

> there appear to be among the Hand-loom weavers, two classes almost wholly distinct from each other; the one, who though they take in work in their own houses or cellars, are congregated in the large manufacturing towns; and the other, scattered in small hamlets, or single houses, in various directions throughout the manufacturing county ... It appears that persons of this description, for many years past, have been occupiers of small farms of a few acres, which they have held at high rents; and combining the business of Hand-loom weaver with that of working farmer, have assisted to raise the rent of their land from the profits of their loom.[6]

Even as late as 1840, W. E. Hickson, the assistant handloom weavers' commissioner, argued that younger men rarely depended solely on the loom.

> They calculate upon field-work in harvest-time; upon the produce of their potato settings; in some districts upon fishing; and occasional employment in various capacities.[7]

Further, though limited, evidence on the link between hand weaving and agriculture in the early nineteenth century can be adduced from contemporary diaries. They show that David Whitehead, a fustian weaver in Rossendale used to milk in the morning and at night, whilst William Varley, a weaver of Higham, near Burnley, kept a pig and hens, and also tended a small garden.[8]

An alternative contemporary viewpoint on the extent and durability of the link between agriculture and textile production was expressed, however. It appears in the writings of Peter Gaskell, a young surgeon living in the Stockport area around 1830. Referring to the middle decades of the eighteenth century, he distinguishes three rural groups who were directly affected by the expanding textile industry. The group with the highest socio-economic status, composed of yeomen and small freeholders, worked entirely in agriculture. Below this group was a class of superior artisans who were engaged primarily in manufacturing, but who held some land from which they derived a subsidiary income. The group with the lowest status comprised inferior artisans who depended entirely upon manufacturing.[9]

According to Gaskell, each of these groups became more involved in textile production as spinning machinery was introduced from the 1770s onwards. The improved supply of yarn, he maintains, benefited the artisan groups particularly, since it allowed them to work more regularly at the loom. Indeed, the superior artisan group gave up agricultural work altogether, despite losing social status by relinquishing land. The yeoman, too, found textile work profitable and, for a time, produced a large quantity of yarn. Generally, therefore, textile production in rural districts became increasingly a specialist activity.

In assessing the contemporary evidence, historians have offered varying interpretations as to the importance of the non-specialist weaver. Writing in 1904, S. J. Chapman accepted that the association of 'small farming with manufacturing' was common, even as late as the mid-1820s. He suggests, though, that from Radcliffe's time onwards, the number of specialist weavers was growing at the expense of those weavers who possessed small farms or allotments or who hired themselves out for harvest work. Several explanations of this change are advanced, including an increased demand for weavers following the introduction of the jenny and the onset of depression in agriculture which hit small farmers and led to the displacement of much casual farm labour. He argues, too, that the invention of more complex appliances, not least handlooms, created the need for greater specialisation and prompted weavers to leave the countryside for large villages or towns where skilled mechanics could be found to undertake repairs. In most cases where weaving and farming were combined, he contends, the latter would be regarded as by-employment.[10]

A more cautious and qualified acceptance of the extent to which hand weavers were agriculturalists was offered in 1920 by G. W. Daniels. He points out that not all of them could have been:

In the first place, for obvious reasons, we must rule out the great majority of those engaged in industry who lived in Manchester and its immediate neighbourhood and also those in the other centres of congregated population ... In the eighteenth century, as in the early nineteenth, agriculture and industry have to be sought in the country districts such as that to which Radcliffe refers.

He goes on to consider Radcliffe's distinction between the small farmers who derived income partly from weaving and the cottagers who were specialist weavers, except for a few weeks at harvest time. The latter, he feels, could not be regarded as agriculturalists in any reasonable sense, even when they had small gardens attached to their cottages. He concedes that it is impossible to know the proportion of farmer weavers to cottager weavers, but suggests it is 'extremely probable' that the latter were in a considerable majority.

Turning to a detailed consideration of Gaskell's ideas, he concurs that the specialist weaver became increasingly common. He regards Gaskell's analysis of industrial transition as 'undoubtedly trustworthy', noting that its importance lies chiefly in the indication it gives of the extent to which rural textile workers were connected with agriculture. He concludes:

But when we take into account the total number engaged in the Lancashire textile industry in the towns and in the country districts, the conclusion that the relative number of part-time agriculturalists was small would seem to have abundant justification. They can hardly be regarded as the typical workpeople.[11]

In 1927, a sub-regional contribution was made to the debate by G. H. Tupling. Using parish register data he plotted the location of woollen areas in early eighteenth century Rossendale and found

no signs of that concentration of artisans in congested areas which accompanied the development of the textile industries at the end of the century, and which was indicative of a population divorced from the soil and wholly dependent on its work in the shop or factory.

However, further plots based on data extracted from the Haslingden register during the mid-eighteenth century revealed clusters of weavers around the church and at Laneside, 'the nuclei from which Haslingden grew'. These weavers represented a class of textile operatives 'almost wholly, if not completely, divorced from agricultural employment'. Whilst domestic spinning and weaving continued to provide part-time occupations for agricultural workers, both processes were increasingly performed, he thought, by full-time artisans living in the emerging towns of Haslingden, Bacup and Newchurch.[12]

During the early 1930s, two further contributions to the debate were advanced. The first, by J. H. Clapham, strongly backs the revisionist view and goes as far as to observe that the farmer/weaver was 'half-mythical'.[13] The second, a carefully-considered account by A. P. Wadsworth and J. de Lacy Mann, reviews and adds to the contemporary evidence. They acknowledged that Clapham may have been correct, but stress that contemporary comments about the strength of the link between farming and weaving was 'everywhere the same'. Using lease and inventory evidence, they seek to demonstrate a general association between land and industry during the first half of the eighteenth century. They note, too, the frequency with which advertisements in local newspapers during the late eighteenth century refer to the sale of farms with loomshops attached. In concluding, they express concern about Daniels' notion that landless weavers comprised a considerable majority and suggest the situation probably varied a good deal in different parts of Lancashire.

They also declare that the notion would not be as true of the earlier years of the century as of the later.[14]

More recent response to the debate has come from John Lyons and Duncan Bythell. The former is in broad sympathy with the revisionist line, arguing that the strong comparative advantage of cotton weaving led to it being adopted on a more full-time basis. Farmer/weavers could still be found in the 1830s, but, by the following decade, urban hand weavers predominated.[15] In contrast, Bythell takes a traditionalist stance, observing that hand weaving was often combined with other jobs, in many cases with agriculture. He agrees that industrial outwork only occupied part of the family for part of the time and that this tradition continued throughout the Industrial Revolution. He stresses that in country districts hand weavers would be 'pressed into fieldwork' at harvest time and that, in consequence, Clapham's notion that the farmer/weaver was 'half-mythical' by 1830 cannot be sustained. In urban areas, meanwhile, workers in a variety of trades would turn to weaving when their business was slack. Nevertheless, Bythell acknowledges that there were men who worked as full-time weavers. Prominent among them were the skilled fancy weavers at Bolton or Paisley; the heads of households in country villages where little part-time farm work and no other industrial employment were available; and weavers in handloom sheds. Finally, he points to the prominence of women and children in the handloom weaving labour force. 'The real importance of cotton handloom weaving in the industrial revolution', he urges, was that

> it furnished the kind of by-occupation for the aged, the unmarried sisters and daughters, and the growing children in a family ... For these people, weaving was the best way of making some contribution to the family income; but instead of following it as a full-time trade, they wove only when time and inclination suited, or necessity compelled them, to make such a contribution.[16]

Given the incompleteness of the available evidence and the impressionistic nature of the contemporary accounts, it is hardly surprising that opinions on the importance of the farmer/weaver during the Industrial Revolution era should differ. That the farmer/weaver existed at this time is not in dispute; what is in doubt is how often he occurred and what proportion of his income he derived from weaving.

The first point to bear in mind is that, as is suggested in Chapter 1, the majority of hand weavers may have been town dwellers by the 1820s; clearly, few of this group would have been able to find agricultural jobs. Compared with their rural counterparts, however, they may have been better placed to find other types of part-time occupation, since the number and range of job opportunities would have been far greater in towns than in the countryside. Even so, it is by no means certain that part-time work was commonly offered by urban employers, or that hand weavers would have sought it. Much would have depended on the general employment situation and there can be no doubt that urban weavers (as well as those in the country) had great trouble obtaining alternative employment during trade recessions. Thus, in 1826, it was reported that in three districts of Blackburn

(Nova Scotia, Little Islington and Grimshaw Park) almost 600 out of around 2,000 weavers, the great majority of whom would have worked at the handloom, were unemployed.[17]

If urban hand weavers were largely specialists, what of their rural counterparts? Is it likely, as such contemporaries as Aikin and Eden imply, that they commonly farmed? Alternatively, is it safer to support Peter Gaskell and G. W. Daniels and argue that rural hand weavers achieved an increasingly high degree of specialisation?

One obvious consideration here is whether rural weavers owned or leased land, however small their plots. That they often did so is undeniable, as can be seen from numerous references in local newspaper advertisements to the sale of farmhouses with loomshops. Yet such evidence is easy to overstate. In the first place, even a cursory glance at these advertisements reveals that by no means every farm offered for sale in the textile districts was necessarily equipped with a loomshop. Joseph Livesey, the teetotal pioneer, was surely guilty of exaggeration when, referring to his childhood in the early nineteenth century, he maintained: 'all the small farms in Walton, Penwortham, and the adjoining country places were "weaving farms", having a shop attached to hold a . . . number of looms.'[18] Secondly, both field observation and map evidence reveal row after row of rural hand weavers' cottages with little or no land attached. At the front, these cottages frequently open directly on to the road and where gardens are to be found, either at the front or back, they are mostly small.[19] Whether the occupiers of these dwellings can be regarded, to borrow Professor Daniels' phrase, as agriculturalists in any reasonable sense, is unlikely. Thirdly, Poor Law Commission returns show that in one major upland weaving centre, Padiham (near Burnley), few cottages were provided with gardens.[20] Lastly, since most country weavers' cottages date from the late eighteenth and early nineteenth centuries, when incomes derived from hand weaving were likely to have exceeded those obtained from farming by a considerable margin, the incentives for rural handloom weavers to specialise would have been strong.[21] Looked at another way, specialising in the weaving trade would have enabled rural workers to earn much more than they could have earned by combining farming and weaving and with a good deal less effort.

Even where a handloom weaver did own or lease land, it is by no means certain that its produce yielded him any appreciable return. Not only would the size of the plot have been important here, but also its elevation and aspect; the fertility of its soil; and the climatic vagaries to which it was subjected. As has been demonstrated in the previous chapter, most of the heaviest concentrations of handloom weavers in the early nineteenth century occurred in upland pastoral districts, where land holdings were often small and where cereal and vegetable crops could prove difficult to raise. Indeed, it is evident from sale notices in local newspapers that most upland farms with hand weaving facilities were under ten acres in extent and the land was invariably in pasture or meadow. For example, four hand weaving farmsteads near Haslingden, offered for sale at the beginning of 1828, were all concerned with cattle rearing, three of them having just above seven acres of land each and the other around five.[22] No indication is given as to the capacity of the loomshops in these farms, though other advertisements show that from two to four was common.[23] This suggests that it was usual for several members of the family to weave and that a sizeable proportion of the family income was derived from this source.

Not all rural hand weavers were concentrated in upland areas, of course, and it may be that those in the lowlands were better placed to supplement family income from agricultural activity. Physical conditions would certainly have proved more favourable for growing food crops and cottage gardens may normally have been provided. Some indication of this comes from the early 1830s Poor Law Commission returns, which divulge that small gardens for potato growing were common at North Meols and that gardens were general in Kirkham parish, with many cottagers keeping a pig.[24] In fact, large gardens can still be seen in Fylde villages where hand weaving was of some importance, most notably at Elswick, north of Kirkham.[25] Further, the Poor Law returns state that Kirkham women and children who were old enough to work were employed in reaping during the harvest period and in weaving at other times.[26] All this suggests a more active interest in agricultural pursuits in lowland than in upland weaving areas, though lowland families specialising in hand weaving cannot be ruled out, especially when the economic incentive was strong. As late as 1851, quite a number of lowland weaving families concentrated heavily, if not entirely, on hand weaving and can have had no more than a marginal interest in agricultural work.[27]

It can also be too readily assumed that rural handloom weavers who had the opportunity to grow food crops and to rear animals actually wished to do so or did so efficiently. One contemporary, the agriculturalist R. W. Dickson, thought them to have been severely wanting in this respect. Writing of the handloom weavers who had land attached to their cottages, he drew attention to 'the uncultivated and slovenly state in which such lands are almost invariably found'. He continued:

Men of this stamp are quite unfit for the management of land; and besides, they have neither the capital nor knowledge necessary for rendering land productive and beneficial. Whatever they perform about it, is commonly done in the worst and most irregular manner, and they seldom attend at all to any sort of improvements. In short, it appears to me from a pretty full examination of the subject, that in this district, nothing can be more prejudicial to the interests of the landed proprietor, or more injurious to the community, than the practice of annexing lands as small farms to cottages designed for weaving and other mechanical labours.

Hand weavers, he felt, were only capable of growing potatoes and other garden vegetables and of raising a few 'half-starved animals'.[28]

Since home-grown produce could provide useful additions to family income and nutritional levels, Dickson's remarks seem rather ill-judged. His stance certainly differs from that of his fellow agriculturalist J. Binns, who enthused about the societies to promote fruit growing formed by hand weavers in the Darwen area.[29] No doubt, as at Darwen, many hand weavers did farm or garden successfully, especially where soils and climate were favourable. Yet Dickson does highlight the possibility that weavers might gain little from land at their disposal; that they owned or rented land did not necessarily mean they used it to the best advantage or even that they used it effectively.

Further evidence on the extent to which hand weavers were specialist or non-specialist workers is hard to find. Parish register entries seldom give handloom weavers with dual occupations, but parish clerks may have recorded predominant, as well as specialist occupations. The same is true of a list made in 1826 of several hundred poor relief recipients at Great Harwood, near Blackburn. In this case, though, as Bythell has pointed out, several men who combined weaving with another trade were noted.[30] Even so, of the large number of weavers included in the list, relatively few were given with dual occupations.

There are strong indications that, by the early nineteenth century, the great majority of Lancashire hand weavers relied little on alternative forms of employment. Families could still earn a living from combining weaving with agriculture, but their ranks had been thinned by a substantial margin. At the root of this change was the locational shift in handloom weaving as the trade became increasingly urbanised. At the same time, the rural hand weavers specialised to an increasing extent, taking advantage of the much higher earnings available in domestic outwork than in other occupations. The growing number of rural colonies of handloom weavers, still such a prominent feature of the Lancashire landscape, had little if anything to do with farming. To satisfy the rapid and sustained growth of the unmechanised weaving industry required not only a massive force of hand weavers, but also one which was prepared to maximise its rewards, or to minimise its workload, through specialisation.

## 2 The change to cotton weaving

Wadsworth and Mann have demonstrated that, by the end of the seventeenth century, three areas of localised textile production could be found in Lancashire. In the central parts of the county the manufacture of fustians (cloths usually having a linen warp and a cotton weft) had grown to prominence, largely at the expense of coarse woollens. As a result, woollen manufacture had become largely confined to the eastern border regions. In the western lowland districts, meanwhile, the emphasis was on linens, the production of which had spread into the Manchester area, again replacing woollens.[31]

If goods made entirely from cotton were produced in Lancashire during the late seventeenth century, Wadsworth and Mann argue, it could only have been on an extremely small scale.[32] Indeed, it was not until the later decades of the eighteenth century that cotton wares assumed prominence, the trade growing rapidly, M. M. Edwards points out, in the 1780s and 1790s. It was in the later decade, he suggests, that the price reduction on cottons 'most dramatically exerted itself on linen and woollen manufactures.' As a result, manufacturers in these trades either began losing labour to the cotton industry or turned to cotton production themselves.[33]

Something of the inroads made by the cotton producers during the late eighteenth and early nineteenth centuries can be gauged from contemporary observations. For example, writing of Mellor, near Stockport, in the 1770s and 1780s, William Radcliffe noted 'a change in the woollen looms to fustians and calico, and the linen early gone, except the few fabrics in which there was a mixture of cotton.' So complete was this change to cotton production that, Radcliffe maintained, the ensuing fifteen-year period could be referred to as the 'golden age of this great trade.'[34]

A more general picture of the conversion to cotton fabrics may be obtained from the account of John Aikin's perambulations through Lancashire, published in 1797. More often than not, Aikin's comments lack detail, but they show clearly that cotton production had made appreciable headway in many parts of the county. In the north-east, for example, cotton had been 'of late' introduced at Colne, with dimities and calicoes being added to the traditional range of woollen and worsted goods. At nearby Burnley, a similar situation prevailed. 'Its trade,' Aikin notes, 'was formerly only in woollen and worsted goods, but the cotton manufactures are now introduced in it.'[35] Further west, in the Blackburn area, cotton may already have made substantial progress. 'The town', Aikin relates:

was formerly the centre of the fabrics sent to London for printing called Blackburn greys, which were plains of linen warp shot with cotton. Since so much of the printing has been done near Manchester, the Blackburn manufacturers have gone more into the making of calicoes. The fields around the town are whitened with materials lying to bleach.[36]

A few miles south of Blackburn, at the village of Over Darwen, the manufacturers were making 'a large quantity of cotton goods', whilst at Haslingden, about eight miles to the south-east, 'much of the cotton trade' had been introduced, though the wool trade had also expanded during the previous twenty years.[37]

In the main towns of central Lancashire, cotton had also assumed significance. At Preston, Aikin found that linens were still sold, but that 'of late the cotton branches have obtained possession.' One local firm, Watson and Co., was manufacturing dimities, muslins and calicoes 'from the raw cotton to the printing . . .'[38] He recorded, too, that there were cotton mills at Chorley and that at Wigan, cotton was intruding on the staple trade in checks.[39]

Aikin also reported that cotton goods were being made in the south-east Lancashire towns, Manchester included, though to a varying extent. At Leigh, he was told that fustians had formerly been produced, but that 'latterly, they have made here fine wide-yard jeans, in imitation of India, with figured and flowered drawboys.'[40] In the neighbouring town of Bolton, which was still celebrated for its fustians, he found that 'the muslin trade is that which seems to answer best at present', whilst further to the east, at Bury, he discovered that wool was still being produced, though cotton manufacture was 'carried on very extensively in most of its branches.'[41] On visiting Middleton, to the north of Manchester, he was informed that silk weaving was giving way to 'the more profitable branches of muslin and nankeen' and at Ashton-under-Lyne, that the inhabitants had of late 'fallen more into the practice of making twists and warps for velverets, cotton thicksets, etc.'[42] At Rochdale, he found that the staple trade was still the manufacture of woollens, though even here, the cotton trade had 'spread greatly in the neighbourhood.'[43] At neither Oldham nor Stalybridge, however, did Aikin record cotton manufacturing. In the former town, he noted that strong fustians were 'carried on to a considerable extent'; in the latter that the woollen trade continued to flourish.[44] This was true, also, at Tyldesley, near Leigh, where new woollen mills were being erected. Yet cotton weaving was firmly established in the village, its 976 inhabitants using 325 looms in the 'cotton manufactures of Marseilles quiltings, dimities, corduroys, velvets, velveteens, thick sets, muslins, muslinets and new stripes for furniture.'[45]

Lastly, mention should be made of the cotton manufacturing observed by Aikin in two south-west Lancashire towns, namely Warrington and Ormskirk. At the former, he reported, sailcloth made from linen, or from linen and hemp, had developed into a major product. But he also noted that several manufacturers had recently

> exerted themselves to introduce the cotton branches here, and succeeded to a considerable degree. As the coarser cotton goods were those chiefly attempted, many of the sail-cloth weavers, for the sake of more employment and better wages, turned their hands to the new manufacture, which caused a considerable decline of the old; but since the commencement of the war, the case has been reversed.[46]

At the latter, Aikin was informed that the only trades were cotton spinning for Manchester manufacturers, along with the production of thread for sailcloth.[47] No mention was made of cotton production at Kirkham, in the southern Fylde, though, Aikin maintained, the town's chief trade was in coarse linens, especially sailcloth.[48]

With a few possible exceptions, it is evident from Aikin's survey that, by the mid-1790s, cotton production was mounting a growing, and in some places, a powerful challenge to the established fabrics throughout the Lancashire textile districts. It is not possible from Aikin's account to assess the relative importance of the cotton spinning and weaving branches in each of these districts, though he makes it plain that cotton weaving was widespread; that a varied range of cotton cloths was being produced; and that, in some places — Tyldesley provides one instance — a high degree of dependence on cotton weaving had already been attained.

It is instructive to compare Aikin's survey with that compiled a quarter of a century later by Edward Baines. In common with Aikin, Baines does not chart the progress of cotton manufacturing very closely and, all too often, fails to quote the sources from which his evidence was derived. Nevertheless, comparison of the two accounts enables some assessment to be made of the extent to which, district by district, cotton manufacturing developed in Lancashire during the early decades of the nineteenth century.

The importance Aikin ascribes to cotton manufacturing in north-east Lancashire is fully confirmed by Baines. In the Blackburn area, Baines relates, manufacturers had increasingly turned to calico production during the late eighteenth century, with the result that, by the mid-1820s, the town 'enjoyed the advantages of this branch of the cotton business more perhaps than any other place in Lancashire.' He estimated that 49,200 pieces of cotton goods were produced weekly there, giving employment to 10,000 people.[49] William Feilden, a Blackburn witness to the 1826 Select Committee on Emigration, expressed similar views, stating that production of calicoes in Blackburn had extended considerably, 10,000 pieces more per week being woven than a decade previously.[50] Baines also notes that cotton had gained ascendancy in and around Burnley (formerly a woollen area), where weekly production of calico amounted to 25–30,000 pieces.[51] He thought cotton had also become the major manufacturing industry at Colne, with some 12,600 calico pieces being produced there each week, chiefly for sale to printers.[52] Baines gives no details of cotton manufacturing at Darwen,[53] but mentions that cotton production had become more important than wool production at Haslingden.[54]

A similarly progressive record is evident in central Lancashire towns. At Preston, Baines maintains, the cotton trade was conducted on a relatively small scale prior to 1791, despite the endeavours of Messrs Collison and Watson. In that year, the Horrocks family opened their first mill in the town and soon built others. By 1824, there were some forty cotton spinning mills in Preston and neighbourhood, along with a 'very numerous' body of weavers.[55] Baines also relates that cotton manufacturing was carried on 'to a great extent' at Chorley, muslins being the principal fabric manufactured,[56] whilst at Wigan calicoes were produced along with the traditional linens and fustians.[57]

Baines points to other strongholds of cotton production in the south-east part of the county. He notes that Manchester and Stalybridge were particularly concerned with cotton spinning; Middleton with a range of cotton cloths, including calicoes, nankeens, ginghams and checked handkerchiefs; Leigh with muslins; and Bolton with quiltings, muslins, counterpanes and dimities.[58] He states, too, that cotton had become the principal manufacturing activity at Bury, though woollen manufacture was still carried on there,[59] whilst at Oldham there were no less than sixty-five cotton mills, all but two of which had been built since 1800.[60] Here, it seems, was the reason why Aikin did not mention cotton production as being important in the town during the mid-1790s. Baines also reports that cotton spinning had become well established at Rochdale, but that woollen production remained a major interest there, some 6,000 pieces of flannel being made weekly in the town and neighbourhood.[61]

Elsewhere in the county, cotton manufacturing appears to have taken place on a relatively modest, though by no means insignificant, scale. At Kirkham, Baines relates, some 2,000 pieces of cotton cloth of 'different descriptions' were produced weekly, besides considerable amounts of sailcloth and of fine and coarse linens.[62] A similar level of cotton cloth production had been attained at Clitheroe, the trade having 'gained ground yearly' since 1800.[63] Other cotton producing towns mentioned by Baines include Lancaster, where sailcloth production had fallen to only twenty pieces per week, and Garstang, where little general manufacturing took place, but where a number of looms was in use for weaving linen and cotton goods.[64] Finally, he draws attention to the calicoes, muslins and velveteens produced at Warrington,[65] as well as to small amounts of unspecified cotton wares made at Ormskirk and Prescot.[66]

Little additional documentary evidence on the extent to which cotton weaving had developed in Lancashire by the mid-1820s is to be found. Parish register entries seldom mention the type of fabric woven and, where they do, the references are too scattered and too infrequent to allow any firm conclusions to be drawn. The sole exception occurs in the Haslingden baptism register for 1813. In that year, the first 118 entries consistently distinguish between cotton and wool weavers, the former being four times as numerous as the latter.[67]

One further indicator of the growth to prominence of cotton hand weaving in Lancashire must be considered. It is provided by the numerous premises specially designed for cotton handloom weaving. The point has already been made that domestic weavers' cottages used in the cotton trade normally contained loomshops at groundfloor or cellar level in order to maintain adequate humidity.[68] Numerous cottages of this type have survived throughout central Lancashire, the loomshops often being distinguished by rows of three, yard-square windows at front and rear. In many examples, some or all of the lights have been blocked in, but seldom skilfully enough to obliterate all traces. This is so, for instance, with the impressive terrace at Top o'th' Lane, Brindle (near Preston), where, despite extensive alterations to several cottages, twenty former dwellings built for hand weavers can be seen (Plate 6). Most had loomshops on the ground floor, situated at the side of the living accommodation.[69] Photographs of demolished examples also reveal the presence of groundfloor or cellar loomshops, as, for instance, at Cleaver Street and Copy Nook, Blackburn[70] and at Edge's Court, Kirk Street and Velvet Walks, Bolton.[71]

It is probable that a great many more handloom weavers' cottages used in the cotton trade have yet to be identified. In the main, they would have housed small loomshops, with space for only one or two looms. There is evidence in the Brandwood Account Books to show that such loomshops would probably have been situated in the rear downstairs room of two-up-two-down cottages.[72] Since the external wall of these rooms has often been altered by the addition of a kitchen extension, the original window arrangement by which the former loomshop may be recognised is obscured. The problem is compounded by the fact that loomshops

6  Former hand weavers' cottages, Top o'th' Lane, Brindle. The cottage on the left still displays the characteristic triple-window arrangement at ground-floor level. So, too, does the third cottage along, though the central of the window openings has been deepened. It is likely that the garage of this cottage was formerly the loomshop attached to the second cottage, which is now single-fronted.

7 Rear loomshop weavers' cottages, Lower Darwen.

## Nature of the hand weaving labour force

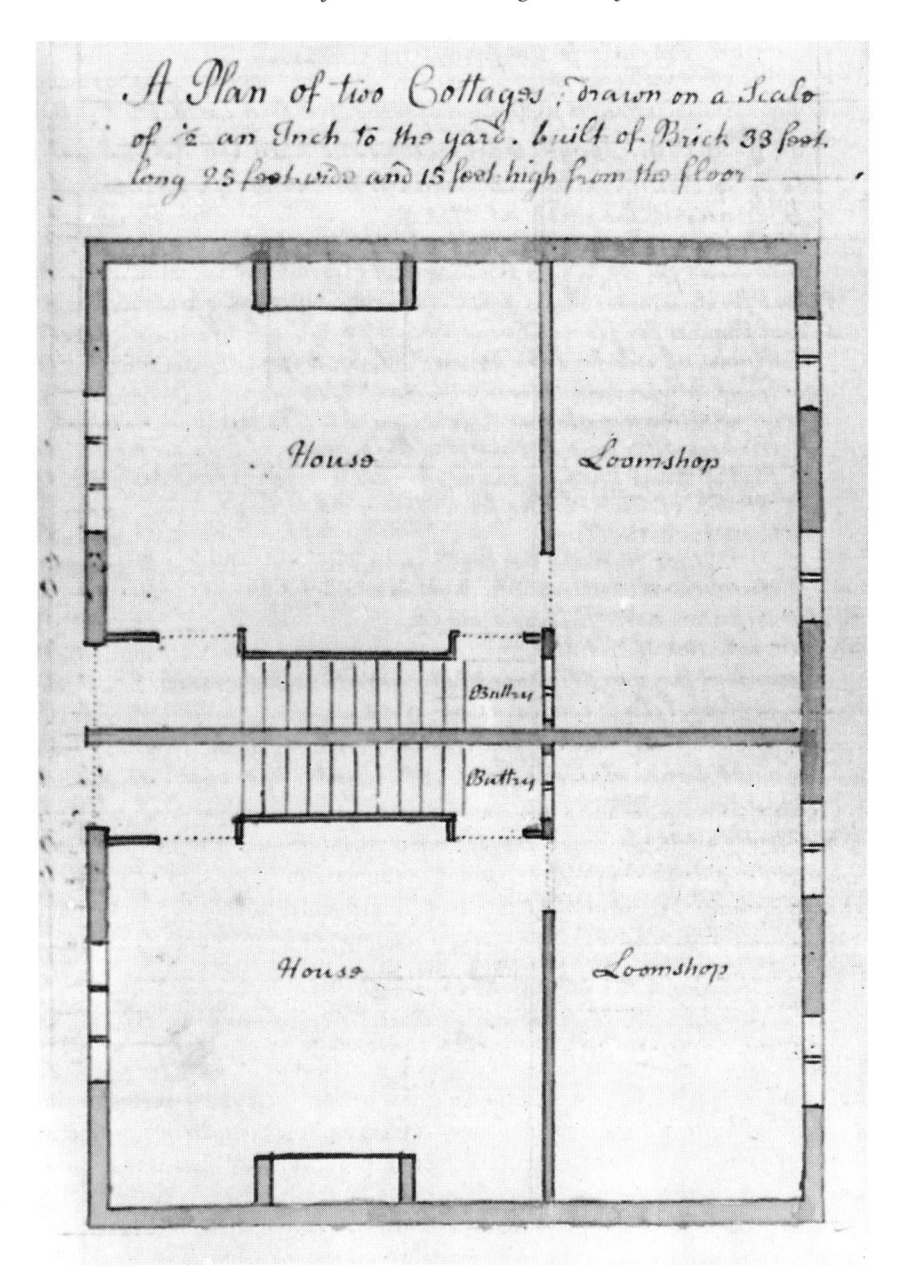

*A Plan of two Cottages; drawn on a Scale of ½ an Inch to the yard. built of Brick 33 feet long 25 feet wide and 15 feet high from the floor*

House | Loomshop
Buttry
Buttry
House | Loomshop

8  The Brandwood plan again reveals that access to the loomshop was via the house; there were no back doors. The photograph of cottages at Lower Darwen, near Blackburn, shows cottages of this type, the rear downstairs rooms of which may have been used for weaving.

of this size occurred frequently, even though the four-loom shop predominated.[73] As a result, field investigation is likely to understate the importance of the smaller groundfloor loomshops, unless supportive documentary evidence as to their existence can be adduced.

What must be stressed here is that, for the most part, upper-storey loomshops in Lancashire were confined to eastern districts, where wool weaving predominated, and to the silk areas; neither of these fabrics needed a humid atmosphere to be woven.[74] Elsewhere in the county very few have been discovered, either as extant examples or from photographic records. In the cotton districts, the groundfloor or cellar loomshop held sway.

There is, however, an important qualification to make, relating to Colne and the villages around. It has been shown that cotton weaving predominated in this area by the mid-1820s.[75] Yet most of the surviving hand weavers' cottages in the area, of which there are substantial numbers, appear to have contained upper-storey loomshops (Plate 9). Characteristically, these cottages have two windows at back and front on the upper floor, but only one back and front window on the lower floor.[76] Thus, the upper storey was better lit by means of natural light than the lower and would have comprised the loomshop. Why, then, were such cottages used for cotton weaving?

It does not seem likely that all these cottages would have been built before cotton weaving spread into the district to supersede wool and worsted. To deny that substantial numbers of weavers' cottages were erected in the Colne area as cotton weaving grew rapidly is to stretch credulity beyond the limit. Nor is it probable that only upper-storey examples have survived. Far more compelling as an explanation is the idea that the cotton woven in these cottages was of a coarse variety, which would have been less demanding than the finer cottons with regard to atmospheric requirements. Accordingly, upper-storey loomshops could be provided. These gave less obstruction to natural light than those at groundfloor level or, more particularly, in cellars, a consideration of some importance.[77] Thus, Robert Heywood, a handloom manufacturer from Bolton, received a complaint that trees he had planted would interfere with the light in an adjoining loomshop. Heywood conceded the point and allowed the branches to be cropped.[78]

That lower grade cloths were being woven at Colne in the early 1830s is confirmed by James Thomas, a Clitheroe calico printer.[79] He drew the distinction between the depressed state of the Colne weavers and the comparative prosperity of those weaving finer cloths in central Lancashire. What is also clear is that cotton hand weaving declined early in the Colne area, as the hand weavers changed to alternative fabrics and the powerloom took over in cotton; both processes were virtually complete by mid-century.[80] Evidently, then, the Colne area followed a different tradition from central Lancashire with regard to the type of cotton cloth woven and this is reflected in the contrasting design of its domestic loomshops.

Although it cannot be determined exactly how quickly cotton superseded other fabrics in Lancashire during the late eighteenth and early nineteenth centuries, it

9 Cottages built with upper-storey loomshops, Blacko, near Colne.

had certainly become the predominant fibre in almost every part of the county's textile zone by the mid-1820s. The production of fustians shrank fairly quickly into relative insignificance and only in parts of eastern Lancashire did the manufacture of woollen cloth manage to retain any importance. As new opportunities arose, the hand weaving labour force was prepared, and able, to adapt to the production of new types of fabric, a practice which their children and grandchildren were often to emulate.[81]

## Notes

1  W. English, *The Textile Industry* (1969), p. 68.
2  J. Aikin, *A Description of the Country from Thirty to Forty Miles Round Manchester* (1968 reprint of 1795 edition), p. 244.
3  Sir F. M. Eden, *The State of the Poor* (1966 edition of 1797 text), vol. 1, p. 296.
4  W. Radcliffe, *Origin of the New System of Manufacture* (1828), p. 59.
5  J. Butterworth, *An Historical and Descriptive Account of the Town and Parochial Chapelry of Oldham* (1817), p. 101.
6  *PP*, 1826/7 (237) V, p. 5. Quoted in J. H. Clapham, *An Economic History of Modern Britain*, 1 (1967 reprint of 1926 edition), p. 180.
7  *PP*, 1840 (639) XXIV, p. 649. Quoted in D. Bythell, *The Handloom Weavers* (1969), p. 58.
8  D. Whitehead, *Autobiography* (typescript edition, 1956), p. 3; W. Bennet, *History of Burnley* (1948), vol. III, p. 383. Both are quoted in Bythell, *op. cit.*, pp. 58–9.
9  P. Gaskell, *Artisans and Machinery* (1968 reprint of 1836 edition), pp. 26–30. See, also, G. W. Daniels, *The Early English Cotton Industry* (1920), pp. 136–9.
10  S. J. Chapman, *The Lancashire Cotton Industry* (1904), pp. 9–10.
11  Daniels, *op. cit.*, pp. 139–43.
12  G. H. Tupling, *The Economic History of Rossendale* (1927), pp. 179, 189 and 201.
13  Clapham, *op. cit.*, p. 552. Quoted in Bythell, *op. cit.*, p. 60.
14  A. P. Wadsworth and J. De Lacy Mann, *The Cotton Trade and Industrial Lancashire, 1600–1780* (1931), pp. 316–20.
15  J. S. Lyons, 'Family responses to economic decline: handloom weavers in early nineteenth century Lancashire', *Research in Economic History*, 12 (1989), pp. 49–50 and 78.
16  Bythell, *op. cit.*, pp. 58–61.
17  *BM*, 15.3.1826. The leading Blackburn cotton spinner and manufacturer, William Feilden, testified that there was very little power weaving in Blackburn at this time (*PP*, 1826/7, 337, V, p. 463. See also B. Lewis, *Life in a Cotton Town, Blackburn, 1818–48* (1985), pp. 5–6.
18  J. Livesey, 'The editor's autobiography', *The Staunch Teetotaller*, 13 (1868), p. 197.
19  Examples include the sizeable hand weavers' colonies at Top o'th' Lane, Brindle and Chapel Lane, Hoghton, both near Preston.
20  *PP*, 1834 (44) XXXI, p. 284.
21  For examples of the earnings of hand weavers during the late eighteenth century, see Bythell, *op. cit.*, p. 94 *et seq.*
22  *BM*, 21.1.1828.

23 J. G. Timmins, 'Handloom weavers' cottages in central Lancashire: some problems of recognition', *Post-Medieval Archaeology*, 13 (1979), pp. 266–7.
24 *PP*, 1834 (44) XXXI, pp. 283 and 292.
25 Hand weavers still comprised about one in ten of the working population at Elswick in 1851.
26 *PP*, 1834 (44) XXX, p. 282.
27 At Freckleton, near Kirkham, for instance, 17 out of the 57 households with hand weavers were in this position.
28 R. W. Dickson, *General View of the Agriculture of Lancashire* (1815), p. 107.
29 J. Binns, *Notes on the Agriculture of Lancashire* (1851), pp. 128–9.
30 LRO, Great Harwood Relief Registers, 1825–26. Quoted in Bythell, *op. cit.*, p. 60.
31 Wadsworth and Mann, *op. cit.*, pp. 23–4.
32 *Ibid.*, p. 111.
33 M. M. Edwards, *The Growth of the British Cotton Trade* (1962), pp. 33–4.
34 Radcliffe, *op. cit.*, pp. 61–2.
35 Aikin, *op. cit.*, pp. 278–9.
36 *Ibid.*, p. 270.
37 *Ibid.*, pp. 273 and 276.
38 *Ibid.*, p. 287.
39 *Ibid.*, pp. 289 and 294.
40 *Ibid.*, p. 297.
41 *Ibid.*, p. 262.
42 *Ibid.*, pp. 245 and 233.
43 *Ibid.*, p. 249.
44 *Ibid.*, pp. 237 and 230.
45 *Ibid.*, p. 299.
46 *Ibid.*, pp. 302–3.
47 *Ibid.*, p. 315.
48 *Ibid.*, p. 42.
49 E. Baines, *History, Directory and Gazetteer of the County Palatine of Lancaster*, 1 (1968 reprint of 1824 edition), p. 505.
50 *PP*, 1826/7 (237) V, p. 434.
51 Baines, *op. cit.*, p. 567.
52 *Ibid.*, p. 620.
53 However, there were several manufacturers of calicos and cambrics at Over Darwen in 1828 (Pigot & Co., *National Commercial Directory*, 1829, p. 219).
54 Baines, *op. cit.*, p. 664.
55 *Ibid.*, vol. 2, pp. 484–5.
56 *Ibid.*, vol. 1, p. 601.
57 *Ibid.*, vol. 2, p. 661.
58 *Ibid.*, vol. 2, pp. 134, 556, 429, 45 and vol. 1, p. 534.
59 *Ibid.*, vol. 1, p. 579.
60 *Ibid.*, vol. 2, p. 440.
61 *Ibid.*, vol. 2, p. 534. However, the 1831 census compilers pointed out that the manufacture of woollen articles in Lancashire was relatively unimportant. See *PP*, 1833 (149) XXXVL, p. 308.

62  *Ibid.*, vol. 1, p. 656.
63  *Ibid.*, vol. 1, p. 612.
64  *Ibid.*, vol. 2, p. 26 and vol. 1, p. 640.
65  *Ibid.*, vol. 2, pp. 590, 455 and 467.
66  *Ibid.*, vol. 2, pp. 134–5. During the early 1830s, Ormskirk weavers were producing cloth of a very inferior description (*PP*, 1834, 44, XXXVI, p. 706).
67  LRO, Haslingden Baptism Registers, PR 3016.
68  See pp. 52–6.
69  J. G. Timmins, *Handloom Weavers' Cottages in Central Lancashire* (1977), p. 64.
70  *Ibid.*, pp. 29–30; Lewis, *op. cit.*, p. 18.
71  W. E. Brown, *Bolton As It Was* (1972), pp. 21 and 37; C. H. Saxelby, *Bolton Survey* (1971), final plate.
72  TTM, Brandwood Account Book.
73  J. G. Timmins, 'Handloom weavers' cottages in central Lancashire: some problems of recognition', *Post-Medieval Archaeology*, 13 (1979), pp. 266–7.
74  J. G. Timmins, *Handloom Weavers' Cottages in Central Lancashire* (1977), pp. 20–3.
75  See p. 81.
76  Upper-storey loomshops in wool handloom weavers' cottages tend to have rows of windows.
77  But upper-storey loomshops, and many of those in cellars, were more inconvenient in terms of access, a point made by N. K. Scott, *The Architectural Development of Cotton Mills in Preston and District* (MA thesis, 1952), p. 60.
78  BAS, Heywood Papers, ZHE 46/83.
79  *PP*, 1833 (690) VI, Q.3,970.
80  See pp. 139–40.
81  See pp. 137–42.

# Chapter 4

# THE ONSET OF DECLINE IN COTTON HAND WEAVING

In Chapter 1, it is suggested that contemporary estimates of numbers employed in cotton hand weaving provide an unsatisfactory basis on which to assess the onset of decline in the trade. It is also noted that historians have generally concluded that the decline was under way during the 1820s, despite the lack of progress made by the powerloom.

Here, an alternative interpretation is offered. It is argued that hand weaver numbers in Lancashire, both generally and in the cotton trade alone, did not show any marked decline before the late 1830s. The contention is examined from two standpoints, one looking at the onset of decline in relation to general movements in the trade cycle and the other in relation to particular localities within the county.

The former approach points to the conclusion that the upsurge in business activity during the mid-1830s was powerful enough to maintain overall hand weaver numbers at, or close to, their peak level. So strong was this upturn that neither hand nor power weaving capacity could meet demand for cottons of all types or for other fabrics. Besides, the powerloom could not as yet weave more than a limited range of wares on a commercial basis. For a time, therefore, rivalry between new and traditional sectors diminished.

The latter approach reveals a marked variation in the intra-regional onset of decline, the earliest falls of any significance being in the south Lancashire towns, where the powerloom made its greatest initial impact. Here, hand weaver numbers were falling by the early 1830s, whereas in other districts, including some urban areas, numbers held up well until the closing years of the decade. Using new figures derived from parish register counts, it is argued that the losses incurred at local level were not particularly heavy by the mid-1830s and that they were confined to a few districts. Support is thus lent to the idea that overall numbers had shown little decline. In explaining these variations, the importance of the type of fabric being woven is stressed, since it was in those districts producing the plainer and coarser grades of cotton that the powerloom gained early acceptance, with consequent effects on the size of the hand weaving labour force.

## 1  The impact of the mid-1830s trade upturn

That employment opportunities for handloom weavers were greatly enhanced during the mid-1830s is abundantly evident from contemporary newspaper accounts and from the comments of witnesses before the Select Committee on Hand Loom Weavers' Petitions. Throughout this period, references abound to the briskness of the cotton trade, to the shortages of handloom weavers, and to advances in their piece rates. After several years of depressed conditions, the hand weavers were once more able to enjoy a measure of prosperity.

The general direction in which the trade cycle moved during the 1830s and the overall impact it had on the prosperity of hand weaving, are soon dealt with. In the early months of 1834, as the upswing gained momentum, there were reports from several Lancashire towns of the rising demand for woven goods, those of Bolton, for example, being 'anxiously enquired for'.[1] By June, Edmund Ashworth, the leading factory owner from Egerton, near Bolton, could tell Edwin Chadwick that handloom weavers in his locality were much wanted.[2] During the succeeding month, it was reported that calico hand weavers at Colne were 'held in much demand',[3] and that at Oldham, Ashton and elsewhere in the Manchester area, cotton handloom weavers were fully employed.[4] Trade remained buoyant throughout the autumn and winter of 1834–35 and although Robert Gardner, a cotton spinner and manufacturer, discerned 'a slackness of demand for labour' during the early summer of 1835, the overall improvement was maintained throughout that year.[5] In October, hand weavers were still wanted at Bolton and the fancy trades there were busy, with weavers being offered bounties to meet an extensive demand for fancy quiltings.[6] During the following month, the *Bolton Chronicle* could announce notable progress in the fancy trades at Chorley, Preston, Blackburn and Darwen, the report concluding that there was 'a most unprecedented demand for 9–8 jaconets, for printing'.[7]

The new year brought further good cheer. In January, the manufacturing trade at Bolton was described as being 'all animation'[8] and the following month brought notice that the silk trade in the Manchester area was continuing its revival, the previous year having been one of 'unexampled activity'.[9] Towards the end of July, a local newspaper correspondent was writing that the demand for handloom weavers was 'scarcely ever so brisk as at the present moment'.[10] The general position was summarised by Henry Ashworth, brother and business partner of Edmund, when he observed that 'the year 1836 was remarkable for great activity in the cotton trade.'[11]

It was not until the early months of 1837 that the inevitable recession took place. In April, trade at Bolton had become very dull and manufacturers were laying off weavers as their warps were finished.[12] Similar reports came from other parts of the county. In the Preston neighbourhood, for example, a 'considerable portion' of the hand weavers were out of work,[13] whilst at Mawdesley and Croston, weaving villages situated to the west of Chorley, the handlooms were nearly all at a standstill.[14] Some improvement did occur during the second half of the year,[15] but the upturn was not particularly strong and before the end of the year trade at Bolton was reported as stagnating, whilst at Wigan the handloom weavers were described as 'not having more than half employment'.[16] Speaking generally of the winter of 1837–38, 'the year of the American panic', William Hickson observed:

A greater number of looms had been thrown out of employment than for a long time had been remembered and that, in consequence, some thousands of families had been plunged into the greatest distress.[17]

Another brief revival took place during the summer and autumn of 1838, with Hickson reporting that a large factory of handloom weavers at Manchester, which had stopped entirely during the winter, now had eighty-eight looms employed. But the respite was short. By the early months of 1839, local newspapers were again reporting that business was slack.[18] At the end of July, the *Blackburn Standard* carried an article noting the poor state of trade since the beginning of the year.[19] In September, trade was still said to be 'drooping' in cloths woven both by hand and by power.[20] Overall, 1839 proved to be a year of recession, one local paper referring in November to 'cheerless and gloomy trade throughout Lancashire'.[21]

In judging the economic impact of these trade cycle movements on the handloom weaving trade, two major issues arise. The first concerns the extent to which the trade revival at mid-decade curbed the decline in overall hand weaver numbers. The growing, but limited, use of powerlooms during the 1820s and early 1830s, coupled with the fall in demand for woven goods during the depression of 1829–33, would have reduced employment opportunities for hand weavers, even if the lack of alternative jobs meant that the overall size of the hand weaving labour force showed little, if any, diminution. The second issue concerns the variation in the impact of the cycle on different sections of the hand weaving labour force. Given that the rate of powerloom investment would have quickened during the mid-1830s, especially in urban areas, the question arises as to whether the urban hand weaver benefited less from the trade upturn than his rural counterpart. Given, too, that the impact of the powerloom would have been greatest with regard to the cheaper grades of cotton cloth, the possibility must be raised that weavers of fine and fancy wares were the chief beneficiaries of the upturn, perhaps enjoying the highest employment levels they ever attained. Was it the case indeed that, as William Hickson believed, the demand for hand-woven cloth remained little diminished?[22]

In addressing these issues, it is necessary at the outset to comment on the magnitude and duration of the mid-1830s cyclical upturn, since this helps to shed light on the degree to which additional jobs were created, both for handloom and for powerloom weavers. Once more, contemporary observation is highly instructive, even though it is fragmentary and sometimes imprecise.

The importance of the mid-1830s cyclical upturn in the economic life of Britain and, for that matter, of other countries, has long been appreciated. It formed the peak of one of the country's few major trade cycles, distinguished in terms of both amplitude and duration from the more minor cycles that came before and after.[23] It is associated with a marked rise in investment, not least in the early railway system. Its impact was felt strongly throughout British industry, leading to a substantial extension in the country's fixed capital assets and being instrumental in promoting an industrial growth rate of 47.2 per cent during the 1830s, the highest decennial growth rate to be achieved in Britain throughout the nineteenth century.[24]

In the cotton industry, investment rose sharply. From 1835–37, steam engine horse power in Lancashire cotton mills probably expanded by 50 per cent and the amount of capital equipment employed by 20 per cent.[25] Rises in output were also impressive. From the trough year of 1832 to the peak year of 1836, total production of cotton goods increased by 37 per cent and piece goods by 38 per cent.[26] For individual firms, there were welcome and very marked improvements in profitability. In 1836, for example, the Ashworths of Egerton recorded an impressive return of 22.5 per cent on capital employed at their New Eagley Mill and 17.3 per cent at Egerton. These figures were greatly in excess of their normal returns during the 1830s and 1840s, which averaged only some 5 per cent.[27] Throughout the industry, firms were benefiting from rising yarn and cloth prices without a corresponding increase in the cost of raw cotton.[28]

That the trade upturn brought a sharp rise in the demand for handloom weavers can be judged from the labour shortages that emerged in the trade. In part, these may have been exacerbated by some fall in numbers during the early 1830s. Yet they would not have occurred in the absence of the upsurge. Nor would they have been as extensive as they proved. Thus, as the cycle approached its peak in the summer of 1836, a local correspondent of the *Preston Chronicle* claimed that some of the largest handloom manufacturers were advertising widely throughout the country districts of Lancashire for additional hands. They placed advertisements which commonly asked for as many as 500 or 1,000 new weavers.[29] Again, during the summer of 1835, it was reported that, at Bolton, weavers of fancy cords had been laid off, but had easily found new work in making fine jaconets, for which handloom weavers were 'not to be had'.[30] Not only, therefore, did severe general shortages of handloom weavers arise, but in some branches of the trade, especially those producing finer and fancier grades of cottons, as well as non-cottons, they became particularly acute. It was in these branches that the powerloom was as yet uneconomic.

The extent of the rising demand for handloom labour during the mid-1830s is also reflected in the size of the wage increases that were secured. As early as June 1834, Edmund Ashworth noted that hand weavers' wages had been advanced by as much as 10 per cent.[31] During the next two years, further rises were made and in July 1836, the *Preston Chronicle* correspondent observed that where 4s was paid a month ago, manufacturers 'now give 5s, and where 5s now 7s.'[32] Other references were also to rises of a shilling or two per piece, again suggesting that the percentage change was substantial.[33] To these advances may be added the bonuses that could be secured for prompt delivery. For example, in March 1836, an advance of 0.5d per yard was being offered on chequered sarcenets (a silk fabric), besides a bonus of 2s for every piece returned within a twenty-one-day period.[34]

Indices of calico hand weavers' piece rates compiled by Bythell and Lyons tell a similar story. Thus, from a low point of 33 in 1832, Bythell's index rises to a peak of 44 in 1835. During the following year it falls away slightly, reaching a low point of 29 in 1837. On this evidence, the effect of the mid-1830s upturn was to bring calico piece rates back to the levels attained in 1827 and 1828.[35]

How powerful these incentives proved in maintaining the size of the hand weaving force, or even of extending it, would have depended to some extent on the level of wage rises that occurred in other occupations. Data are lacking, but in a report presented to the Poor Law Commission in 1835, Dr James Phillips Kay maintained that wages of hand weavers were higher than for several years past, whilst the wages of mill hands had not advanced. Accordingly, the earnings of the former were not 'greatly inferior' to those of the latter and the economic incentive for hand weavers to enter factory work had diminished.[36] When the hand weavers' preference for domestic work and the difficulties they might encounter in finding alternative jobs, especially in country districts, are taken into account, it is quite apparent that there was little encouragement for them to abandon their trade during the mid-1830s.[37]

One further point should be made about the benefits brought by the trade upturn to hand weavers in general. It is that the prosperity engendered lasted for quite some time. As early as 1833, the upward pressure on wages was apparent and it was more than three years before any significant downturn occurred. As they became accustomed to comparative prosperity, the confidence of the hand weavers in the future of their trade would have been heightened and their willingness to remain with it would have strengthened. That numerous children of hand weavers were still entering the trade at this time serves only to reinforce this view. Their presence is shown in the 1841 and later sets of census schedules, families commonly being recorded which depended entirely on the handloom, especially in country areas.[38] Moreover, that the downturn of 1837 was short-lived, may have led some hand weavers to believe that years of progress would outnumber those of depression, thereby reinforcing their confidence in the long-term viability of hand weaving. In such circumstances, they would have chosen to stay with the trade rather than to seek new opportunities.

Turning to consider the impact of the mid-1830s trade improvement on particular sections of the hand weaving labour force, it seems likely that experience varied. For the purposes of discussion, two broad groups may be distinguished, namely those weaving cheap, plain cottons and those concentrating on finer and fancier cottons or on non-cottons. Each will be taken in turn.

For those producing the cheaper grades of cotton, who would have comprised the majority, it might be thought that the 1830s upturn was more detrimental than beneficial. After all, it was with them that the powerloom was in the greatest competition and it was they who stood to lose out most as increasing numbers of powerlooms were installed. Indeed, that cotton manufacturers experienced such acute shortages of labour in the mid-1830s would have prompted many to extend their existing powerloom capacity or to install powerlooms for the first time, as in the cases of Horrocks & Company of Preston and James Grimshaw of Barrowford, near Colne. The powerloom capacity of the former concern rose from 576 in 1833 to 764 in the following year and of the latter from 44 in 1835 to 168 in 1836.[39]

Such reasoning must be questioned, however, not least because it can be too readily assumed that the demand for hand weavers of cheap cottons did not expand significantly. Yet this seems doubtful. In the first place, the piece rate indices for calico weaving compiled by Bythell and Lyons rose, respectively, by one-third and one-fifth during the mid-1830s. Secondly, at the height of the cyclical upturn in the summer of 1836, it was reported that the manufacturers advertising for large numbers of extra hand weavers were 'hawking their work which is chiefly of a common description'.[40] Evidently, if they had expanded their powerloom capacity, they had not done so to a sufficient extent. Nor can the reluctance of some manufacturers to rely too heavily on machines they regarded as imperfect be ruled out. After all, the major technical breakthroughs achieved by Kenworthy and Bullough were still several years away.[41] It is all too easy to assume that manufacturers usually had sufficient confidence in the powerloom during the mid-1830s to rely completely upon it. Perhaps, too, the decision to invest in new powerlooms was sometimes made rather too late to take full advantage of the trade upturn. Accordingly, total weaving capacity became severely stretched and manufacturers had little option but to try and maximise the input made by traditional technology, even in producing the cheaper grades of cloth.

Regarding those weaving the more expensive cottons and the non-cottons, it is plain that the demand for their services grew extremely strongly during the mid-1830s and references to the growing need for additional weavers in particular branches of these trades are not difficult to find. For instance, during August 1835, it was reported that a revival had recently taken place in the demand for handloom piece goods at Bamber Bridge, Clayton Green and Chorley, especially in ginghams, on which an advance of two shillings per piece had been given. It was felt, too, that there were prospects of further improvement.[42] Again, towards the end of 1835, the Bolton bed quilt and counterpane trades were said to be 'uncommonly brisk' and all kinds of fancy quiltings were still in great demand.[43] Outside cotton, the position was similar. In March 1836, for example, the rise in demand for chequered sarcenets was so great that several houses would each have been pleased to hire three or four hundred additional weavers if they could have been speedily obtained.[44] The wool trade, centred in the Rochdale area, had also revived after being badly hit by the imposition of the American tariff. It was reckoned that some hundreds of flannel hand weavers had left the trade, but that those remaining were now 'well employed'.[45]

In all these trades the numbers of handloom weavers would have increased appreciably during the mid-1830s. Competition from the powerloom was as yet fairly limited, whilst the growth in demand for their products rose to high, perhaps unprecedented, levels. Indeed, it is apparent that these trades spread to new areas of Lancashire as manufacturers sought additional labour and weavers responded to the high wages on offer. Thus, early in 1834, silk weaving was said to be extending rapidly in the Oldham area,[46] whilst in October of the following year it was reported that the trade had lately been introduced at Chorley on a considerable scale.[47]

There is strong reason to believe, therefore, that the sharp trade improvement of the mid-1830s served to stem any decline in hand weaver numbers that may already have set in. The overall demand for woven goods showed a dramatic increase, which was sustained for several years and which could only be partially met by the powerloom sector. This was so even with regard to the cheaper grades of cotton cloth. In other branches, which were still largely free from the competition of the powerloom, the benefit of the general trade upturn for hand weaving was probably even more pronounced. Beyond doubt, the hand weaving sector had a major role to play in coping with the additional output required during the mid-1830s.

By the end of the 1830s, however, a very different picture had emerged. The growth in powerloom capacity during the middle years of the decade had reached the stage where factory weavers could meet a high proportion of the diminished demand for cheaper cottons as the business cycle went into recession. To service their fixed costs, manufacturers needed to keep their powerlooms running as much as possible and so began to lay off handloom weavers in considerable numbers.[48] Since the great majority of powerlooms were in urban mills, it was the urban hand weavers who suffered particularly. And their position was made worse because investment in powerlooms still occurred, albeit at a much slower rate, and output of cotton goods continued to rise, with a resultant downward pressure on product prices and wage rates.[49] Even so, the decline of hand weaving was to prove a lengthy affair, particularly in the finer and fancier grades of cotton and in non-cottons. Weavers in these branches, many of whom were urban based, remained a significant element in the labour force until well into the mid-Victorian era.

## 2 Intra-regional variation

The approach adopted in this section is to examine the onset of decline in handloom weaving from district to district and then to assess the overall position across the county. In so doing, local estimates of hand weaver numbers made during the

*The last shift*

Table 4.1 *Handloom weaver totals in south Lancashire towns, 1834–36*

| Town | % age of pop'n examined | Number of weavers |
| --- | --- | --- |
| Manchester | 64 | 2,811 |
| Salford | 74 | 381 |
| Bury | 72 | 275 |
| Ashton | 82 | 320 |
| Stalybridge | 90 | 32 |
| Dukinfield | 95 | 19 |

1830s are compared with the parish register estimates for the early 1820s. For some districts, the former are not available, but it is nevertheless possible to consider the situation in most of Lancashire's major textile districts. Accordingly, a reasonably comprehensive analysis can be attempted.

It has been previously noted that the powerloom made its strongest initial impact in urban areas, especially in south-east Lancashire.[50] It is not unexpected, therefore, to find that contemporaries singled out this district as one where the handloom experienced an early decline. In 1834, James Brennan, a Manchester weaver, recounted that the 112 looms in his street had sunk to 46 and that, in Manchester as a whole, there had formerly been a great many more weavers than the 3–4,000 that remained.[51] A large-scale, house-to-house survey made by the Manchester Statistical Society between 1834–36 also pointed to small numbers of hand weavers in Manchester, as well as in the neighbouring towns of Salford, Dukinfield, Stalybridge, Ashton and Bury.[52] The results, some of which are reproduced in Table 4.1, must be viewed with care, however, because many of those questioned did not give their occupations. In fact, at Manchester and Salford, where more than three-quarters of those examined resided, only some two-thirds did so. Additionally, though the society claimed to have covered very nearly the whole working population below the rank of shopkeeper, except in Manchester, it remarked that the register of occupation 'could be considered accurate only in the sum total'. The number of handloom weavers, therefore, could have been considerably understated in each of the towns.

Despite these uncertainties, it is instructive to compare the society's figures with those obtained from the parish register estimates for the early 1820s. This indicates a substantial fall in numbers at Manchester, from about 20,000 to around 3–4,000, though the actual reduction was probably smaller. In the other towns, falls were less spectacular, because the absolute number of hand weavers was not so high. For example, at Ashton-under-Lyne, it was from around 5,000 to perhaps 400–500.[53] Plainly, the powerloom was making its presence felt in the south-eastern towns, though in one of Manchester's main working-class districts, 2,060 hand weavers were counted in 1835, compared with only 608 power weavers.[54]

## Onset of decline in cotton hand weaving

At nearby Stockport, meanwhile, handloom weavers and jenny spinners were said to have been the two principal groups of workers that had 'decayed',[55] bringing, according to the local weaver William Longson, a drop in the number of hand weavers from 5,000 in 1818 to only 400 in 1834.[56] It should be noted, however, that Longson thought Stockport to be an exception, he never having heard of 'one-fifth part of the diminution of numbers in any other place.'[57] Nevertheless, Gilbert Henderson, the poor law assistant commissioner, spoke of the diminishing number of handloom weavers in all the large towns by the mid-1830s, although he conceded that the rate of decline varied.[58]

Another major town where contemporaries thought that hand weaver numbers fell early was Preston. In 1834, two local weavers, Robert Crawford and John Lennon agreed that some 3,000 hand weavers were to be found in the town, less than there had been fifteen years or so before, Lennon thought.[59] Unfortunately, no figure by which to estimate the extent of decline was offered. However, by assuming their estimate was reasonably correct (though clearly it was an approximation) there is substance in their claim. The parish register figures suggest a total of between 3,500 and 4,500 in the early 1820s, so that numbers may have reduced by one-third at the most.

Crawford also suggested that in the district of Preston, as many as 13,000 hand weavers could still be found in 1834.[60] He gave no precise definition of the area he included, though it did not embrace Blackburn. Nor did he mention whether the number had fallen in recent years. Seemingly, he included the whole of Preston parish, with its several thousand hand weavers in the early 1820s and perhaps extended into districts south of the Ribble. Whatever the truth of this, his evidence does indicate that a sizeable hand weaving labour force was still to be found in the Preston area in the mid-1830s and one that may not have been dramatically reduced. The bulk would have been in rural locations, a reflection of the limited impact of the powerloom outside urban centres.

Whilst hand weaver numbers were falling in some parts of Lancashire by the 1830s, this was by no means the case throughout the county. Indeed, in certain districts, the talk was still of an overall increase. Thus, in 1833, James Grimshaw, a cotton master from Barrowford, remarked that 'of late years' the number of handloom weavers had risen in the Colne district, the main hand weaving stronghold in north-east Lancashire.[61] It seems that in the town of Colne, there were still no powerlooms as late as 1840.[62] Again, during 1834, William Longson, a silk weaver, spoke of increases in the countryside around Stockport.[63] Growing numbers were also mentioned in the Bolton neighbourhood where, according to Richard Needham and William Pilling, handloom weavers from the town, there were more hand weavers to be found in 1833 than there had been in 1817. This was true, they believed, both within the borough of Bolton and within the division of Bolton, which included the borough as well as several surrounding townships.[64] In the following year, John Makin, a Bolton textile manufacturer, expressed similar views, suggesting that the number of handloom weavers in the borough had increased over the last ten or fifteen years.[65] A fourth Bolton hand weaver, Philip Halliwell, did not entirely agree with his colleagues, but did state that there were as many hand weavers in Bolton as there ever had been.[66]

Needham and Pilling also gave estimated numbers of hand weavers in their locality. According to their calculations, there were 23,500 in the division of Bolton and 7,000 in the borough. Without knowing the precise coverage of the former area, it is difficult to identify an appropriate parish register estimate to check against the Needham and Pilling figure. As far as the borough is concerned, however, the parish register estimates suggest a figure of between 6,000 and 7,500 in the early 1820s. Hence, the suggestion of the contemporaries that the Bolton borough numbers were stable or rising in the mid-1830s is highly plausible. Moreover, since the powerlooms in Bolton parish were mainly to be found within the town area, it is likely that handloom weaver numbers in the division of Bolton were also undiminished.[67] Here, then, was a major group of Lancashire handloom weavers, perhaps as many as one in every seven, which was as yet largely unaffected by the appearance of the powerloom.

If hand weaver numbers were still rising in Bolton into the 1830s, the question remains as to when they began to fall. Quite possibly, numbers would have been maintained during the mid-1830s economic upsurge, though another Boltonian, the muslin and cotton manufacturer Jonathan Hitchen, thought they were 'lessing very much' by 1835. Even so, he still quoted a figure of about 7,000.[68] It is unlikely, therefore, that any marked decline became apparent before the end of the decade. Some indication that this was the case is provided by the results of a survey undertaken by Dr James Black in 1837. From house-to-house enquiries, Black was able to enumerate 5,658 hand weavers, of whom, he found, 960 were counterpane weavers and 390 were bed quilt weavers.[69]

With regard to the other major centres of hand weaving, namely Blackburn, Rochdale, Oldham and Wigan, the position is uncertain. No representatives from Rochdale and Wigan were called before the parliamentary enquiries and those from Blackburn and Oldham did not comment on any change in handloom weaver numbers.[70] Robert Gardner, sometime a Manchester cotton spinner and manufacturer, thought that numbers had fallen in Manchester and several neighbouring towns, including Oldham, but felt unable to attempt any quantification.[71] At Rochdale, too, it seems that some reduction had occurred in the numbers of woollen weavers, but again precise details are not given.[72] The most likely situation is that within each of these towns, Rochdale excepted, numbers of cotton hand weavers were falling as competition from powerlooms intensified, but that sizeable groups could still be found in surrounding rural districts. As the mid-nineteenth century census figures indicate, this may have been more the case in the Blackburn area than at Oldham or Wigan.[73]

For the districts where hand weavers were less heavily concentrated, little evidence is available. Testifying to the 1834 Committee, James Ashworth, a woollen manufacturer who was acquainted with the Rossendale, Padiham and Burnley area,

## Onset of decline in cotton hand weaving

remarked only that the number of woollen hand weavers in Rossendale had fallen during the previous decade or so.[74] Yet, as late as 1842, W. C. Taylor reckoned that the number of hand weavers in Rossendale was as great as it ever had been.[75] At Heywood, meanwhile, the powerloom had virtually taken over.[76] As to the position elsewhere, including the Chorley and Leyland area, where hand weaving was the major occupation, the witnesses remained silent. Nevertheless, any substantial fall in numbers seems improbable, since this area developed an early interest in weaving high-quality cloths,[77] and still contained a high proportion of fancy handloom weavers during the mid-1830s.[78]

In explaining the varying pace of powerloom investment from district to district, the economic advantages of site enjoyed by textile manufacturers in north Cheshire and south Lancashire have been highlighted. A. J. Taylor, for instance, argues that capital for powerloom investment came almost entirely from owners of spinning mills, who were more numerous and larger in the Manchester area than further north. He maintains, too, that the facilities to produce powerlooms were more readily available in south Lancashire than elsewhere.[79] Similarly, Duncan Bythell has argued that master spinners in the Manchester area had the experience of dealing with machines, the buildings in which to house them and the resources for their purchase. He believes that such advantages were conspicuously lacking amongst manufacturers in other parts of Lancashire.[80]

Such arguments express the locational advantages acquired by the textile industry as it developed apace in the south Lancashire towns. Yet advantages of this type were not confined to the south of the county. The 1835 Factory Returns show that there were many more powerlooms in the parishes of Blackburn and Preston (4,256 and 2,356 respectively) than in those of Wigan (where there were 1,532) and of Bolton (where they totalled 1,699). Even the Lancaster parish total of 1,144 was not far short of the Bolton and Wigan figures.[81] Evidently, therefore, the arguments of Bythell and Taylor are incomplete; what they have overlooked is the type of fabric being woven. It is this which is crucial in explaining the variations in early powerloom development within the county.

Useful guidance on this matter is provided by Edward Baines. For the mid-1830s, he has compiled a table showing the particular types of cotton cloth woven in various parts of the county and whether hand or powerlooms were employed. Altogether, he distinguishes twenty-five groups of fabrics, of which only one, stout printing calicoes, was woven entirely on the powerloom. The production of this fabric was centred in south-east Lancashire and north-east Cheshire, principally at Hyde, Stockport, Dukinfield, Stalybridge, Manchester and Ashton.

Three other categories, were woven chiefly by power. They were stout calicoes for domestic purposes, which were woven at Todmorden and elsewhere; cotton shirtings, the product of Stockport, Manchester, Preston and other places; and smallwares, a Manchester speciality. The only other wares to be woven by power were cotton velvets and similar fabrics, which were manufactured at Oldham, Warrington, Manchester, Bury and Heywood.[82] No mention is made of Blackburn amongst Baines' power weaving towns, but a witness before the 1834 Commission noted that one leading handloom manufacturer there had specialised in producing a strong, plain calico.[83] It is known, too, that the stronger types of cotton goods, including fustians, were being woven at Oldham in the post-Napoleonic years.[84]

Although the picture is incomplete, there is enough to show that the powerloom gained early ascendancy in those districts where the coarser and cheaper types of cottons and fustians had become the leading fabrics and that not all of these districts were in the south of the county. Conversely, in districts where the powerloom had made little impact, including Bolton and Chorley, products that could not as yet be woven economically by power, including muslins and ginghams, held sway. And some of these districts were in the south of the county. As well, that such towns as Blackburn produced a range of cotton fabrics helps to explain why the handloom continued to be responsible for an appreciable amount of production there, despite the inroads made by the powerloom.[85]

Before summarising the evidence from the various localities, another consideration must be briefly aired. It concerns the growing practice amongst hand weavers in some districts of switching from cotton to other fabrics as the powerloom gradually extended its capabilities. This tendency was already evident in the pre-Victorian period and was ultimately to constitute one of the main ways in which domestic outwork continued to survive in the Lancashire textile industry well into the second half of the century. The theme will be developed in depth at a later stage when census evidence is adduced.[86] Here it may be noted that the parliamentary enquiries into hand weaving make several references to such developments, especially to silk hand weaving in the Manchester area and at Leigh and Middleton.[87] They mention, too, the growth of hand-woven mixture cloths, such as mousseline-de-laine, a light dress fabric made from cotton and wool.[88] It is clear that the practice of diversifying into silk was well established by the early 1840s, Edwin Butterworth's figures for 1841 giving 5,000 silk hand weavers at Leigh and 2,000 at Middleton.[89]

One of the key points to emerge from this analysis is that the available evidence suggests a general decline in the numbers of cotton hand weavers in Lancashire's major towns by the mid-1830s, Bolton excepted. Only in the case of Manchester, however, was the extent of the fall particularly large. Here, upwards of 16,000 hand weavers may have left the trade during the 1820s and early 1830s; elsewhere, figures of a few thousand were usual. At the most, therefore, Lancashire's population of urban hand weavers would have been 25–35,000 fewer by the mid-1830s. As a proportion of the 170,000 or so that were to be found in the county during the early 1820s, this was extremely modest. At the most, it represented a fall of about one in five.

Whether this represented an overall decline in Lancashire's hand weaver numbers remains to be considered. At least one contemporary, Robert Gardner, thought it did. In his view, the cotton hand weaving labour force was one-third smaller in 1835 than it had been ten or twelve years before. His reasoning was based on the notion that the powerloom had taken over in several towns around Manchester, leaving no more than one in ten of the handlooms there weaving cotton. He also maintained that handlooms were idle elsewhere, as at Bolton, where the figure was as high as one in four.[90]

The validity of Gardner's claims must be doubted, however. This is partly because the towns he selects were mainly small, Stockport and Oldham being the exceptions, whilst not all were in Lancashire. It is also because, given the progress of powerlooms in urban areas, it may be anticipated that a proportion of urban handlooms would have been idle by the mid-1830s. Plainly, there is not enough substance in Gardner's reasoning to justify his conclusion. It is much more likely that the alternative view advanced by William Hickson, the handloom weavers' commissioner, is correct. Following his visit to Lancashire in the autumn of 1838, he found that not only were considerable numbers of cotton hand weavers still at work, but that, from 'universal testimony', the numbers were almost as great as at any former period.[91]

Contemporary views apart, there are several reasons arising from the analysis of particular localities to suggest that the number of hand weavers in Lancashire was maintained until the late 1830s. In the first place, it is probable that, as the cotton trade continued to expand during the 1820s and 1830s, the rural handloom weavers, largely immune from the growing threat of the powerloom, could have continued to increase in number. Nor can it be safely assumed that this increase would have been confined to those weaving the finer and fancier grades of cotton. Secondly, in at least two major hand weaving centres, Bolton and Colne, the indications are that cotton hand weaving was still expanding, albeit to a relatively small extent. Thirdly, the growth in domestic silk weaving was already making a notable impact during the 1830s. Any overall fall in hand weavers by the middle of the decade would therefore have been marginal and, even as far as cotton was concerned, it would not have gone far. Given that the mid-1830s trade upsurge would have acted beneficially on handloom weaving, it may be concluded that no significant reduction in Lancashire's hand weaving labour force would have occurred prior to the late 1830s, though important changes were becoming evident in its distribution.

### Notes

1 *MSA*, 11.1.1834.
2 *PP*, 1835 (500) XXXV, p. 322.
3 *PC*, 19.7.1834.
4 *Ibid.*, 26.7.1834.
5 *PP*, 1835 (341) XIII, Q.2027.
6 *PC*, 31.10.1835.
7 *Ibid.*, 28.11.1835.
8 *PC*, 16.1.1836.
9 *Ibid.*, 13.2.1836.
10 *Ibid.*, 23.7.1836.

11 H. Ashworth, 'An enquiry into the origin, progress, and results of the strike of the operative cotton spinners of Preston, from October, 1836 to February, 1837', *Memoirs of the Literary and Philosophical Society of Manchester*, IV (1837), p. 2.

12 *PC*, 1.4.1837.

13 *BS*, 26.4.1837.

14 *PC*, 15.4.1837.

15 *Ibid.*, 2.9.1837. The main body of hand weavers were reported to be in a comparatively comfortable condition, work being 'somewhat plentiful' and payment a 'living remuneration'.

16 *Ibid.*, 21.10.1837 and 11.11.1837.

17 *PP*, 1840 (639) XXIV, p. 4.

18 See, for example, *BS*, 1.3.1839.

19 *Ibid.*, 31.7.1839.

20 *Ibid.*, 2.10.1839.

21 *Ibid.*, 20.11.1839.

22 *PP*, 1840 (639) XXIV, p. 12. Hickson took the view that the powerloom had, at that time, created its own market.

23 W. W. Rostow, 'Cycles in the British economy, 1790–1914', in D. H. Aldcroft and P. Fearon, *British Economic Fluctuations, 1790–1939* (1972), pp. 77–80.

24 F. Crouzet, *The Victorian Economy* (1982), p. 49.

25 R. C. O. Matthews, *A Study of Trade-Cycle History* (1954), p. 135.

26 *Ibid.*, p. 151.

27 R. Boyson, *The Ashworth Cotton Enterprise* (1970), p. 30.

28 Matthews, *op. cit.*, p. 134.

29 *PC*, 23.7.1836.

30 *BS*, 8.7.1835.

31 *PP*, 1835 (500) XXXV, p. 322. Letter from Edmund Ashworth to Edwin Chadwick.

32 *PC*, 23.7.1836.

33 For example, ginghams in the Chorley area were advanced 2/- per piece in the late summer of 1835 (*Ibid.*, 1.8.1835).

34 *PC*, 5.3.1836.

35 D. Bythell, *The Handloom Weavers* (1969), p. 105. Lyons' index shows identical movement, rising from a low point of 60.4 in 1832 to a high of 72.5 in 1835. See J. S. Lyons, 'Family response to economic decline: handloom weavers in early nineteenth century Lancashire', *Research in Economic History*, 12 (1989), p. 51.

36 *PP*, 1835 (500) XXXV, p. 298.

37 See pp. 161–70.

38 See p. 133.

39 LRO, Cost Book, DDHs 75; MCLA, Farrer Collection L1/16/3/7.

40 *PC*, 23.7.1836.

41 For details see p. 23.

42 *PC*, 1.8.1835.

43 *PrP*, 31.10.1835.

44 *PC*, 5.3.1836.

45 *Ibid.*, 6.2.1836.

46 *MSA*, 8.2.1834.

47 *PrP*, 31.10.1835.

48  See, for example, the comments from Samuel Courtauld to the Handloom Weavers' Commission (*PP*, 1840, 43–1, XXIII, p. 227).
49  Matthews, *op. cit.*, pp. 139–40.
50  See p. 22.
51  *PP*, 1834 (556) X, Q.6,525.
52  Manchester Statistical Society, *Report on the Condition of the Working Classes, in an Extensive Manufacturing District in 1834, 1835 and 1836*, (1838). The survey was undertaken by four agents, each paid the not inconsiderable sum of 16/- per week. For further details see T. S. Ashton, *Economic and Social Investigations in Manchester, 1833–1933* (1977 reprint of 1934 edition), pp. 21–2.
53  For the early 1820s estimates, see pp. 37–8.
54  The survey was undertaken by an agent employed by the Manchester Statistical Society. The district was 'inhabited more than any other in the town by the working classes and by those of the poorest description. The population of the district was 42,135 in 1831. See E. and T. Kelly, *A Schoolmaster's Notebook* (1957), p. 117 and Ashton, *op. cit.*, pp. 20–1.
55  *PP*, 1833 (690) VI, Q.10,565.
56  *PP*, 1834 (556) X, Q.6,741. He was more certain about the accuracy of the earlier figure than of the later.
57  *Ibid.*, Q.6,771.
58  *PP*, 1834 (44) XXVIII, p. 910. Quoted in Bythell *op. cit.*, p. 265.
59  *PP*, 1834 (556), QQ.5,862 and 6,244.
60  *Ibid.*, Q.5,867.
61  *PP*, 1833 (690) VI, Q.10,171.
62  *PP*, 1840 (220) XXIV, p. 607.
63  *PP*, 1834 (556) X, Q.6,772.
64  *PP*, 1833 (690) VI, QQ 11,782–9. The division of Bolton included Bolton borough and several surrounding townships.
65  *PP*, 1834 (556) X, Q.5,054.
66  *Ibid.*, QQ.5,746–7.
67  See p. 22.
68  *PP*, 1835 (341) XIII, Q.2,929.
69  J. Black, *A Medico-Topographical, Geographical and Statistical Sketch of Bolton and Its Neighbourhood* (1837).
70  See *PP*, 1833 (690) VI, Q.11,090 *et seq.* and *PP*, 1834 (556), Q.6,883 *et seq.*
71  *PP*, 1835 (341) XIII, Q.1,743.
72  *PC*, 6.2.1836.
73  See J. G. Timmins, *The Decline of Handloom Weaving in Nineteenth Century Lancashire* (PhD thesis, University of Lancaster, 1990), Appendix B5.
74  *PP*, 1834 (556) X, QQ.7646–8.
75  W. C. Taylor, *Tour of the Manufacturing Districts of Lancashire* (1842), p. 71.
76  *PP*, 1835 (341) XIII, Q.2,241.
77  A. M. Warnes, 'Early separation of houses from workplaces and the urban structure of Chorley, 1780–1850', *THSL&C*, 112 (1970), pp. 110–1.
78  *PP*, 1834 (44) XXXVI, p. 736.
79  A. J. Taylor, 'Concentration and specialization in the Lancashire cotton industry, 1825–1850', *EcHR*, 1 (1949), p. 117–18.

80 Bythell, *op. cit.*, p. 91.
81 *PP*, 1836 (24) XLV, p. 5.
82 E. Baines, *History of the Cotton Manufacture in Great Britain* (1966 reprint of 1835 edition), p. 418.
83 *PP*, 1834 (556) X, Q.6,886.
84 J. Butterworth, *An Historical and Descriptive Account of the Town and Parochial Chapelry of Oldham* (1817), p. 6.
85 See p. 141.
86 See pp. 137–41.
87 See, for example, *PP*, 1833 (690) VI, QQ.5,128–36 and *PP*, 1840 (639) XXIV, p. 14.
88 *PP*, 1839 (159) XLII, p. 5.
89 E. Butterworth, *A Statistical Sketch of the County Palatine of Lancaster* (1841), pp. 50 and 94.
90 *PP*, 1835 (341) XIII, QQ.1,759 and 2,241.
91 *PP*, 1840 (639) XXIV, p. 12.

## Chapter 5

# THE SURVIVAL OF HAND WEAVING IN THE MID-VICTORIAN PERIOD

It has been shown that disagreement exists amongst historians about the rate at which hand technology in cotton weaving was displaced. At one extreme are those who favour the views of Duncan Bythell and maintain that the process was virtually complete by the mid-nineteenth century. At the other, are those in the tradition of S. J. Chapman, who, taking a more gradualist stance, argue that hand technology remained significant in the cotton industry as late as the mid-Victorian era.[1] In this chapter, the question is re-examined, using fresh evidence drawn from census enumerators' schedules.

The chief drawback with this evidence is the failure amongst enumerators to distinguish consistently between hand and power weavers, despite being instructed so to do.[2] Nevertheless, it does permit important new insights to be obtained into the size and structure of Lancashire's hand weaving labour force at, and beyond, mid-century. In particular, it enables its economic significance to be closely assessed, not only by considering the extent to which the trade had declined since the peak years, but also by examining the degree to which it still contributed to the Lancashire economy. It is this latter aspect which has received scant attention from historians, with the result that discussion on the survival of hand weaving in Lancashire has been rather narrowly focused. Yet, using census evidence, the significance of the mid-Victorian hand weavers can be considered in relation to the working population as a whole and with regard to the growing body of powerloom weavers. The first section of this chapter is devoted to these issues.

In part, the economic significance of mid-Victorian hand weaving would have depended upon the composition of the labour force. Other things being equal, the higher the proportion of adult male workers in a domestic trade, the greater would labour productivity and output have been. This is not because women usually worked less efficiently than men (though young children normally did) but because, as contemporaries relate, domestic duties impinged upon the time available for paid employment, especially for married women with families. For instance, the wife of William Gifford, a Bolton hand weaver, sometimes worked at the handloom, but since she had three children to care for, she could only earn a third to a half as much as her husband.[3] Such matters, which lead into considerations of the importance of child labour and family working groups, can also be addressed using census evidence. They are discussed in the second section of this chapter.

Several conclusions emerge from the analysis. The first is that hand weaving in Lancashire remained economically important in the 1850s and 1860s to a much greater extent than has been realised, even though it had declined substantially. The second is that whilst the balance had swung decisively from hand to power weaving in the major Lancashire towns by mid-century, albeit to a varying degree, numerous rural districts continued to rely greatly on domestic weaving. Only gradually was this dependency relinquished in the 1850s and 1860s, as powerlooms were adopted by more and more rural manufacturers. Finally, hand weaving continued to provide a great many jobs for women and children, emphasising the durability of family working groups. That hand weavers were able to benefit from family income is crucial in explaining how so many managed to stay in their trade, despite the falling piece rates they were forced to endure.

## 1 Overall numbers and dependency

Estimates of hand weaver numbers listed in the 1851 to 1871 census enumerators' schedules for Lancashire are given in Table 5.1. To facilitate comparison, the geographical areas are the same as those used for the parish register weaver totals recorded in Chapter 2. The figures for 1851 are presented in rank order, according to the numbers of hand weavers that are estimated to have survived.

The figures must be treated with caution. Those for major urban areas are subject to sampling error, whilst many others are derived by narrowing down the ranges given by the census counts, using the criteria discussed in Appendix A2. This procedure is more straightforward with the 1851 than with later data, because the enumerators in 1851 distinguished more fully than their successors between hand and power weavers. Indeed, entries become less explicit in this respect from census to census, the enumerator perhaps taking the view that he did not need to differentiate once hand weaving had virtually ceased in his district. As a result, the 1851 figures are, in most cases, rather more reliable than those for later years.

Even so, concern arises with several sets of 1851 figures, because large numbers of census schedules have been destroyed. The main shortfalls occur in Manchester parish, where details relating to over 180,000 people (some 40 per cent of the total population) are missing; at Ashton-under-Lyne, where more than 40,000 entries (about 80 per cent) are unobtainable; and at Eccles, where lost entries amount to about 17,000 (around 60 per cent).[4]

There is uncertainty as to whether the figures understate or overstate hand weaver numbers. That they may be too low is partly because of the missing

Table 5.1 *Estimates of handloom weavers in Lancashire, 1851–71*

| Parish; parish district or group | 1851 No. | % | 1861 No. | % | 1871 No. | % |
|---|---|---|---|---|---|---|
| Blackburn | 5,411 | 7 | 3,253 | 3 | 1,304 | |
| Manchester* | 4,456 | 2 | 2,216 | – | 948 | |
| Bolton | 4,203 | 5 | 3,080 | 3 | 1,137 | |
| Leigh | 4,096 | 16 | 3,161 | 11 | 1,517 | |
| Colne | 3,741 | 17 | 411 | 2 | – | |
| Central Lancashire | 3,054 | 11 | 1,403 | 5 | 536 | |
| Preston | 2,929 | 4 | 1,517 | 2 | 146 | |
| Wigan | 2,697 | 4 | 1,576 | 2 | 329 | |
| Middleton | 2,694 | 18 | 2,203 | 12 | 1,259 | |
| Oldham | 2,433 | 3 | 1,664 | 2 | 776 | |
| Winwick | 1,912 | 10 | 1,281 | 5 | 630 | |
| Deane | 1,872 | 6 | 1,240 | 4 | 826 | |
| Rochdale | 1,833 | 2 | 1,148 | – | – | |
| Bury | 1,532 | 2 | 432 | – | – | |
| Eccles* | 1,147 | 5 | 619 | – | – | |
| Ribchester | 1,101 | 28 | 451 | 12 | 126 | |
| Prestwich | 1,086 | 8 | 699 | 4 | 411 | |
| West Central Lancs | 965 | 12 | 544 | 6 | 195 | |
| Penwortham | 710 | 12 | 192 | 4 | 76 | |
| North Meols | 623 | 7 | 450 | 3 | 47 | |
| Standish | 592 | 7 | 95 | 1 | – | |
| Walton-le-Dale | 527 | 8 | 266 | 4 | 191 | |
| Flixton | 508 | 25 | 110 | 5 | 23 | |
| Newchurch-in-Pendle | 501 | 21 | 38 | 2 | – | |
| Newchurch-in-R'dale | 500 | 3 | 394 | 2 | – | |
| Kirkham | 499 | 5 | 179 | 2 | – | |
| Haslingden | 489 | 3 | 268 | 1 | – | |
| Burnley | 467 | 1 | 20 | – | – | |
| Padiham | 417 | 6 | 39 | – | – | |
| Church | 401 | 4 | 167 | 1 | – | |
| Ormskirk | 278 | 2 | 185 | 1 | 19 | |
| St Michael's-on-Wyre | 197 | 4 | 55 | 1 | 31 | |
| Warrington | 163 | 1 | – | | – | |
| Clitheroe | 121 | 1 | – | | – | |
| Ashton-under-Lyne* | 100 | 1 | – | | – | |
| East Bolton | 91 | 1 | – | | – | |
| Accrington | 78 | 1 | – | | – | |
| Downham | 60 | 11 | – | | – | |
| Whalley | 47 | 2 | – | | – | |
| Tarleton | 19 | 1 | – | | – | |
| Altham | 4 | | – | | – | |
| Total | 54,554 | | 29,356 | | 10,527 | |

* Incomplete returns, 1851

schedules, though this is not a problem beyond 1851. It is also because schedules were not examined from areas where weaver concentrations were low during the peak years; where it becomes apparent from census schedule counts that hand weaving had become insignificant; and where workhouse returns are concerned, since it is not clear whether inmates described as weavers gave their former or current occupation.[5] A further reason is that the undifferentiated weavers who could not be identified with reasonable confidence as hand weavers were assumed to have been power weavers. This proves a greater problem in 1871 and 1881 than in earlier years, when enumerators commonly drew the distinction. It should also be noted that several sets of urban schedules in 1861 and beyond were searched only in areas where hand weaving was concentrated.[6] Some hand weavers would therefore have been missed, though numbers cannot have been large. In all, underestimation probably amounts to a few thousand in each year, especially in 1851 and 1861 when hand weaver numbers were still considerable.

That the figures may be overestimates is largely because undifferentiated weavers working with mixtures, silks and fancy cottons are assumed to have been hand weavers, irrespective of age. For those recorded in the 1851 census, this is not an unreasonable view; at that date, as is shown in Chapter 1, the powerloom had made little progress in manufacturing non-cottons, with the exception of worsted. For those listed in later censuses, though, the position is less clear. There is no doubt that the powerloom was increasingly applied to non-cottons during the third quarter of the nineteenth century. Yet, in the silk districts especially, progress was far from rapid, as the following section demonstrates. Given, too, that silk weavers comprised the majority of Lancashire's non-cotton hand weavers, any exaggeration of the totals given in Table 5.1 will not be substantial. In any case, over-recording will be partly cancelled out by under-recording. Where the balance lies remains conjectural, but, if anything, the figures are on the low side.

Bearing these qualifications in mind, it is suggested that, in 1851, between 39,358 and 77,488 handloom weavers could still be found in Lancashire. From this range, an estimate of 54,554 is made, about two-thirds working with cotton. By 1861, the number still attained around 30,000 (half in cotton), the trade showing surprising resilience in a number of districts, including the cotton weaving areas of central Lancashire. Even as late as 1871, some 10,000 remained and it was not until the following decade that hand weaving in Lancashire became virtually extinct. Remarkably, hand weavers were still recorded in the 1881 census, though numbers cannot have been large. They included cotton weavers at Ribchester and Mellor in the Ribble Valley, forty-three of whom were listed. Most were middle-aged or elderly, but some were only in their twenties and thirties.[7] Quite plainly, Bythell's small, isolated groups of elderly cotton hand weavers belong to these years, rather than to the late 1840s.[8]

It is difficult to compare these estimates with any given by previous writers. This is because they relate to Lancashire rather than to the country as a whole and cover other types of fabric in addition to cotton. However, it will be suggested in the following chapter that, in 1851, around 32,000 of Lancashire's hand weavers were still manufacturing cotton cloth and a further 5,000 or so cotton mixture cloths.[9] For the country as a whole, Wood's estimate for that year is 40,000.[10] Since, according to Norman Murray's calculations, there were some 20,000 cotton hand weavers in Scotland at mid-century, the Wood estimate is far too low.[11] The national figure would have comfortably exceeded 50,000.

Taking a longer-term perspective on this decline, it is evident that substantial numbers left the trade during the second quarter of the nineteenth century. Given that no significant reduction occurred before the late 1830s, as is shown in the previous chapter, the 1840s must have been the crucial period. If the 1821 figure of 165,000 hand weavers is reasonably correct, then upwards of 100,000 hand weaving jobs were lost in Lancashire during this decade. These losses reflect the large-scale investment in new powerloom capacity during the major business cycle upturn of the mid-1840s, as well as the contemporaneous advances achieved in the techniques of power weaving.[12]

As the figures in Table 5.2 demonstrate, the rate of decline between districts varied appreciably. It is again necessary to stress that the local figures cannot be taken too literally and to reiterate that the 1851 figures for Manchester, Ashton-under-Lyne and Eccles may be wide of the mark. Nevertheless, in parishes with the greatest numbers of hand weavers during the peak years (Manchester, Rochdale, Blackburn, Bolton and Oldham) substantial job losses in hand weaving arose, amounting, collectively, to perhaps 50,000. Thus, the downward trend in hand weaver numbers, evident in most major towns by the mid-1830s, remained a distinctive feature during the following decade. Even in these parishes, however, there were rural districts which, though relatively sparsely populated, still depended greatly on hand weaving at mid-century. This was so, for instance, at Failsworth in Manchester parish, where the 1,335 hand weavers comprised no less than 30 per cent of the total population. It was also the case at several districts in Blackburn parish, especially those in the Ribble Valley, as Table A2.1 reveals.[13]

In other districts, less striking declines took place. They included parts of north-east Lancashire, centred on Colne; of central Lancashire, especially to the south of Preston, embracing the Penwortham, Chorley and Walton-le-Dale areas; and of south Lancashire, most notably in Leigh and Middleton parishes. Here, reductions in hand weaver numbers were comparatively small, always amounting to less than 20 per cent; indeed, in some cases, as at Ribchester, and Middleton, it may be that small increases occurred.

It is not necessarily the case that in areas where hand weaving had declined slowly by mid-century, the powerloom had made little progress. This was sometimes true, as at North Meols and Ribchester, where no power weavers were recorded in 1851 and may still have been absent in 1861.[14] Indeed, in some of these localities, including Samlesbury, to the east of Preston, powerlooms were never

Table 5.2  *Hand weaver numbers, 1821 and 1851*

| Parish; parish district or group | 1821 total | 1851 total | % change |
|---|---|---|---|
| Accrington & Altham | 1,005 | 82 | −92 |
| Ashton-under-Lyne | 4,915 | 100 | −98 |
| Blackburn | 14,750 | 5,411 | −63 |
| Bolton | 14,623 | 4,203 | −71 |
| Burnley | 3,222 | 467 | −86 |
| Bury | 8,604 | 1,532 | −82 |
| Central Lancashire | 5,529 | 3,054 | −45 |
| Church | 1,887 | 401 | −79 |
| Clitheroe | 396 | 121 | −69 |
| Colne | 7,146 | 3,741 | −48 |
| Deane | 4,330 | 1,872 | −57 |
| Downham | 269 | 60 | −78 |
| East Bolton | 849 | 91 | −89 |
| Eccles | 6,618 | 1,147 | −83 |
| Flixton | 693 | 508 | −27 |
| Haslingden | 2,505 | 489 | −80 |
| Kirkham | 1,967 | 499 | −75 |
| Leigh | 6,170 | 4,096 | −34 |
| Manchester | 20,797 | 4,456 | −79 |
| Middleton | 2,519 | 2,694 | +7 |
| Newchurch-in-Pendle | 1,203 | 501 | −58 |
| Newchurch-in-R'dale | 2,505 | 500 | −80 |
| North Meols | 363 | 623 | +72 |
| Oldham | 11,467 | 2,433 | −79 |
| Ormskirk | 670 | 278 | −59 |
| Padiham | 1,481 | 417 | −72 |
| Penwortham | 1,651 | 710 | −57 |
| Preston | 3,910 | 2,929 | −25 |
| Prestwich | 4,198 | 1,086 | −74 |
| Ribchester | 986 | 1,101 | +12 |
| Rochdale | 10,708 | 1,833 | −83 |
| St Michael's-on-Wyre | 462 | 197 | −57 |
| Standish | 1,538 | 592 | −62 |
| Tarleton | 137 | 19 | −86 |
| Walton-le-Dale | 1,259 | 527 | −58 |
| Warrington | 1,377 | 163 | −88 |
| West Central Lancs | 1,151 | 965 | −16 |
| Whalley | 410 | 47 | −89 |
| Wigan | 7,047 | 2,697 | −62 |
| Winwick | 3,986 | 1,912 | −52 |
| | | Average | −67 |

More detailed figures for both 1821 and 1851 can be found in J. G. Timmins, *The Decline of Handloom Weaving in Nineteenth Century Lancashire* (PhD thesis, University of Lancaster, 1990), Appendices B3–B6.

installed.[15] Often, though, fairly substantial numbers of power weavers were to be found in these districts at mid-century. They probably took over in cheaper grades of cotton, forcing the remaining hand weavers to concentrate on more expensive cottons or on silk or mixtures. Thus, new and traditional sectors remained complementary.

To illustrate this development, the township of Bedford (near Leigh) may be taken. In the 1820s, cambric muslins were the main fabrics woven in the area,[16] but, by 1851, nearly all the Bedford hand weavers, numbering around one thousand, produced silk.[17] Few cotton hand weavers were left, most being middle-aged or elderly, perhaps unwilling at a late stage in their working lives to make the transition to weaving alternative fabrics. In fact, Bedford's cotton industry, which remained substantial, had become almost entirely mechanised; the 1851 enumerators counted about 330 power weavers engaged in the trade. In contrast, they noted only around 70 power weavers working with silk.

That the handloom was superseded much more quickly in some parts of Lancashire than in others was strongly influenced by the degree to which the workforce was willing and able to secure alternative work. The point is considered more fully in Chapter 7. Here it is sufficient to note that the rate of decline was slower when high-quality cloths were being produced and when rural rather than urban locations were involved. Indeed, numerous rural communities in Lancashire which still depended heavily on hand weaving during the 1850s had by no means relinquished their interest during the following decade.

Some idea of the extent of this dependency may be gauged from the percentage figures in Table 5.1. In each case, they relate to the total population of the district and need to be increased by a third or a half to obtain figures relating to the working population.[18] It can be seen that, as late as 1851, hand weavers could still constitute over 20 per cent of the total population and in several other cases between 10 and 20 per cent. Such areas were in the more rural parts of the county, where the encroachment of the powerloom remained limited. In each of the major urban parishes, by contrast, hand weavers formed only a few per cent of the total population; in comparative terms, they had ceased to be a major element in the urban workforce, though at Bolton and Blackburn, they were by no means insignificant. By the mid-nineteenth century, cotton cloth output in urban Lancashire was largely the product of powerlooms.

To examine more fully how dependent mid-Victorian rural areas could be on the handloom, a case study may be undertaken of several enumeration districts situated to the south of Preston; they are listed in Table 5.3. Settlement in these districts was generally dispersed, the largest village, Leyland, having a population of less than 4,000. Most settlements fell into the 500 to 1,500 range.[19] In each of the districts, the 1851 enumerators consistently distinguished between hand and power weavers, whilst those of 1861 normally did so.[20] Cotton was the main fabric woven and there appears to have been little switching into mixtures.[21] For each district, the hand weaver total is given as a proportion of the estimated labour force.[22]

Table 5.3 *Hand and power weavers in central Lancashire, 1851 and 1861*

(a) 1851

| District | Total labour force | Hand weavers | | Power weavers | |
|---|---|---|---|---|---|
| | | No. | % | No. | % |
| Brindle | 734 | 372 | 51 | 4 | 1 |
| Hoghton | 834 | 358 | 43 | 69 | 8 |
| Hoole | 533 | 214 | 40 | – | – |
| Croston | 821 | 311 | 38 | – | – |
| Bretherton | 436 | 133 | 31 | – | – |
| Ulnes Walton | 291 | 91 | 31 | – | – |
| Samlesbury | 912 | 262 | 29 | – | – |
| Leyland | 1,805 | 510 | 28 | 250 | 14 |
| Penwortham | 786 | 199 | 25 | 81 | 10 |
| Clayton-le-Woods | 420 | 105 | 25 | 46 | 11 |
| Eccleston and Heskin | 555 | 96 | 17 | 4 | 1 |
| Farington and Cuerden | 1,274 | 71 | 6 | 404 | 32 |

(b) 1861

| District | Total labour force | Hand weavers | | Power weavers | |
|---|---|---|---|---|---|
| | | No. | % | No. | % |
| Brindle | 820 | 251 | 31 | 60 | 7 |
| Hoghton | 706 | 206 | 29 | 108 | 15 |
| Hoole | 583 | 88 | 15 | 95 | 16 |
| Croston | 916 | 257 | 28 | 95 | 10 |
| Bretherton | 418 | 77 | 18 | 3 | 1 |
| Ulnes Walton | 288 | 41 | 14 | 4 | 1 |
| Samlesbury | 726 | 167 | 23 | 2 | – |
| Leyland | 1,937 | 196 | 10 | 434 | 22 |
| Penwortham | 793 | 78 | 10 | 154 | 19 |
| Clayton-le-Woods | 415 | 57 | 14 | 77 | 19 |
| Eccleston and Heskin | 694 | 42 | 6 | 80 | 12 |
| Farington and Cuerden | 1,412 | 26 | 2 | 394 | 28 |

Overall, some 2,700 people residing in these districts in 1851 were described as hand weavers. They constituted almost 30 per cent of the total labour force and, in several places, formed the largest single occupational group. At Brindle, where the labour force exceeded 700, they were still more numerous than those in all other occupational groups taken together. Only at Farington, with Cuerden, did

## Survival in the mid-Victorian period

power weavers exceed hand weavers.[23] Overall, power weavers numbered 858, less than a third of the hand weaving labour force; in several districts, power weavers had yet to appear.

By 1861, hand weaver numbers in the area had almost been halved, leaving a total of 1,486, whilst power weavers had risen by around 75 per cent, to reach a total of 1,506. In overall terms, power weavers were now slightly more numerous than hand weavers, though, of course, their output would have been far greater. Only at Bretherton, Ulnes Walton and Samlesbury had the powerloom failed to make any appreciable impact, but in some of the more rural districts, including Hoghton, Brindle, and Croston, there were still relatively few power weavers. Indeed, at each of these places, more than one in four workers continued at the handloom, compared with, at the most, 15 per cent who worked at the powerloom. At Brindle, to take the extreme, almost one in three employed people worked at the handloom. It is plain, therefore, that hand weavers remained a major occupational group in such districts and may still have comprised the most numerous element in the labour force. Moreover, even where the powerloom had made substantial progress, as at Leyland, hand weavers had by no means been displaced. Their numbers may have been much reduced, but they continued to form a significant group of workers.

Beyond 1861, inadequacies in the occupational descriptions recorded by census enumerators make the balance between hand and power weaving more difficult to assess. Nevertheless, in the adjoining chapelry of Walton-le-Dale, an 1864 survey shows that eighty-two hand weavers headed households and that they were still as numerous as household heads given as powerloom weavers.[24] Moreover, in the selected districts, whilst power weavers had gained a marked numerical ascendancy by the early 1870s, the hand weavers had by no means disappeared. As far as can be judged, some 300 or so would still have been working, mainly at Croston, Hoghton and Brindle.[25] Perhaps they were helped to survive by the major trade cycle upturn of the early 1870s.[26] As in the mid-1830s, pressure on overall weaving capacity may have been sufficiently strong for manufacturers to maintain, or even to extend, their interest in hand weaving, even though powerloom capacity would doubtless have expanded. Any such respite would have been short-lived, though, and it seems reasonable to assume that most of the remaining hand weavers would have been displaced during the mid and late 1870s. Certainly, very few are to be found in the 1881 census schedules.[27]

It was not only in the countryside, however, that the decline of hand weaving could prove a protracted event. Even in some of the small towns, hand weavers might continue to form one of the largest, perhaps even the most numerous, occupational groups, well into the mid-Victorian era. At Middleton, for example, about 2,300 hand weavers could be found out of an 1851 population total of under 9,000, perhaps one in three of the working population. Again at Colne, where the total population was of a similar size to that of Middleton, there remained at least 1,600 handloom weavers in 1851. A decade later, numbers had fallen substantially

*The last shift*

Table 5.4 *Proportions of hand and power weavers in Lancashire's major textile towns, 1851 and 1861*

| Year | Town | Weaver percentage | | Sample size |
|------|------|------|------|------|
| | | (a) hand | (b) power | |
| 1851 | Ashton-under-Lyne | – | 12.2 (±10) | 41 |
| 1851 | Blackburn | 3.8 | 26.3 | – |
| 1861 | Blackburn | 1.8 (±1.6) | 16.8 (±4.4) | 279 |
| 1851 | Great Bolton | 4.9 (±1.7) | 3.0 (±1.4) | 609 |
| 1861 | Bolton | 3.5 (±2.0) | 4.1 (±2.1) | 341 |
| 1851 | Bury | 1.2 (±0.9) | 10.0 (±2.6) | 508 |
| 1851 | Manchester | 1.5 (±1.5) | 3.8 (±2.3) | 264 |
| 1851 | Oldham | 0.6 (±1.2) | 6.6 (±3.8) | 167 |
| 1851 | Preston | 4.1 (±2.0) | 12.4 (±3.4) | 370 |
| 1861 | Preston | 1.9 (±1.6) | 15.7 (±4.3) | 268 |
| 1851 | Rochdale (Spotland) | 1.6 | 10.3 | – |
| 1851 | Wigan | 4.4 (±2.1) | 4.1 (±2.0) | 363 |
| 1861 | Wigan | 2.5 (±1.8) | 1.8 (±1.5) | 286 |

at Colne (only about 200 were to be found), but at Middleton, almost 2,000 remained, representing almost one in every five inhabitants.[28]

In most of the major towns, meanwhile, the powerloom had gained a clear ascendancy over the handloom. This can be judged from Table 5.4, which is based mainly on the results obtained from sampling urban populations (see Appendix A2). The figures can only be regarded as rough estimates, since most are subject to sampling error and all are based on the assumption that undifferentiated weavers under the age of forty would have worked at the power loom. Also, the sample size for Ashton is not large enough to express the power weaver proportion within a relatively small degree of error. As a rule, the figures may tend to overstate the importance of power weaving.

Allowing for these drawbacks, however, there is every indication from census evidence that, in Lancashire's major textile towns, powerloom weavers outnumbered handloom weavers to an appreciable extent by the early 1850s. Wigan and Bolton, however, proved exceptions to this rule. In both these towns, the proportion of hand weavers still exceeded that of power weavers, even if the former were much inferior in terms of the volume of output and, to a lesser extent, in terms of value added. The Wigan finding may reflect the strength of alternative investment opportunities in non-textile work, especially coal mining, whilst at Bolton, the concentration on fine and fancy cottons perhaps gave less scope for local textile entrepreneurs to invest in powerlooms. Inevitably, however, the powerloom became increasingly used in both towns, though even in the early 1860s, it may have provided fewer jobs than the handloom at Wigan.[29] Power weaving may have made substantial inroads into the production of higher-grade cotton cloths, but had not yet entirely taken over.

Despite the advances of the powerloom, hand weaving had by no means been displaced in the major towns by 1850, as the figures in Table 5.4 reveal. It is true that in some of these towns, the survival rate was extremely low, and that where hand weavers' colonies had once thrived, only the occasional representative of the trade could be found. This was the case at Oldham and Bury, for example. In other towns, however, appreciable numbers of handloom weavers remained, probably on the outskirts. For example, in 1851, several hundreds were enumerated in the Mile End and Revidge area to the north-west of Blackburn. The Mile End settlement comprised fifty-three households in 1851, in forty-four of which hand weavers were still to be found. In thirty-three of the households, moreover, no other source of income than hand weaving was disclosed. Altogether, there were 130 hand weavers, all working with cotton and they comprised about 80 per cent of the labour force.[30] Imprecise census entries make the post-1851 position in these settlements hard to assess, but it is likely that in and around most major towns, hand weavers' colonies would have been much depleted, even if they had not been entirely superseded.[31]

The demise of hand weaving took place at the time the major textile towns showed a marked degree of physical expansion.[32] As a result, hand weavers' terraces built on the periphery of pre-Victorian towns became increasingly occupied by non-domestic workers. Sometimes, these cottages contained groundfloor loomshops situated at the side of the domestic accommodation. Once hand weaving ceased, the loomshop and room above were divided from the rest of the property to make a separate house.[33] Cellar loomshops might be utilised in a similar manner, though they were often difficult to subdivide because direct outside access could not always be provided.[34] Many fell into disuse, therefore.[35] Redundant loomshops could thus provide useful additions to housing stock as urban populations continued to increase rapidly.[36]

In considering the extent of dependency on hand weaving during the mid-Victorian period, a further aspect arises. It concerns the employment opportunities hand weavers gave to others, both within and beyond their own working groups. A number of possibilities may be suggested, including the transportation of raw materials and finished products; distribution and collection work at warehouses; maintenance of looms and loom parts; and pirn winding. Some of these services may have been provided largely, if not solely, by the weavers themselves.[37] However, pirn winding created a sizeable domestic labour force. The process involved using a simple hand machine to wind weft on to shuttle pirns.[38] Usually, winding was done by children and elderly people.[39] They are often mentioned in census schedules, though it is rarely made clear that they worked specifically for hand weavers; power weavers, too, required their services. The most notable exception to this rule occurs at Pilkington, near Bury, in 1851. Here, 42 winders served 215 hand weavers, a ratio of about one to five.[40] More than one-third were under fifteen, the youngest being nine. This may give weight to Cunningham's view that young children found it hard to find employment,[41] though the early Victorian schoolmaster, David Winstanley, maintained that children he taught left school at the age of six or eight to assist with pirn winding.[42] There is no means of telling how representative the Pilkington data are, but they do indicate that winders working for hand weavers may have numbered tens of thousands when the trade was at its peak and could still have formed a sizeable labour force at mid-century.

This section has assessed the changing importance of hand weaving in Lancashire on the basis of employment levels. It is argued that the first major reductions in numbers took place in urban areas during the 1840s, as powerloom investment rose strongly. Yet some urban hand weavers still formed quite numerous groups at mid-century and not only in the smaller towns. In many country districts, meanwhile, dependency on hand weaving remained remarkably high, the powerloom making very limited impact. It was only gradually during the mid-Victorian years that rural hand weavers were displaced.

## 2  Age/sex distribution

In discussing the age/sex structure of the hand weaving labour force, historians have advanced two hypotheses which appear to be contradictory. One concerns the extent to which women and children became numerically predominant in the trade. It has been suggested that this had already occurred by the early nineteenth century and that it grew more pronounced as the trade went into long-term decline. The other relates to recruitment of young people into the trade. The assumption has been made that this had fallen markedly by the mid-nineteenth century, giving rise to a labour force with a high and growing proportion of elderly people. Both hypotheses have been used to downgrade the economic significance of the hand weaving labour force, which, runs the argument, would have achieved enhanced output levels had it contained a higher proportion of young men. However, the hypotheses rest on shaky foundations and have not been tested against the available evidence, a task to which this section is devoted.

Turning first to the issue of the predominance of women and children in the trade, it will be helpful to outline a selection of the comments that historians have made. For example, Duncan Bythell has remarked that the proportion of women and children in handloom weaving probably rose steadily during the early nineteenth century. He cites evidence to suggest that they may have comprised half the total number of weavers and, in one locality at least, as many as 75 per cent.[43] Norman Murray has taken a similar line. Writing of the Scottish hand weavers, he concludes that 'a sizeable proportion without doubt would have been ... women and children'. He also argues that the proportion of female and child weavers would probably have risen over time 'when, with falling living standards, all available family members were put to work'.[44] Both Bythell and Murray confirm the views of earlier commentators, including Baines and Clapham. The former claimed that

Table 5.5  *Female and child handloom weavers in selected districts, 1851 and 1861*

| District | Total weavers | | Female & child (%) | |
|---|---|---|---|---|
| | 1851 | 1861 | 1851 | 1861 |
| Croston | 311 | 257 | 50 | 57 |
| Salesbury | 180 | 126 | 66 | 66 |
| Wheelton | 237 | 73 | 59 | 46 |
| Hoghton | 358 | 204 | 66 | 64 |
| Samlesbury | 262 | 167 | 63 | 60 |
| Much Hoole | 206 | 85 | 59 | 54 |
| Flixton | 319 | – | 56 | – |
| Foulridge | 405 | – | 64 | – |

there were 'large departments' of hand weaving which were almost entirely the province of women and children.[45] The latter, referring to families in upland Lancashire, suggested that it was customary for husbands and sons to work as farmers, while wives and daughters operated handlooms.[46] Taking a more general stance, Maxine Berg argues that the major source of labour for domestic industry was the women and children of the family.[47] Berg's comments apply to the eighteenth and early nineteenth centuries, but are echoed by Pamela Horn with regard to later years. She maintains that where cottage industries survived into the Victorian era, it was usually women and girls who predominated in them.[48]

Much of the attraction of such labour to entrepreneurs lay in its availability and cheapness, issues which are analysed in the final chapter.[49] The task here, though, is to establish more exactly the importance of child and female labour in the Lancashire hand weaving trades and to analyse the extent and causes of any changes that occurred in the age and gender balance as these trades went into long-term decline.

In many districts, the problem of deciding whether undifferentiated weavers recorded in census enumerations worked at hand or power looms makes it hazardous to compute reliable age/sex distributions for the weaving trades during the mid-Victorian era. However, useful insights can be obtained by taking case studies from areas where reasonably full records were made at successive censuses and where high concentrations of handloom weavers were still to be found. A number of such areas can be distinguished in the 1851 and 1861 returns, but none which also embraced those of 1871. Even so, data are available from various parts of the county (in some cases for 1851 only) and a selection are presented in Table 5.5. Males aged eighteen and above are deemed to have been adults.

The figures reveal that, as previous writers have observed, women and children were well represented amongst the hand weaving labour force. In the districts selected, they averaged 60 per cent of the total in 1851 and 58 per cent in 1861. Yet

Table 5.6  Handloom weavers by age group and gender in selected districts, 1851 and 1861

| District | Year | Age groups (%) | | Gender (%) | |
| --- | --- | --- | --- | --- | --- |
|  |  | 10–29 | 50 & over | male | female |
| Croston | 1851 | 54 | 11 | 59 | 41 |
|  | 1861 | 40 | 17 | 47 | 53 |
| Salesbury | 1851 | 59 | 9 | 48 | 52 |
|  | 1861 | 54 | 9 | 48 | 52 |
| Wheelton | 1851 | 39 | 21 | 50 | 50 |
|  | 1861 | 7 | 41 | 54 | 46 |
| Hoghton | 1851 | 43 | 18 | 43 | 57 |
|  | 1861 | 30 | 35 | 40 | 60 |
| Samlesbury | 1851 | 53 | 16 | 47 | 53 |
|  | 1861 | 46 | 18 | 43 | 57 |
| Much Hoole | 1851 | 66 | 8 | 54 | 46 |
|  | 1861 | 33 | 20 | 49 | 51 |

the highest figure, 66 per cent at Hoghton and Salesbury in 1851, was well short of the 75 per cent mentioned by Bythell and proportions considerably below the average occurred. It is also true that a rather lower percentage would have been obtained by taking a lower age than eighteen to define when males ceased being children. The general conclusion would not have been fundamentally altered, however.

Whether the higher figure in each district was the maximum ever attained is unclear. Yet, in only one instance was the 1861 figure higher than that for 1851. This raises doubt about the validity of Norman Murray's contention that the ratio of women and child hand weavers may have increased as their trade declined. Perhaps this did happen for a time, but a peak would eventually have been reached once child recruitment into the trade began to slacken. According to J. S. Lyons, this was taking place from the 1830s onwards. Thereafter, he argues, the employment of children as hand weavers became negligible, or at least much reduced, and young people increasingly left the trade. Lyons bases his view on the notion that children of hand weavers were quickly absorbed into factory jobs, whilst their parents were unable to find alternative work. Accordingly, he reasons, the hand weaving labour force became increasingly an occupation followed by adults.[50]

In order to examine the validity of this hypothesis more closely, several of the data sets used in Table 5.5 can be broken down into finer detail. For each district, young age groups (10–29 years old) and elderly age groups (50 and above years old) may be distinguished and the proportion they comprised of the total hand weaving labour force is calculated.[51] Overall proportions of male and female hand weavers are also computed. The results are given in Table 5.6.

## Survival in the mid-Victorian period

It is evident that the proportion of young handloom weavers in the selected districts diminished appreciably in the mid-Victorian years. During the 1850s, the overall proportion of those aged 10–29 fell from 51 per cent to 38 per cent. At the same time, the proportion of those who were fifty and above rose from 14 per cent to 20 per cent.[52] Quite clearly, the hand weaving labour force was aging, as young people turned increasingly to alternative jobs. No doubt this was the case more generally, though the rate at which it happened is easy to exaggerate. In some of the selected districts the fall in the proportion of young weavers during the 1850s was surprisingly small, a result of the powerloom making little headway and of the failure of rural districts to generate a broader economic base. Indeed, as at Samlesbury and Salesbury, hand weavers under thirty still formed around half the employees in their trade as late as the early 1860s. Moreover, even in areas where hand weaving had virtually died out, at least some of those left in the trade might be comparatively young. For example, in the village of Eccleston, near Chorley, thirty-two hand weavers were to be found in 1861, of whom two were teenagers, four were in their twenties and four more in their thirties.[53]

The continuing presence of young people in hand weaving reflects the durability of family working groups, with children being prepared to follow in their parents' footsteps, even when the hand weaving trade in their district was approaching extinction. The 1851 and 1861 census schedules frequently record households in which several members of the family, including unmarried sons and daughters, still worked at the handloom. It is a theme which is addressed in detail in the following chapter.[54]

The maintenance of family working groups makes it by no means evident that negligible numbers of young people became hand weavers during the early Victorian years, even in cotton weaving. There can be no doubt, of course, that overall recruitment of children into hand weaving did decrease considerably at this time. Yet one of the most striking features of the data shown in Table 5.6 is the relative youthfulness of the labour force, especially in 1851; around half were under the age of thirty. It is clear that, in some parts of the textile districts, numerous children were still entering hand weaving well into the mid-Victorian period. And this was as true in cotton as it was in non-cotton districts.

Other considerations to emerge from Table 5.6 concern the gender balance in handloom weaving. In the selected districts, female handloom weavers outnumbered males more often than not, though seldom to any marked degree; the difference was normally measured by only a few per cent and did not exceed 20 per cent. Moreover, there are indications that, as competition from the powerloom intensified, males assumed the majority. In the later stages of the trade's history, indeed, females may have been in a distinct minority.

To support these propositions, two sets of census data may be cited, both of which are obtained from districts where enumerators distinguished consistently between hand and power weavers. The first, extracted from the 1851 returns, relates to nine adjoining districts in the Ribble Valley. Here powerlooms had yet

Table 5.7 *Proportions of male and female hand weavers in districts with power weaving sheds, 1861*

| District | Weaver totals | | Hand weavers (%) | |
| --- | --- | --- | --- | --- |
| | male | female | male | female |
| Penwortham | 43 | 34 | 55 | 45 |
| Wheelton | 40 | 33 | 54 | 46 |
| Harwood | 62 | 48 | 56 | 44 |
| Rumworth | 56 | 44 | 56 | 44 |
| Walton-le-Dale | 105 | 85 | 55 | 45 |
| Leyland | 64 | 34 | 65 | 35 |
| Colne | 43 | 18 | 71 | 29 |
| Wigan (part of) | 102 | 11 | 90 | 10 |

to appear. In total, 1,224 handloom weavers were returned, 54 per cent of whom were female. In only one district did males outnumber females.[55] The second, taken from the 1861 census schedules, is recorded in Table 5.7.[56] It is drawn from districts where power weavers exceeded hand weavers and shows that the ratio of male to female hand weavers was consistently in favour of males, sometimes to a striking degree. Here is a marked contrast with the preponderance of females revealed by the 1851 data and with the growing importance of women that was evident in textile weaving during the late eighteenth and early nineteenth centuries.[57]

At first sight, this result may seem surprising. After all, it might be expected that adult females would have found hand weaving to be amongst the type of occupations which could be most easily accommodated within the household duties required of them and might have been seen as a more respectable type of employment than factory work.[58] The former argument might have particular force as far as married women with young children are concerned, though unmarried daughters may also have carried a heavy burden of domestic responsibility, especially if the mother wove; if there were young children in the family; if the household head was a widower; or if the family was large.[59] Why, then, did women hand weavers eventually become numerically less important than men hand weavers?

In seeking explanation, account must be taken of the position of adult male hand weavers. It will be argued in the final chapter that it was often hard for this group to find new work, as Lyons argues, despite their willingness to do so as their piece rate fell.[60] Thus, they had little option but to remain at the handloom throughout their working lives; at any stage in the history of hand weaving, adult males were well represented.

Adult female hand weavers, however, were differently placed, especially those who were married and had children. Ivy Pinchbeck suggests that these women gave up work once children came along, so that family income declined at a time when it was most needed, with dire results.[61] It is more probable, though, that they would not have ceased weaving until the income they had foregone was recouped from children's earnings, assuming this was possible. Indeed, census schedule evidence shows that it was common for women with children to remain at the handloom even when several of their children were wage earners. This was especially so in areas where hand weaving remained prominent. Thus, at Osbaldeston in the Ribble Valley, thirty-nine out of forty-nine households enumerated at the 1851 census contained hand weavers and in just four cases was the wife given as not having an occupation.[62] Two of these wives were in their forties and two in their fifties, pointing to the economic difficulties that young wives could experience by giving up their jobs. By contrast, married women at Lower Darwen, near Blackburn, were frequently without paid employment at this time, even when part of their family income was derived from hand weaving. In one enumeration district, twenty-eight wives were listed, only ten of whom were in paid employment.[63] The difference in these patterns of female employment reflects the more diversified economic base at Lower Darwen, where factory occupations ensured higher family earnings, thereby freeing married women to concentrate on domestic work.[64]

The point to be emphasised in this discussion is that married women did tend to give up handloom weaving as their families grew older. Contrary to Ivy Pinchbeck's belief, however, the stage at which this occurred varied considerably, much depending on the level of family earnings that could be achieved. Thus, in families dependent on hand weaving, the wife often continued to work at the handloom into middle age, whilst in families with a more diversified range of income she might cease hand weaving in her twenties or thirties. Sooner or later, though, she did give up the loom. Accordingly, handloom weaving became more the province of men than of women. This was especially true as far as middle-aged and elderly hand weavers were concerned, since women of that age were in a position to leave the trade but, in many cases, men were not. In general, wives of hand weavers were no different from most working-class women, including those working in cotton mills, in ceasing paid work once they married and had children.[65] That they were often living in more impoverished circumstances than other women meant that it could take them much longer to achieve this goal.

One question to arise from this analysis concerns the extent to which the heavy dependency of hand weaving on child and female labour affected overall output in the trade. Duncan Bythell has argued that such labour was mainly casual, that it comprised an unskilled, part-time element with a low earning potential. Essentially, it provided a by-occupation for elderly members of the family, for unmarried daughters and sisters and for growing children. It was only when 'time and inclination suited, or necessity compelled' that these people would turn to the loom.[66]

Two responses may be made to these remarks. Firstly, it is by no means certain that all women and children were in fact part-time workers. The reality is impossible to judge, but it is quite conceivable that unmarried sisters and daughters, especially those who had attained adulthood, would often have been expected to work long hours at the loom, as well as to undertake domestic duties. If they were not full-time weavers, they may not have been too far distant from being so. Maybe this was also true of wives, particularly when the needs of young children made heavy demands on the family budget; when trade recession intensified poverty levels; and when a sick or improvident husband placed a severe strain on family resources. Secondly, even if Bythell's argument has substance with regard to the late eighteenth and early nineteenth centuries, it is surely less convincing when applied to later years. This point will be examined more fully in Chapter 7, but it may be suggested here that there would have been a general tendency for hand weavers to work longer hours as their piece rates fell. The argument has particular strength as far as those weaving families who found it difficult to diversify income were concerned, of which numerous examples could still be found in the mid-Victorian period.[67] As to 'growing children', they might well have been able to approach or match the output of adults, especially when they reached their mid or late teens.

The evidence presented in this section supports the contention that nineteenth century hand weavers were mainly women and children. Even so, men formed a significant minority, perhaps as much as 40 per cent of the total, rather more than is generally acknowledged. It also appears that females outnumbered males, though not to any marked extent, with males eventually coming to predominate. It is evident, too, that although the hand weaving labour force gradually aged, in many districts heavy recruitment of children continued to occur well into the mid-Victorian period. The reliance on women and children may have restricted output and hence diminished the relative importance of the trade, though, given the frequency with which adult male hand weavers were to be found, too much should not be made of this argument. Nor is it certain that, taking both quality and quantity into account, women and older children were markedly inferior hand weavers to men and any differences there were could well have narrowed as the trade went into long-term decline. Accordingly, care must be taken not to over-emphasise the limiting influence that the age and gender of hand weavers had on the level of output they were able to attain.

## Notes

1  See pp. 27–32.

2  The instructions issued to the 1851 enumerators stressed that 'the particular branch of work, and the material, are always to be distinctly expressed' (*PP*, 1851, 1339, XLIII, p. 38).

3  *PP*, 1824 (51) V, p. 399. See also R. Guest, *A Compendious History of the Cotton Manufacturer* (1968 reprint of 1823 edition), pp. 47–8.

4  That hand weaving probably declined relatively quickly in Lancashire's south-east towns makes these losses less serious than they might otherwise have been.

5  A study of seven poor law unions in central Lancashire concludes that the imposition of workhouse tests was unsuccessful, so that workhouses became 'largely voluntary

workhouses for the sick and aged' (R. Boyson, 'The new Poor Law in north-east Lancashire, 1834–71', *TL&CAS*, 70, 1960, p. 44). It is known, too, that hand weaving was largely abandoned in the Preston Poor Law Union workhouses during the late 1830s (W. Proctor, 'Poor Law administration in Preston Union, 1838–1848', *THSL&C*, 117, 1966, p. 156).

6   For details, see footnote 6, Appendix A2.
7   Mellor Census Returns, 1881, ED 6; Ribchester Census Returns, 1881, ED 6.
8   See p. 30.
9   See p. 136.
10  See p. 28.
11  N. Murray, *The Scottish Handloom Weavers, 1790–1850* (1978), p. 22.
12  See pp. 21–3.
13  See p. 226.
14  In neither place do the 1861 census enumerators make specific mention of power weavers.
15  R. Eaton, *History of Samlesbury* (1936), p. 178.
16  E. Baines, *History, Directory and Gazetteer of the County Palatine of Lancaster*, 2 (1968 reprint of 1824–25 edition), p. 45.
17  Around three-quarters of them were specifically described as hand weavers.
18  For instance, census schedules reveal that the working population at Tockholes in 1851 comprised some 600 people out of a total of 939.
19  The population figures are given in W. Farrer and J. Brownbill (eds), *A History of the County of Lancaster*, 2 (1908), pp. 337–8.
20  Undifferentiated weavers are identified as hand or power weavers according to the criteria given in Appendix A2.
21  Croston was the main exception, cotton and worsted cloth being woven by 1861.
22  The labour force figures exclude farmers' wives, since their contribution to paid employment is difficult to assess. Their numbers are relatively small, however.
23  These two districts were grouped because of the small size of the Cuerden population.
24  LRO, Walton-le-Dale Relief Committee Census, 1864, PR 2948/2/8.
25  At Croston, there were at least 72 and probably over 100, the undifferentiated weavers mainly making coloured cloth (Croston Census Returns 1871, ED 5).
26  Acccording to Feinstein, UK net national product reached its mid-Victorian peak in 1871 at £1.1 million in 1873. This level was not attained again until 1882 (C. H. Feinstein, *Statistical Tables of National Income, Expenditure and Output of the U.K., 1855–1965*, 1976, Table 6).
27  At Brindle, nine are listed in 1881, six in their seventies and the youngest being forty-six. None are given at Hoghton and only one at Croston.
28  The 1861 enumerators at Colne who did distinguish between hand and power weavers make it plain that the powerloom had virtually taken over in the town.
29  The Wigan sample picked out five hand weavers, three power weavers and four weavers. Two of the weavers were aged forty-four and sixty-seven and were assumed to have been handloom weavers.
30  J. G. Timmins, *Handloom Weavers' Cottages in Central Lancashire* (1977), p. 51.
31  For example, at Seven Acre Brook, a colony of nineteen hand weavers' dwellings to the north-west of Blackburn, sixteen hand weavers of cotton were enumerated in 1871, along with four middle-aged weavers (Blackburn Census, 1871, ED 70).

32   The contrast between the area covered by the textile towns on the 1840s and 1890s O.S. maps is striking.

33   For examples, see J. G. Timmins, 'Handloom weavers' cottages in central Lancashire: some problems of recognition', *Post-Medieval Archaeology*, 13 (1979), pp. 252–8.

34   This was possible, however, where weavers' cottages with cellar loomshops were built on a slope, so that the cottage was two-and-a-half storied at the front and three at the back. For examples at Higher Walton, near Preston, see N. K. Scott, *The Architectural Development of Cotton Mills in Preston and District* (unpublished MA thesis, 1952), p. 59.

35   It was said in 1871 that only about 280 cellars in Bolton were occupied, others being much neglected and the receptacle of rubbish and filth (Dr Ballard's *Report on the Sanitary Condition . . . of Bolton*, 1871, p. 6). For similar comment based on personal reminiscence, see A. Foley, *A Bolton Childhood* (1973), p. 79.

36   For example, the population of Blackburn rose by almost 20,000 between 1851 and 1871 (Farrer and Brownbill, *op. cit.*, p. 336).

37   For instance, Reach came across a hand weaver at Middleton who carried his finished cloth to Manchester (C. Aspin, ed., *Manchester and the Textile Districts in 1849*, 1972, p. 101).

38   For a brief description of the process, see *Blackburn Weekly Telegraph*, 9.8.1902.

39   That this was so for the Middleton weavers, see Aspin, *op. cit.*, p. 106.

40   Pilkington Census Returns, 1851, ED 1F.

41   See p. 5.

42   E. and T. Kelly (eds), *A Schoolmaster's Notebook* (1957), p. 42.

43   D. Bythell, *The Handloom Weavers* (1969), pp. 60–62.

44   Murray, *op. cit.*, pp. 28–9.

45   E. Baines, *History of the Cotton Manufacture in Great Britain* (1966 reprint of 1835 edition), p. 494.

46   J. H. Clapham, *An Economic History of Modern Britain*, 1 (1930), p. 180.

47   M. Berg, *The Age of Manufactures* (1985), pp. 134–7.

48   P. Horn, 'Victorian villages from census returns', *The Local Historian*, 15 (1982), p. 26.

49   See pp. 161–70.

50   J. S. Lyons, *The Lancashire Cotton Industry and the Introduction of the Powerloom* (unpublished PhD dissertation, 1977), pp. 42–4; and 'Family response to economic decline: handloom weavers in early nineteenth century Lancashire', *Research in Economic History*, 12 (1989), p. 57.

51   It is unusual to find children aged under ten listed as hand weavers in the census schedules. At Middleton, children were said to begin weaving at age ten or twelve (Aspin, *op. cit.*, p. 104), though winders may have been as young as six or eight (E. and T. Kelly, *A Schoolmaster's Notebook*, 1957, p. 42).

52   They were normally specialist hand weavers, few being given as having dual occupations or being dependent on poor relief.

53   By this time, more than sixty powerloom weavers were to be found in the village.

54   See p. 133.

55   The districts are Balderstone; Cuerdale; Clayton-le-Dale; Dinckley; Osbaldeston; Ramsgreave; Salesbury; Samlesbury; and Wilpshire. Males predominated at Dinckley, where the total number of hand weavers was only sixty-eight.

56 For Harwood and Wheelton, the entire data are used. For the rest, data from several districts are selected.

57 I. Pinchbeck, *Women Workers and the Industrial Revolution, 1750–1850* (1930), pp. 162–6.

58 On the alleged immorality of factory women see, for example, W. F. Neff, *Victorian Working Women* (1966 reprint of 1929 edition), pp. 53–7; Aspin, *op. cit.*, p. 19; and Pinchbeck, *op. cit.*, pp. 196–201.

59 Households showing one or more of these features are not difficult to find amongst census schedules. Thus, in 1851, Thomas Ireland's household at Dutton, near Blackburn, contained himself, his wife and eight children. All the children were female and the four eldest, along with their parents, wove. The four youngest children were aged from one month to six years.

60 See pp. 161–2.

61 Pinchbeck, *op. cit.*, p. 179.

62 Moreover, only one of the four came from a household depending solely on hand weaving.

63 Lower Darwen Census Returns, 1851, ED 4a.

64 By 1851, the working population in the village was around 2,000, of whom 613 were employed in the cotton spinning and weaving mill owned by Thomas Eccles (Lower Darwen Census Returns, 1851, ED 4c, schedule 53).

65 For instance, Anderson's 1851 sample of Preston's population revealed that only 26 per cent of wives living with their husbands worked. For the most part, they were younger wives with few or no children (M. Anderson, *Family Structure in Nineteenth Century Lancashire*, 1972, pp. 71–2). For similar findings in the Deansgate area of Manchester, see J. H. Smith, 'Ten acres of Deansgate', *THSL&C*, 80 (1980), pp. 51–3. General comment is in J. Rule, *The Labouring Classes in Early Industrial England* (1986), pp. 178–9; H. Perkin, *The Origins of Modern English Society* (1969), pp. 150–1; and Pinchbeck, *op. cit.*, pp. 196–201.

66 Bythell, *op. cit.*, p. 61.

67 They were mainly in rural areas and were unwilling to move to towns.

# Chapter 6

# THE MEANS OF SURVIVAL

In the previous chapter, it is suggested that handloom weavers were able to survive in considerable numbers during the mid-Victorian period because they could depend on family income. The first section of this chapter develops the theme, piecing together evidence derived from various contemporary sources. The argument is proffered that handloom weavers often continued to belong to households in which several family members were wage earners and in which hand weaving was the sole source of income. In this way, they could hope to maintain an adequate standard of living, though, for many, periods of extreme poverty would have been all too frequent.[1] Whilst it is acknowledged that hand weaving families increasingly diversified income as competition from the powerloom intensified, it is also argued that, with surprising frequency, they remained highly dependent on the trade well into the mid-Victorian years. It is this latter aspect that has escaped notice, mainly because it has been too readily assumed that the entry of children into the trade had all but ceased by mid-century.

In the second section of the chapter, the other main strategy hand weavers adopted to remain at their trade is analysed. This is the tendency to move into finer and fancier cottons or into silks or mixtures. Once more, new evidence is adduced, especially from census schedules, the compilers of which were instructed to record the type of fabric woven.[2] Inevitably, not all of them did so, but sufficient detail was entered to show that a growing proportion of the declining labour force in handloom weaving turned to non-cotton fabrics during the mid-Victorian era, especially silk. Yet, until the 1860s, cotton hand weavers continued to predominate, probably making higher-grade cloths in the main. These developments reflect the slowness with which the technical difficulties of weaving certain fabrics economically by power were overcome. They also point to the ability of some groups of hand weavers to obtain an adequate income from weaving them.

*The means of survival*

## 1 Hand weavers and family income

The part played by family income in the economic livelihood of handloom weavers has received some attention from Duncan Bythell and John Lyons. Bythell's discussion is brief, highlighting individual case histories drawn from the Parliamentary enquiries into hand weaving. It serves only to qualify his general conclusions about the declining living standards of cotton hand weavers during the first half of the nineteenth century. By contrast, Lyons' contribution is fundamental to his analysis, forming a major element in his explanation of why cotton hand weaving proved such a durable trade.

Bythell's comments lead him to two main conclusions. The first is that, even as late as the early Victorian years, when piece rates for hand weaving had been very much reduced, a small hand weaving family with most of its members in work would have been 'fairly comfortable'.[3] Examples quoted are of a family of six earning 22/6*d* per week (3/9*d* per person) and another of eight with an income totalling 25/9*d* (about 3/3*d* per person). The former relied on four wage earners and the latter on five. Secondly, he argues that families deriving their income from hand weaving did not necessarily earn a great deal less than families who found employment in other trades. Accordingly, it was only in a 'very relative sense' that many hand weavers' families were more impoverished than other families.[4]

Not all the evidence Bythell cites relates to families which were totally dependent on hand weaving. In fact, the two families whose earnings are detailed both relied on contributions from children working in factories. In one case, the fifteen-year-old son earned more from factory work each week (7/-) than his hand weaver father (6/6*d*). Possibly, therefore, Bythell's argument may have less force when applied to families which relied totally on hand weaving. Indeed, such families may normally have earned appreciably less than those which were able to diversify their income.

Only a limited amount of contemporary evidence is available to test the validity of this proposition. In part, it comes from the results of a door-to-door enquiry undertaken amongst handloom weaving households at Miles Platting, on the Manchester outskirts, in 1835. It shows that families depending entirely on hand weaving could obtain the income levels that Bythell suggests were needed to maintain a reasonable degree of comfort. For example, John Turner's family earned 20/- per week from four looms (5/- per loom) producing ginghams. There were six in the family, giving an income per person of 3/4*d*. To take another case, Adam Johnson's family realised an income of 32/- per week from weaving fine quiltings. This amounted to no less than 8/- per loom and 4/- per person.[5] Such sums were also earned by hand weavers employed by the Horrocks' of Preston. For instance, Thomas Wilding of Longton, along with his wife and two teenage children, earned 28/1*d* or 7/- per loom during a thirteen-week period in 1835, whilst J. Caton of Preston and his three teenagers averaged 27/4*d* (6/10*d* per loom) during an eleven-week period.[6]

These earnings, however, were at the higher end of the domestic workers' wage range. The Horrocks' weavers were regarded as being amongst the most industrious the firm employed, whilst the earnings of the two Miles Platting families were much higher than those attained by most of their neighbours. In fact, weekly sums of 1/6d to 2/6d per person were common at Miles Platting, whilst several families obtained less than 1/-. Such differences stem from the type of fabric woven, as well as from the number of looms and the size of family. At one extreme, Robert Dudson made 15/- per week from a single loom weaving silks, but this was exceptional. At the other, William Mosley's two looms yielded only 6/- per week from the production of coarse ginghams.

These figures indicate that, by the mid-1830s, families relying completely on hand weaving would normally have been unable to earn as much per capita as those who could diversify into alternative occupations. Other wage statistics from the early 1830s help to confirm this view. They were compiled by the Manchester Chamber of Commerce and relate to the weekly earnings of men, women and children working in various occupations at Manchester. A selection are presented in Table 6.1.[7]

The figures show that child handloom weavers received roughly the same wages as children in other textile occupations, sometimes more. No details are given of the earnings of child powerloom weavers, but they would scarcely have been higher than those of women in the trade. Probably, therefore, child hand and power weavers would have received much the same amount. If anything, the differential would have been in favour of power weavers, but it would not have been marked. Consequently, there may not have been any strong incentive for hand weaving parents to send their children into factories. This said, it cannot be assumed that even small variations in the earning capacity of children were unimportant. Much would have depended on the economic situation in which individual hand weavers found themselves and should this have worsened, the temptation to enhance family income from child factory work may have proved overwhelming. Yet it must be stressed that, as the figures in Table 6.1 reveal, the assumption that child factory workers were necessarily better paid than their hand weaving counterparts cannot be sustained, at least during the early 1830s. In particular, the piecers and scavengers employed in spinning mills, the former a substantial group of child workers, may often have earned appreciably less.[8]

With regard to adult handloom weavers, the position was different. The figures in Table 6.1 demonstrate that this group was placed firmly on the lower rungs of the wages ladder. Amongst adult males, no other group of workers received less than 10/- per week. As far as adult females were concerned, the wage differentials between occupations were less marked than in the case of males, the highest levels attained being 15/-.Despite this, adults may generally have experienced stronger financial incentives than children to leave hand weaving. Whether they wished to do so, or were able to find alternative jobs, are issues to be addressed in the following chapter.[9]

Table 6.1 *Weekly earnings in Manchester trades, 1832*

| Occupation | Weekly earnings (shillings) | | |
|---|---|---|---|
| | men | women | children |
| Textile | | | |
| Spinners | 20.0–25.0 | 10.0–15.0 | – |
| Piecers | – | – | 4.6– 7.0 |
| Scavengers | – | – | 1.7– 2.7 |
| Card room hands | 14.5–17.0 | 9.0– 9.5 | 6.0– 7.0 |
| Dyers and dressers | 15.0–20.0 | – | 5.0–10.0 |
| Power weavers | 13.0–16.8 | 8.0–12.0 | – |
| Nankeen hand weavers: | | | |
| (a) fancy | 9.0–15.0 | – | – |
| (b) common | – | 6.0– 8.0 | 6.0– 8.0 |
| (c) best | 10.0–13.0 | – | – |
| Check hand weavers: | | | |
| (a) fancy | 7.0– 7.5 | | |
| (b) common | – | | 6.0– 7.0 |
| Cambric hand weavers | 6.0– 6.5 | 6.0– 6.5 | 6.0– 6.5 |
| Quilting hand weavers | 9.0–12.0 | 9.0–12.0 | – |
| Non-textile | | | |
| Porters | 14.0–15.0 | | |
| Shoemakers | 15.0–16.0 | | |
| Carpenters | 24.0 | | |
| Stone masons | 18.0–22.0 | | |
| Spadesmen | 10.0–15.0 | | |
| Bricklayers' labourers | 12.0 | | |

How far this reasoning needs modificatiion when the Lancashire textile districts as a whole are considered is uncertain. However, the records of James Grimshaw of Barrowford indicate that power weavers did not always earn the sums that the Manchester figures suggest. During the later half of the 1830s, Grimshaw's weavers generally operated two looms and mostly achieved payments of between 12/- and 20/- per fortnight. Those earning above 20/- per week were three and four loom weavers, of whom there were relatively few.[10] Such depressed rates may have arisen from north-east Lancashire being a low wage area, as well as from Grimshaw's preference for youthful employees. Hand weavers here may also have earned low wages — they certainly wove cheaper grades of cloth — though the differential between hand and power weavers' earnings may have been less than was the case in Manchester, providing a more limited encouragement to abandon domestic work.

Whilst uncertainty remains about the relative earnings of hand and power weavers, during the immediate pre-Victorian years, families depending either wholly or in part on hand weaving could earn per capita incomes sufficient to maintain a fairly comfortable existence. This was so despite deductions they had to make from gross wages to cover working expenses, including replacement or repair of healds and shuttles; purchase of flour for warp dressing; and heating and lighting for loomshops.[11] Variations in family circumstances would have been endless, but even allowing for the minimum levels given in Table 6.1, a family of six relying entirely on four handlooms could still return a total gross income of 24/- or 4/- per head. This was well above the 3/6$d$ per head which one hand weaver estimated was the sum necessary to provide some degree of comfort.[12]

But what of the 1840s and beyond? Could appreciable numbers of hand weaving families, including those working with cotton, still earn enough at their trade to maintain a reasonable standard of living, at least during the more prosperous years? Or was the reality that it soon became necessary for some members of hand weaving families to find other, more lucrative jobs? Increasingly, such jobs would have included power weaving, which would have become more rewarding as three or four looms per weaver became the norm.[13]

Consideration of these issues is hampered by a paucity of information on handloom weavers' earnings throughout the early and mid-Victorian eras. Even G. H. Wood, compiler of the most comprehensive study of nineteenth-century cotton workers' wages, is unable to produce figures other than those given in the hand weavers' enquiries of the 1830s. He resorts to the unsubstantiated argument that cotton hand weavers' earnings changed little during the middle decades of the century, standing at around 6/3$d$ per week,[14] a figure close to those given by Bamford and Engels for the mid-1840s,[15] and by Dodd for the early 1840s,[16] but rather more than the 5/- maximum quoted for those at Manchester in 1849.[17] Such data lend support to John Lyons' conclusion that, at mid-century, the mass of cotton hand weavers earned perhaps 5/- to 6/- a week.[18] Even so, the more skilled amongst them could make substantially more than this. A survey carried out for the Statistical Society of London between 1839 and 1859, relating to over 200 trades in Lancashire, gives sums of 15/- to 16/- for handloom weavers in the fancy cotton trades.[19]

As to mixed cloths, Leonard Horner discovered that mousseline-de-laine weavers could achieve as much as 14/- to 20/- per week at mid-century.[20] Sums of around 20/- a week were also earned in the early 1840s by hand weavers in the employ of Smith and Wiseman at Barrowford. These, however, were the best paid, others earning only about half this amount or less. Thus, whereas William Greenwood of Colne averaged around 21/- per week between November 1841 and April 1842, Olive Bottomley of Colne earned only around 7/- per week during the same period. The fabric they wove is not clear, but may well have been mousseline-de-laine.[21] Meanwhile, a hand weaver of gros-de-Naples (a thick silk) received 8/- per week at Blackley, near Manchester, in 1844,[22] whilst silk handloom weavers at

Middleton told Angus Reach in 1849 that it took 'a very clever weaver to make 10/- a week as a general thing'; 8/- or 9/- was more usual and 12/- to 14/- was possible with some types of cloth.[23] Similar sums were quoted for Macclesfield, though Jacquard hand weavers of figured silks could average 10/- to 11/-.[24]

Despite the fragmentary nature of these data, there are enough to show that some groups of hand weavers, including those in silks and high-grade cottons, could still earn the levels of wages at mid-century that prevailed fifteen years or so before. No figures are available to show the amounts paid to child hand weavers at this time, but even if they earned only a few shillings per week, families depending solely on the handloom might make a tolerable living. That this was commonly the case is indicated by the frequency with which hand weaving families survived into the mid-Victorian era. For instance, in the Ribble Valley districts of Balderstone, Osbaldeston and Dutton, the 1851 census enumerators recorded 159 families in which at least one member was a handloom weaver. Of these, 70 (40 per cent) relied totally on the handloom and a further 40 (25 per cent) earned the bulk of their income from it.[25] At Tockholes, near Blackburn, a similar proportion depended solely on the handloom (38 out of 99 hand weaver households), whilst at Hoghton, near Chorley, the figure was 71 out of 139 (51 per cent) and at neighbouring Brindle, as high as 92 out of 151 (60 per cent). In each of these districts, as elsewhere, three or four members of the family were often hand weavers and sometimes up to six or more, including many teenagers. Consequently, even though individual earnings might be low, total family income was often sufficient to achieve a subsistence level, assuming that the looms could be kept in fairly regular use.

Although families relying entirely on hand weaving were still common in many parts of Lancashire during the mid-nineteenth century, they were obviously becoming less so as hand weaving continued to decline. Increasingly, hand weaving families were forced to diversify their economic base in order to make ends meet. This point was been strongly propounded by J. S. Lyons, who declares that cotton hand weavers sent their children into factories, whilst they remained as domestic workers. Entry of children into the trade ceased and, by implication, middle-aged and elderly hand weavers became dominant. And he argues that rural hand weaving families often moved into towns, so that the children might find work in cotton factories, whilst their parents continued at the handloom.[26]

As far as urban hand weavers are concerned, the Lyons' thesis has much applicability. For the children of urban handloom weavers, work was frequently available in cotton factories and, in numerous instances, full advantage was taken of the opportunities. This was so, for example, at Over Darwen. Here, fifty households with parent handloom weavers can be identified in the central area of the town from the 1851 census. Of these, thirty-eight contained children working in mills, mainly as power weavers.[27] Taking an alternative viewpoint, urban hand weavers were chiefly adult by the 1850s. For instance, of 63 Blackburn hand weavers living at Snig Brook, Blakey Street and Winter Street in 1851, the age range was 23 to 89 years, only 13 being under 40.[28] Yet it is false to assume that, by the mid-nineteenth century, all urban children had ceased hand weaving. Thus, in the Chapel Street area of Little Bolton, 16 out of 93 hand weavers (17 per cent) listed in the 1851 census returns were teenagers.[29] Nor is it true that every urban adult who remained in hand weaving did so by sending his or her children into factory or other work. Many hand weavers did not live as part of a nuclear family, but lodged or boarded, sometimes with kin. In one district of Wigan, for example, 30 out of 113 hand weavers in 1861 were lodgers, mostly male and nearly all middle-aged and elderly.[30] There were instances, too, of unmarried children continuing at the handloom as part of a family group until reaching middle age and of hand weavers employing non-household members to weave for them.[31]

The tendency for children of hand weavers to undertake non-domestic work also extended to some rural districts, normally in the vicinity of major towns. Not infrequently, jobs were available in textile factories, including powerloom sheds. Coal mining, too, provided numerous employment opportunities for boys.[32] In contrast to the position in urban areas, however, child hand weavers were still to be found in considerable numbers during the mid-nineteenth century. For example, at Salesbury, near Blackburn, 47 of the 177 hand weavers (27 per cent) enumerated in 1851 were aged sixteen or under.[33] In 1861, the figure was still as high as 21 per cent.

Yet it was not in every rural district that factory or colliery jobs could be obtained by children during the 1840s and 1850s. This was so, for instance, throughout much of the Ribble Valley. Here, children generally worked either as hand weavers or in agriculture. In fact, it was not uncommon to find fathers employed as farmers or as agricultural labourers, whilst their children wove at the handloom. The explanation for this pattern of family work lies partly in the limited size of land holdings. Often, the family farm comprised only a few acres and did not require the labour of several hands.[34] Accordingly, children could be otherwise occupied and, in the absence of factory work, they had little option but to become domestic weavers, unless they were prepared to move.[35] Besides, a child may have been able to earn more as a hand weaver than as an agricultural labourer. It may also be noted that a mother might be the only hand weaver in a household, a reflection of the comparative ease with which the job could be accommodated within the domestic responsibilities demanded of her.

That a child may have earned more from hand weaving than from farming is one instance of a broader concern that arises with Lyons' analysis. If, as he contends, hand weaving parents were behaving in an economically rational manner, they would have sent their children into factories in order to enhance, perhaps to maximise, family earning potential. That this policy brought success is by no means certain, however. It has already been shown that earnings of factory children could be low during the mid-1830s and, if Reach's observations are correct, the position had not changed by the late 1840s. He spoke with twelve Manchester children who worked in textile mills, all aged from 10 to 16 years, most of whom were paid no more than 6/- per week. The best paid received 8/- and the worst paid 2/10$d$.[36] And Wood's estimate for child piecers in 1850 was 5/6$d$, rising to 6/6$d$ in 1860 and 7/- in 1870.[37] It is true that these sums were often higher than earnings in other trades, but it cannot be taken for granted that child hand weavers during the mid-Victorian years always earned less than children working in textile factories, or in many other occupations. For some hand weaving parents, the rational economic decision could have been to put their children into domestic work, however short-sighted this may have proved.

It remains only to note that one other way in which hand weavers could diversify family income as their trade declined was to revert to a non-specialist role. How far this took place, though, cannot be satisfactorily judged. Some people recorded in the census schedules, usually heads of household, did combine hand weaving with another job, such as farming, innkeeping, carting or, to quote the most bizarre case, grave digging. But it is not certain that this practice occurred as a response to falling income. Nor is it clear how far opportunities arose for hand weavers, child or adult, to supplement their incomes on a temporary basis. This must have occurred to some extent, as it always had, and could have been sufficient to make a useful, perhaps even a vital, contribution to family income.[38]

It is plain from this analysis that family income helped numerous handloom weavers to continue at their trade beyond the mid-nineteenth century. Increasingly, the sources from which this income was obtained were diversified, especially as far as children were concerned. As early as the 1840s, it may have been quite rare for the children of urban hand weavers not to have moved away from domestic work. In many country districts, however, this process took a good deal longer, as the economic base was slow to diversify. Well into the mid-Victorian era, child hand weavers remained common in rural Lancashire, as did families who relied solely or largely on handloom weaving. The existence of such families has not been previously acknowledged, despite the frequency with which they were found. Yet they demonstrate that sufficient income could still be earned from hand weaving to allow families to subsist without having to send some members into alternative work. No doubt the pressure to do this became increasingly strong, but, in a surprising number of cases, the temptation to break up the family working unit was long resisted.

## 2 Type of fabric

Historians have often contended that as the powerloom took over from the handloom in the production of coarser cottons during the 1830s and 1840s, Lancashire's hand weavers turned increasingly to finer and fancier cottons, as well as to silks and mixtures. Yet no detailed analysis has been undertaken to establish the degree to which this took place and why it occurred more strongly in some parts of the county than in others. Such an analysis is none the less important, in that it

Table 6.2  *Hand weavers by fabric type, 1851–71*

| Fabric type | Census year | | |
| --- | --- | --- | --- |
| | 1851 | 1861 | 1871 |
| Cotton: | | | |
|   Weaver numbers | 17,636 | 14,769 | 4,397 |
|   Weaver % | 32  (59) | 50  (52) | 42  (44) |
| Silk and satin: | | | |
|   Weaver numbers | 15,212 | 12,179 | 5,744 |
|   Weaver % | 28  (29) | 41  (42) | 55  (55) |
| Wool, worsted and flannel: | | | |
|   Weaver numbers | 2,064 | 1,326 | 29 |
|   Weaver % | 4  (4) | 5  (5) | –  – |
| Mixtures and others:* | | | |
|   Weaver numbers | 2,184 | 328 | 44 |
|   Weaver % | 4  (10) | 1  (1) | –  – |
| Unspecified: | | | |
|   Weaver numbers | 17,463 | 779 | 328 |
|   Weaver % | 31  (–) | 3  (–) | 3  (–) |

\* This group includes linen and fustian.

provides further insights into the means by which hand weavers were able to prolong their trade during the mid-Victorian era.

In addressing the issue, census schedules once more provide a good deal of help. For each census year, they enable estimates to be prepared of the numbers and proportions of hand weavers producing various types of cloth. These are given in Table 6.2.

Three considerations should be borne in mind about the estimates. Firstly, although census enumerators normally specified the type of cloth woven, they did not always do so. Secondly, the weaver numbers used in the table are themselves estimates and are thus subject to error.[39] Lastly, the urban samples provide too few hand weavers to assess with precision the numbers weaving a particular type of cloth. This most affects the figures for Bolton, Manchester, Wigan and Preston, in which towns relatively large numbers of hand weavers would have been found in 1851.[40] At best, therefore, weaver numbers according to fabric type can only be approximated.

To distribute the unspecified weavers amongst the other groups is to risk compounding the degree of error in the estimates. Yet, in doing so, guidance is available from fuller enumerations in districts neighbouring those where unspecified weavers were found. Further, in the case of the urban samples, the type of fabric is sometimes stated. Using this evidence, along with other details gleaned from contemporary sources, revised estimates may be made.[41] They are given in parentheses in Table 6.2, expressed in percentage terms. If anything, they exaggerate the importance of cotton weaving, since this presumed to be the predominant fabric in the great majority of cases.

One hypothesis the estimates help to confirm is that diversification from cotton had a significant influence on the survival of the Lancashire hand weaving trades. The process had not gone too far by 1850, when only about two-fifths were working with non-cottons, especially silks and mixtures. Thereafter, however, the proportion increased, approaching perhaps half by 1861 and maybe 60 per cent in the early 1870s. The change reflects a more rapid decline in cotton than in silk hand weaving, numbers in the latter trade attaining a peak during the 1850s. In part, this was due to the growing use of powerlooms in silk weaving, though relatively few powerloom silk weavers are mentioned in the census schedules. It was also affected by the general decline in the silk trade, following the removal of tariff protection in 1860.[42]

Two major questions arise from these observations. Why is it that non-cotton hand weaving became important in certain parts of Lancashire and why did cotton handloom weaving continue to be well represented elsewhere in the county? To start with, the development of silk weaving is considered.

The growth of the silk trade at Manchester and in the Bolton/Leigh area during the second quarter of the nineteenth century has been outlined by Duncan Bythell. He quotes the view of J. F. Foster, a local magistrate, to show that some 8,000 silk weavers were already at work in Manchester by the late 1820s.[43] This seems to have been an exaggeration, however. Another contemporary, a Macclesfield silk weaver named Thomas Cope, undertook a five-day survey in 1833 which showed that the figure was 6,000 for Lancashire as a whole and no more than 950 at Manchester and Salford.[44] Half of Cope's weavers resided in the Leigh area, where, Bythell notes, the change-over from cotton to silk weaving was taking place rapidly. By the late 1830s, the trade was thriving so well there that the older-established silk weavers in Manchester and Middleton were complaining about the competition that had developed. They were particularly aggrieved, it was alleged, because piece rates of a halfpenny less than those which they received were being paid to the Leigh weavers.[45]

Comtemporary writings shed further light on these matters. According to an elderly hand weaver whom Angus Reach interviewed in 1849, the silk trade was introduced into Middleton around 1820.[46] Edward Baines agrees. Writing in 1824, he notes that whilst cotton was the major trade in the town, silk was making considerable headway.[47] Thereafter, it continued to grow and by the early 1840s, Edwin Butterworth could rank silk weaving alongside cotton weaving as the town's principal manufactures. In total, he estimated, some 2,000 silk weavers could be found there.[48]

At Leigh, meanwhile, silk weaving appears to have made particularly rapid progress, as Bythell suggests. It has been noted that cambric muslins were the town's leading product during the mid-1820s,[49] but, a decade and a half later, Butterworth maintained that as many as 5,000 silk weavers were to be found there. He believed that, as at Middleton, silk could be classed on a par with cotton.[50]

The extent to which the silk hand weaving industry ultimately developed in both the Middleton and Leigh areas may be broadly judged from the 1851 census schedule entries. In the former area, heavy concentrations were to be found immediately to the north and east of Manchester, centred on Chadderton, Middleton, Failsworth and Droylesden. Here, around 6,500 silk hand weavers were recorded in 1851. In the latter area, the bulk were to be found at Leigh and at several townships to the north, including Westhoughton, Hindley and Atherton. There were also notable concentrations to the south of Leigh at Lowton and Culcheth. Altogether in the Leigh area, the census enumerators listed some 7,000 silk hand weavers in 1851.

In explaining the rise of silk weaving in Lancashire, the fillip given to silk production generally in Britain from the sharp reductions in import duties on raw silk must be noted. These took place during the mid-1820s, bringing the level down from 4/- per pound for Indian raw silk and 5/6$d$ for that of other countries, to only 1$d$ per pound.[51] Under this stimulation, raw silk imports into Britain rose from an annual average of 1.1 million lbs in 1815–17 to one of 3.1 million lbs in 1829–31.[52] These reduced costs no doubt fed through into final product prices, with a consequent impact on sales, though since silk products would have been sold to high income groups, demand for them may have been highly price inelastic.[53]

But why did silk weaving develop in some parts of Lancashire rather than others? One explanation was offered by the old weaver to whom A. B. Reach spoke in 1849. According to his account, manufacturers from Spitalfields began to put out silk at Middleton at a time when the powerloom had brought heavy unemployment in the town. Their aim was to 'bate down' the wages paid to Spitalfield weavers. Nor, he maintained, did the matter rest there. Following a dispute with the Middleton weavers, masters began to put out at Leigh where redundant cotton hand weavers, glad to obtain work, were prepared to weave silk at cheaper rates.[54]

If the explanation has substance, then two of the areas with the highest concentrations of cotton hand weavers in the early nineteenth century both experienced the impact of the powerloom at an early date. It is not clear when mechanised weaving became widely used at Leigh, but powerlooms had certainly reached Middleton parish by the 1830s, the factory inspectors recording 408 in 1835.[55] Further, from a manufacturer's point of view, the problems and costs of distributing raw materials would have been less acute where weavers were highly concentrated rather than where they were thinly scattered. The closeness of the Leigh and Middleton areas to Manchester would also have been regarded by manufacturers as an additional attraction when extra labour was required. Yet Middleton did not by any means lose its entire silk weaving trade to Leigh. Leigh may have become the more important centre, in part, perhaps, through lower wage costs, but the growth in demand for silk weaving was rapid enough to provide major employment opportunities in both townships. Indeed, that other, rather smaller silk weaving centres developed in Lancashire, including Ormskirk, North Meols and Darwen is further testimony to the tremendous growth in demand for silk cloth generated during the 1830s and 1840s.[56] And, once more, silk manufacturers may have favoured these districts because unemployed cotton hand weavers were available, at least some of whom were used to working with fine cloths.[57]

Little evidence is available from the censuses about the types of silk cloth that were woven. Occasional reference is made to weavers of satin and of silk plush, the latter a fabric having extra warp threads used to form a pile (or plush) on the surface.[58] Presumably, these plush cloths would have catered for the needs of the more discerning buyer and that few plush weavers were mentioned in the census would have been partly because their numbers were relatively small. But in any case, the enumerators were not required to go into any detail beyond the general description of cloth types that they normally gave.

Two further comments on the types of silk cloth woven on the handloom may be made. Firstly, although both plain and fancy lines were being produced, the latter may have predominated by the mid-1830s. Supportive evidence comes from a local newspaper report which notes that figured sarcenets (very fine silk cloths) then comprised the leading silk fabric manufactured in Lancashire and that chequered sarcenets were next in importance. The report also states that plain sarcenets were still produced in quantity, with some 'exceedingly fine reeds' being worked, but that bandannas, once a major product, were 'now seldom seen in the loom.'[59] It may be, as S. R. H. Jones maintains, that customer preferences were switching towards finer silk fabrics.[60] This was certainly so with bandanna handkerchiefs. In conversation with a Macclesfield silk weaver in 1849, Angus Reach was told that bandanna weaving was harder work than it had been twenty years ago, because a finer weft thread was now being used and this required much greater care to be taken.[61]

The second comment is to note that, given the apparent importance of figured hand silk weaving, the Jacquard loom must have been used to an appreciable extent. Reach certainly observed them operating both domestically and in weaving sheds, though, in Macclesfield at least, he found that manufacturers were keen to ensure that the finer sorts of fancier goods were woven in factory sheds, so as to obtain closer supervision of the workforce.[62] Their importance should not be exaggerated, however, since they would not have been required to weave the plain and check cloths.

Whilst silk was the fabric to which displaced cotton hand weavers most frequently turned, considerable numbers of them also switched to mixture cloths. By far the most important was mousseline-de-laine, a dress fabric with a cotton warp and a worsted weft. Bythell has shown that the fabric began to be woven at Colne in north-east Lancashire during the later 1830s and that it soon came to employ large numbers.[63] Indeed, census data show that it quickly replaced cotton as the major fabric. By 1851, perhaps 3,500 of the Colne area hand weavers were producing mousseline-de-laine, compared with a few hundred weaving cotton. Some mousseline-de-laine weavers were to be found elsewhere in Lancashire, but numbers were insignificant compared with those at Colne.

Much uncertainty arises in explaining why the production of mousseline-de-laine became so heavily localised. Perhaps it had a good deal to do with the availability of a substantial, trained labour force, the services of which were no longer required for manufacturing the printing calicoes in which the area specialised.[64] The powerloom had certainly reached Colne by the early 1840s and quite a number of cotton powerloom weavers were recorded in the area by the 1851 census enumerators.[65] No doubt, too, the enterprise of local manufacturers played its part, with many of them seeing the opportunities presented by diversification. Whatever, the reasons, it is plain that the introduction of mousseline-de-laine prolonged the life of the hand weaving trade in and around Colne for at least one decade and perhaps for two.

The rapidity with which handloom weavers turned to mousseline-de-laine during the 1840s was matched by the swiftness with which they abandoned the fabric during the following decade, at least in the main production area. No precise data at which this began can be established, but census returns show that relatively few survived until the early 1860s. One influence here was the powerloom. Failure amongst census enumerators to distinguish hand from power weavers makes the overall position hard to judge, but it is likely that, by 1861, mousseline-de-laine had become largely a product of the powerloom in the Colne district. It certainly had at Trawden. Here, in the main, the enumerators did separate hand from power weavers. Amongst the former, they counted only fifteen or so who might still have woven mousseline-de-laine; amongst the latter, the number was in excess of 150.[66] Whether the overall level of demand for mousseline-de-laine had also declined substantially by the early 1860s is unclear, but it is certain that any changes in market conditions bore more heavily on hand weavers in the Colne area than on power weavers.

In other parts of Lancashire, meanwhile, the weaving of mousseline-de-laine on the handloom was sometimes more prolonged. This was so, for example, at Mellor, near Blackburn, where reference was made in 1861 to a man who managed seventy-one handlooms used for weaving fancy cotton and worsted cloth.[67] Yet here, as elsewhere, those involved in the trade were relatively few and all had disappeared from the scene by the early 1870s.

Other mixture cloths were also made on Lancashire handlooms, though not as extensively as mousseline-de-laine. They embraced a variety of fibre combinations, as Richard Muggeridge found.[68] Amongst them, silk and cotton was the most prominent.[69] This was woven in several parts of central Lancashire, for example, including the Croston area, where it helped hand weaving to continue until at least the early 1870s. According to the 1871 census schedules, upwards of a hundred hand weavers were at work there — the total population was 808 — and around one in five were given as cotton and silk weavers.[70]

Whilst the mid-Victorian hand weaving industry in Lancashire became increasingly dependent on non-cotton fabrics, census records show that cotton was by no means replaced. In 1851, if not beyond, cotton hand weavers may still have retained their majority, as the figures in Table 6.2 suggest. What explanation can be offered?

Perhaps the most compelling possibility, definitely the most frequently advanced, is that the cotton hand weavers concentrated increasingly on finer and fancier grades of cloth.[71] These, it is held, were not only unecomonic to weave on the powerloom, but could also yield reasonably high earnings for hand weavers. Advantages arose, therefore, to both employers and employed in maintaining production of these cloths on the handloom. Evidence to support this view is admittedly fragmentary, but is none the less sufficient for a supportive case to be mounted.

The surest instance of dependency on high-quality cotton cloths in a major hand weaving centre is at Bolton. As early as the mid-1830s, a local newspaper reported that the production of coarse cloths on the town's handlooms was 'very limited'. Instead, the emphasis was on the fancy trades, with various types of muslins, quilts and counterpanes being prominent.[72] The Black Survey of 1837 showed that as many as 960 counterpane weavers and 390 quilt weavers were to be found in the town, about a quarter of the hand weaving labour force.[73] Census evidence reveals that these products remained important into the 1850s and 1860s, though the sampling techniques used to analyse the census data do not allow any precise quantification to be made. According to one commentator, however, the number of caddow counterpane hand weavers in the town actually rose during the mid-nineteenth century, from 1,000 in 1833 to 1,700 in 1862.[74] At the time of the 1871 census, only 103 counterpane weavers and 40 quilt weavers received mention at Bolton, though there may have been others who were not specifically described as such.

Further evidence of any early switch to finer fabrics was reported at Blackburn. It comes from a newspaper report on a meeting of handloom weavers which took place in January 1834. The correspondent noted that calico weaving in the town had been taken over by the powerloom, with the result that hand weavers were driven to working 'the finer cloths and fancy muslins'.[75] Whether the remark applied also to those in the rural districts around Blackburn, especially in the Ribble Valley, is unclear, though a handloom muslin manufacturer was listed at Ribchester in 1881.[76] What is certain is that Blackburn township was one of the most important powerloom centres in Lancashire by the mid-1830s,[77] whilst in the Ribble Valley settlements its appearance was belated.[78] Possibly, therefore, the Ribble Valley weavers did concentrate on higher-grade wares.

If Bolton and Blackburn, two of the major centres of cotton hand weaving, had moved into the production of finer cloths by the early Victorian years, what of the smaller centres? Evidence is again hard to unearth, though some help is provided by Edwin Butterworth. Writing in the early 1840s, he reported that in the central Lancashire parishes of Brindle, Hoole, Leyland and Penwortham, the emphasis was on light cotton cloths. He also observed that at Flixton parish, the weaving of fancy cottons prevailed.[79] It may be mentioned, too, that census schedules make occasional reference to hand-woven cotton cloths other than those at Bolton. They include check weaving (presumably a type of gingham) which took place in the Entwistle area to the north of Bolton and the weaving of coloured cottons (and of other types of coloured fabric), which was practised at Croston, near Chorley.[80] Yet it seems probable that many such specialities went unrecorded in the censuses, including the so-called 'blue bratting', an all cotton or cotton and linen cloth woven in half-inch squares, which, during the mid-nineteenth century, was manufactured on handlooms at Samlesbury, near Preston.[81]

It is unfortunate that all these references to high-quality cotton cloths relate almost exclusively to the central Lancashire cotton districts. Of the type of cotton specialisms that occurred elsewhere in the hand weaving areas, evidence is lacking. Accordingly, the possibility cannot be entirely ruled out that some mid-Victorian cotton hand weavers still produced coarser cloths. In fact, John Lyons has shown this was so in the case of the Horrocks concern at Preston, which, until 1853, produced medium cambrics by both hand and power.[82] Why Horrocks adopted this policy is uncertain, but they may have preferred to convert gradually to power weaving, recognising that, for the types and qualities of cloth they wove, advantages arising from using traditional technology long remained significant.

There is reason to suppose, then, that hand-woven cloth produced in Lancashire during the mid-Victorian period was often of a relatively high value. This was probably true of silks and mixtures, as well as of at least certain types of cotton and this helps to explain why cotton continued to be woven on the handloom. In all probability, many of the higher-grade cloths succumbed only gradually to the powerloom and, in some districts, continued to provide considerable employment opportunities for hand weavers beyond mid-century. Furthermore, numerous hand weavers were able to remain in domestic work because, in common with their forebears, they were prepared and able to switch to alternative fabrics as circumstances changed. Handloom weavers may have adopted conservative attitudes in seeking to defend the lifestyle they preferred; yet they often took advantage of new opportunities which allowed them to do so.

### Notes

1   For a discussion, see D. Bythell, *The Handloom Weavers* (1969), ch. 10.
2   The instruction was to include the fabric in parentheses after the occupation (*PP*, 1851, 1339, XLIII, p. 6).
3   Bythell, *op. cit.*, p. 136.
4   *Ibid.*, p. 137.

## The means of survival

5  *PP*, 1834 (556) X, pp. 607–9. The survey was undertaken by a visitor, well acquainted with the area (E. and T. Kelly, eds, *A Schoolmaster's Notebook*, 1957, pp. 123–4).

6  *PP*, 1835 (341) XIII, Q.1,756. See also *PP*, 1840 (220) XXIV, p. 601 *et seq*., but examples given may not relate to families totally dependent on handlooms.

7  E. Baines, *History of the Cotton Manufacture in Great Britain* (1966 reprint of 1835 edition), p. 439.

8  A Manchester Statistical Society survey of 1834 noted occupations of 7,789 local people. Piecers numbered 1,087 and formed the largest single occupational group after hand weavers (Kelly, *op. cit.*, p. 118).

9  See pp. 161–70.

10  MCLA, Grimshaw's Wages Book, L1/16/3/7.

11  For details, see Bythell, *op. cit.*, pp. 120–2.

12  He was James Orr, a Paisley weaver (*ibid.*, p. 128).

13  See pp. 157–8.

14  G. H. Wood, *History of Wages in the Cotton Trade during the Past Hundred Years* (1910), pp. 112–13.

15  F. Engels, *The Condition of the Working Class in England in 1845* (1971 reprint of 1845 edition), p. 157; S. Bamford, *Walks in South Lancashire and on Its Borders* (1972 reprint of 1844 edition), p. 64.

16  W. Dodd, *The Factory System Illustrated* (1968 reprint of 1841–42 edition), p. 126. Dodd quotes figures for two Wigan weavers who probably wove cotton, one earning 5/- to 6/- per week and the other about 6/-. Trade was, however, depressed at this time.

17  W. and R. Chambers, *The Cotton Metropolis* (1972 reprint of 1844 edition), p. 30.

18  J. S. Lyons, 'Family response to economic decline: handloom weavers in early nineteenth century Lancashire', *Research in Economic History*, 12 (1989), p. 76.

19  D. Chadwick, *On the Rate Wages . . . in the Manufacturing District of Lancashire . . . from 1839–1859* (1859), p. 24. The data were obtained from circulars and visits.

20  *PP*, 1850 (1239) XXIII, p. 278. Quoted in Bythell, *op. cit.*, p. 262.

21  LRO, Wiseman's Wages Book, DDWm (uncatalogued).

22  Bamford, *op. cit.*, p. 252. This weaver, however, was working with inferior thread, which slowed him down appreciably.

23  C. Aspin (ed.), *Manchester and the Textile Districts in 1849* (1972), p. 101.

24  *Ibid.*, pp. 89 and 93.

25  Judging by the relative number of wage earners in the family who were hand weavers.

26  J. S. Lyons, *The Lancashire Cotton Industry and the Introduction of the Powerloom* (unpublished PhD dissertation, 1977), p. 47. Judy Lown notes a variation of this practice with regard to families of silk weavers in Essex. Here, husbands remained as domestic weavers, often being given care of young children, whilst their wives and older children worked in the mill (J. Lown, *Women and Industrialisation: Gender at Work in Nineteenth Century England* (1990), p. 216.

27  Only families in which the husband and wife are clearly recorded as hand weavers are included.

28  Blackburn Census Returns, 1851, ED 1M.

29  Little Bolton Census Returns, 1851, ED 5 & 9.

30  Wigan Census Returns, 1871, ED 9.

31  One instance, that of William Pearce of Bolton, is recorded in *PP*, 1842 (77) XXXV, p. 3. However, such journeymen hand weavers were uncommon (*PP*, 1841, 296, X, p. 2).

32  Eccleshill, to the south of Blackburn, provides one instance. In 1851, boys here were commonly employed in coal mines and girls in cotton factories as piecers or weavers. Some boys were also power weavers.

33  Indeed, hand weaving was still by far the most usual occupation for children.

34  On the larger farms, by contrast, children tended to be employed on the land rather than in hand weaving.

35  Thus, thirteen heads of household are listed as small farmers at Balderstone in 1851 (ED 4a), but only four of their children were probably farm workers, compared with twenty-nine who worked at the handloom.

36  Aspin, *op. cit.*, pp. 48–9.

37  Wood, *op. cit.*, p. 131.

38  M. Anderson, *Family Structure in Nineteenth Century Lancashire* (1971), pp. 75–6.

39  They are based on the figures given in Table 6.1.

40  Nevertheless, mention of fabrics other than cotton in the census entries for these towns seems to be infrequent.

41  An 1849 sanitary report for Wigan gives one instance of the help provided by contemporary sources. This states that the staple industries of Wigan were coal and cotton (spinning, hand weaving and power weaving) along with a little silk weaving (G. T. Clark, *Report to the General Board of Health on ... the Borough of Wigan*, 1849, p. 6).

42  S. R. H. Jones, 'Technology, transaction costs, and the transition to factory production in the British silk industry, 1700–1870', *JEH*, XLVII (1987), p. 90.

43  Bythell, *op. cit.*, p. 260.

44  *PP*, 1831/2 (678) XIX, Q.11,712. Quoted in Sir F. Warner, *The Silk Industry of the United Kingdom: Its Origins and Development*, p. 150.

45  Bythell, *op. cit.*, p. 261.

46  Aspin, *op. cit.*, p. 103.

47  E. Baines, *History, Directory and Gazetteer of the County of Lancaster*, 2 (1968 reprint of 1824 edition), p. 429.

48  E. Butterworth, *A Statistical Sketch of the County Palatine of Lancaster* (1841), p. 94.

49  See p. 81.

50  Butterworth, *op. cit.*, p. 50.

51  *PP*, 1831/2 (678) XIX, p. 11.

52  *Ibid.*, p. 9.

53  See B. Murphy, *A History of the British Economy, 1740–1970*, 1 (1973), p. 438 and J. Butt and I. Donnachie, *Industrial Archaeology of the British Isles* (1979), p. 76.

54  Aspin, *op. cit.*, p. 103.

55  *PP*, 1836 (24) XLV, p. 5.

56  About 550 silk hand weavers were to be found at North Meols in 1851, around 250 at Ormskirk and about 240 in the Darwen area.

57  Butterworth, *op. cit.*, pp. 97 and 100.

58  W. S. Murphy, *The Textile Industries* (1910), IV, pp. 116–20.

59  *PC*, 2.4.1836.

60  Jones, *op. cit.*, p. 93. The author refers to the post-1860 period, when the removal of tariff protection brought a major threat to the British silk industry.

61 Aspin, *op. cit.*, p. 96.
62 *Ibid.*, p. 92.
63 Bythell, *op. cit.*, pp. 261–2.
64 See p. 81.
65 There were several hundred in Colne and Barrowford.
66 Though cotton power weavers predominated in the village.
67 Mellor Census Returns, 1861, ED 4.
68 *PP*, 1840 (220) XXIV, p. 578.
69 Another was silk and worsted, for winter garments, which was introduced at Bolton in 1835 (*PrP*, 28.11.1835).
70 The proportion may have been higher given that quite a number of the Croston hand weavers were undifferentiated.
71 See for example, J. H. Clapham, *An Economic History of Modern Birtain* (1967 reprint of 1926 edition), p. 554 and A. J. Taylor, 'Concentration and Specialization in the Lancashire cotton industry, 1825–50', *EcHR*, 1 (1948–49), p. 117.
72 *BS*, 28.10.1835.
73 J. Black, *A Medico-Topographical, Geographical and Statistical Sketch of Bolton and Its Neighbourhood* (1837).
74 W. P. Crankshaw, *Industrial Bolton* (1927), p. 37.
75 *BC*, 25.1.1834.
76 See p. 175.
77 See p. 22.
78 At Mellor, for instance, powerloom weaving was not introduced until 1878 (T. Counsell, *Mellor in Blackburnshire: a Short History*, 1929, p. 141).
79 Butterworth, *op. cit.*, pp. 14, 41, 51, 104, and 34.
80 Precise details of the nature of these cloths are not recorded.
81 R. Eaton, *History of Samlesbury* (1936), p. 179.
82 J. S. Lyons, 'Technological dualism, rivalry and complementarity: handicrafts in the transition to modern industry' (forthcoming), p. 34.

# Chapter 7

# MID-VICTORIAN HAND WEAVERS: REASONS FOR SURVIVAL

The first part of this chapter is historiographical. It provides a critical assessment of historians' explanations for the survival of outwork in the British cotton textile industry during the middle decades of the nineteenth century. The aim is to establish an appropriate context within which a discussion on the durability of Lancashire's hand weaving trades can be set. Building on the ideas outlined in the introduction, attention is focused on supply-side explanations, namely the technical shortcomings of the powerloom; the abundance of cheap labour available for domestic weaving; and the inability of entrepreneurs in the hand weaving trade to raise the finance necessary for mechanisation. It is these aspects which textile historians have emphasised. Consideration is also given to demand-side influences, about which comparatively little has been written.

In the second section, these arguments are developed in order to explain why handloom weaving remained important in mid-Victorian Lancashire. They are tested against an empirical background, drawing on a range of neglected evidence, including that derived from business records and trade directories. It is held that whilst the general arguments used by historians to explain the survival of outwork can be usefully applied to domestic weaving, they need to be carefully qualified and extended.

Turning firstly to technological aspects, it is argued that these strongly influenced the durability of handloom weaving. This is largely because the technical shortcomings of powerlooms took longer to overcome than has been generally conceded, especially regarding fine and fancy cottons and non-cottons. To a minor extent, it is also because the productivity gains arising from using improved handlooms have been too readily discounted.

Of importance, too, is the argument about labour abundance. Well into the Victorian era, hand weavers remained a numerous element in the Lancashire labour force, especially in rural areas. They often continued to work together in family units, favouring a traditional way of life and expressing a strong distaste for the alternatives. It is these aspects which, in recent writings at least, have been underplayed; too much attention has been given to explanations based on the inability of hand weavers to find new employment. Such arguments have credence, but they do not allow sufficiently for the diversity of circumstances in which hand weavers and their families found themselves.

As to the notion that handloom manufacturers were generally unable to raise the capital they needed for powerloom investment, strong reservations are expressed. No doubt this was the case in some instances, but it is shown that it was not only the more marginal producers that clung to traditional methods. So, too, did many soundly-based concerns, the proprietors of which continued to live in some opulence. Indeed, they might still employ appreciable numbers of hand weavers beyond mid-century. Accordingly, neither the level of profitability a firm achieved, nor the scale on which it operated, provides a sufficient explanation of the positive attitudes towards hand weaving which entrepreneurs often retained.

Finally, consideration is given to demand-side aspects. Lack of evidence makes it difficult to assess their importance, but there is sufficient to suggest that not only did mid-Victorian hand weavers continue to benefit from periodic short-term rises in demand for their product, but that employers retained at least some handlooms to cope with short production runs, the consequence of the volatile market conditions under which they operated.

## 1  Historiographical issues

In perusing contemporary comment on the impressive productivity advances achieved by early powerlooms, it is at first sight surprising that so few were in use by the 1820s. Richard Guest, for example, writing in 1823, maintained that a boy or girl aged fourteen to fifteen could manage two powerlooms and could weave three and a half times as much cloth as the best hand weaver. He argued, too, that the powerloom produced cloth of a higher quality than the handloom. This was because the hand weaver could not draw back his lathe with constant force as he wove, with the result that his cloth inevitably varied in thickness. Conversely, the steam-loom lathe gave a steady, constant blow, achieving a much more regular weave.[1]

A decade later, an unnamed manufacturer was making even more striking comparisons between the performance of hand and powerlooms.

A very good hand weaver, 25 or 30 years of age, will weave two pieces of 9-8 shirtings per week, each 24 yards long, containing 100 shoots of weft to the inch; the reed of the cloth being a 44 Bolton count . . .

In 1823, a steam-loom weaver, about 15 years of age, attending two looms, could weave seven similar pieces in a week . . .

## The last shift

In 1833, a steam-loom weaver, from 15 to 20 years of age, assisted by a girl about 12 years of age, attending to four looms, can weave eighteen similar pieces in a week; some can weave 20 pieces.[2]

Whether four steam-looms were commonly operated by a weaver and a child assistant (known as a tenter) at this time is doubtful, however. Taking evidence from factory inspectors' returns, Blaug suggests two was the norm in 1835, rising to between 2.5 and 3 by 1860 and to four by 1887.[3] This squares with the findings of G. H. Wood, who maintains two looms were usual in the 1830s and four very unusual.[4] Further, in conversation with elderly weavers and overlookers, Wood discovered that one-loom weavers were not at all uncommon until after 1860. And even in the United States, which might be expected to have been ahead of Britain in weaving technology, two looms per weaver was still customary in 1840.[5] Yet there can be little doubt that the pre-Victorian powerloom greatly speeded up production of certain types of cloth and more consistently wove fabrics of an even texture.

Despite these advantages, cotton manufacturers might still be reluctant to install powerlooms, since, as von Tunzelmann points out, their investment decisions were influenced by economic as well as technological considerations. In this respect, much depended on cloth quality, contemporaries declaring powerlooms to be less economic than handlooms for finer grades. The example is cited of a leading Bolton firm finding it unprofitable to use powerlooms for 60-reed cloth, a relatively coarse fabric. More generally, cloths graded as 100s on the Manchester count (equalling 60 on the Bolton) were woven more economically by power, whereas cloth with counts of 120 were not.[6]

Calculations made by von Tunzelmann support such views. For the mid-1830s, he compares costs and benefits of making a 50-reed cambric, a coarser cloth than the 60-reeds, by power and hand. He includes labour, capital and material costs, which all proved appreciably higher with powerlooms. After allowing for absorption of most of the capital costs in the first year of operation, he finds little return accrued from weaving this fabric on powerlooms above that earned on handlooms. He notes the former could weave finer cloths, but one weaver was needed per loom, presumably to cope with more frequent breakages of thread. As a result, production rates were little higher than those achieved by hand. 'In sum,' he concludes, 'the powered technique could be applied to finer or fancier cloths, but could not yet be profitable on them'.[7]

As von Tunzelmann admits, however, his analysis has limitations, much depending on the accuracy of his assumption that powerlooms in the mid-1830s wove five pieces of 50-reed cambric per week. If the true figure was only four, the powerloom would have earned a net loss over its lifetime, whereas an extra half piece per week would have converted an annual return of 3.5 per cent into one of about 14 per cent. He acknowledges, too, that manufacturers might have been tempted to install powerlooms for reasons other than those entering into his calculations. These included the higher prices obtained for cloth with a more regular weave; the quicker turnover of stock; the greater certainty with which delivery dates could be met; and savings from eliminating embezzlement of yarn. At least some of these advantages, though, would have arisen by bringing hand weavers into workshops.

In concluding, von Tunzelmann argues that technical improvements made to the powerloom during the 1840s tilted the balance in its favour, even for finer cloths. These improvements, associated particularly with Kenworthy and Bullough, comprised devices to stop the loom automatically when the weft broke or the shuttle needed refilling; a means of keeping the woven cloth at its proper width (the roller temple); and a method of adjusting the take-up motion which kept the speed of weaving constant. Such advances may have halved weaving labour costs. At the same time, reductions in fuel costs made it economic to run steam engines and hence powerlooms at faster rates, thereby consolidating the advantages of the powerloom.[8] Nor, von Tunzelmann believes, was any scope left to reduce cotton hand weavers' wages, even in the finer branches, so weakening one of the main incentives to remain with the traditional technology.

Criticism of von Tunzelmann's analysis has been voiced by J. S. Lyons. In particular, he points to a significant error von Tunzelmann makes in calculating the amounts of value added in hand and power weaving. This error, which arises from assuming that value added per piece was over twice as high in the former trade as in the latter, highlights the inadequacy of the data available for this type of calculation and leads Lyons to observe that it cannot be concluded that the profitability of the powerloom in the mid-1830s was as low as von Tunzelmann suggests.[9] Moreover, he argues that the sharp upturn in powerloom productivity that occurred in the 1840s was due to technical modifications in the powerloom rather than to the impact of power cost reductions. Indeed, these technical improvements were designed to eliminate problems that arose when looms were operated at higher speeds.[10]

The importance von Tunzelmann and Lyons attach to Kenworthy and Bullough's inventions has certainly been accepted by fellow historians. Richard Marsden, for example, maintains that, in their absence, the powerloom could never have entirely displaced the handloom. Before their introduction, the 'closest and most unremitting attention' was required of the weaver to ensure that the loom was stopped when the weft thread broke or when the shuttle pirns became empty. Consequently, one loom was the most that many weavers could manage and two the maximum for the most skilful weavers.[11] If this was indeed the case, then doubt arises as to whether two looms per weaver actually was the norm during the 1830s.

Whilst the utility of Kenworthy and Bullough's inventions must be recognised, so, too, must their limitations. Thus, D. A. Farnie points out that the full potential of the powerloom depended on improvements in the preparatory processes, especially power warping, invented in 1843, and slasher-sizing, introduced as late as 1853.[12] Again, Richard Marsden cautions that much ingenuity had still to be expended in further improving the powerloom during the next half century.[13] This was especially so with regard to fancy cottons and non-cottons. As far as the former are concerned, neither the Jacquard nor dobby (small Jacquard) was adapted to power weaving until 1860 and even then took time to perfect.[14] As to the latter, S. R. H. Jones suggests that the pace of technological change was a major determinant of the speed with which the factory system evolved in the silk trade. He reasons that the move into factory production lagged just behind major technological advances in both throwing and weaving, thus strongly suggesting a causal relationship. That throwing became a factory industry long before weaving strengthens the argument since, if other than technological change had yielded substantial economies, factory production would have been adopted much earlier than it was.[15]

Historians have thus made a strong case for seeing technological change as decisive in promoting mechanised factory weaving; in its absence, the transition only took place to a limited extent. And numerous outwork weavers may have been found in the Lancashire textile trades during the mid-Victorian years because the powerloom took much longer to perfect than has been generally conceded. Indeed, the significance of technical progress in power weaving during the 1840s may have been greatly overstated.

Before becoming too enthusiastic about this line of reasoning, however, it is as well to remember that other explanations for the durability of domestic weaving must be considered. The possibility cannot be ruled out that even when particular fabrics could be economically woven by the powerloom, they remained for some time the product of the handloom, at least in part.

To start with, Habakkuk's factor cost approach may be taken. An outline of his general theme is given in the introduction, but mention should also be made of the benefits he thinks arose to textile manufacturers from maintaining at least some handloom weavers. One concerns increased productivity levels. He suggests that falling piece rates would have prompted hand weavers to increase output, thereby diminishing the relative cost advantages of powerlooms. During the 1820s, productivity rises amongst cotton hand weavers may have amounted to 25 or 30 per cent, a figure based on estimates of changes in weaver numbers and output assuming only handlooms were in use.[16] The resultant increase in output, Habakkuk believes, kept cloth prices and factory sector profits at comparatively low levels, thereby reducing the incentive and the ability of manufacturers to invest in powerlooms; they would only have done so 'under the stimulus of increased demand or because innovation reduced the cost of powerloom products.' Further, because hand weavers were prepared to accept lower wages, the labour costs of producing by handloom fell more than those of producing by powerloom. Given these developments, it was not until the 1850s that the balance of advantage swung decisively away from hand weaving and manufacturers went over 'more or less entirely' to the powerloom.

Apart from highlighting productivity improvements in hand weaving, Habakkuk conjectures that textile manufacturers were slower to invest in powerlooms than

*Reasons for survival*

they might have been because of the sheer number of hand weavers at their disposal. He remarks that:

the existence of a large sector of the weaving industry organised on the domestic system acted as a brake which periodically pulled up the mechanisation of the industry.[17]

Others, including E. P. Thompson, share this view, stressing also the cheapness of hand weaving labour.[18]

Inevitably, these propositions have not escaped criticism. With regard to productivity increases, Bythell maintains these would not have been considerable because of 'the essentially casual, part-time attitude to work' amongst many of the women and children employed at the handloom. He also suggests that even though weavers may have worked longer hours at the loom as their trade declined, they did not necessarily increase output proportionally. This was because the monotony of their work necessitated frequent stoppages and, in any case, they became too depressed and listless to work intensively for lengthy periods. Nevertheless, he thinks Habakkuk's estimate of increased hand weaver productivity is plausible. His view contrasts with that of Lyons, who deems it 'not proven'.[19]

Bythell and Lyons are equally critical of Habakkuk's point about hand weaver availability holding back powerloom investment. The former considers Habakkuk weakens his case by supposing hand weaver numbers scarcely declined before 1830 and fell only slowly thereafter. In reality, the decline 'began earlier, and was affected more quickly, than has usually been supposed.' His only concession to Habakkuk is to agree that, to some extent, hand weaving would have declined more quickly had the supply of labour been less abundant than it actually was,[20] a view also expressed by Ivy Pinchbeck.[21] As to Lyons, he formulates his criticism around the propositions that, for the argument to apply, hand weaving labour would not have been able to find alternative work and wage falls in hand weaving would have taken place without effect on wages in the factory sector. Both occurrences are unlikely to have applied. He concludes that the loss of labour from the hand weaving trades assisted factory industry and other growing trades by releasing labour to them and that the continued existence of handloom weavers 'attests only to the willingness of workers to accept low and declining wages for lengthy periods . . .'.[22] Why this was so is unresolved.

But how valid are these criticisms? With regard to hand weaver productivity, it is true, as Bythell observes, that there would always have been a physical limit on the output a hand weaver could achieve, but it is arguable whether this had generally been reached by the 1830s. In the first place, weavers in the finer and fancier branches, who were relatively well paid, may have worked shorter hours than other hand weavers whilst remaining at, or above, subsistence level. There may still have been scope, therefore, to extend the length of their working day. Secondly, it is by no means certain that, as hand weaving went into long-term decline, women and children continued to regard themselves as essentially casual, part-time workers. Faced with reducing piece rates and, in certain parts of the

151

county at least, with a dearth of alternative employment opportunities, attitudes to work may have changed significantly. For women and children, longer and more regular working hours at the loom may have bcome increasingly common and the pace of work may have quickened. Further, children may have started to work at an earlier age than was customary, perhaps, as Michael Sanderson suggests, being withdrawn entirely from formal schooling.[23] Indeed, there may be much in Ivy Pinchbeck's remark that, by the 1840s, the working hours of child handloom weavers were almost always excessive.[24] The possibility cannot be lightly dismissed that handloom weavers continued to improve their productivity, albeit to a diminishing extent, well into the Victorian period and this may have played no minor part in explaining why manufacturers remained interested in employing them.

A further question about productivity also arises. It concerns the idea that higher output per worker in hand weaving during the 1840s and 1850s may have resulted partly from improved handloom technology, especially as the dandy loom became more widely used. Both von Tunzelmann and Bythell have noted that the introduction of the dandy loom during the early nineteenth century may have enabled hand weavers to achieve a 50 per cent increase in output. Both are doubtful, however, that dandy looms were widely used. The latter also mentions that the dandy loom was only suited to weaving plain, coarse cloths, which were the first to succumb to the powerloom. For this reason, the dandy loom had a relatively ephemeral impact, those in Blackburn being given up by the late 1830s. Nor, he believes, was the use of the dandy loom widespread.[25]

Yet reservations must be expressed about these views. This is partly because evidence on the extent to which dandy looms were favoured is sparse. Further, as will be demonstrated in the following section, what evidence there is has been used rather selectively.[26] It may be that firm conclusions on the importance of the dandy loom cannot be drawn, but more can certainly be said.

With regard to the criticisms of arguments about the durability and cheapness of handloom labour, doubts must again be raised. In the first place, it should be emphasised that the census schedule evidence presented in Chapter 5 confirms that Habakkuk's ideas on the rate at which hand weaving declined are far more accurate than those of Bythell. This being so, the notion that abundant supplies of handloom labour formed an important element in the decision of manufacturers to remain with traditional technology has a firm historical basis; it is not mere supposition. Secondly, as the wage data in Chapter 6 suggest, hand weaving labour was appreciably less expensive than power weaving labour, at least as far as adults were concerned. Moreover, in the absence of strong union organisation, it was extremely difficult for hand weavers to avoid falling victim to wage abatement – the practice of demanding discounts on piece rates, generally on the allegation of poor workmanship – or to 'wage flexibility' – the policy of diverting work to districts where the lowest wages could be paid.[27] Finally, whilst it is undoubtedly true that substantial numbers of hand weavers did find alternative jobs, especially during the early Victorian years, the argument is easy to overstate. By no means all of them could do, especially those in the older age groups who lived in rural districts where employment opportunities were limited.

Another concern about this argument is that it fails to take account of the positive attitudes hand weavers continued to hold towards their work and the distaste with which they viewed alternatives. These have often been commented upon by historians. For instance, J. F. C. Harrison argues that hand weaving remained popular because of the freedom it gave from the pace and discipline of factory work, as well as satisfying 'the old artisan craving for independence',[28] and E. P. Thompson that hand weavers resented factory discipline and the way in which it disrupted the 'whole pattern of family and community life.'[29] Such ideas, however, have been dismissed by John Lyons. He prefers an alternative which emphasises the reactions of handloom weavers to changing economic circumstances. He writes:

Those who remained at the loom did so because that was a reasonable response to the complex of opportunities and constraints which impinged on their lives. It is therefore precisely because the children of many weavers were able to find jobs in the cotton mills, and because it was rather difficult for adult weavers to find clearly advantageous alternatives, that handloom weaving remained a viable occupation ... through the 1850s.[30]

He acknowledges that factory owners preferred to employ children rather than adults, since the former were not only readily available and relatively cheap, but also much easier to absorb into the factory work regime.[31] For him, therefore, rational economic behaviour on the part of both employed and employer explains the durability of hand weaving and the argument that hand weavers were reluctant to enter the factory becomes 'almost totally vitiated'.

Amongst the difficulties with this line of argument is the stress it places on hand weavers' children finding factory jobs rather than, as was so often the case during the 1840s and 1850s, remaining in domestic weaving, even in the cotton trade. That they commonly comprised part of a family working group depending solely, or largely, on income derived from hand weaving, suggests a different, more traditional form of rational behaviour, based not on maximising family income, but on securing an adequate level of family earnings. And the argument certainly necessitates a review of the attitudes that hand weavers held towards domestic work and its alternatives. These have not been considered by historians in any depth and in recent writings they have been largely overlooked.

Aside from considerations of technology and labour availability, the other supply-side issue historians have raised to explain the survival of hand weaving concerns entry costs into mechanisation. Two aspects arise. The first is that handloom manufacturers found it difficult to secure the investment funds needed to begin power weaving, perhaps because they were small-scale, marginal concerns. The cost of powerlooms was not inordinately high, Edward Baines quoting prices of £7 10s to £8 10s for the mid-1830s, Montgomery of £9 for 1840 and Lyons of £7 for 1850 though, as Berg observes, the costs were multiplied by expenditure on equipment for preparatory processes.[32] The second is that fixed costs in the powerloom trade were borne entirely by the manufacturer, whereas in handloom weaving they could be largely passed on to the labour force; hand weavers rather than their employers were expected to provide loomshops and major items of working equipment, including looms, shuttles and healds.[33] In consequence, handloom manufacturers not only saved on initial fixed capital expenditure, but also avoided having to meet the costs of maintaining under-employed machines and buildings during trade recessions. To borrow Bythell's words, the 'chief losses of the old system fell on the weavers.'[34] Given a reasonably elastic labour supply, especially the almost unlimited number of females who could be moved with ease into and from the labour market, employers in the hand weaving trade could expand or contract production without any major anxieties about their ability to cover fixed capital costs.[35] In the economic climate of the 1840s and 1850s, when years of depressed trade were all too frequent, such an advantage would not have been lightly foregone. This is the more so when it is realised that the ratio of fixed to working capital in the cotton industry had risen from 25 to 50 per cent before 1815 to 66 per cent by the mid-1830s.[36]

In appraising the argument about whether handloom manufacturers could afford to mechanise, two further considerations should be borne in mind. One relates to the West Riding textile trade. Pat Hudson has shown that a marked difference arose between the speed with which the worsted and woollen branches of this trade succumbed to mechanised weaving. As late as 1850, powerlooms were few and far between in wool weaving, whereas they were widely used for worsteds. The contrast reflected variation in the structure of the two trades. In the wool trade, the master clothiers with limited capital reserves remained dominant and the artisan resilient. In the worsted trade, however, capital accumulated in the hands of entrepreneurs controlling a putting-out system which was relatively inefficient and uneconomic.[37] Accordingly, in terms of both means and motive, the incentive to mechanise was greater in worsteds than in woollens. Other influences were also at work to explain the differing rates at which mechanisation took place, including the problem of preventing thread breakage when weaving wool on the powerloom, the result of spinning woollen yarn much more softly than other types of yarn.[38]

The second consideration is that relatively small firms predominated in the mid-nineteenth century cotton trade. According to V. A. C. Gatrell, there was no concentration of production in the industry during the early decades of the century[39] and R. Lloyd-Jones and A. Le Roux estimate that median firms in the spinning and weaving branches employed only 120 hands by the 1840s.[40] The latter also conclude that medium-sized firms were becoming more important at the expense of both large and small concerns. By 1841, the median numbers employed by Manchester cotton firms had reached 174, compared with 54 in 1815. Out of a total of 128 Manchester cotton firms in 1841, 37 (almost one in three) employed fewer than 100 people and 71 (above half) fewer than 200.[41] For Lancashire as a whole, 423 out of 975 firms (about two in five) had fewer than 100 employees and

680 (more than two-thirds) fewer than 200.[42] Small firms would not necessarily have been unprofitable, but their ranks may well have included numerous concerns which were not in a sound enough financial position to move into, or extend, their investment in powerlooms and which may therefore have been forced to maintain their interest in hand weaving. Thus, although the Lancashire hand weaving trades developed a putting out system similar to that of the Yorkshire worsted trades, they may have mechanised less rapidly because, in part at least, they remained characterised by relatively small-scale enterprise.

It is all too easy to assume, though, that small firms, including those owned by specialist handloom manufacturers, were barred from using powerlooms through financial constraints. As D. A. Farnie points out, entry costs into mechanised weaving could be minimised by renting both looms and power and by securing yarn on credit. Only a few hundred pounds would be needed to set up as a powerloom manufacturer.[43] Moreover, Gatrell maintains, credit was abundant to cotton producers of all sizes, at least during the 1820s and 1830s. He suggests, too, that opportunities were opening up for small firms to operate on commission work for larger concerns, especially in weaving.[44] Here, perhaps, was one potential source from which credit could be obtained to start or extend power weaving activity.

One more point about the financial well-being of cotton enterprises must be made. Whilst it has often been assumed that specialist handloom weaving concerns struggled to survive during the Victorian period, little in the way of supportive evidence has been adduced to demonstrate this was so. In those branches which were declining it might be thought many would have been, as Bythell suggests.[45] Yet not every Victorian handloom manufacturer was in dire economic straits, even if the maintenance of economic viability was becoming increasingly hard. Much hinged on the type of fabric woven and, therefore, on the acuteness of the competition from powerlooms and on whether any diversification could be achieved. Thus, Robert Heywood of Bolton, who was a cloth finisher as well as a handloom manufacturer specialising in fine quiltings, accumulated a fortune of £100,000 by the time he died in 1868.[46] Other mid-Victorian handloom manufacturers were also well placed financially, as is clearly indicated by evidence from census schedules, a theme covered in the next section.

That hand weaving concerns might transfer successfully to power weaving must not be overlooked. As in the case of William Feilden of Blackburn, some were leading firms which mechanised at an early stage.[47] More generally, J. S. Lyons argues, most new entrants to power weaving in the early decades of the nineteenth century were already combining spinning with hand weaving.[48] Other references are to specialist handloom manufacturers, some of whom did not take up power weaving until the 1840s or 1850s. Several have been identified in Blackburn, including John Abbot, who purchased Greenbank Mill in 1841 and James Pemberton, who bought King Street Mill in 1847. The financial sources they tapped are unclear, but both were long-established manufacturers and may not have resorted to external funding. Abbot's move appears to have been ill-timed and he soon failed. However, his successor Edward Briggs, another local handloom manufacturer, proved successful, adding a new weaving shed and converting the older buildings to spinning.[49] How frequently hand weavers themselves set up in power weaving is uncertain, though instances have been recorded.[50]

One final aspect of the discussion on the cost advantages manufacturers could secure from sticking with traditional technology must be mentioned. This is the contention that savings could be made on fixed capital expenditure during trade recessions, referred to by Lyons as the 'buffer' effect. By laying off hand weavers as the downturn intensified, they could hope to keep their powerlooms in use, earning at least enough to meet fixed capital costs. Lyons, though, doubts this was possible, citing the comments of Leonard Horner to show that numerous power weaving concerns were at a standstill or working short time in 1841.[51] How far firms could make savings in this way clearly depends on the extent of sales reduction; the balance they maintained between new and traditional techniques; and the type and quality of fabric they produced.

It remains to consider historians' comments as to how far hand weaving continued to thrive because of demand-side considerations. Unfortunately, such comments are few. Bythell's suggestion that periodic upsurges in general demand for woven goods would have been sufficiently strong to absorb hand weaving capacity and encourage powerloom installation has already been noted.[52] No doubt this was the case, as the severe shortage of hand weavers during the major trade upturn of the mid-1830s indicates.[53] Even so, the process clearly took longer to achieve than he envisages. At times of acute labour shortage, moreover, there was every incentive to draw on all available labour, domestic and factory alike.

It may also have been the case, as Maxine Berg has suggested, that some manufacturers used powerlooms to meet normal requirements and hired hand weavers to cope with exceptional demands.[54] These demands would not necessarily have provided sufficient encouragement to install additional powerlooms; nor would they have been confined to the more specialised fabrics. Accordingly, temporary opportunities would have been provided for 'reserve' hand weavers to produce the same grade of cloth as power weavers, even though the latter could do so far more efficiently. As well, where a manufacturer did become confident enough to extend powerloom capacity, he might still need the additional services of handloom weavers until his new machines were fully operational, if not longer. Where new premises were required to accommodate these extra machines, the hand weavers may have continued to find employment for a considerable time.

Of consumer preferences for hand-woven rather than machine-woven cloths, historians have been virtually silent. Bythell has mentioned that institutional demand for certain types of fabrics made by hand might endure because of customer conservatism.[55] As an example, the caddow (or knotted) counterpanes produced at Bolton can be cited. For technical reasons, these were never successfully woven on powerlooms and were much demanded by hospitals and workhouses, because of their strength and durability. A large-scale trade in caddows developed with Russia, but this was curtailed during the Crimean War.[56]

To summarise, it is quite apparent that historians have undertaken very little analysis of the reasons why hand weaving remained important in mid-Victorian Lancashire. This is partly because, as in the case of Duncan Bythell, they have sought to explain the demise of hand weaving rather than its survival. It is also because those who have recognised that large numbers of hand weavers were still to be found beyond the mid-nineteenth century, including S. J. Chapman and J. H. Clapham, were not dealing with the hand weaving trades in any depth.[57] Moreover, the one scholar who has approached the matter in detail, namely John Lyons, has taken a stance which has only been tested against a limited amount of empirical data. Accordingly, there is scope to undertake a more systematic analysis of the available evidence and, in so doing, to set the survival of hand weaving more firmly in the context of the major explanations about the survival of outwork generally in Victorian Britain.

## 2 New perspectives

This section begins with an analysis of how far the survival of hand weaving in mid-Victorian Lancashire can be atrributed to technical inadequacies of the powerloom. It is argued that this explanation has been underplayed, because the slowness with which the powerloom was developed has not been sufficiently emphasised. Nor have the advances in handloom weaving technology. These are unlikely to have had a profound effect in delaying mechanisation, but, at least as far as the dandy loom is concerned, they were not without significance.

Discussion on technological advance in power weaving during the mid-nineteenth century has centred on the achievements of Kenworthy and Bullough in the early 1840s. Some of the limitations of their improvements are noted above,[58] but further evidence can be adduced to demonstrate that, despite the significant progress they made, the powerloom left much to be desired in producing a range of fabrics.

To start with, the limited short-term impact of Kenworthy and Bullough's developments can be noted. In a press advertisement appearing in the spring of 1844, three years after their patent was secured, they claimed that over 12,000 looms had been fitted with their mechanisms.[59] Exactly how many powerlooms were to be found in the country at this time is unknown, though there were over 100,000 in the cotton trade alone during the mid-1830s.[60] Even conceding that Kenworthy and Bullough did not exaggerate, it is clear that their inventions had reached no more than a small minority of looms then in operation.

The impact on productivity achieved by the Kenworthy and Bullough techniques must also be questioned. It will be recalled that, according to Richard Marsden, their improvements meant that the powerloom became a perfect machine only in principal.[61] According to him, one loom per weaver had been common prior to their introduction and two the maximum. This is probably an exaggeration, however. During the mid-1830s, weavers at Grimshaw's shed at Barrowford nearly all worked two looms and a few three or four.[62] A decade later, Samuel Bamford found a similar situation in a weaving shed at High Crompton (near Oldham),[63] whilst in the mid-1850s, the diarist weaver, John O'Neil, operated three looms.[64] Nevertheless, there is much substance in Marsden's contention. As late as the mid-1870s, one commentator observed that although the weft stop motion and many minor parts of the powerloom had been improved to the point of becoming 'comparatively perfect', it was the opinion of 'many competent men' that the powerloom remained an imperfect machine and that considerable changes were still required before it could be used to full advantage.[65] Writing at the same time, another authority maintained that the richest and most delicate fabrics would probably always be woven on the handloom.[66]

Further backing for Marsden's view is evident from perusing abstracts of patent submissions relating to the powerloom.[67] Hundreds are to be found for the mid-Victorian years, giving credence to the idea that the variety and volume of patents concerning weaving were then more numerous than those relating to any other art.[68] In itself, this is testimony to the imperfections that still existed in the powerloom. Yet, contrary to the beliefs of their proposers, it is likely that most of these submissions were not of fundamental importance, at best being no more than alternative arrangements to those which were already operating in a reasonably effective manner. Others, though, were significant, and illustrate that, despite the major technological advances made, imperfections remained which delayed appreciably the universal application of power weaving.

Two examples may be cited. The first concerns a patent granted to Valentine, Foster and Haworth in October 1855. A report on the patent stated that fine or weak yarn was liable to break in powerlooms when, with the shed open, the weft was driven up by the reed against the finished cloth. The problem was that the tension of the warp threads varied as the healds were raised and lowered. The patentees introduced a device which took up the slack yarn when the shed closed and let it out again when the shed opened. As a result, the warp was always kept at the required tension and because the weft was more easily driven up, the friction on the yarn was reduced.[69]

This example reveals that the powerloom was still not economically viable with regard to fine or weak threads as late as the mid-1850s and perhaps beyond. Because thread breakages were still more frequent than with stronger yarns, the possibilities of using a reduced labour input per loom remained limited. Unfortunately, the types and strengths of threads to which the patentees referred was not given, but muslins and other light cottons would have been included. The same was true of silk and wool. In the early 1840s, both were seen as rather delicate for the powerloom, being subject to constant breakages. With wool weaving, for example, W. A. Miles, the assistant handloom commissioner for Gloucester, argued that a delicacy of blow was required which the powerloom did not possess. The warp threads had to be spun very carefully to avoid breakages, thereby adding to expense, and a warp of such quality could anyway have been woven as fast on the handloom.[70] As late as 1851, George White was writing that the fabrics to which the powerloom had been applied with most success included calicoes, heavy domestics, sheetings, shirtings, furniture cloth, and moleskins; all were cloths in the production of which there was little fear of yarn breakage. He stated, too, that the powerloom had not proved suitable in the heaviest work, such as sailcloth manufacture, where the yarn in the loom had to be rigid.[71]

The second example refers to a refinement of the weft stop motion. It was patented in August 1859, by W. Hollins and F. Hyde of Glossop. According to a report on their patent, once the weft fork stopped the loom when a broken thread was picked up, the momentum of the fly-wheel and other moving parts caused the loom to pick once or twice without any weft being entered. The cloth, however, would still be taken up, causing a 'thin place' in the weave. Their device was designed to disengage the loom before this could happen, thereby ensuring a cloth of even texture.[72]

Irrespective of the utility of such improvements, these examples make it plain that, through technical inadequacy, the mid-Victorian powerloom did not always have a marked economic advantage over the handloom. The main actions undertaken by the hand weaver had been mechanised, but the powerloom could not respond as flexibly or as quickly as the hand weaver in correcting faults that arose during weaving. Accordingly, the high quality of power woven cloth could not be guaranteed, as the cotton manufacturer H. S. Gibbs found to his cost,[73] and the product was not always superior to that of the handloom. The argument has less weight when applied to coarser, plainer fabrics, especially cottons and worsteds, which comprised the bulk of output. Yet it does help to explain why some types of cloth were slow to succumb to mechanised weaving.

To take this line of argument is not to ignore the inadequacies of cloths woven on the handloom. Much skill was demanded on the part of the handloom weaver to produce the highest-grade cloths and a considerable variation in quality would doubtless have arisen. Indeed, the correspondence of Robert Heywood, a quilting manufacturer from Bolton, reveals that the quality of his hand-woven cloths could leave a great deal to be desired. During the early 1850s, he was receiving complaints that some of the welts he was supplying to a London customer easily split. The problem, it was suggested, was that too fine a warp was being used.[74] In striving to produce a fabric which differed from those offered by his competitors, Heywood seems to have overlooked some of the constraints that arose in selecting appropriate thread and shedding combinations.

It is not only the shortcomings of the powerloom which feature in the technical aspects of the discussion on hand weaver survival. So, too, do improvements in handloom technology. The attention paid to the dandy loom in this respect has been pointed out, the suggestion being offered that its significance has been underplayed.[75] Thus, whilst Bythell states that dandy looms were still being installed

## The last shift

in Bolton during the early 1830s,[76] he does not mention the claim made by John Makin, a Bolton manufacturer, that this increase was large and that it was still taking place at least as late as 1834.[77] Nor does he note the testimony of a Preston weaver, Robert Crawford, that numbers of dandy looms had also risen considerably in his town during this period.[78]

Doubt must also be thrown on Bythell's assumption that the use of dandy looms was neither widespread nor long-lived. He provides evidence to show that they had been given up at Blackburn during the late 1830s, but that they continued to be used at Wigan in 1841.[79] Yet it is clear that they could still he found in various parts of the county during the mid-Victorian period. Thus, Jonathan and George Ramsbottom of Higher Booths, Rossendale, were paying rates on a warehouse and dandy shop as late as 1849,[80] whilst a group of about twenty dandy weavers was recorded in the 1851 census returns for Chorley.[81] In 1851, George White observed that the dandy loom was still 'a good deal used in the factory system'.[82] Even as late as 1868, a weaving shop at Kirkham, which contained twenty-six dandy looms, was being auctioned as a going concern. Equipment on offer included new shuttles for handlooms.[83]

That the dandy loom was installed in workshops rather than domestic premises has often been remarked upon. Accordingly, it is quite possible that references to looms in hand weavers' workshops were to dandy looms, as in the case of the weaving shop established at Mellor, near Blackburn during the mid-1850s.[84] Furthermore, dandy looms wove coarser grades of cloth, so their continued use would have provided one way by which cloths that could be woven on the powerloom remained as hand-produced items.

Evidence that other improvements in the handloom served to stave off the adoption of the powerloom is hard to unearth. Some success seems to have been achieved with looms weaving double-width cloths, though it is unlikely they were widely used.[85] There is also evidence of individuals attempting to improve handlooms, including, as late as 1860, Benjamin Croasdale, a tackler, and William Harling, a machine joiner, both of Blackburn. They built a working model of their loom for display, but no details survive of the improvements they made. Extravagant claims were, none the less, made on their behalf, including the calculation that, with the assistance of one boy, a hand weaver using their system might work four looms.[86]

To summarise, technological considerations had a major impact on the rate at which powerlooms were installed in Lancashire mills, especially in those parts of the county that specialised in fine and fancy cottons and in non-cottons. Only gradually were manufacturers convinced that the powerloom was an economic proposition in the manufacture of such fabrics. However, the force of this argument must not be overstated. It is by no means certain that cheap, lower-grade cottons did not continue to be woven on the handloom beyond mid-century. And even if the handloom had become confined to the production of high-quality goods, it does not necessarily follow that manufacturers would be quick to adopt mechanisation once this became an economic proposition. Other influences were also at work.

Amongst them must be counted the availability of a hand weaving labour force which was relatively cheap, plentiful and responsive. It is suggested in Chapter 5 that this is an important consideration, since hand weaver numbers remained significant in mid-Victorian Lancashire, especially in rural areas. What is required, however, is a closer analysis of why this was so.

Explanations offered by historians include the difficulties hand weavers experienced in switching to factory work, a view not always shared by contemporaries. For example, James Thomson, a calico printer from the Clitheroe area, found work for many of them as dyers, washers and labourers.[87] Similarly, W. R. Greg, the leading cotton spinner and manufacturer, hired some to work as power weavers, a practice also known to the Bolton handloom weavers, Richard Needham and William Pilling.[88] And John O'Neil, the diarist hand weaver, obtained work as a linen power weaver aged forty-four.[89] Yet the overall impression left by contemporaries supports Lyons' contention that the majority of hand weavers were unable to obtain factory jobs. John Lennon, a Preston hand weaver, reckoned no more than one in six were able to do so,[90] whilst John Fielden, the Todmorden factory master, refused numerous applications from hand weavers seeking jobs in his factories.[91] Taking a more general line, the economist and mathematician, Charles Babbage, observed that those hand workers who became redundant were not always qualified to take up the new, machine-orientated labour and that considerable time would elapse 'before the whole of their labour' was wanted.[92] Again, Andrew Ure, the factory advocate, declared that it was nearly impossible to convert persons past the age of puberty into factory hands.[93] Further weight was added to such views by Peter Gaskell, the Manchester surgeon, and Richard Muggeridge, the assistant hand weavers' commissioner. The former observed that the question was often raised as to why domestic workers did not become the first to weave on steam-looms or to find other factory jobs,[94] whilst the latter asserted that, for adult male weavers, powerloom factories did not 'furnish an adequate extent of employment to them which it deprives them of'.[95]

If, as contemporary opinion implies, millowners were often reluctant to find jobs for hand weavers, what were their reasons? Did they fear, perhaps, that it would prove extremely difficult to retrain people who were unaccustomed to the demands of factory work, especially those of more mature years? How strong is the evidence, in fact, to suggest that age did matter in this respect? And what of other considerations, not least the opposition that factory workers may have voiced to their ranks being swelled by former hand weavers? Did the former see the latter as serious competitors for factory jobs?

That employers did regard age as an important factor in recruiting power weavers is confirmed both by contemporary comment and by census evidence. Amongst the former is the testimony of John Marshall, the Leeds flax magnate, who, responding to a question about the likelihood of hand weavers obtaining jobs in textile mills, remarked: 'the young people can but the older people cannot . . .'.[96] W. R. Greg broadly agreed, though he thought that the transfer from hand to power weaving was not confined to the young, those aged twenty-five to forty making the best weavers.[97] Peter Gaskell wrote in similar vein, but exaggerated his case by maintaining that steam-loom manufacturers depended solely on young women and girls.[98]

With regard to census evidence, it transpires that mid-Victorian enumerators listed comparatively few power weavers above the age of forty, the great majority being in their teens and twenties.[99] Moreover, it is doubtful that the older power weavers were new or recent entrants to the trade. In all probability, they were recruited as young people and sustained their ability to work effectively at the powerloom for a longer period than was usual. For this reason, greater numbers of middle-aged power weavers can be anticipated with each successive census. It may also be mentioned that of thirty-nine former hand weavers who can be traced in the 1861 census returns for Brindle, near Preston, the three men and two women who became power weavers were all aged thirty or under. Such evidence is hardly conclusive, but it is consistent with the notion that only young hand weavers normally found work at the powerloom.

As a rule, then, adult hand weavers, especially those who had reached middle age, did find difficulty in obtaining factory work. Faced with the choice of hiring either young, inexpensive and adaptable people who, it might be reasonably expected, had a long working life before them, or those in middle age, who would demand adult wages and who might hold fixed attitudes to working practices, the employers' course was clear. Perhaps the choice was often less stark than this, but it is hard to conceive that the factory owner would normally have been more favourably disposed towards the older person than the younger. Only when labour shortages became acute, as during major trade cycle peaks, would his attitude have softened.

However, it was not merely on grounds of age that factory employment was hard to secure. Needham and Pilling, the Bolton hand weavers, and Richard Marsden, the hand weaver and Chartist leader, asserted that workers in certain trades operated a closed shop against hand weavers' children. Further, should a master take a hand weaver's child as apprentice, his workforce would turn out against him.[100] Behind this action was the desire of factory workers to secure jobs for their own children, an expression, perhaps, of the importance they attached to maintaining kinship links.[101]

It is quite possible, though, that these observers overstated their argument, since there is nothing to suggest that their comments were based on anything more than a limited number of instances with which they were familiar. In as far as pressure was exerted in this way, however, it would doubtless have been pursued with greater vigour during trade recessions when jobs were scarce. Conversely, following major upturns in the economy, the ability of family working groups to meet labour shortages may have proved woefully inadequate, so that hand weavers' children would have been accepted as factory workers with far less hostility than was customary. Maybe this helps to explain why they were often recorded as having factory jobs in the mid-nineteenth century censuses.[102]

The question must also be raised as to whether any discrimination against the employment of handloom weavers' children in factories had a racial dimension. As is well known, growing numbers of Irish in Lancashire's textile towns during the mid-Victorian years helped to fuel social tension, especially when trade was slack.[103] Yet, as Bythell has shown, it is easy to overstate the importance of the Irish as an element in the handloom weaving labour force. In every cotton town except Manchester, they did not form more than a small proportion of the population and they were even less evident in rural districts.[104] Examination of the 1851 census returns from several country areas around Blackburn shows few people of Irish origin and none in hand weaving, despite the importance of the trade in the local economy. Nevertheless, immigrant status would scarcely have helped families to obtain factory work and, from time to time, must have acted as a positive hindrance, even if relatively few were affected.

There is also a further dimension to the question. It concerns the extent to which hand weavers obtained jobs other than in textile factories, a task which, according to Lyons, adults amongst them found 'rather difficult'. As far as contemporaries are concerned, opinions differ over the matter. George Smith, the Manchester cotton master, reckoned that they could not generally do so,[105] an opinion shared by Needham and Pilling.[106] Conversely, the Stockport weaver William Longson, thought that many in his area did turn to 'various other employments'.[107] John Lennon from Preston noted that hand weavers could find agricultural work during the summer months, but had to return to the handloom in winter. He, too, thought they did not find it easy to obtain new employment on a permanent basis.[108] There is also the point that available alternatives might be shunned. Thus, Joseph Fletcher, the assistant hand weavers' commissioner for the Midlands, maintained that female hand weavers were most reluctant to enter domestic service, a comment he might with equal conviction have made of young females in general. So strongly were they attracted to the 'freedom of control' which accompanied domestic labour, that recruitment of good domestic servants was difficult to achieve.[109]

Despite the pessimism of these comments, it is clear that non-textile jobs were found by hand weavers, as the Brindle census schedules confirm. They demonstrate that various opportunities were open to former hand weavers and not merely to the youthful ones. For instance, between 1851 and 1861, three of the more elderly became small-scale farmers, with holdings ranging in size from three to ten acres. Amongst other non-textile jobs they obtained were railway platelayer and labourer; clogger; house servant; painter; stone quarrier; and farm labourer. Such evidence lends weight to Bythell's conclusion that, according to aptitude and ability, former hand weavers might enter any of a whole range of occupations. How frequently they did so, however, is uncertain. Known examples are very few and quite insufficient to allow any meaningful generalisation about numbers that were likely to have found particular types of jobs. Only through detailed local investigation using census schedule and parish register evidence will a clearer picture emerge.

One consideration to arise from this analysis is the possibility that rural hand weavers encountered greater difficulty than their urban counterparts, and were less successful, in securing replacement jobs. In mid-Victorian Lancashire, the contrast between the rapid growth of towns and the stagnation of rural settlements could be stark, reflecting distinct variations in economic growth rates and hence in the development of alternative employment. This is clearly illustrated by A. J. Taylor's research. Using factory return figures, he shows that between 1838 and 1850, the horse-power generated by Lancashire's water-powered cotton mills, most of which were in rural districts, diminished by 5 per cent, whilst that available in steam-driven mills, which were mainly in towns, rose by more than 50 per cent.[110] It might be added that whilst population growth was widespread throughout rural Lancashire during the first two or three decades of the nineteen century, the reverse was true during the early and mid-Victorian years.[111]

Of course, not all rural districts which depended heavily on hand weaving failed to develop new industries. Those in more accessible locations, perhaps situated on the outskirts of major towns and possessing good communications, might acquire a number of steam-driven textile factories, as well as intensifying their interests in other types of manufacturing and in extractive industry. Labour availability in declining hand weavers' colonies would have proved attractive to entrepreneurs, at least as far as juveniles were concerned. Yet caveats must be entered. In the first place, many rural settlements, especially those in the northern parts of the textile districts, either did not acquire alternative industry, or, where they did, new jobs becoming available proved insufficient for replacement needs. Secondly, substitute industry did not always appear until hand weaving was in an advanced state of decay. Lastly, new jobs may have been mainly for young people, even in the non-textile sector. This may have been more pronounced with regard to women, a number of those at Brindle continuing to weave during the early years of marriage, but becoming housewives in their thirties and forties. However, whether they did so through choice or through necessity is uncertain.

The impact of limited rural development in textile Lancashire during the mid-Victorian years was probably exacerbated through a measure of geographical immobility on the part of hand weavers. It was certainly a problem that vexed the relieving officer of the Chorlton Poor Law Union, who, having failed to convince local hand weavers about the benefits of moving, was driven to complain

> the handloom weavers who live in the out districts seem to expect the trade to go to them; I have urged upon people repeatedly, and offered to find them a house if they would follow me to Manchester, that I would undertake to find them subsistence, but they prefer staying eight or nine miles off.[112]

Not all handloom weavers were as unwilling to move as those at Chorlton; the steady decline of many rural populations in the weaving districts during the mid-Victorian period provides ample testimony to this. Much would have depended, though, on whether they could obtain employment elsewhere; whether they were willing to sever established social links; and whether they regarded alternative environments, especially those in towns, as at all palatable. The safety net of out relief, frequently granted in mid-Victorian Lancashire, despite the best endeavours of those who framed the 1834 Poor Law Amendment Act, may also have encouraged some immobility, as would the private relief funds generated during major trade depressions. There are occasional census references to handloom weavers receiving poor relief, including several elderly ones at Holcombe, near Bury, who each drew 1/6*d* per week at the time of the 1851 census,[113] rather less than the 2/- per week paid to Preston handloom weavers in the late 1830s.[114] It is known, too, that relief in aid of wages was commonly granted at Bolton, a major hand weaving centre, during the mid-1840s.[115] Such payments would scarcely have encouraged handloom weavers to move, the more so if they were elderly and if the payments they received were regular and sustained.

For rural hand weavers choosing not to move, there would often have been little option but to continue with their trade. Furthermore, it may not have been possible to find alternative work for their children in the locality. Several contemporaries drew attention to this, leading Richard Muggeridge, the assistant hand weavers' commissioner, to observe:

The weaving is so ill-requited, that no man, who has the opportunity of bringing up his child to any other trade, will put him to the weaving; most country weavers, however, still bring their children up to the loom, for lack of such opportunity of otherwise providing for them.[116]

Although Muggeridge wrote at the start of the 1840s, his argument would have still been applicable in the 1850s and 1860s. During these decades, as is shown in Chapter 5, rural children continued to become hand weavers and, in certain districts, they were surprisingly numerous. It is impossible to know how far family constraints prevented them from moving away to seek other employment. However, the comments of Muggeridge and others, which are couched in terms of fathers being responsible for choosing the type of job their children undertook, may be taken to imply that this was sometimes, perhaps often, the case.

To explore the theme in a little more detail, it is useful to apply Michael Anderson's notion of calculative and normative constraints. Following Anderson, it might be argued that normative considerations would have acted more powerfully on individual and group behaviour in traditional rural society than in emerging urban/industrial society, leading rural children to consider carefully their familial responsibilities and the hardships that might beset their parents should they leave home at an early age.[117] For instance, should they have felt that losses to family income arising from their departure would leave their immediate family in dire financial circumstances, they might have felt duty-bound to remain at home. Taking a calculative perspective, however, it might be argued that country hand weavers would be included amongst those parents who, because their earnings were meagre, would not have been able to exercise a strong enough influence over their offspring to prevent a move taking place.[118] Weight would be added to the argument if, as may often have happened, children could reasonably anticipate finding rewarding jobs elsewhere, the earnings from which would enable them to achieve a higher living standard than was possible by staying with their parents.

Gender considerations may have further complicated the issue. It might be proposed, for instance, that daughters from rural handloom weaving families would have been less likely to leave home at an early age than sons, if only for the calculative reason that, from the mid-teenage years, females received appreciably lower wages for factory work than males.[119] To test the idea, data on hand weavers' children aged 16 to 19 who still lived with their parents may be extracted from the 1851 census schedules. Thus, at Hoghton and Brindle, rural districts to the southeast of Preston, 138 such children can be identified, of whom a small majority, 56 per cent, were female. Possibly, therefore, girls from rural hand weaving families were only marginally more geographically immobile than boys.

In moving from country to town, or to new jobs in the same district, hand weavers had to consider possible losses that might arise to family income. The issue was aired by William Hickson in his 1840 report.

A mechanic employed in the manufacture of steam-engines has no use for the labour of his wife and daughter; but not so the weaver ... The wife and children of a weaver in most cases contribute very materially to their own support. This is one reason why a weaver will cling to his trade longer than prudence would appear to dictate. His own earnings may be 7s, but, with the assistance of his wife and children, that 7s may be made 21s. To give up his loom and take to day labour, would be therefore to place himself in an inferior position, unless other employment for his wife and children could be obtained.[120]

What is puzzling from Hickson's comments is the implication that wives and children would have been forced to give up handloom weaving once their husbands did so. In certain circumstances this may indeed have happened. For instance, with the father working full-time in another job, it may no longer have been possible for any member of the family to have collected thread from the manufacturer or to have returned finished cloth to him. Again, where wives and children alone were not in a position to undertake more than a minimal amount of hand weaving, or to achieve a satisfactory standard, difficulty may have been experienced in obtaining thread from the employer. But it is hard to know if situations of this nature were commonplace. Perhaps Hickson's argument is more telling when applied to those in the weaver's family who were solely engaged in ancillary tasks, principally winding. Should the most productive weaver in the family have vacated his or her loom, the situation could have arisen where ancillary workers were capable of producing more than the remaining weavers needed; a functional imbalance would have developed within the family working group. This would also have been so if the sole hand weaver in a household turned to another occupation. In the first case, the ancillary workers would at best become under-employed; in the second, they might well become unemployed.

The question remains, though, of how much would have been lost from family income through the reduced earning capacity of ancillary workers once the most productive hand weaver in a household ceased to operate. As far as winders were concerned, such losses would probably not have been great. Most were children or elderly people, who would hardly have generated a substantial proportion of family income. Even so, for families existing at or near subsistence level, earnings at the margin would have been vitally important and would not have been lightly forgone. Further, these earnings could have been available from an early age – perhaps before a child was of legal age for factory work – as well as from people who would otherwise have been beyond retirement age.[121] As far as part-time weavers were concerned, however, potential income losses may have been substantial. Compared with winders, their earning capacity would have been relatively high, perhaps sufficient to attain the three to one ratio suggested by Hickson. In such circumstances, the temptation to remain with hand weaving would have been strong. Indeed, assuming a reasonable degree of economic rationality prevailed, the hand weaver would not have been prepared to take alternative work unless he was confident that a net gain to family income would result.

To summarise this part of the discussion, it may be concluded that adult hand weavers who gave up their trade were often excluded from factory work on grounds of age and lack of adaptability. Not infrequently, however, they were able to find alternative work as an expanding economy continued to present new and varied opportunities. This was more difficult in rural than in urban areas, though Lancashire's country districts often developed replacement industries as hand weaving declined. Many rural handloom weaving families did move into areas where employment prospects were better, but many others stayed where they were and continued to depend solely or largely on handloom weaving. Those remaining in some rural districts had little option to do otherwise.

In analysing why hand weavers remained at their trade, it is necessary to examine not only the economic circumstances in which they found themselves, but also the attitudes they held to their work and way of life, as well as to the alternatives with which they were faced. It has been noted that these attitudes have been regarded as significant in explaining the reluctance of hand weavers to seek change, but that the available evidence has not been presented and discussed in any depth.[122]

Some of this evidence is first hand and is contained in comments made by witnesses called before the Parliamentary enquiries into hand weaving. As such, it is open to the charge that the opinions expressed were not representative of the general body of employees in the trade.[123] That no female or child witnesses were called may be seen as especially worrying in this respect. For the rest, reliance has to be made on the observations of those who met with hand weavers, either frequently, as in the case of their employers, or irregularly and perhaps fleetingly, as with the handloom weavers' commissioners. Again, there is concern about the reliability of such evidence, though it is informed by direct contact with weavers and must express the views of some of them.

The most considered and thorough contemporary analysis of handloom weavers' attitudes is provided by assistant commissioner Muggeridge. He toured the Lancashire weaving districts during the spring and summer of 1838, holding a succession of public meetings at which weavers and other interested parties submitted testimony.[124] These meetings took place in each of the main textile towns.

Muggeridge contended that hand weavers were keen to cling to their trade for three main reasons, despite enduring 'scanty and inadequate remuneration'. Firstly, more than most other groups of workers, the hand weaver enjoyed a high degree of freedom from external supervision; he was 'master of his own time, and sole guide of his actions', being free to 'play or idle, as feeling or inclination leads him'. Secondly, he could work as part of a family group, in which each member had a common interest; the 'fate of one being the fate of all, it is borne, be it harsh or otherwise, without repining'. Lastly, some hand weavers believed their trade would revive and 'the good old days' would again return.[125]

Reservations must be expressed about these comments, however. Foremost amongst them is Muggeridge's tendency to offer a rather fanciful interpretation of hand weavers' living and working conditions. It is unlikely, for example, that they would have taken quite such a positive view of their position vis-à-vis other workers, especially by the 1840s. Faced with the need to minimise income losses as piece rates fell, they would have been forced to work more intensively and, as far as market conditions allowed, more regularly, thereby curtailing the freedom they hitherto enjoyed. Indeed, references to the lengthy hours worked by handloom weavers during the 1830s and beyond are not difficult to find.[126] Moreover, there would have been many hand weavers, most notably, perhaps, married women with young children to look after, who would have failed to recognise themselves in Muggeridge's somewhat romanticised description. For them, the opportunity to escape at will from the daily round of work-related and domestic chores would have been greatly circumscribed, the more so during trade recessions when their earnings would have proved more vital than usual in maintaining family income levels.

This said, it would be wrong to dismiss Muggeridge's ideas out of hand. If he was guilty of exaggeration or even of wishful thinking, it does not follow that the arguments he expounded were without foundation, nor that the opinions he sought to portray were not sincerely held. Besides, other contemporaries advanced similar ideas. For example, Muggeridge's fellow commissioner, William Hickson, frowned on the irregular habits of the hand weaver. 'At any moment,' he declared, 'the domestic weaver can throw down his shuttle and convert the rest of the day into a holiday or busy himself with some more profitable task'.[127] Travers Twiss, Professor of Political Economy at Oxford, felt this practice to be nothing less than an evil and averred that it would never happen under the disciplined regime of the factory. Yet, he conceded, 'this liberty of excess has its charms for the domestic workman'.[128] It looks, too, as if freedom from day-to-day control could allow hand weavers considerable latitude regarding the time they took to complete an order. John Kingan, a Scottish muslin manufacturer, maintained that two or three months might be taken to weave a piece which, under contract terms, should have taken six weeks. The manufacturer would make little comment about the delay, whilst the extended time enabled the weaver to undertake additional work if opportunity arose.[129]

Muggeridge's attempts to explain why hand weavers remained at their looms despite earning extremely meagre wages were couched mainly in terms of the benefits that were thought to have arisen from domestic work. Other commentators, however, broached the topic from the point of view of the disadvantages which, they believed, beset factory employment and which, in consequence, deterred hand weavers from seeking such work both for themselves and their children. The most comprehensive statement of these views was provided by John Scott, a handloom weaver from Manchester. Understandably embittered by the death of his young son in a spinning-mill accident, he expressed unqualified opposition to children working in factories, a line he professed to have taken before the fatality occurred. His objections, though, extended beyond the risk of accidents to embrace general damage to factory children's health from exhaustion and from breathing impure air.[130] Furthermore, he urged, factory work posed a real threat to their morality.

They have to be in the factories from six in the morning to eight at night, consequently they have no means of instruction; and a parcel of boys congregated together cannot get any solid information, the natural inclination of the mind being bent to that which is evil instead of good; there is no good example shown them; they have no opportunity of receiving any education.

His comments are much in accord with those of Muggeridge concerning the value and desirability of family working groups, reflecting an ideal which transcended class boundaries. Essentially, both men adopted a traditionalist outlook, which did not hide their disquiet about the fundamental changes through which society was passing.

Parents suffering similar experiences to John Scott may have been equally reluctant to send their children into textile mills. Whether such people were numerous is doubtful, however, despite the frequency with which factory accidents occurred.[131] Scott apart, witnesses appearing before the hand weaving commissions made little of alleged threats to either health or morality. Nor, generally, was comment sought by the inquisitors, an indication in itself that the issues were not of paramount concern. Moreover, it is not hard to find handloom weaver parents whose children were working in textile mills at the time of the 1851 census. Maybe some of them still objected to factory work, but, albeit reluctantly, had come to recognise that their children's future no longer lay with hand weaving. Since child earnings could be vital in keeping working-class families above subsistence level, high-minded principle may have been increasingly sacrificed to the harsh dictates of economic necessity.

As to other concerns handloom weavers harboured about factory work, little evidence is available. There was brief mention by contemporaries that some hand weavers could not tolerate the noise in factory weaving sheds and that some found factory discipline irksome.[132] Feeling was also expressed that factory hours were long and that more leisure time could be taken under the domestic system.[133] Such issues were probably of greatest concern to those weavers who had already spent many years as domestic workers and who were too set in their ways to change fundamentally. Younger people, by contrast, may have been far more adaptable, a point that would not have been lost on employers.

Whilst it is plain from this discussion that concerns about the evils of factory work and the desirability of domestic work are of some account in explaining the longevity of hand weaving, evidence is far too thin to say how influential they were. Yet it is hard to see how they lack validity. In Lancashire, as elsewhere, hand weavers often maintained a traditional way of life, relying solely on domestic labour. The earnings they could achieve as family units gave them an adequate living and this enabled them to follow a lifestyle they preferred, rather than one which they found unfamiliar and distasteful.

The other supply factor influencing the survival of hand weaving may now be assessed. This is the issue of how far mid-Victorian handloom manufacturers were held back from transferring into mechanised weaving because they were unable to obtain the finance they required.

To begin with, it is necessary to identify firms which were likely to have been relying on handlooms rather than powerlooms at mid-century, in order to trace their progress in subsequent years. Trade directories form the main source of evidence and the numbers obtained for each district are given in Table 7.1.

Altogether 414 handloom manufacturers can be identified during 1851, Manchester excluded.[134] Most were weaving cottons, with muslins, ginghams and nankeens all receiving mention, along with counterpanes and quilts at Bolton. The most numerous non-cotton group was the woollen manufacturers at Rochdale and Bury, whilst mousseline-de-laine producers were well represented at Colne.

Having established these totals, individual firms may be traced through from one directory to the next in order to establish how many transferred to power weaving. As Table 7.1 shows, only a small minority, 42 (10 per cent), can be distinguished with reasonable certainty as having done so. Evidently, new entrants into power weaving were mostly drawn from other business sectors, as in the case of Robert Parkinson, John Anderton Alston and John Alston. The three became proprietors of a powerloom mill at Blackburn in 1854, working previously as draper, cotton spinner and bookkeeper respectively.[135] In fact, as is well established, J. A. Alston was following a path trodden by numerous cotton spinners before him, including such leading enterprises as the Ashworths of Egerton and the Gregs of Styal.[136]

Table 7.1  *Mid-Victorian handloom weaving manufacturers*

| District | 1851 total | Number changing to powerlooms |
|---|---|---|
| Ashton | 1 | – |
| Bacup | 2 | – |
| Blackburn | 28 | 2 |
| Bolton | 62 | 4 |
| Burnley | 7 | 2 |
| Bury | 30 | 4 |
| Chorley | 23 | 5 |
| Clitheroe | 2 | – |
| Colne | 31 | 4 |
| Darwen | 4 | 1 |
| Denton | 11 | – |
| Didsbury | 4 | – |
| Haslingden | 21 | 4 |
| Kirkham | 4 | – |
| Leigh | 18 | – |
| Leyland | 2 | – |
| Middleton | 6 | – |
| Newchurch | 17 | 1 |
| Ormskirk | 2 | – |
| Padiham | 4 | – |
| Preston | 15 | 1 |
| Radcliffe | 22 | 6 |
| Ramsbottom | 3 | – |
| Ribchester | 4 | – |
| Rochdale | 58 | 7 |
| Tyldesley | 1 | – |
| Whalley | 6 | – |
| Wigan | 23 | 1 |
| Worsley | 3 | – |
| Total | 414 | 42 |

That mid-Victorian handloom manufacturers seldom moved into power weaving may appear to lend support to the notion that they were usually small-scale, marginal concerns, unable to muster the finances required. All too often, it might be thought, they survived for relatively short periods, prospering modestly when trade was good, but, over the long term, generating insufficient reserves to cope with the leaner years. Faced with low, even diminishing product prices, they could only hope to enhance revenue by expanding sales volume. However, as the powerloom relentlessly encroached into the production of an ever-widening range of cloths, opportunities to do so would only have lessened. Indeed, the tendency for all handloom manufacturers, large as well as small, may have been to shed labour. But only the former could hope to adopt such a policy for any appreciable length of time. Handloom manufacturers such as William Parkinson of Livesey, near Blackburn, and William Dickinson of Little Bolton, who employed only six people between them in 1851, obviously had little to gain from this approach.[137]

To portray Lancashire's mid-Victorian handloom manufacturers in this way is to over-simplify greatly, however. In particular, it cannot be assumed that their failure to mechanise usually arose from an inability to raise adequate funds. Many were producing specialised, high-quality goods and remained prosperous concerns, with little need, or incentive, to change. They often lived in some affluence, occupying houses in the more fashionable parts of towns and making ample provision for themselves and their families. This did not, of course, apply in every case, not even, perhaps, in the majority, but the frequency with which it did is striking and has certainly escaped notice.

To support these contentions, handloom manufacturers residing at Bolton, Chorley and Blackburn may be considered. They comprised three of the most numerous groups of cotton manufacturers in Lancashire at mid-century, numbering over one hundred. Most were town based, but they included some in surrounding rural areas. All can be distinguished with reasonable certainty, especially at Chorley, where directory compilers consistently separated them from powerloom manufacturers. In some cases they can also be traced in census schedules, the entries occasionally giving employee numbers.

The indications are that few of the firms operated on a large-scale basis; employees were usually given in tens rather than hundreds. Amongst them were firms which disappeared relatively quickly, perhaps, as with Hugh Brody & Son of Bolton, because they were forced into bankruptcy, or, as with Jonathan Hitchen, also of Bolton, they were elderly men who wished to retire.[138] Some may also have left because they were in danger of becoming, or had already become, loss makers. Yet, in the early 1850s at least, many others remained profitable concerns, enabling their proprietors to obtain a fairly high standard of living. Thus, of the 45 households belonging to the group which can be traced in census schedules, 20 (44 per cent) contained at least one resident servant (some had two or three), a benefit available to only a small minority of Lancashire households. Again, the rateable values of their houses often exceeded the norm two- or three-fold, reflecting their large size and superior location. And they frequently provided well for their children, some finding employment in the family firm, perhaps as weavers or warpers, but also in sales or clerical work. Others were able to obtain a lengthy education, remaining at school well into their teenage years. As a rule, manufacturers' wives were not in paid employment and in several households, children of working age, usually daughters, were similarly placed, probably undertaking domestic duties. Without doubt, many mid-Victorian handloom manufacturers provided a comfortable existence for their families and gave them social and economic advantages which comparatively few would have enjoyed.

The prosperity of other handloom manufacturing concerns in mid-Victorian Lancashire is indicated by the scale upon which they operated. In 1851, for example, Henry Crook of Westhoughton employed 250 silk hand weavers, whilst at Freckleton in the southern Fylde, the Mayor Brothers' sailcloth and sack weavers exceeded 200.[139] At the same time, John Chadwick of Middleton, another silk manufacturer, was putting out to no less than 501 'outdoor' weavers, in addition to employing 103 people in other occupations,[140] and Samuel Catlow of Colne was finding work for 500 people weaving mousseline-de-laine.[141] Once more, these men lived in some style, all running households with at least one living-in servant. That they lacked the means to enter powerloom weaving had they so wished is hard to believe. There were also textile manufacturers with premises in several towns, again indicating quite large-scale operations, as well as a desire to absorb cheap labour. The two most prominent were Tootal, Broadhurst and Lee, who were at Bolton and Chorley during the early 1850s and Critchley, Armstrong and Company, who were at Bolton, Colne and Chorley.[142]

That inadequate finance did not necessarily prevent handloom manufacturers from mechanising is also indicated by the continuing involvement in the trade of combined spinning and weaving firms. Instances are not easy to identify, since there is uncertainty as to when these firms completed their transfer to mechanised production. Nevertheless, there are indications that, for some firms, this may not have been until well into the Victorian period, as in the case of Horrocks and Company of Preston.

During the late eighteenth and early nineteenth centuries, this concern developed an extensive putting-out system in the surrounding rural districts, with warehouses at several places, including Longridge, Ormskirk, Leyland, Kirkham and Hutton. Receipts were paid regularly from these warehouses, though the individual sums involved were less than those obtained from the firm's Preston warehouse. For example, in January 1832, receipts from Longridge amounted to £750; from Ormskirk £600; from Hutton £300; Leyland £560; and Kirkham £170. This compared with £1,503 from Preston.[143] Assuming these receipts related only, or very largely, to earnings from hand weaving, then Horrocks' interests in outwork had a strong urban dimension.

Horrocks' involvement in power weaving began in the mid-1820s. The capacity of their new weaving shed is unknown, but further installations of powerlooms took place during the 1830s, reaching a total of 764 by 1836.[144] In consequence, the hand weaving trade was run down, at least in the country areas. By the late 1830s, the firm retained only its Preston and Ormskirk warehouses, though it had opened a new one in Manchester.[145] However, as Lyons has shown, the firm did not cease hand weaving until the early 1850s.[146]

Another combined concern, that owned by John W. Dall of Samlesbury, near Preston, appears to have eschewed mechanised weaving altogether. Until the mid-1850s, when he ceased trading, Dall operated a water-powered spinning factory and put out to local hand weavers, employing 171 people in 1851.[147] Perhaps an anachronism amongst Lancashire's mid-Victorian cotton masters, he none the less made his business pay and lived in some style. In the early 1850s, he employed two resident female servants, one a cook and dairymaid, the other a housemaid. Moreover, the elder of his two sons had graduated from Trinity College, Dublin, and the younger was employed as a bookkeeper, probably by his father. Neither Dall's wife, nor his eighteen-year-old daughter, were in paid employment. Whether other country cotton firms continued to operate on a similar basis during the 1850s, and achieved such prosperity, is unknown, but Dall's case once more illustrates that those in the Lancashire textile trades who retained traditional means of production, might operate profitably to a surprisingly late period. Certainly water-powered mills could prove remarkably durable, reflecting, as in the case of the Gregs' mill at Styal, useful locational advantages, not least a cheap and regular source of power.[148]

The policy of transferring gradually into power weaving may not have been unusual prior to the major technological improvements made to the powerloom in the early 1840s. However, as manufacturers gained confidence in the technical efficiency of the powerloom, they may have become more willing to switch directly from the traditional technology. One instance of this was reported at Rochdale in 1842 by E. C. Tufnell, the Assistant Poor Law Commissioner. Following a visit to the Wuerdale and Wardle district, he wrote that a local textile manufacturer had recently built a steam-powered factory, to which he 'at once transferred ... production'.[149]

Whilst handloom manufacturers often remained soundly based in the early 1850s, the possibility arises that they eventually became loss makers and, as a result, were unable to transfer into more profitable activities. This may have been true, for example, of Richard Leeming of Ribchester, who employed only thirteen hand weavers in 1861 and does not appear to have enjoyed a particularly opulent lifestyle.[150] Age, too, was against him, for he was then in his late sixties. He, and others in a similar position, may have had neither the means nor the will to extend or modernise his business. His aim may simply have been to eke out a modest living and, if possible, to put at least something aside for retirement years.

Other handloom manufacturers did diversify successfully, however. For instance, William Marsden of Longridge not only moved into power weaving, but also into linen drapery and groceries. By 1861, he was employing his wife as a shop worker, as well as a shop assistant who lived in and a house servant.[151] Again, Kenneth McKenzie of Chorley, a manufacturer of fancy ginghams in 1851, had become a solicitor's clerk by 1861. Although no longer an employer, his household remained prosperous, depending on his income and that of his sister and aunt who both taught. They maintained one resident servant.[152] Lastly, John Cairns of Chorley, who employed 110 muslin hand weavers in 1851,[153] began a comfortable retirement at his fashionable Park Road residence. In 1861, his private income supported his four unmarried daughters and he, too, continued to employ a servant.[154]

The type of strategy handloom manufacturers could employ when moving into power weaving can be illustrated in the cases of James Grime of Over Darwen and James Fisher of Blackburn. The former economised on fixed capital expenditure by equipping three house cellars (perhaps built for hand weaving) as a power weaving shop.[155] His may have been a cottage factory similar to those identified in Coventry by J. Prest.[156] The latter took over Daisyfield and Plantation Mills at Blackburn during the mid-1840s as a mortgagee. The sum he advanced to the proprietors is not disclosed, though quite sizeable amounts would have been involved to make the conveyance worthwhile from the point of view of the mortgagors. Indeed, in another instance of this practice, that of the Alstons and Parkinson in 1854, the mortgage advance was no less than £2,000.[157] So here is a further indication that handloom manufacturers in mid-Victorian Lancashire continued to prosper.

As a final point, it should be noted that entrepreneurs still felt confident enough to enter Lancashire's hand weaving trades during the mid-Victorian years. This is well exemplified in the case of Blackburn. Five are given in the 1871 directory list for the town, none of whom were recorded in 1851.[158] No doubt there were those whose confidence was misplaced, but that the industry continued to attract risk capital strongly implies that profits were there to be earned. And even as late as 1881, they were still to be found in census schedule entries, including Joseph Whittaker and Martin Margerison of Ribchester. The former lived with his wife and eight children, the two eldest daughters being dressmakers, the elder son a joiner and one of the younger daughters a pupil teacher. As in earlier years, good provision could be made for children. The latter, aged only forty-one, was described as a muslin manufacturer employing twenty hand weavers.[159]

It is plain, then, that the argument linking failure to mechanise weaving with inadequate investment funds cannot be taken too far. To portray Lancashire's mid-nineteenth century handloom manufacturers solely as a group of small-scale, impoverished employers is an exaggeration. The reality is that although comparatively few switched to mechanised production and although their ranks did contain many marginal concerns (some making only an ephemeral appearance) many, perhaps most, remained soundly-based enterprises, able to compete effectively with powerloom manufacturers. If their profitability was eroded as the powerloom grew to prominence, it is by no means evident that they chose to remain with hand weaving because they could not afford to do otherwise. Moreover, those that did make the transition including Horrocks of Preston, did not necessarily do so at a single step. Instead, they might prefer to retain at least some handloom weavers, and may have done so for a considerable period of time.

It remains to assess what impact demand-side influences had on the survival of Lancashire's handloom weavers. Of course, a considerable, though diminishing, quantity of hand-woven goods continued to be purchased during the middle decades of the nineteenth century, but it is impossible to know how far this reflected a lack of satisfactory alternatives rather than a declared customer preference for hand-woven products.

There are indications, however, that manufacturers may have wished to continue with the production of hand-woven goods because of the nature of demand in the markets they served. At the root of this issue lie the sharp fluctuations in demand for woven goods. These could arise across a range of products for a limited period of time, reflecting general variations in economic activity. They could also occur for particular products as the fickle dictates of fashion changed consumer preference swiftly from one type of fabric to another. In these circumstances, the manufacturer was often confronted with the situation where the demand for his products was likely to be limited and where expenditure on additional capacity in the form of powerlooms seemed highly risky in relation to anticipated revenue. This was the more so with high-quality fine and fancy goods, in the production of which the powerloom may still have been regarded as relatively inefficient. For coarser, plainer goods such as cotton sheetings and shirtings, a much larger and enduring demand could be anticipated, so that investment in powerlooms could be more easily justified. It is no surprise, therefore, to find that William Bashall of Farington, near Preston, who probably specialised in the production and distribution of shirtings, owned over 300 powerlooms as early as the mid-1830s.[160]

Some contemporary comment is available on these matters. For instance, William Hickson, the assistant hand weavers' commissioner, argued that handlooms would always continue to exist, because the demand for some fabrics was so limited and uncertain that it would never pay to 'erect complicated and costly machinery'.[161] Again, a Macclesfield silk hand weaver with whom the journalist Angus Reach conversed in 1849 declared that a great deal depended on fashion and because fashions altered so much, it was difficult 'either for master or men to suit the market'. He went on to stress the sudden changes in taste that could occur for fancy articles. Thus, a manufacturer might give out orders to weavers for goods of a certain pattern. By the time these were finished, consumer taste could have altered, leaving the manufacturer with a good deal of unsold stock. As a result, manufacturers were reluctant to place large orders, so that work available to hand weavers could fluctuate appreciably.[162]

Indications of similar marketing problems at the level of the individual firm are evident in the records of Robert Heywood, the Bolton quilting manufacturer. He was weaving higher-grade cloths and, taking into account various combinations of fineness, pattern and colour, his product range was enormous. His was also a fashion trade and it is evident from business correspondence with his customers that he relied greatly on market intelligence with which they supplied him. For instance, in 1846, one of his London buyers, John Goodman, sent samples of coloured checks and stripes which were much in demand. Goodman was unable to obtain the supplies he required, being 'fairly ashamed to see my customers they are so pressing for them'.[163] At the same time, Messrs Harrison and Son, also London buyers, were sending samples of white quiltings of a quality and pattern which, they maintained, Heywood had never produced.[164] What is clear is that Heywood manufactured non-standard cloths, the production runs of which were often limited. For this reason, if for no other, it would not have paid him to have employed powerlooms across his entire product range.

It must also be noted that market uncertainties continued to arise from fluctuations in business activity and that these might remain a deterrent to manufacturers from developing their interests in power weaving. This was the more so since a sizeable body of hand weavers could still be found. During major upturns in trade, demand may have risen sufficiently to outstrip the available powerloom capacity, so that more reliance would have to be placed on traditional technology. This was the case, for example, during the mid-1840s, when local newspapers carried reports on the general rise in demand for cloths which could not be met by existing capacity. In Manchester, both wholesalers and drapers were buying extensively, urged on by their belief that the harvest would be 'propitious'.[165]

More minor rises in demand could also benefit handloom weavers, at least on a local level. For instance, following depressed trade in 1855, a revival occurred during the following year, leading the *Blackburn Standard* to comment that hand weavers were weekly more in demand and that they were being remuneratively paid for their labour. It was at this time, indeed, that the old workhouse at Mellor was fitted out as a hand weaving shop.[166] There is even one instance reported of a revival taking place during a general depression in the cotton trade. This was at Preston in 1847, when handloom weaving was said to be uncommonly brisk.[167]

Inevitably, these improvements in demand brought only temporary respite to the hand weavers, but there can be little doubt that they were influential in delaying the rate at which their trade declined. Perhaps, too, they helped to encourage amongst hand weavers the belief to which Muggeridge alluded regarding the restoration of the former prosperity of their trade.[168]

As to precisely which markets continued to generate a demand for hand woven products, very little can be said. Only occasional references can be found in the contemporary literature and they are insufficient to enable anything more than a sketchy analysis. What does seem reasonably certain, however, is that the mid-Victorian hand weaving trades benefited appreciably from the demand for luxury items. For example, the fancy quiltings and welts supplied by Robert Heywood were used for gentlemen's waistcoats,[169] whilst Reach's Macclesfield weaver was making cloth for silk handkerchiefs.[170] It is also likely that such cloths as mousse-line-de-laine, widely woven on handlooms in north-east Lancashire, were destined for luxury products, in this case ladies' dresses.[171]

There is no way of judging the balance between home and overseas sales of hand-woven goods in the mid-Victorian years. However, some insights can be obtained into the destination of exports. Thus, as far as hand-woven muslins were concerned, Richard Marsden maintains that the sole remaining market was in the western states of America and in Canada, but that this trade was terminated during the Civil War.[172] It is also known that Robert Heywood's quiltings were being sold abroad, if not always with success. In 1851, he received a letter from Bates, Jamieson and Company of Mexico, regretting that they had only been able to dispose of one case of quiltings which had been received three years previously. They laid the blame squarely on the local preference for cheaper goods, which in any case attracted a lower import duty.[173] It may be noted in passing that Robert Heywood travelled extensively abroad, but that he seems to have viewed his trips as pleasure rather than business activities.[174] In this respect he may have belonged to that much-maligned group of entrepreneurs who stand accused of failing to exploit their overseas opportunities to the maximum extent.

It may be concluded, therefore, that whilst markets continued to be found for hand-woven goods during the mid-Victorian years, it is uncertain as to how far this arose through consumer preference. However, that the powerloom only gradually became an economic proposition in weaving all but the coarser and plainer grades of cotton suggests that, for quite a range of cloths, the consumer was not given the choice between the hand and the machine-made article. As the new technology became increasingly capable of weaving economically the finer and fancier cottons, as well as the non-cottons, it was not always the case that manufacturers were quick to respond. Only in a limited number of cases was this due to financial constraints; of far greater importance was the continued availability of a cheap and responsive labour force. This was the product of both geographical and occupational immobility, which in turn was influenced by the difficulties handloom weavers experienced in obtaining factory employment and by the positive attitudes they continued to hold towards domestic work, despite the poor remuneration it so often yielded.

## Notes

1   R. Guest, *A Compendious History of the Cotton Manufacture* (1968 reprint of 1823 edition), p. 46.

2   E. Baines, *History of the Cotton Manufacture in Great Briatin* (1966 reprint of 1835 edition), p. 240.

3   M. Blaug, 'The productivity of capital in the Lancashire cotton industry during the nineteenth century', *EcHR*, XIII (1961), pp. 365–6.

4   G. H. Wood, *The History of Wages in the Cotton Trade during the Past Hundred Years* (1910), p. 30.

5   J. Montgomery, *Cotton Manufacture of the United States of America* (1969 reprint of 1840 edition), p. 107.

6   *PP*, 1834 (556) X, QQ.5,728 and 6,748. Quoted in G. N. von Tunzelmann, *Steam Power and British Industrialization to 1860* (1978), p. 196.

7  *Ibid.*, pp. 198–9.
8  *Ibid.*, p. 202.
9  J. S. Lyons, 'Powerloom profitability and steam power costs', *EEH*, 24 (1987), pp. 397–400.
10  *Ibid.*, pp. 401–3.
11  R. Marsden, *Cotton Weaving: Its Development, Principles, and Practice* (1895), p. 95.
12  D. A. Farnie, *The English Cotton Industry and the World Market, 1815–1896* (1979), p. 282.
13  Marsden, *op. cit.*, p. 97.
14  See p. 232.
15  S. R. H. Jones, 'Technology, transaction costs, and the transition to factory production in the British silk industry, 1700–1870', *JEH*, XLVII (1987), p. 94.
16  H. J. Habakkuk, *American and British Technology in the Nineteenth Century* (1962), p. 147.
17  *Ibid.*, p. 149.
18  E. P. Thompson, *The Making of the English Working Class* (1963), p. 309.
19  D. Bythell, *The Handloom Weavers* (1969), p. 117; J. H. Lyons, *The Lancashire Cotton Industry and the Introduction of the Powerloom, 1815–1850* (unpublished PhD thesis, 1977), p. 13.
20  Bythell, *op. cit.*, p. 81.
21  I. Pinchbeck, *Women Workers and the Industrial Revolution* (1930), p. 179.
22  J. S. Lyons, 'Technological dualism, rivalry, and complementarity: handicrafts in the transition to modern industry' (forthcoming), esp. pp. 12–15.
23  M. Sanderson, 'Social change and elementary education in industrial Lancashire, 1780–1840', *Northern History*, III (1968), p. 139.
24  Pinchbeck, *op. cit.*, p. 182.
25  Bythell, *op. cit.*, p. 84.
26  See pp. 159–60.
27  *PP*, 1840 (639) XXIV, pp. 592–600.
28  J. F. C. Harrison, *The Early Victorians, 1832–51* (1971), p. 29.
29  Thompson, *op. cit.*, pp. 337–9. See also, P. Mathias, *The First Industrial Nation* (1969), p. 207 and M. Thomis, *The Town Labourer and the Industrial Revolution* (1974), p. 91.
30  J. S. Lyons, *The Lancashire Cotton Industry and the Introduction of the Powerloom, 1815–1850* (unpublished PhD thesis, 1977), p. 45.
31  *Ibid.*, p. 26.
32  Baines, *op. cit.*, p. 509; Montgomery, *op. cit.*, p. 210; M. Berg, *The Introduction and Diffusion of the Power Loom, 1780–1842* (MA thesis, 1972), pp. 24–5; Lyons, *op. cit.*, p. 219.
33  Bythell, *op. cit.*, pp. 120–1.
34  *Ibid.*, p. 80.
35  With reference to outwork generally, Bythell suggests there was a constant turnover of women. They entered and left the labour force as personal circumstances dictated (D. Bythell, *The Sweated Trades*, 1978), p. 166.
36  V. A. C. Gatrell, 'Labour, power, and the size of firms in Lancashire cotton in the second quarter of the nineteenth century', *EcHR*, 30 (1977), p. 103.
37  P. Hudson, 'Proto-industrialisation: the case of the West Riding wool textile industry in the 18th and early 19th centuries', *HWJ*, 12 (1981), pp. 46–52.

38  Ibid., p. 46. See also D. T. Jenkins and K. G. Ponting, *The British Wool Textile Industry, 1770–1914* (1982), p. 113.
39  Gatrell, *op. cit.*, pp. 96–102.
40  R. Lloyd-Jones and A. A. Le Roux, 'The size of firms in the cotton industry: Manchester, 1815–41', *EcHR*, 33 (1980), p. 74 (footnote 2).
41  Ibid., pp. 74–5.
42  Gatrell, *op. cit.*, p. 98.
43  Farnie, *op. cit.*, pp. 284–5.
44  Gatrell, *op. cit.*, pp. 104–5.
45  Bythell, *op. cit.*, p. 80.
46  W. E. Brown, *Robert Heywood of Bolton, 1786–1868* (1970) p. 63.
47  R. D. S. Wilson, *The Feildens of Witton Park* (n.d.), p. 14; B. Lewis, *Life in a Cotton Town: Blackburn, 1818–48* (1985), pp. 5–6.
48  J. S. Lyons, 'Vertical integration in the British cotton industry 1825–50: a revision', *JEH*, XLV (1985), pp. 420–2.
49  M. Rothwell, *Industrial Heritage: A Guide to the Industrial Archaeology of Blackburn*, 1 (1985), pp. 19 and 21.
50  D. Bythell, 'From handloom to powerloom: corporation and co-operation in the English cotton industry in the mid-nineteenth century', *Proceedings of the VIII Congres International D'Historie Economique* (1982).
51  J. S. Lyons, 'Technological dualism, rivalry, and complementarity: handicrafts in the transition to modern industry' (forthcoming).
52  See p. 8.
53  See pp. 94–5.
54  M. Berg, *The Machinery Question and the Making of Political Economy, 1815–1840* (1980), p. 229.
55  D. Bythell, *The Sweated Trades* (1978), p. 197.
56  W. P. Crankshaw, 'Famous Bolton cotton fabrics', *Supplement to the Textile Manufacturer* (June 1927), p. 37.
57  See p. 10.
58  See p. 149.
59  *BS*, 29.5.1844.
60  See p. 20.
61  See p. 149.
62  MCLA, Grimshaw's Wages Book, L1/16/3/7.
63  S. Bamford, *Walks in South Lancashire and on Its Borders* (1972 reprint of 1844 edition), p. 64.
64  M. Brigg, 'Life in East Lancashire, 1856–60: a newly-discovered diary of John O'Neill (John Ward) weaver of Clitheroe', *THSL&C*, 120 (1969), p. 101.
65  *Engineering*, 25.6.1875, p. 536.
66  *Ibid.*, 24.4.1874, p. 302.
67  They appear as a regular feature in the journal *The Engineer*, sometimes being assessed in appreciable detail.
68  *Engineering*, 25.6.1875, p. 536.
69  *The Engineer*, 18.7.1856, p. 380.
70  *PP*, 1840 (220) XXIV, pp. 434–6.
71  G. White, *A Practical Treatise on Weaving by Hand and Power Looms* (1851), p. 96.

72  *The Engineer*, 9.3.1860, p. 160.
73  H. S. Gibbs, *Autobiography of a Manchester Cotton Manufacturer* (1887), p. 69.
74  BAS, Heywood Correspondence, ZHE 47/2.
75  See p. 152.
76  Bythell, *op. cit.*, p. 84.
77  *PP*, 1834 (556) X, QQ.5,037 and 5,042.
78  *Ibid.*, Q.5,880.
79  Bythell, *op. cit.*, p. 84.
80  RRL, Higher Booths Rate Book, 1849.
81  Chorley Census Returns, 1851, EDs 1a, 1c and 11.
82  White, *op. cit.*, p. 129. It was used for coarse goods only.
83  *PG*, 10.10.1868. The shop belonged to Richard Baines, who was 'declining business'.
84  J. Bailey & Co. of Preston operated 160 handlooms as well as powerlooms on their premises in 1840 (*PP*, 1840, 639, XXIV, p. 8).
85  Bythell, *op. cit.*, p. 83.
86  *BS*, 31.10.1860.
87  *PP*, 1833 (690) VI, Q.3,976.
88  *Ibid.*, Q.11,364 and Q.11,837.
89  Brigg, *op. cit.*, pp. 87 and 97.
90  *PP*, 1834 (556) X, Q.6,416.
91  J. Fielden, *The Curse of the Factory System* (1969 reprint of 1836 edition), p. 68.
92  C. Babbage, *On the Economy of Machinery and Manufactures* (1832), p. 229.
93  A. Ure, *The Philosophy of Manufactures* (1967 reprint of 1835 edition), p. 15.
94  P. Gaskell, *Artisans and Machinery* (1968 reprint of 1836 edition), p. 35.
95  *PP*, 1840 (220) XXIV, p. 607.
96  *PP*, 1833 (690) VI, Q.2,411.
97  *Ibid.*, Q.11,366.
98  Gaskell, *op. cit.*, p. 36.
99  See p. 231.
100  *PP*, 1833 (690) VI, Q.11,790; J. E. King, *Richard Marsden and the Preston Chartists* (1981), p. 5.
101  For a discussion, see M. Anderson, *Family Structure in Nineteenth Century Lancashire* (1971), ch. 9.
102  See p. 133.
103  See, for example, J. Walton, *Lancashire, A Social History, 1558–1939* (1987), pp. 252–3.
104  Bythell, *op. cit.*, pp. 63–5.
105  *PP*, 1833 (690) VI, Q.9,465.
106  *Ibid.*, Q.11,794.
107  *PP*, 1834 (556) X, Q.6,744.
108  *Ibid.*, QQ.6,248–52.
109  *PP*, 1840 (220) XXIV, p. 71.
110  Taylor, *op. cit.*, p. 115.
111  This is evident in the decennial census figures summarised in W. Farrer and J. Brownbill (eds), *History of the County of Lancaster*, 2 (1908), pp. 331–48.
112  *PP*, 1843 (402) VII, Q.1,109. Quoted in Bythell, *op. cit.*, pp. 252–3.

113 Tottington LE Census Returns, 1851, ED 2D.

114 W. Proctor, 'Poor Law administration in Preston Union, 1838–1848', *THSL&C*, 117 (1966), p. 157. They were also given bedding and looms.

115 R. Boyson, 'The new Poor Law in north-east Lancashire', *THSL&C*, LXX (1960), pp. 41–3.

116 *PP*, 1840 (220) XXIV, p. 605.

117 Anderson, *op. cit.*, pp. 88–9.

118 *Ibid.*, pp. 92–6. Anderson's argument is conducted largely in the context of Lancashire's farming families being able to pay wages sufficient to keep offspring at home.

119 See p. 131.

120 *PP*, 1840 (639) XXIV, p. 12.

121 See pp. 117–18.

122 See p. 153.

123 For comment, see Bythell, *op. cit.*, p. 18 and 'The hand-loom weavers in the English cotton industry during the industrial revolution: some problems', *EcHR*, (1964). See also P. Richards, 'The state and early industrial capitalism: the case of the handloom weavers', *P&P*, 83 (1979), pp. 92–115.

124 *PP*, 1840 (220) XXIV, p. 577.

125 *Ibid.*, pp. 601–2.

126 For comment, see D. Bythell, *The Handloom Weavers* (1969), pp. 116–17.

127 *PP*, 1840 (220) XXIV, p. 648.

128 T. Twiss, Two Lectures on Machinery (1971 reprint of 1844 edition), p. 28.

129 *PP*, 1834 (556) X, Q.165.

130 *PP*, 1835 (341) XIII, QQ.2,637–48.

131 Richard Marsden, the hand weaver Chartist leader, was forced to send his daughters into factory work. One died from consumption, which he attributed to her long hours in the mill and her unhealthy working conditions (King, *op. cit.*, p. 39). Factory inspectors' reports provide accident statistics from the 1830s. Thus, for the half year to 30 April 1850, Leonard Horner noted as many as 888 accidents in the north of England, 6 of them fatal, 85 necessitating amputations and 128 causing fractures (*PP*, 1850, 1239, XXIII, p. 270). For numerous examples of accidents in Lancashire factories, see W. Dodd, *The Factory System Illustrated* (1968 reprint of 1842 edition).

132 See, for example, *PP*, 1834 (556) X, Q.5,473; 1835 (341) XIII, Q.2,103; and 1835 (500) XXXV, p. 298.

133 *PP*, 1840 (639) XXIV, p. 9.

134 There may have been some handloom manufacturers left in Manchester at mid-century, but the great majority listed in directories were country concerns with Manchester warehouses. For details of the problems involved in using trade directories to compute numbers of handloom manufactures, see J. G. Timmins, *The Decline of Handloom Weaving in Nineteenth Century Lancashire* (PhD thesis, University of Lancaster, 1990), Appendix B7.

135 BlMu, Mortgage Deed, Feilden Papers, 845.

136 R. Boyson, *The Ashworth Cotton Enterprise* (1970), pp. 59–60; M. B. Rose, *The Gregs of Styal* (1978), pp. 10–11. But is should be remembered that early Victorian powerloom manufacturers were drawn from a variety of backgrounds. See A. Howe, *The Cotton Masters, 1830–1860* (1984), p. 14.

137 Livesey Census Returns, 1851, ED 3d, schedule 40; Little Bolton Census Returns, 1851, ED 8, p. 5.

138  For Brody's bankruptcy see *BC*, 10.11.1855. Hitchen was seventy-eight years old in 1851 (Little Bolton Census Returns, 1851, ED 19, p. 15).
139  Westhoughton Census Returns, 1851, ED 1a, schedule 64; Freckleton Census Returns, 1851, ED 1a, schedule 41.
140  Middleton Census Returns, 1851, ED 1a, schedule 186.
141  Colne Census Returns, 1851, ED 4F, schedule 28.
142  *Slater's Directory* (1851), pp. 34, 50, 80 and 92.
143  LRO, Cash Book, DDHs, 18 (1).
144  LRO, Cost Book, DDHs, 75. This is confirmed by the 1835 Factory Inspectors' Returns (*PP*, 1836, XLV, p. 4).
145  LRO, Cash Book, DDHs, 18 (2).
146  J. S. Lyons, 'Family response to economic decline: handloom weavers in early nineteenth century Lancashire', *Research in Economic History*, 12 (1989), p. 76.
147  Samlesbury Census Returns, 1851, ED 8, schedule 1.
148  M. Rose, *The Gregs of Quarry Bank Mill* (1986), p. 144.
149  *PP*, 1842, XXXVa, p. 176.
150  Ribchester Census Returns, 1861, ED 5, p. 9.
151  Dilworth Census Returns, 1851, ED 8a, schedule 6 and 1861, ED 3, schedule 32. He built a mill at Longridge in 1851. Arriving in the village in 1832, he put out to local hand weavers on behalf of Horrocks & Co. of Preston. See T. C. Smith, *A History of Longridge and District* (1888), p. 105.
152  Chorley Census Returns, 1851, ED 1c, schedule 81; and 1861, ED 2, schedule 197.
153  Chorley Census Returns, 1851, ED 1a, schedule 35.
154  Chorley Census Returns, 1861, ED 2, schedule 39.
155  BIRL, Manchester Fire & Life Company Policies, 1, no. 29,568.
156  J. Prest, *The Industrial Revolution in Coventry* (1960), ch. 6.
157  BlMu, Mortgage Deed, Feilden Papers, 845.
158  *Slater's Directory* (1871), p. 60.
159  Ribchester Census Returns, 1881, ED 5, p. 4 and ED 6, p. 1.
160  LRO, Stock Account, DDX 819/1. The firm may have owned more powerlooms than this. The stock-taking reference is to 315 pieces of cloth in the loom.
161  *PP*, 1840 (639) XXIV, p. 13.
162  C. Aspin (ed.), *Manchester and the Textile Districts in 1849* (1972), p. 95.
163  BAS, Heywood Correspondence, ZHE 42/17.
164  *Ibid.*, ZHE 42/16.
165  *BS*, 24.7.44.
166  *BS*, 13.2.1856.
167  *BS*, 22.9.1847.
168  *PP*, 1840 (220) XXIV, p. 601.
169  W. E. Brown, *Robert Heywood of Bolton, 1786–1868* (1970), p. 8.
170  Aspin, *op. cit.*, p. 94.
171  The fashion for this material had recently developed. See *PP*, 1839 (159) XL11, p. 5.
172  Marsden, *op. cit.*, p. 232.
173  BAS, Heywood Correspondence, ZHE 47/79.
174  Brown, *op. cit.*, pp. 10–11.

# CONCLUSION

The mid-Victorian period saw significant growth in the British cotton industry. The value of final product rose well over two-fold, from £45.7 million in 1849–51 to £104.9 million in 1869–71. Exports gained in importance, rising from 60.8 per cent of final product value to 67.1 per cent. To generate the additional output, spinning and weaving capacity virtually doubled, the 21 million spindles of 1850 expanding to 38.2 million in 1870 and powerlooms from 250,000 to 441,000.[1]

This growth was accompanied by further structural change in the industry, comprising a move away from the formation of integrated spinning and weaving concerns, which characterised the second quarter of the nineteenth century, towards the development of firms specialising in either process.[2] There was also a continuing, if rather modest growth in the size of firms,[3] and a reinforcement of the urban emphasis in spinning and weaving, as the remaining water-powered spinning mills were gradually abandoned and as rural hand weaving areas failed to develop replacement industry on a sufficient scale. Associated with these changes were advances in textile mill design, including the introduction of single-storey power weaving sheds, the familiar saw-tooth roofs of which took advantage of northern light and were angled to avoid direct penetration of sunlight in British latitudes.[4] This was the period, too, when the vernacular tradition in textile mill architecture became less pronounced and, under the influence of William Fairbairn, a much more conscious attempt was being made to erect spinning blocks and weaving sheds which were visually impressive.[5]

These developments show that, as in earlier decades, the extent and pace of change in the cotton textile industry was appreciable and may be seen to reinforce the view that this industry proved exceptional in an economy marked by limited technological change and low levels of productivity. Yet, as this study has shown, such a view should not be overemphasised. In particular, the mechanisation of cotton weaving took place over a much lengthier time period than is usually acknowledged. Well into the mid-Victorian period, cotton hand weavers had not

## Conclusion

been superseded and, at local level, dependency on the product of the cotton handloom could remain remarkably high. And the continuing importance of hand weaving in mid-Victorian Lancashire is enhanced when the narrow focus of cotton is abandoned and a wider perspective taken, embracing the silks and mixture cloths to which cotton hand weavers increasingly turned.

Attempts to quantify the overall numbers of Lancashire hand weavers during the mid-Victorian period are hindered by the inadequacy of contemporary records. Nevertheless, census evidence shows that, taking all types of fabric into account, as many as 55,000 were still at work in the early 1850s and over 60,000 could have been. A decade later, they still numbered upwards of 30,000 and youthful ones amongst them were by no means uncommon. By the early 1870s, numbers had shrunk to around 10,000, but it was not until the 1880s that Lancashire hand weavers became virtually extinct.

How these figures compare with those of earlier years can be assessed using estimates derived from parish registers. These reveal around 170,000 hand weavers in Lancashire during the early 1820s, the time when the trade was at, or near to, its peak. With such a massive number of workers, the trade was providing a far greater number of jobs than any other throughout the county's textile region. And its importance was accentuated because, in contrast with the proto-industrial period, the great majority of its employees were specialists, many of whom lived in urban areas. Indeed, hand weavers' colonies constituted a major element in the formation of rural and urban settlement in late Georgian Lancashire, giving rise to a new and distinctive type of dwelling, equipped with well-lit loomshops at groundfloor or cellar level.

It is unlikely that any substantial reduction in the overall number of Lancashire's hand weavers occurred prior to the late 1830s. In fact, it was not until the following decade that hand weaving jobs began to be lost with any rapidity. During the mid-1840s especially, the pace of investment in powerlooms quickened markedly, as a major upturn in trade gave entrepreneurs the opportunity to reap the benefits of fundamental advances in powerloom technology, which affected particularly the production of cheaper-grade cottons. It was not until then that the competitive balance within the trade swung decisively in favour of mechanisation.

There was also a marked intra-regional variation in the rate at which hand weaving declined in Lancashire. At mid-century, the lowest rates of survival amongst hand weavers occurred mainly in those areas where the powerloom had made a relatively quick beginning, most notably in the major towns. It was here that the main concentrations of hand weavers arose during the late eighteenth and early nineteenth centuries and it was their livelihood that was particularly threatened by the large-scale adoption of the powerloom in the 1840s.

The position was complicated, however, by the tendency amongst cotton hand weavers to change to the production of alternative cloths, most notably silk, once those they had traditionally woven became the province of the power loom. Moreover, numerous cotton hand weavers could still earn a living, even quite an adequate one, by concentrating on finer and fancier grades of cotton. As with outworkers generally, the productivity of these workers remained low, but the value added they achieved was often substantial and this was reflected in the piece rates they received.

In maintaining their interest in outwork, though, hand weavers did not rely solely on producing the more profitable fabrics. In many instances they were able to remain at their looms because they continued to form part of a family unit which depended on more than one wage earner, often on several. They were thus maintaining a long tradition of family working groups, often relying on the earnings of young children to attain subsistence. Where alternative types of jobs were available, they might diversify the sources from which income was drawn, perhaps allowing young teenagers to take factory work. Where the local economy showed little diversification, however, reliance had often to be placed on joint earnings from handloom weaving. In this way an adequate living could be made, especially if several workers were available and if better qualities of cloth could be woven. Indeed, what is striking in mid-Victorian census schedule entries, and what has escaped comment, is the frequency with which the children of hand weavers continued to follow their parents' trade, especially in rural areas, even into the last quarter of the century.

Hand weavers, then, could often find the means to continue at their trade. Why they did so can be partly explained in terms of the positive attitudes they retained towards outwork, especially the comparative freedom it gave them, and the apprehensions they harboured about factory work, not least the unhealthy and immoral working environment they perceived it to have for their children. It was these motives that informed contemporaries stressed in explaining the survival of outwork and it is the durability of family working groups, especially at a time when the wages of individual hand weavers were low, that gives credence to them. Had such traditional attitudes not been important to hand weavers, they would have sought to a far greater extent the alternatives which, if not in power weaving, were often available. Moreover, even when they did send their children into non-domestic jobs, as frequently they did, they were not necessarily doing so because they no longer preferred that they and their children should work together. It is one thing to have in mind a lifestyle that is considered more desirable than others, but quite another to achieve it, the more so when the work it offered was being inexorably transformed into a mechanised, factory-based activity. And even if these arguments did not apply, it cannot be assumed that, in terms of family income, hand weavers were necessarily better off by placing their children in factory or other types of jobs, than by keeping them at home as hand weavers. The wages paid to young factory children were often low and, at least in some branches of the textile trades, may have been equalled or surpassed by children working in domestic weaving.

Hand weaving also endured because entrepreneurs wanted it to. In assessing their attitudes to outwork, reliance must be placed on a small number of responses, which, for the most part, do not address directly the issues involved. What does emerge, though, is that manufacturers still found substantial cost advantages in making certain types of fabric on the handloom, even as late as the 1850s and 1860s, especially the finer and fancier grades of cotton and the silks and mixture cloths. This was partly because the powerloom still proved uneconomic in weaving such cloths. It was also because, as census schedule evidence so strikingly demonstrates, they could continue to take advantage of plentiful supplies of labour, especially in rural areas. That this was, in the main, child and female labour, kept overall wage costs low. Furthermore, for the less scrupulous or hard-pressed manufacturer, there was still some scope to reduce labour costs through abatement of wages. How far, additionally, manufacturers were also able to benefit from improved labour productivity is conjectural, but in the face of reducing piece rates, hand weavers had a powerful incentive to work longer hours and at a quicker pace. Moreover, a measure of improved productivity would certainly have occurred where the dandy loom was employed. The vast majority of Lancashire's mid-Victorian hand weavers remained domestic workers, however, suggesting that, as S. R. H. Jones surmises, major technological change, and not just the savings on transaction costs, was needed before factory industry was adopted.

It can be seen, therefore, that of the arguments offered by historians to explain the survival of outwork in Victorian Britain, those concerning an abundant and flexible labour supply and inadequate technology have particular value in the case of the Lancashire handloom weaving trades. Some, perhaps quite a number, of handloom manufacturers would have been deterred from investing in powerlooms because they could not meet the required expenditure, but their ranks contained many relatively prosperous men who were in quite a different position. Besides, the possibility of renting room, power and machinery was often available, so that the initial outlay required to mechanise could be quite modest. Nor is it evident that most consumers continued to prefer the hand-made product once the machine-made alternative became available. Some may, but the majority would have appreciated the lower prices and improved quality that the powerloom brought.

The major point to emphasise from this discussion is that the Lancashire textile trades were far less of an exception to the general pattern of industrial development in Britain than has been conceded. The pace of change in these trades was generally quicker than in most other industries, but, well into the mid-Victorian period, significant sections of the weaving branch were characterised by lack of innovation and saw comparatively little in the way of productivity improvements. They remained dependent on production techniques which had endured for generations, and, in rural areas especially, weavers clung to a way of life which, in many respects, resembled that of their grandparents or great-grandparents. Eventually, their trade became obsolete as the powerloom achieved commercial efficiency in the production of an ever-wider range of cloths. However, in Lancashire, as in other British textile districts, the handloom weaver remained a familiar sight for a surprisingly lengthy period of time.

## Notes

1  P. Deane and W. A. Cole, *British Economic Growth, 1688–1959* (1962), pp. 187 and 191.
2  R. Church (ed.), *The Dynamics of Victorian Business* (1980), p. 167 *et seq.*
3  D. A. Farnie, *The English Cotton Industry and the World Market, 1815–1896* (1979), pp. 214–15 and 286.
4  T. W. Fox, *The Mechanism of Weaving* (1894), p. 584.
5  W. Fairbairn, *Treatise on Mills and Millwork*, pt. II, (1861), pp. 114–15.

# BIBLIOGRAPHY

### A  Manuscript sources

#### (a)  At Blackburn Museum

Feilden Papers

#### (b)  At Blackburn Reference Library

Policies of the Manchester Fire & Life Office, Blackburn Agency (B368 MAN)
Blackburn Rate Books

#### (c)  At Bolton Archive Service

Heywood Papers (ZHE)

#### (d)  At Chorley Reference Library

Chorley Town's Book (copy), 1781–1818

#### (e)  At Lancashire Record Office

*(i)  Business records*
William Bashall & Co., Farington (DDX 819)
Horrocks, Crewdson & Co., Preston (DDHs)
Wiseman of Barrowford (DDWm)

*(ii)  Parochial records*
Anglican baptism and marriage registers (PR) or bishops' transcripts (DRB, DRL & DRM)
   for Lancashire (excluding Furness), 1813–22
Padiham relief committee papers, 1824–27 (PR 2863/4)

## The last shift

Selected Catholic and Nonconfirmist registers (MF), 1813–22
Walton-le-Dale, relief of distress committee minutes and census, 1862–64 (PR 2948)

(*iii*) **Other**
Blackburn and Preston Turnpike Trust: case for the promoters, 1824 (TTJ)
Chorley rate books (MBCh)

(*f*)   *At Manchester Central Library, Archives Department*

Farrer Collection: Grimshaw Papers

(*g*)   *At Rawtenstall Reference Library*

Higher Booths Rate Books

(*h*)   *At Turton Tower Museum*

James Brandwood's Account Books

(*i*)   *At Lancashire, Greater Manchester and Merseyside Libraries*

Microfilm copies of census enumerators' schedules, 1841–1881

### B   Parliamentary papers

*PP.*   1819 (301) XVI. An Account of Cotton Twist or Yarn Exported from Great Britain.
*PP.*   1822 (502) XV. Census of Great Britain: Abstracts of Answers and Returns ... in 1821.
*PP.*   1824 (51) V. Report of Select Committee on Artisans, Machinery and Combinations.
*PP.*   1826/7 (237) V. Second Report of the Select Committee on Emigration from the United Kingdom.
*PP.*   1831/2 (678) XIX. Report from the Select Committee ... into the Present State of the Silk Trade.
*PP.*   1833 (149) XXXL. Abstract of Population Returns of Great Britain.
*PP.*   1833 (690) VI. Report from the Select Committee on the Present State of Manufactures, Commerce and Shipping in the United Kingdom.
*PP.*   1834 (44) XXX and XXXI. Reports from the Poor Law Commission.
*PP.*   1834 (556) X. Report from the Select Committee on Handloom Weavers' Petitions.
*PP.*   1835 (341) XIII. Report from the Select Committee on Handloom Weavers' Petitions.
*PP.*   1835 (500) XXXV. First Annual Report of the Poor Law Commissioners.
*PP.*   1836 (24) XLV. A Return of the Number of Power Looms used in Factories in the Manufacture of Woollen, Cotton, Silk, and Linen in each County of the United Kingdom respectively, so far as they can be collected from the Returns of the Factory Commissioners.
*PP.*   1839 XLII and 1840 XXIII and XXIV. Royal Commission on Handloom Weavers; Reports from Assistant Commissioners.

*Bibliography*

     1839 (159) XLII. J. C. Symons, South of Scotland.
     1840 (43–1) XXIII. Report by J. Mitchell.
     1840 (220) XXIV. Reports from Joseph Fletcher, Midlands; W. A. Miles, West England and Wales; and R. M. Muggeridge on the Condition of the Hand Loom Weavers of Lancashire, Westmorland, Cumberland and parts of the West Riding of Yorkshire.
     1840 (639) XXIV. Copy of Report made by Mr Hickson on the Condition of the Hand Loom Weavers.
*PP.*   1841 (296) X. Report of the Commissioners on Hand-loom Weavers.
*PP.*   1842 (89) XXXVa. . . . Report made by Mr Tufnell . . . as to the State of the Poor in the Borough of Rochdale.
*PP.*   1842 (77) XXXVc. Distress in Bolton. Copies of Communications . . .
*PP.*   1843 (402) VII. Report of the Select Committee on the Labouring Poor (Allotments of Land).
*PP.*   1844 (587) XXVII. Abstract of the Answers and Returns . . . of the Population of Great Britain; Occupation Abstract, 1841.
*PP.*   1844 (583) XXVIII. Reports of the Inspectors of Factories for the half year ending 31st December, 1843.
*PP.*   1845 (639) XXV. Reports of the Inspectors of Factories for the quarter ending 30th September, 1844.
*PP.*   1846 (661) XXXVIc. A Copy of Reports Received by thee Poor Law Commissioners in 1841 on the State of the Macclesfield and Bolton Unions.
*PP.*   1850 (745) XLII. Returns of the Number of Cotton, Woollen, Worsted, Flax, and Silk Factories subject to the Factories Act in each County.
*PP.*   1850 (1239) XXII. Reports of Inspectors of Factories for the half year ending 30th April, 1850.
*PP.*   1851 (1339) XLIII. Forms and Instructions . . . for the Use of the Persons Employed in Taking an Account of the Population of Great Britain.
*PP.*   1852–3 (1690) LXXXIX. Population Census of Great Britain: Religious Worship (England and Wales).

### C  Contemporary newspapers and journals

*Blackburn Mail*
*Blackburn Standard*
*Bolton Chronicle*
*Engineering*
*Manchester and Salford Advertiser*
*Preston Chronicle*
*Preston Pilot*
*The Engineer*

### D  Trade directories

E. Baines, *History, Directory and Gazetteer of the County Palatine of Lancaster* (Liverpool, 1824–25), 2 vols.
Kelly & Co., *Post Office Directory of Lancashire* (London, 1858).

*The last shift*

P. Mannex & Co., *History, Topography & Directory of mid-Lancashire* (Preston, 1854).
Pigot & Co., *National Commercial Directory* (London, 1829).
*Slater's Royal National Commercial Directory of Lancashire* (Manchester, volumes for 1851, 1855, 1858, 1861, 1865, 1871–72).

### E  Contemporary maps

(i) Lancashire County maps; Yates, 1786; Greenwood, 1818; Hennet, 1828.
(ii) 1840s first edition O.S. maps, six inches to the mile and five feet to the mile.

### F  Other contemporary books, pamphlets and articles

*Abstract of the Returns made by the Overseers of the Poor of the Several Parishes, Townships and Places in the County of Lancaster* (Preston, 1821).
J. Aikin, *A Description of the County from Thirty to Forty Miles Round Manchester* (1968 reprint of 1795 edition).
H. Ashworth, 'An enquiry into the origin, progress, and results of the strike of the operative cotton spinners of Preston, from October, 1836 to February, 1837', *Memoirs of the Literary and Philosophical Society of Manchester*, vol. IV (1837).
C. Aspin (ed.), *Manchester and the Textile Districts in 1849* (Helmshore, 1972).
C. Babbage, *On the Economy of Machinery and Manufactures* (London, 1832).
E. Baines, *History of the Cotton Manufacture in Great Britain* (1966 reprint of 1835 edition).
Dr Ballard, *Report upon the Sanitary Condition of the Registration District of Bolton, Lancashire* (1871).
S. Bamford, *Passages in the Life of a Radical* (1967 reprint of 1844 edition).
—— *Walks in South Lancashire and Its Borders* (Manchester, 1844).
J. Binns, *Notes on the Agriculture of Lancashire* (Preston, 1851).
J. Black, *A Medico-topographical, Geographical and Statistical Sketch of Bolton and Its Neighbourhood* (Extract from the *Transactions of the Provincial Medical and Surgical Association*, 1837).
E. Butterworth, *A Statistical Sketch of the County Palatine of Lancaster* (London, 1841).
J. Butterworth, *An Historical and Descriptive Account of the Town and Parochial Chapelry of Oldham* (Oldham, 1817).
D. Chadwick, *On the Rate of Wages in 200 Trades and Branches of Labour in Manchester and Salford and the Manufacturing District of Lancashire, during the 20 Years from 1839 to 1859* (Paper read before the Statistical Society of London, December, 1858).
W. R. Chambers, *The Cotton Metropolis* (1972 reprint of 1849 edition).
G. T. Clark, *Report to the General Board of Health on a Preliminary Enquiry into the Sewerage, Drainage and Supply of Water, and the Sanitary Condition of the Inhabitants of the Borough of Wigan* (Wigan, 1849).
R. W. Dickson, *General View of the Agriculture of Lancashire* (London, 1815).
W. Dodd, *The Factory System Illustrated* (1968 reprint of 1841–42 edition).
Sir F. M. Eden, *The State of the Poor* (1966 edition of 1797 text), vol. 1.
T. Ellison, *The Cotton Trade of Great Britain* (1968 reprint of 1868 edition).
F. Engels, *The Condition of the Working-Class in England in 1845* (1958 reprint of 1845 edition).
W. Fairbairn, *Treatise on Mills and Millwork* (London, 1861).
J. Fielden, *The Curse of the Factory System* (1968 reprint of 1836 edition).

## Bibliography

P. Gaskell, *Artisans and Machinery* (1968 reprint of 1836 edition).
H. S. Gibbs, *Autobiography of a Manchester Manufacturer* (London, 1887).
R. Guest, *A Compendious History of the Cotton Manufacture* (1968 reprint of 1823 edition).
J. Holt, *General View of the Agriculture of the County of Lancaster* (1969 reprint of 1795 edition).
W. Lee, *Report to the General Board of Health on a Preliminary Inquiry into the Sewerage, Drainage, and Supply of Water, and the Sanitary Condition of the Inhabitants of the Township of Over Darwen* (London, 1853).
J. Livesey, 'The editor's autobiography', *The Staunch Teetotaller*, (1868), 13.
Manchester Statistical Society, *Condition of the Working Classes, in an Extensive Manufacturing District in 1834, 1835 and 1836* (London, 1838).
J. Montgomery, *Cotton Manufacture of the United States of America* (1969 reprint of 1840 edition).
J. Murphy, *A Treatise on the Art of Weaving* (Glasgow, 1827).
W. Radcliffe, *Origin of the New System of Manufacture* (Stockport, 1828).
W. C. Taylor, *Notes of a Tour in the Manufacturing Districts of Lancashire* (London, 1842).
T. Twiss, *Two Lectures on Machinery* (1977 reprint of 1844 edition).
A. Ure, *The Philosophy of Manufactures* (1967 reprint of 1835 edition).
J. Watson, *The Theory and Practice of the Art of Weaving by Hand and Power* (Glasgow, 1873).
G. White, *A Practical Treatise on Weaving by Hand and Power Looms* (London, 1851).
D. Whitehead, *Autobiography* (n.d.; typescript edition, 1956).

### G  Secondary books, pamphlets, articles and theses

#### (a)  Books and pamphlets

D. H. Aldcroft and P. Fearon, *British Economic Fluctuations, 1790–1939* (London, 1972).
M. Anderson, *Family Structure in Nineteenth Century Lancashire* (Cambridge, 1971).
O. Ashmore, *The Industrial Archaeology of Lancashire* (Newton Abbot, 1969).
T. S. Ashton, *An Economic History of England: the 18th Century* (London, 1955).
—— *Economic and Social Investigations in Manchester, 1833–1933* (1977 reprint of 1934 edition).
C. Aspin, *Lancashire, the First Industrial Society* (Helmshore, 1969).
C. Aspin and S. D. Chapman, *James Hargreaves and the Spinning Jenny* (Helmshore, 1964).
W. Bennet, *History of Burnley* (Burnley, 1948) vol. 3.
M. Berg, *Technology and Toil in Nineteenth Century Britain* (London, 1979).
—— *The Age of Manufactures* (London, 1985).
—— *The Machinery Question and the Making of Political Economy, 1815–1840* (Cambridge, 1980).
M. Berg, P. Hudson and M. Sonenscher, *Manufacture in Town and Country Before the Factory* (Cambridge, 1983).
R. Boyson, *The Ashworth Cotton Enterprise* (Oxford, 1970).
C. P. Brooks, *Cotton Manufacturing* (London, 1892).
Sir C. Brown, *Origins and Progress of Horrocks and Company* (Preston, 1925).
W. E. Brown, *Bolton As It Was* (Nelson, 1972).
—— *Robert Heywood of Bolton, 1786–1868* (Wakefield, 1970).

J. Butt and I. Donnachie, *Industrial Archaeology of the British Isles* (London, 1979).
D. Bythell, *The Handloom Weavers* (Cambridge, 1969).
—— *The Sweated Trades* (London, 1978).
H. Catling, *The Spinning Mule* (Newton Abbot, 1970).
J. D. Chambers, *The Workshop of the World* (Oxford, 1961).
S. D. Chapman, *The Cotton Industry in the Industrial Revolution* (London, 1972).
—— *The History of Working-class Housing* (Newton Abbot, 1971).
S. J. Chapman, *The Lancashire Cotton Industry* (Manchester, 1904).
J. H. Clapham, *An Economic History of Modern Britain* (1967 reprint of 1926 edition), vol. 1.
L. A. Clarkson, *Proto-Industrialization: The First Phase of Industrialization?* (London, 1985).
T. Counsell, *Mellor in Blackburnshire: a Short History* (Blackburn, 1929).
J. C. Cox, *The Parish Registers of England* (London, 1910).
N. F. R. Crafts, *British Economic Growth During the Industrial Revolution* (Oxford, 1985).
F. Crouzet, *The Victorian Economy* (London, 1982).
G. W. Daniels, *The Early English Cotton Industry* (Manchester, 1920).
Darwen WEA Local History Group, *The Darwen Area During the Industrial Revolution* (1987).
P. Deane and W. A. Cole, *British Economic Growth, 1688–1959* (1962).
R. Dennis, *English Industrial Cities of the Nineteenth Century* (Cambridge, 1984).
M. Drake (ed.), *Population Studies from Parish Registers* (Matlock, 1982).
R. Eaton, *History of Samlesbury* (Blackburn, 1936).
M. M. Edwards, *The Growth of the British Cotton Trade* (Manchester, 1967).
W. English, *The Textile Industry* (London, 1969).
D. A. Farnie, *The English Cotton Industry and the World Market, 1815–1896* (Oxford, 1979).
W. Farrer and J. Brownbill, *A History of the County of Lancaster* (London, 1908), vols 2–8.
C. H. Feinstein, *Statistical Tables of National Income, Expenditure and Output of the U.K., 1855–1965* (Cambridge, 1976).
R. Floud, *An Introduction to Quantitative Methods for Historians* (London, 1973).
R. Floud and D. McCloskey (eds), *The Economic History of Britain Since 1700* (Cambridge, 1981) vol. 1.
A. Foley, *A Bolton Childhood* (Manchester, 1973).
J. Foster, *Class Structure and the Industrial Revolution* (London, 1974).
T. W. Fox, *The Mechanism of Weaving* (London, 1894).
T. W. Freeman, H. B. Rodgers and R. H. Kinvig, *Lancashire, Cheshire and the Isle of Man* (London, 1966).
A. D. Gilbert, *Religion and Society in Industrial England* (London, 1976).
H. J. Habakkuk, *American and British Technology in the Nineteenth Century* (Cambridge, 1967).
J. L. and B. Hammond, *The Town Labourer* (London, 1917).
J. B. Harley, *William Yates' Map of Lancashire, 1786* (Liverpool, 1968).
J. F. C. Harrison, *The Early Victorians, 1832–51* (London, 1971).
E. Higgs, *Making Sense of the Census* (London, 1989).
R. L. Hills, *Power in the Industrial Revolution* (Manchester, 1970).
D. Hogg, *A History of Church and Oswaldtwistle, 1760–1860* (Accrington, 1971).
W. G. Hoskins, *Local History in England* (London, 1959).
A. Howe, *The Cotton Masters, 1830–1860* (Oxford, 1984).

## Bibliography

P. Hudson (ed.), *Regions and Industries* (Cambridge, 1989).
J. R. T. Hughes, *Fluctuations in Trade, Industry and Finance* (Oxford, 1960).
S. Jackson (ed.), *Industrial Colonies and Communities* (Liverpool, 1988).
D. J. Jenkins and K. G. Ponting, *The British Wool Textile Industry, 1770–1914* (London, 1982).
P. Joyce, *Work, Society and Politics* (London, 1980).
E. and T. Kelly, *A Schoolmaster's Notebook* (Manchester, 1957).
J. E. King, *Richard Marsden and the Preston Chartists, 1837–1848* (Lancaster, 1981).
P. Kriedte, H. Mendick and J. Schlumbohm, *Industrialization Before Industrialization* (Cambridge, 1981).
D. Landes, *The Unbound Prometheus* (Cambridge, 1969).
R. Lawton, *The Census and Social Structure* (London, 1978).
D. Levine, *Family Formation in an Age of Nascent Capitalism* (London, 1977).
B. Lewis, *Life in a Cotton Town, Blackburn, 1818–48* (Blackburn, 1985).
R. Lloyd-Jones and M. J. Lewis, *Manchester and the Age of the Factory* (Beckenham, 1988).
D. H. Longton, *A History of the Parish of Flixton* (Manchester, 1898).
J. Lown, *Women and Industrialisation; Gender at Work in Nineteenth Century England* (Cambridge, 1990).
J. Lunn, *Leigh: The Historical Past of a Lancashire Borough* (Leigh, n.d.).
R. Marsden, *Cotton Weaving. Its Development, Principles and Practice* (London, 1895).
P. Mathias, *The First Industrial Nation* (London, 1969).
P. Mathias and J. A. Davis, *The First Industrial Revolutions* (Oxford, 1989).
P. Mathias and M. M. Postan (eds), *The Cambridge Economic History of Europe*, 2 (Cambridge, 1978).
R. C. O. Matthews, *A Study in Trade Cycle History* (Cambridge, 1954).
A. Milward and S. B. Saul, *The Development of the Economies of Continental Europe, 1850–1914* (London, 1977).
B. R. Mitchell and P. Deane, *Abstract of British Historical Statistics* (Cambridge, 1962).
J. Mokyr (ed.), *The Economics of the Industrial Revolution* (London, 1985).
N. Morgan, *Vanished Dwellings* (typescript, 1988).
B. Murphy, *A History of the British Economy, 1740–1970* (London, 1973).
W. S. Murphy, *The Textile Industries* (London, 1910).
N. Murray, *The Scottish Handloom Weavers* (Edinburgh, 1978).
A. E. Musson, *The Growth of British Industry* (London, 1978).
W. F. Neff, *Victorian Working Women* (1966 reprint of 1929 edition).
P. O'Brien and C. Keyder, *Economic Growth in Britain and France, 1780–1914* (London, 1978).
S. Pearson, *Rural Houses of the Lancashire Pennines, 1560–1760* (London, 1985).
H. Perkin, *The Origins of Modern English Society, 1780–1880* (London, 1969).
I. Pinchbeck, *Women Workers and the Industrial Revolution* (London, 1930).
J. Porter, *The Making of the Central Pennines* (Ashbourne, 1980).
J. Prest, *The Industrial Revolution in Coventry* (Oxford, 1960).
S. J. Price, *Building Societies, Their Origins and History* (London, 1958).
A. Redford, *Labour Migration in England, 1800–1850* (1964 reprint of 1926 edition).
J. Richardson, *The Local Historian's Encyclopedia* (New Barnet, 1974).
M. Rose, *The Gregs of Styal* (Styal, 1978).
—— *The Gregs of Quarry Bank Mill* (Cambridge, 1986).
W. W. Rostow, *The Stages of Economic Growth* (Cambridge, 1960).

M. Rothwell, *Industrial Heritage: A Guide to the Industrial Archaeology of Accrington* (Accrington, 1979).

—— *Industrial Heritage: A Guide to the Industrial Archaeology of Blackburn*, 1 (Hyndburn, 1985).

—— *Industrial Heritage: A Guide to the Industrial Archaeology of Oswaldtwistle* (Hyndburn, 1980).

—— *Industrial Heritage: A Guide to the Industrial Archaeology of the Ribble Valley* (Accringtion, 1990).

J. Rule, *The Labouring Classes in Early Industrial England, 1750–1850* (London, 1986).

S. B. Saul, *Technological Change: The United States and Britain in the 19th Century* (London, 1970).

C. H. Saxelby (ed.), *Bolton Survey* (1971 reprint of 1953 edition).

J. A. Schmiechen, *Sweated Trades and Sweated Labour* (Beckenham, 1984).

C. Singer, E. J. Holmyard, A. R. Hall and T. I. Williams, *A History of Technology*, IV (Oxford, 1958).

N. J. Smelser, *Social Change in the Industrial Revolution* (London, 1959).

J. H. Smith (ed.), *The Great Human Exploit* (London, 1973).

T. C. Smith, *A History of Longridge and District* (Preston, 1888).

D. J. Steel, *National Index of Parish Registers: General Sources of Births, Marriages and Deaths before 1837*, 1 (Chichester, 1968).

J. Swain, *Industry before the Industrial Revolution* (Manchester, 1986).

W. Tate, *The Parish Chest* (Cambridge, 1946).

J. Thirsk, *The Rural Economy of England* (Cambridge, 1984).

M. Thomis, *The Town Labourer and the Industrial Revolution* (London, 1974).

E. P. Thompson, *The Making of the English Working Class* (Harmondsworth, 1963).

J. G. Timmins, *Handloom Weavers' Cottages in Central Lancashire* (Lancaster, 1977).

G. N. von Tunzelmann, *Steam Power and British Industrialization to 1860* (Oxford, 1978).

G. H. Tupling, *The Economic History of Rossendale* (Manchester, 1927).

A. P. Wadsworth and J. De Lacy Mann, *The Cotton Trade and Industrial Lancashire, 1600–1780* (Manchester, 1931).

J. K. Walton, *Lancashire, a Social History, 1558–1939* (Manchester, 1987).

Sir F. Warner, *The Silk Industry of the United Kingdom: Its Origins and Development* (London, 1921).

R. D. S. Wilson, *The Feildens of Witton Park* (Blackburn, n.d.).

G. H. Wood, *The History of Wages in the Cotton Trade* (London, 1910).

E. A. Wrigley, *Nineteenth Century Society* (Cambridge, 1972).

E. A. Wrigley and R. S. Schofield, *The Population History of England, 1541–1871* (London, 1981).

(*b*)  Articles

M. Blaug, 'The productivity of capital in the Lancashire cotton industry during the nineteenth century', *EcHR*, XIII (1963), pp. 358–81.

M. Brigg, 'Life in East Lancashire, 1856–60: a newly-discovered diary of John O'Neill (John Ward) weaver of Clitheroe', *THSL&C*, 120 (1969), pp. 87–113.

*Bibliography*

——'The Forest of Pendle in the seventeenth century', *THSL&C*, 113 (1961), pp. 65–96.

R. Boyson, 'The new Poor Law in north-east Lancashire, 1834–71', *THSL&C*, 70 (1960), pp. 35–56.

D. Bythell, 'The hand-loom weavers in the English cotton industry during the industrial revolution: some problems', *EcHR*, 17 (1964), pp. 339–53.

——'From handloom to powerloom: corporation and co-operation in the English cotton industry in the mid-nineteenth century', *Proceedings of the VIII Congress International D'Historie Economique* (1982).

R. Church, 'Labour supply and innovation, 1800–1860: the boot and shoe industry', *BH*, XII (1970), pp. 25–45.

D. C. Coleman, 'Proto-industrialization: a concept too many', *EcHR*, (1983), pp. 435–48.

N. F. R. Crafts, 'British economic growth during the Industrial Revolution: some difficulties of interpretation', *EEH*, 24 (1987), pp. 245–68.

——'Economic growth in France and Britain, 1830–1910: a review of the evidence', *JEH*, XLIV (1984), pp. 49–67.

W. P. Crankshaw, 'Famous Bolton cotton fabrics', in *Industrial Bolton: The Crompton Centenary Supplement to the Textile Manufacturer* (London, 1927), pp. 29–42.

H. Cunningham, 'The employment and unemployment of children in England, c.1680–1851', *P&P*, 126 (1987), pp. 115–50.

J. P. Dodd, 'South Lancashire in transition: a study of the crop returns for 1795–1801', *THSL&C*, 117 (1966), pp. 89–107.

A. J. Field, 'On the unimportance of machinery', *EEH*, 22 (1985), pp. 378–401.

T. W. Fletcher, 'The agrarian revolution in arable Lancashire', *TL&CAS*, 72 (1962), pp. 93–122.

D. Foster, 'Poulton-le-Fylde: a nineteenth century market town', *THSL&C*, 127 (1978), pp. 91–107.

V. A. C. Gatrell, 'Labour, power, and the size of firms in Lancashire cotton in the second quarter of the nineteenth century', *EcHR*, (1977), 30 pp. 95–139.

G. L. Gullickson, 'Agriculture and cottage industry redefining the causes of proto-industrialisation', *JEH*, XLIII (1983), pp. 831–50.

P. Horn, 'Victorian villages from census returns', *The Local Historian*, 16 (1982), pp. 25–32.

R. Houston and K. D. M. Snell, 'Proto-industrialization? Cottage industry, social change, and the Industrial Revolution', *The Historical Journal*, 27 (1984), pp. 473–92.

P. Hudson, 'Proto-industrialisation: the case of the West Riding wool textile industry in the 18th and early 19th centuries', *HWJ*, 12 (1981), pp. 34–61.

S. R. H. Jones, 'Technology, transaction costs, and the transition to factory production in the British silk industry', *JEH*, XLVII (1987), pp. 71–96.

R. Lloyd-Jones and A. A. Le Roux, 'The size of firms in the cotton industry: Manchester, 1815–41', *EcHR*, 33 (1980), pp. 72–82.

J. S. Lyons, 'Vertical integration in the British cotton industry, 1825–1850: a revision', *JEH*, XLV (1985), pp. 419–25.

——'Powerloom profitability and steam power costs', *JEH*, 24 (1987), pp. 419–25.

——'Family response to economic decline: handloom weaving in early nineteenth century Lancashire', *Research in Economic History*, 12 (1989), pp. 45–91.

——'Technological dualism, rivalry and complementarity: handicrafts in the transition to modern industry' (forthcoming).

J. D. Marshall, 'The Lancashire rural labourer in the early nineteenth century', *TL&CAS*, 71 (1961), pp. 90–128.

F. F. Mendels, 'Proto-industrialisation: the first phase of the industrialisation process', *JEH*, 32 (1972), pp. 241–61.

J. Mokyr, 'Has the Industrial Revolution been crowded out? Some reflections on Crafts and Williamson', *EEH*, 24 (1987), pp. 293–319.

A. E. Musson, 'The British Industrial Revolution', *History*, 67 (1982), pp. 252–8.

H. W. Ogden, 'The geographical basis of the Lancashire cotton industry', *Journal of the Manchester Geographical Society* (1927), pp. 8–30.

J. Porter, 'A forest in transition: Bowland, 1500–1650', *THSL&C*, 125 (1974), pp. 40–60.

W. Proctor, 'Poor Law administration in Preston Union, 1838–1848', *THSL&C*, 117 (1966), pp. 145–66.

P. Richards, 'The state and early industrial capitalism: the case of the handloom weavers', *P&P*, 83 (1979), pp. 92–115.

M. B. Rose, 'Social policy and business: parish apprenticeship and the early factory system, 1750–1834', *BH*, 31 (1989), pp. 5–29.

S. Rose, 'Gender at work: sex, class and industrial capitalism', *HWJ*, 21 (1986), pp. 113–131.

R. Samuel, 'Workshop of the world: steam power and hand technology in mid-Victorian Britain', *HWJ*, iii (1977), pp. 6–72.

M. Sanderson, 'Social change and elementary education in industrial Lancashire', *Northern History*, III (1968), pp. 131–54.

J. H. Smith, 'Ten acres of Deansgate', *THSL&C*, 80 (1980), pp. 43–59.

W. J. Smith, 'The cost of building Lancashire loomshops and weavers' workshops: the account book of James Brandwood of Turton, 1794–1814', *Textile History*, 8 (1977), pp. 56–76.

A. J. Taylor, 'Concentration and specialization in the Lancashire cotton industry', *EcHR*, 1 (1948–49), pp. 114–22.

R. F. Taylor, 'A type of handloom weaving cottage in mid-Lancashire', *Industrial Archaeology*, 3 (1966), pp. 251–5.

J. G. Timmins, 'Handloom weavers' cottages in central Lancashire', *Post-Medieval Archaeology*, 13 (1979), pp. 251–72.

G. H. Tupling, 'The turnpike trusts of Lancashire', *Memoirs and Proceedings of the Manchester Literary and Philosophical Society*, 94 (1952–53), pp. 1–23.

W. Turner, 'Patterns of migration of textile workers into Accrington in the early nineteenth century', *LPS*, 30 (1983), pp. 28–41.

A. M. Warnes, 'Early separation of houses from workplaces and the urban structure of Chorley, 1780–1850', *THSL&C*, 122 (1970), pp. 105–35.

M. T. Wild, 'The Saddleworth parish registers,' *Textile History*, 1 (1969), pp. 214–32.

W. Wilkinson, 'Power loom developments', *Journal of the Textile Institute* (special issue, 1927), pp. 122–48.

J. A. Williams, 'A local population study at a college of education', *LPS*, 11 (1973), pp. 23–39.

J. G. Williamson, 'Debating the Industrial Revolution', *EEH*, 24 (1987), pp. 269–92.

O. E. Williamson, 'The organisation of work', *Journal of Economic Behavior and Organisation*, 1 (1980), pp. 5–38.

A. E. Wrigley, 'The changing occupational structure of Colyton over two centuries', *LPS*, 18 (1977), pp. 9–21.

*Bibliography*

(*c*) Theses

M. Berg, *The Introduction and Diffusion of the Power Loom, 1780–1842* (MA thesis, University of Sussex, 1972).

R. K. Fleischman, Jr, *Conditions of Life Amongst the Cotton Workers of Southeastern Lancashire During the Industrial Revolution, 1780–1850* (PhD thesis, University of New York, 1975).

G. N. Gandy, *Illegitimacy in a Handloom Weaving Community: Fertility Patterns in Culcheth, Lancashire, 1781–1860* (PhD thesis, University of Oxford, 1978).

G. Greathead, *A Study of Handloom Weaving Decline in the mid-19th Century* (MA thesis, University of Manchester, 1986).

J. T. Jackson, *Housing and Social Structure in mid-Victorian Wigan and St Helens* (PhD thesis, University of Liverpool, 1977).

W. King, *The Economic and Demographic Development of Rossendale, c.1650–c.1795*, (PhD thesis, University of Leicester, 1979).

J. S. Lyons, *The Lancashire Cotton Industry and the Introduction of the Powerloom, 1815–1850* (PhD Dissertation, University of California, 1977).

N. K. Scott, *The Architectural Development of Cotton Mills in Preston and District* (MA thesis, University of Liverpool, 1952).

J. G. Timmins, *The Decline of Handloom Weaving in Nineteenth Century Lancashire* (PhD thesis, University of Lancaster, 1990).

# Appendix A1

# COMPUTING HAND WEAVER NUMBERS IN EARLY NINETEENTH CENTURY LANCASHIRE

This appendix considers the techniques involved in using parish register data to determine handloom weaver numbers. Attention is concentrated on the decade 1813–22, when parish registration becomes more detailed; when hand weaving was at, or approaching, its peak; and when the registers record relatively few powerloom weavers. The data obtained are grouped into two five-year blocks, so that annual fluctuations can be averaged and results compared.

## 1 Availability and coverage of registers

There is no published list of churches and chapels in use throughout Lancashire between 1813 and 1822. However, Edward Baines records the numbers in each parish for 1825, Nonconformist and Catholic, as well as Anglican.[1] He also names and locates most of them, giving dates of erection and rebuilding.[2] To identify the others, and to check his accuracy, searches must be made in the ecclesiastical sections of the Victoria County History.[3] They exclude Furness.

The searches show that, during 1822, 228 churches and chapels were used in Lancashire for Anglican worship. The original registers for seventy-five of them are preserved in the Lancashire County Record Office, as are bishops' transcripts for a further 131. For the remainder, neither registers nor transcripts are available, their returns probably being included amongst those of the mother church. For the period 1813–22, the vast majority of Lancashire parish register entries can be readily traced.

In deciding whether occupational structure can be more satisfactorily analysed using baptism or marriage entries alone, or whether a combination of both sources is needed, several considerations arise. One is the magnitude of the task. Parish Register Abstracts, despite their probable inaccuracy, reveal that some 280,000 baptism entries were made in Lancashire between 1813 and 1822, compared with around 85,000 marriage entries.[4] Not all record occupations and the work of analysing them can be appreciably lightened by sampling. Even so, searching baptisms is clearly the more formidable procedure.

Another consideration is the completeness of occupational recording. From 1813, fathers' occupations are normally given in Anglican baptism registers, a result of the standardised recording demanded by Rose's Act of the previous year. In Nonconformist registers, however, to which Rose's Act did not apply, occupations appear less consistently. Moreover, in some cases, frequent reference is made to parents living in a different parish from that in which the church or chapel was situated. For example, of seventy-two baptisms listed at Middleton Wesleyan Chapel between 1813 and 1822, at least twenty were to parents from neighbouring parishes.[5] By contrast, only a small proportion of Anglican parents in Middleton were outsiders. Even if occupational details are usually given in Nonconformist registers, therefore, the entries will require a good deal of adjustment before they can be combined with those from Anglican registers.

Perusal of Anglican marriage registers reveals that occupations are commonly given, though important exceptions, including those of the parish churches at Preston and Wigan, occur. None the less, virtually all recorded weddings can be found in these registers, because Hardwicke's Act of 1753 stipulated that marriages taking place in England and Wales would be declared void, unless solemnised in the established church. Exceptions were only to be tolerated in the case of Quakers and Jews.[6] D. J. Steel suggests that Nonconformists complied with the law, so that, until the introduction of civil registration of births, deaths and marriages in 1836, nearly all dissenters' marriages took place in Anglican churches.[7] E. A. Wrigley and R. S. Schofield agree. They observe:

Even in the later eighteenth century, when nonconformist baptisms were common, and non-conformist or non-denominational burial grounds had ceased to be a rarity, Anglican marriages were still an overwhelming majority of all marriages.[8]

Neither marriage nor baptism registers, therefore, allow a complete survey of occupational structure in early nineteenth century Lancashire and it is unclear which permits the fuller analysis.

A third consideration is whether marriage or baptism registers are the more accurately compiled. J. Charles Cox believes that, as a rule, the former were

from the obvious importance to persons of all ranks of possessing a faithful record of their union, both for their own sake and as legal proof of their children's legitimacy.[9]

Cox's view is qualified and intuitively plausible, but lacks supporting evidence. In his favour, it might be argued that the need for bride, bridegroom and clergyman to sign marriage registers made it more difficult to avoid keeping an accurate record than was the case with baptism registers, which parents were not required to sign. At best, however, such argument is conjectural and does not resolve the doubts.

Additional evidence on parish register accuracy is provided by Wrigley and Schofield. On the basis of their 404-parish sample (which includes ten Lancashire parishes) they estimate that, for the period 1813 to 1839, the percentage of months with defective registration is 0.1 in the case of baptisms and 0.4 in the case of marriages.[10] (For comparison, the corresponding figures from 1640 to 1653 are 20.5 per cent and 42.8 per cent respectively.) Contrary to Cox's belief, therefore, marriage records may be more defective than baptism records, but, after 1812, the degree of inaccuracy had sunk to insignificant levels in both. This is not to say that all Lancashire's baptism and marriage registers were accurately kept at this time or that inaccuracies should not be sought. Yet such evidence does suggest that the choice of baptism or marriage registers to analyse occupations cannot be settled on the basis of probable accuracy.

Further inaccuracy may arise from using bishops' transcripts rather than original registers. With any copy, of course, mistakes are likely to occur. However, in the case of bishops' transcripts, accuracy may have been improved by a clause in the 1812 Act. This stipulated that clergy were henceforth to sign a solemn declaration confirming that each year's transcriptions were 'true Copies of all the several Entries in the said several Register Books

*The last shift*

...'.[11] Signed declarations of this type, even when made by clergy, do not eliminate all error, but greater care is probably taken when they are required than when they are not.

Two more points arise concerning transcription errors. Firstly, whether resulting from omission or miscopying, they will not be of undue significance when used to calculate proportionate figures, unless particular groups of data (in this case classes of occupation) are less likely to have been transcribed than others. There is no reason to suppose this would have happened. Secondly, the size of register could have had a bearing on the accuracy of recording, since copying smaller registers would have required less effort and concentration than copying larger ones. Unless the degree of inaccuracy is considerable, however, it makes little difference as far as the calculation of proportionate figures from large registers is concerned.

A final anxiety about using parish register entries to assess occupational distributions is that neither marriage nor baptism records give precise descriptions of occupations. As far as hand weaving is concerned, infrequent mention is made of the fabric woven and the distinction between hand and power weavers is usually overlooked. Consequently, from the mid-1820s, when mechanised weaving began to exert a notable impact in Lancashire, parish register entries list a growing, but indeterminate number of power weavers, especially in urban areas.[12] Hence, they become increasingly less reliable in determining the importance of hand weaving.

To summarise, there is little to choose in terms of accuracy and completeness between baptism and marriage register entries as sources for investigating handloom weaver concentrations. However, considerable difficulties arise in both the analysis and interpretation of baptism entries, whereas the use of marriage entries is comparatively straightforward; the problems associated with religious dissent and birth rate variations can both be avoided. Even so, because bridegrooms' occupations are not always recorded, the use of marriage entries alone allows only a partial analysis. To fill the gaps, it is necessary to make estimates derived from entries in Anglican baptism registers, the only source available giving countywide occupational coverage for a significant element in the labour force. That these entries might understate the importance of handloom weaving does not matter, as long as they do so consistently, since the figures they produce are only required as a basis for estimation, rather than as figures in their own right.

The next stage is to find hand weaver proportions from the marriage registers. The results obtained and the problems arising are considered in the following section.

## 2  Marriage register counts

For the period 1813–22, 109 sets of Lancashire marriage registers can be identified.[13] Of these, sixty-six note bridegrooms' occupations during all or part of the period, allowing counts to be made of hand weaver numbers. The results, presented on a quinquennial basis, are recorded in summary form in Tables A1.1 and A1.2. Marriage totals are also given, along with the proportion of bridegroom weavers listed in each register or group of registers. Bridegrooms not belonging to a particular parish are excluded from the counts for that parish.[14] The area of each parish is shown in Map 4.[15]

It is unlikely any other Lancashire marriage registers were in use between 1813–22. Each parish church, of which there were fifty-seven, held a licence to marry and their registers, though sometimes incomplete, are all available. For the 171 chapels of ease, marriage registers can be found in forty-five instances, the rest probably being too unimportant to hold a marriage licence. Indeed, following the passage of Hardwicke's Act in 1754, which aimed to prevent clandestine weddings, church authorities would have been wary of granting marriage licences unless a convincing need could be demonstrated. This could have proved especially difficult to achieve for chapels of ease serving either sparsely-populated rural districts or growing urban congregations with a parish church nearby. Significantly, such chapels often occurred in early nineteenth-century Lancashire.

Except in the case of St Mary, St Denys and St George, Manchester (the present-day Manchester Cathedral) all marriage registers contain few enough entries to permit exhaustive counting. Most list fewer than one hundred entries per year and over half less than fifty. Manchester Cathedral registers, however, average over 1,500 entries per year between 1813–22, over three times the number in the next biggest register, that of St Peter's, Liverpool. For each year, therefore, a random sample of the Manchester entries is taken, using a sampling fraction of 147. The results, expressed at the 95 per cent confidence interval are accurate to within ±3 per cent of the total number of entries. (Appendix A3 gives further details).

Registers yielding small annual marriage totals — fewer than twenty per year — frequently show monthly gaps in registration, sometimes lasting a year or more. Since most belong to churches in thinly-populated districts, where few weddings took place, significant under-recording is unlikely.

In assessing the accuracy of registers from more populous parishes — those averaging twenty or more entries annually — the working hypothesis is preferred that at least one marriage would have been recorded per month, a stringent test for registers with only twenty or thirty entries per year. However, even allowing for seasonal variation in weddings, upon which historians have often commented, it might be thought that accurately-kept registers with, say, over sixty entries per year, would not be expected to yield any monthly gaps, whilst those with between twenty and sixty would reveal very few.[16]

To test these propositions, searches are made to find monthly gaps in registers averaging twenty or more entries per year. As Table A1.3 shows, only in registers providing 20–39 entries each year are such gaps frequent. Moreover, 39 of the 64 gaps arise in just two registers, Newchurch-in-Pendle and Rainford, which averaged only twenty-two and twenty-four entries each year respectively. There is reason to suppose, therefore, that Lancashire marriage registers share the low levels of defective registration occurring generally in the early nineteenth century.

Statistical tests applied to a sample of these registers enable observed numbers of monthly entries to be compared with expected numbers. Details are given in Appendix A3. In only two of six registers examined is there a significant disagreement at the 1 per cent level. Whether this disagreement indicates register inaccuracy or merely a lack of randomness in the timing of marriages is uncertain. Again, therefore, a high degree of accuracy is indicated.

In preparing Tables A1.1 and A1.2, the data are modified to deal with incomplete occupational recording. This occurs in nearly every register, so that most bridegroom weaver figures obtained lie within a range of values. In reducing these to single-figure estimates, it is assumed that, for each data set, weavers within the unknown range were in the same proportion as those in the known. Thus, if the minimum proportion of bridegroom weavers is 40 per cent, it is held that 40 per cent of those with unspecified occupations were also weavers. The technique usually gives an appropriate result, because the ranges are comparatively narrow. However, this is not always so. At Rivington, for example, it is from 7 per cent to 50 per cent between 1818–22 and at Formby from 7 per cent to 43 per cent.

Table A1.1  *Number of bridegroom weavers recorded in Lancashire Anglican registers, 1813–17*

| Church or group of churches* | Weaver total | Marriage total | Weaver %age |
|---|---|---|---|
| Blackburn Parish | 1,202 | 1,967 | 61 |
| Bolton | 993 | 2,019 | 49 |
| Burnley | 180 | 495 | 36 |
| Bury | 470 | 1,125 | 42 |
| Central Lancashire | 238 | 486 | 49 |
| Colne | 469 | 605 | 78 |
| East Bolton Area | 33 | 112 | 29 |
| Lancaster Area | 18 | 526 | 3 |
| Leigh | 363 | 582 | 62 |
| Liverpool, Christ Church | 0 | 157 | 0 |
| Liverpool Dockland | 20 | 1,402 | 1 |
| Liverpool, Holy Trinity | 2 | 316 | 1 |
| Liverpool, St Anne Richmond | 2 | 1,113 | 0 |
| Liverpool, St John | 5 | 430 | 1 |
| Liverpool, St Paul | 3 | 459 | 1 |
| Liverpool, St Peter | 39 | 2,430 | 2 |
| Liverpool, St Thomas | 2 | 431 | 0 |
| Lune Valley | 3 | 108 | 3 |
| Manchester, St Mary, St Denys and St George | 1,828 | 7,617 | 24 |
| Merseyside | 9 | 326 | 3 |
| Middleton | 315 | 629 | 50 |
| Newchurch-in-Pendle | 83 | 104 | 80 |
| North Fylde | 6 | 151 | 4 |
| Oldham | 457 | 841 | 54 |
| Penwortham | 64 | 110 | 58 |
| Prescot Parish | 48 | 591 | 8 |
| Toxteth Park | 1 | 377 | 0 |
| Walton-le-Dale | 76 | 205 | 37 |
| West Central Lancashire | 69 | 271 | 25 |
| West Fylde | 11 | 170 | 6 |
| West Lancashire Coast | 5 | 134 | 4 |
| West Manchester | 87 | 1,275 | 7 |

\* Churches in Blackburn Parish were Blackburn, Great Harwood and Samlesbury; in Central Lancashire they were Brindle, Chorley and Leyland; in East Bolton they were Ainsworth and Radcliffe; in Lancaster they were Chipping and Lancaster; in Liverpool Dockland they were St George and St Nicholas; in Lune Valley they were Bolton-le-Sands, Halton, Melling, Over Kellet, Tatham, Tunstall and Whittington; in Merseyside they were Hale, Childwall and Walton; in North Fylde they were Cockerham, Pilling

## Computing hand weaver numbers in early nineteenth century Lancashire

Table A1.2  *Number of bridegroom weavers recorded in Lancashire Anglican registers, 1818–22*

| Church or group of churches* | Weaver total | Marriage total | Weaver %age |
|---|---|---|---|
| Blackburn Parish | 1,210 | 2,182 | 55 |
| Bolton | 578 | 1,240 | 47 |
| Burnley | 223 | 622 | 36 |
| Bury | 487 | 1,211 | 40 |
| Central Lancashire | 301 | 685 | 44 |
| Colne | 472 | 696 | 68 |
| Deane | 208 | 550 | 38 |
| East Bolton Area | 51 | 143 | 36 |
| Lancaster | 23 | 501 | 5 |
| Leigh | 434 | 767 | 57 |
| Liverpool, Christ Church | 0 | 180 | 0 |
| Liverpool Dockland | 6 | 1,688 | 0 |
| Liverpool, Holy Trinity | 0 | 302 | 0 |
| Liverpool, St Anne Richmond | 2 | 956 | 0 |
| Liverpool, St John | 3 | 337 | 1 |
| Liverpool, St Paul | 0 | 433 | 0 |
| Liverpool, St Peter | 14 | 2,485 | 1 |
| Liverpool, St Thomas | 1 | 386 | 0 |
| Lune Valley | 3 | 154 | 2 |
| Manchester, St Mary, St Denys and St George | 1,819 | 9,095 | 20 |
| Merseyside | 0 | 375 | 0 |
| Middleton | 314 | 740 | 42 |
| Newchurch-in-Pendle | 94 | 114 | 82 |
| North Fylde | 10 | 129 | 8 |
| Oldham | 529 | 1,119 | 47 |
| Penwortham | 95 | 165 | 58 |
| Prescot Parish | 29 | 584 | 5 |
| Rochdale | 471 | 935 | 50 |
| Toxteth Park | 1 | 395 | 0 |
| Walton-le-Dale | 55 | 133 | 41 |
| West Central Lancashire | 61 | 246 | 25 |
| West Fylde | 13 | 192 | 7 |
| West Lancashire Coast | 1 | 149 | 1 |
| West Manchester | 78 | 1,680 | 5 |

and Stalmine; in Prescot Parish they were Farnworth, Prescot, Rainford and St Helens; in West Central Lancashire they were Croston, Eccleston and Hoole; in West Fylde they were Bispham, Lytham and Poulton; in West Lancashire Coast they were Altcar, Formby, Halsall, Melling and Sefton; and in West Manchester they were St John and St Mary.

*The last shift*

*Map 4* Lancashire parishes, 1822

*Computing hand weaver numbers in early nineteenth century Lancashire*

Table A1.3  *Frequency of monthly gaps in Lancashire marriage registers, 1813–22*

| Annual entries | Number of registers | Registers with monthly gaps | Total of monthly gaps |
|---|---|---|---|
| above 99 | 12 | 0 | 0 |
| 80–99 | 3 | 2 | 4 |
| 60–79 | 3 | 2 | 1 |
| 40–59 | 4 | 4 | 10 |
| 20–39 | 8 | 7 | 64 |

In both cases, the degree of variation is exaggerated by the small number of annual entries, averaging one at Rivington and three at Formby. Altogether, data from six marriage registers combine few entries with a wide range of results, all during the period 1818–22.[17]

One possible drawback with this approach is that it assumes all those for whom no occupation was recorded were actually in work. In general, this assumption is reasonable, since the incomplete entries occur in blocks, suggesting that, over a period of time, clergy simply omitted to enter the appropriate details. Sometimes, however, failure to note occupations is occasional, indicating that the bridegroom or father may have been unemployed. Fortunately, registers suffering from this defect yield fairly precise weaver proportion figures, thus requiring very little adjustment.

A second modification to the data involves grouping quinquennial weaver totals from adjoining parishes in order to overcome any distortions arising from using small databases (Tables A1.1 and A1.2 and Map 5).[18] The figures for the west Lancashire parish of Hoole illustrate the problem. The Hoole registers average only three marriages per year between 1813–22, whilst bridegroom weavers comprised 21 per cent during the first quinquennium and 67 per cent during the second. It is possible that a pronounced upsurge in the importance of handloom weaving took place at Hoole during the post-Napoleonic era, perhaps because a new employer moved into the area. Equally, the small number of entries may give unreliable figures.

It may be that registers yielding small annual marriage totals — say fewer than five on average — distort occupational distributions, both by exaggerating the relative importance of particular jobs and by understating the range of occupations. These problems may be most acute in several of the north Lancashire parishes — Over Kellett, Whittington, Bolton-le-Sands, Claughton, Halton, Tunstall and Tatham — and at Altcar and Formby in the south-west of the region. None provide unexpected results as far as hand weaving is concerned, though this may reflect their location outside the main weaving districts as much as the inherent reliability of their registers.

It remains to find a satisfactory means of calculating bridegroom weaver proportions for parishes where marriage registers omit occupations. The procedures are considered in the next section.

### 3  Gaps in registration

Between 1813–22, about 60 per cent of total entries in Lancashire marriage registers give bridegrooms' occupations. They provide figures of weaver concentration in most parts of

*The last shift*

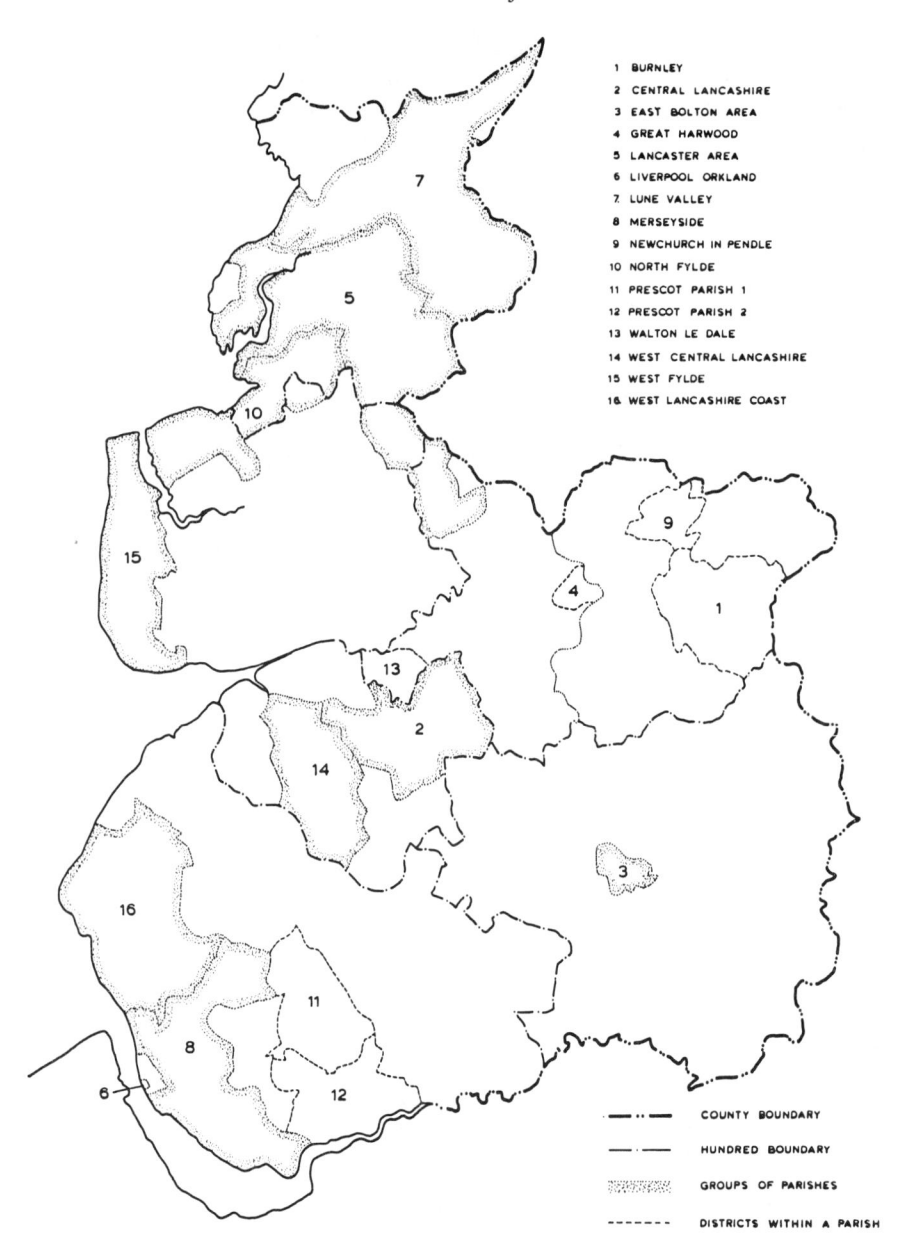

| | |
|---|---|
| 1 | BURNLEY |
| 2 | CENTRAL LANCASHIRE |
| 3 | EAST BOLTON AREA |
| 4 | GREAT HARWOOD |
| 5 | LANCASTER AREA |
| 6 | LIVERPOOL ORKLAND |
| 7 | LUNE VALLEY |
| 8 | MERSEYSIDE |
| 9 | NEWCHURCH IN PENDLE |
| 10 | NORTH FYLDE |
| 11 | PRESCOT PARISH 1 |
| 12 | PRESCOT PARISH 2 |
| 13 | WALTON LE DALE |
| 14 | WEST CENTRAL LANCASHIRE |
| 15 | WEST FYLDE |
| 16 | WEST LANCASHIRE COAST |

— ·· — COUNTY BOUNDARY
— · — HUNDRED BOUNDARY
▒▒▒ GROUPS OF PARISHES
- - - - - DISTRICTS WITHIN A PARISH

*Map 5* Parish groups and parish divisions in the early 1820s

the county, though certain districts, including the Liverpool area, are more fully covered than others. Some of the most serious gaps occur in Whalley parish (north-east Lancashire) where heavy concentrations of hand weavers were found. For this parish, twelve sets of marriage registers are available, but only in three cases are bridegrooms' occupations given.[19] Altogether, fewer than 30 per cent of marriage occupations for north-east Lancashire can be traced. Other significant gaps materialise in several of the more populous parishes in central and south Lancashire, including Preston and Wigan, where relatively high weaver concentrations were again to be found.

To fill the gaps and provide a full picture of weaver concentration in the county, estimates are required of the missing figures of bridegroom weavers. Anglican baptism registers can be used since, as is noted earlier, they record occupations consistently from 1813.[20] Thus, for any Anglican church with surviving registers, fathers' occupations can be obtained even if those of bridegrooms cannot. Given the inadequate recording of occupations in Nonconformist registers, only Anglican registers can be used. Whether, as a result, the figures are affected by any significant geographical variation in the strength of Non-conformity remains to be seen.

In using baptism register entries to determine bridegroom occupations, the working hypothesis is made that the ratio of bridegroom weavers to father weavers recorded in the Anglican registers is reasonably constant; there might be, perhaps, three father weavers to every bridegroom weaver. Since some variation can be expected to either side of this constant, it is appropriate to give precision to the relationship by means of regression analysis. This provides the means by which predictions of the unknown proportions of bridegroom weavers can be made.[21]

The first stage in the analysis is to count the number of weaver baptisms in those parishes for which bridegroom weaver totals are known. To obtain consistent results, the counts include weaver baptisms taking place in dependent chapelries and exclude entries relating to females, mainly, but not exclusively, concerning illegitimate births.[22]

In parishes where weddings took place only at the mother church, linking marriage weaver with baptism weaver entries, including those listed at dependent chapelries, is a straightforward matter. At Penwortham parish, for example, counts of father weavers given in the baptism registers at Penwortham Church and Longton Chapel can be added together and compared with numbers of bridegroom weavers recorded at Penwortham. For the parish as a whole, the ratio of baptism to marriage weavers is 3.8:1 between 1813-17 and 3.1:1 between 1818-22. Men living in Penwortham who married elsewhere, or who had their children baptised elsewhere, are ignored, partly because they are difficult to locate, but mainly because they are few in number.

Where more than one church in a parish was licensed to marry, it can prove difficult to link baptism and marriage entries. Thus, at Liverpool, Lancaster and Walton-on-the-Hill (Merseyside group) not all marriage registers record bridegrooms' occupations, whilst at Ainsworth Chapel (East Bolton) and at Aughton, Arkholme and Leck Chapels (Lune Valley) no father occupations are available. In each case, ratios of father weavers to bridegroom weavers cannot be calculated exactly. This matters little, though, since the numbers of weavers in north Lancashire and in the Liverpool area would have been too few to allow meaningful ratios to be obtained, even if full records had been kept.

Problems are also posed by the data from Manchester parish, where the numbers of bridegroom and father weavers greatly exceeded those in any other parish. In terms of regression analysis based on absolute numbers, the inclusion of such an abnormally high set of figures might lead to significant distortion. Since the regression lines are not to be used to estimate exceptionally large numbers of bridegroom weavers, it is safer to omit the Manchester figures from the analysis.

Usually, complete baptism and marriage figures are available for each five-year period. Where they are not, estimates have to be made in order to ensure that figures used in the regression analysis are compatible. These estimates are based on average figures computed from, and then added to, the known figures. In two instances (Hindley and Bolton-le-Sands) only one year's figures were recorded between 1813–17, so no estimates are attempted.

For two parishes, Prescot and Blackburn, more than one set of father weaver/bridegroom weaver figures can be calculated, thereby increasing the rather small number of variables available for regression analysis. Four of the Prescot parish registers — Farnworth, Prescot, St Helens, and Rainford — give marriage occupations, whilst a fifth set, belonging to Great Sankey chapel, record only baptisms. Since Great Sankey is situated in the south-east corner of the parish and was much nearer to Farnworth church than to other churches in the parish, people living there would either have married at Farnworth or in the adjoining parish of Warrington. However, register entries throughout the county reveal that, for marriages and baptisms, people normally made use of the churches in the parish they resided. Accordingly, the register entries for Farnworth and Great Sankey may be grouped separately from those in other registers at Prescot parish.

In Blackburn parish, two outlying areas, Walton-le-Dale and Great Harwood may be taken as separate districts.[23] Here, the churches catered almost exclusively for the marriage and baptism needs of local people, the registers making few references to people from elsewhere in the parish or from outside. Nor do the registers of Blackburn parish church make more than occasional references to either Walton-le-Dale or Great Harwood inhabitants.

The results of the baptism counts are given in summary form in Table A1.4. Absolute numbers of bridegroom weavers are also noted for comparison.

Scatter diagrams plotting these data show a strong linear relationship (Figure A1.1). Problems arise, however, with the figures for Blackburn and Bolton between 1813–17 and for Blackburn and Rochdale between 1818–22. All lie some distance from a regression line describing the remainder of the data, so that to draw regression lines including these figures might provide a means of predicting bridegroom weaver numbers subject to a wide margin of error. Nor can the degree of error be assessed, since there is no way of establishing whether a high or a low ratio of father weavers to bridegroom weavers would be expected in the deviant areas.

Because of these uncertainties, alternative approaches using percentage figures are tried. One tests the hypothesis that the percentage of bridegroom weavers in a district is nearly the same as the percentage of father weavers recorded in the Anglican baptism registers for that district. The second undertakes further regression analysis.

The first approach reveals that in nearly every district the percentage figure of Anglican father weavers is similar to that of bridegroom weavers. This is evident from Figure A1.2, where the quinquennial figures for each district are plotted as scatter diagrams. Comparison with a forty-five degree line drawn through the origin of each graph, shows that deviations above 10 per cent are infrequent, occurring in only nine out of forty-three instances. The average deviation amounts to 6.6 per cent between 1813–17 and to 6.1 per cent between 1818–22.

Similar results are obtained from the regression analysis. The data for each five-year period show a high degree of correlation (0.94 for 1813–17 and 0.91 for 1818–22) and the regression equations reveal that the bridegroom weaver proportions were no more than 2 or 3 per cent above the father weaver proportions (Appendix A3).

Estimates of bridegroom weaver numbers, therefore, can be more satisfactorily obtained using percentage rather than absolute baptism figures. Neither enable precise estimates to be made, but the former offer a significant reduction in the possible range of error compared with the latter. Since it makes little difference which of the two approaches using percentage figures is chosen, it is assumed that the baptism proportions form an acceptable proxy for the marriage proportions. In this way, around half the figures recorded in Tables A1.5 and 2.2 (page 44) are derived, the remainder being taken from marriage registers.

Comparison of the quinquennial totals suggests that hand weaving had not experienced any appreciable decline by the early 1820s. In general, the percentage figures show small reductions, but this may reflect population rises as much as falling hand weaver numbers. Of course, in districts where relatively large percentage falls did occur, hand weaving could have passed its peak and replacement industry may already have been developing. This was perhaps happening in Rossendale, where an 11 per cent reduction was recorded at Haslingden and one of 10 per cent at Newchurch. At the same time, in districts with rising weaver percentages, including Middleton and Leigh, hand weaving would still have been expanding and may have been some years from attaining its zenith. Given the incomplete nature of the parish register evidence, these conclusions are tentative, but they are consistent with the notions that overall numbers of hand weavers had not yet begun to diminish and that the onset of decline in the trade varied appreciably from district to district.

## 4 Numbers of handloom weavers

In using weaver proportions derived from Anglican baptism registers to estimate absolute numbers of hand weavers, two sets of calculations are required. One is to turn proportionate figures of father weavers into absolute numbers and the second is to determine the proportions these formed of the total weaving labour force. At both stages, formidable difficulties arise and, at best, the results are approximations. None the less, the approach offers perhaps the only means of obtaining new insights into the overall size of the Lancashire hand weaving trade during its peak years, drawing on a source hitherto neglected for the purpose.

The baptism register data is highly age-specific, referring almost exclusively to men in their twenties and thirties. The younger limit is perhaps more certain than the older, but the proportion of fathers aged forty or above would not have been substantial. This being so, it is reasonable to assume that, for each parish, the weaver proportion derived from baptism entries corresponds closely to the proportion of male weavers aged twenty to forty who lived in that parish. Thus, in a parish where one in every three fathers is described as a weaver, a similar ratio is anticipated amongst all males in their twenties and thirties. In effect, it is held that fathers listed in a baptism register during a particular year constituted a fairly random sample of married men drawn largely from the twenty to forty age group.

This argument might be challenged on the grounds that certain occupational groups, including handloom weavers, experienced higher than average birth rates, a reflection of their comparative prosperity. Baptism registers, therefore, may overstate the importance of handloom weaving. Furthermore, because the data are derived from Anglican registers, it might be suggested that distortions will arise if, compared with other occupational groups,

Table A1.4  *Father and bridegroom weaver numbers, 1813–22*

(a) 1813–17

| District | Father weavers | Bridegroom weavers |
| --- | --- | --- |
| Blackburn Area | 2,145 | 1,138 |
| Bolton Parish | 2,224 | 993 |
| Burnley | 455 | 180 |
| Bury Parish | 1,910 | 470 |
| Central Lancs | 1,219 | 238 |
| Colne Area | 1,201 | 469 |
| Great Harwood | 307 | 65 |
| Leigh Parish | 1,521 | 363 |
| Merseyside | 0 | 9 |
| Middleton Parish | 1,329 | 315 |
| Newchurch-in-Pendle | 250 | 83 |
| North Fylde | 34 | 6 |
| Oldham Parish | 2,139 | 457 |
| Penwortham Parish | 304 | 64 |
| Prescot Parish I | 57 | 34 |
| Prescot Parish II | 39 | 14 |
| Toxteth Park | 0 | 1 |
| Walton-le-Dale | 207 | 76 |
| West Central Lancs | 310 | 69 |
| West Fylde | 93 | 11 |
| West Lancs Coast | 15 | 5 |

hand weavers were over-represented amongst Nonconformist sects. This certainly concurs with A. D. Gilbert's view that the Nonconformist in the late eighteenth and early nineteenth century was commonly a handloom weaver or some other type of domestic worker.[24] Possibly, therefore, Anglican register data understate the importance of the handloom weaving trade.

With regard to the first challenge, it has been demonstrated that some proto-industrial groups did indeed experience relatively high birth rates; for them, greater prosperity led to a significant lowering of the marriage age.[25] However, in the absence of detailed research findings, it is not clear whether this was so in the case of the Lancashire handloom weavers. It is true that there is abundant evidence in parish registers to show that population growth in the Lancashire textile districts was appreciable during the eighteenth century.[26] It is also plain that rural as well as urban populations in the county continued to grow during the early decades of the nineteenth century, as printed census returns demonstrate.[27] Yet, if there was a direct relationship between the income levels of hand weavers and the size of their families, it may already have been diminishing in strength during the immediate post-Napoleonic years; by then, the piece rates paid for hand weaving were in long-term decline

(b) 1818–22

| District | Father weavers | Bridegroom weavers |
| --- | --- | --- |
| Blackburn Area | 1,799 | 1,156 |
| Bolton Parish | 2,043 | 578 |
| Burnley | 629 | 223 |
| Bury Parish | 1,903 | 487 |
| Central Lancs | 1,243 | 301 |
| Colne Area | 1,239 | 472 |
| Deane Parish | 1,076 | 208 |
| Great Harwood | 244 | 54 |
| Leigh Parish | 1,549 | 434 |
| Merseyside | 0 | 0 |
| Middleton Parish | 1,188 | 314 |
| Newchurch-in-Pendle | 290 | 94 |
| North Fylde | 68 | 10 |
| Oldham Parish | 2,027 | 529 |
| Penwortham Parish | 291 | 95 |
| Prescot Parish I | 48 | 21 |
| Prescot Parish II | 50 | 7 |
| Rochdale Parish | 2,428 | 471 |
| Toxteth Park | 0 | 1 |
| Walton-le-Dale | 220 | 55 |
| West Central Lancs | 320 | 61 |
| West Fylde | 50 | 13 |
| West Lancs Coast | 6 | 1 |

and had dropped considerably from peak levels.[28] Nor is there reason to suppose that, in the Industrial Revolution era, higher than average birth rates were confined to hand weavers. By this time, there was ample opportunity for other groups of Lancashire working people to achieve earnings as high as those attained in hand weaving. It is hard to make out a convincing case, therefore, to show that, during the early nineteenth century, hand weavers would have had larger families than other occupational groups because of income differentials.

In tackling the second challenge, the 1851 religious census can be used to determine whether, from district to district, the strongholds of Nonconformity coincided with those of handloom weaving.[29] Two sets of data may be extracted from the census. One, figures on numbers of churchgoers, proves difficult to use, because it gives the total number of church attendances on census Sunday rather than the actual number of those attending. The latter would plainly be more useful for the purpose in hand, but can only be derived using unverifiable assumptions about the numbers who attended church more than once.[30] The

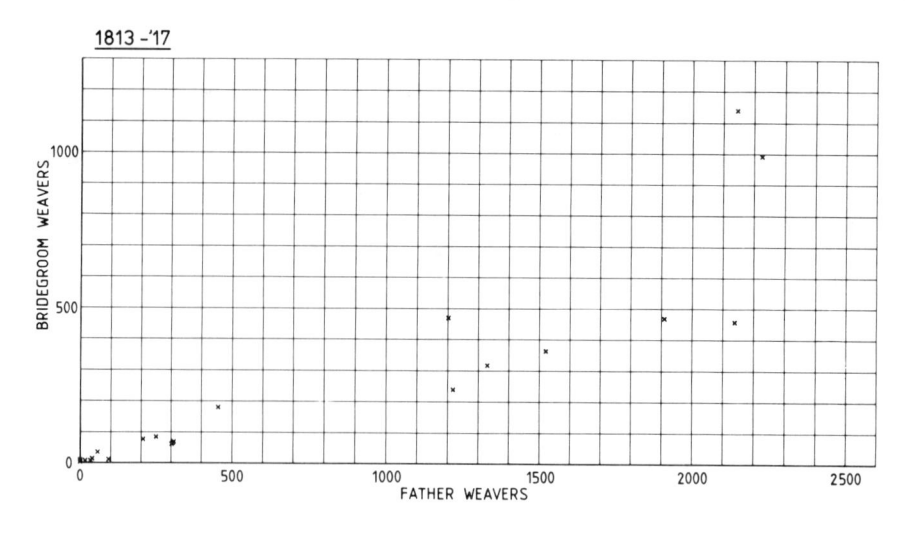

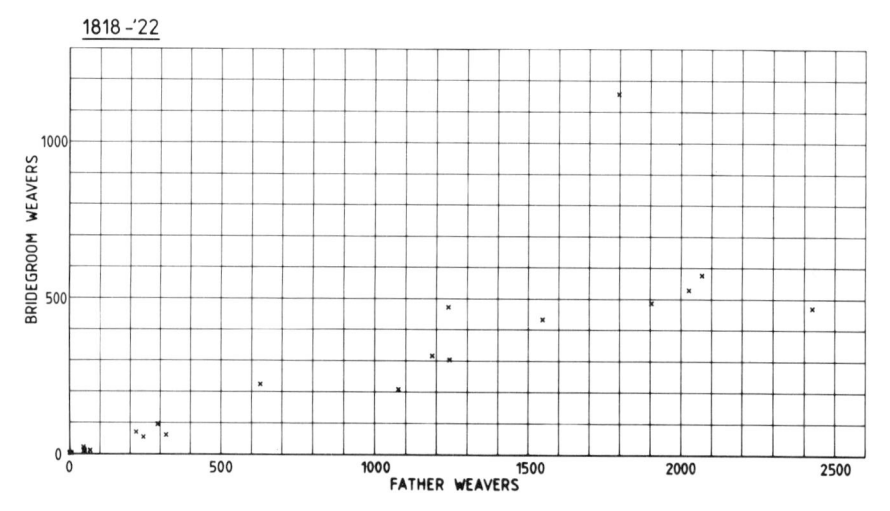

*Figure A1.1* Relationship of father and bridegroom weaver numbers in selected Lancashire districts, 1813–22

second data set, namely numbers of church sittings, also has weaknesses, including incompleteness. Yet it can be used without complicated and perhaps unjustified manipulation and, despite its inaccuracies, it does indicate overall variations in the strength of religious sects from district to district. Thus, a general relationship between religious persuasion and hand weaving can be established, even if it cannot be stated very precisely.

Data on numbers of church sittings in each census district are given in Table A1.6. Non-Anglican totals are grouped and, for each district, the ratio of Anglican to Non-Anglican (mainly protestant) sittings is computed.[31]

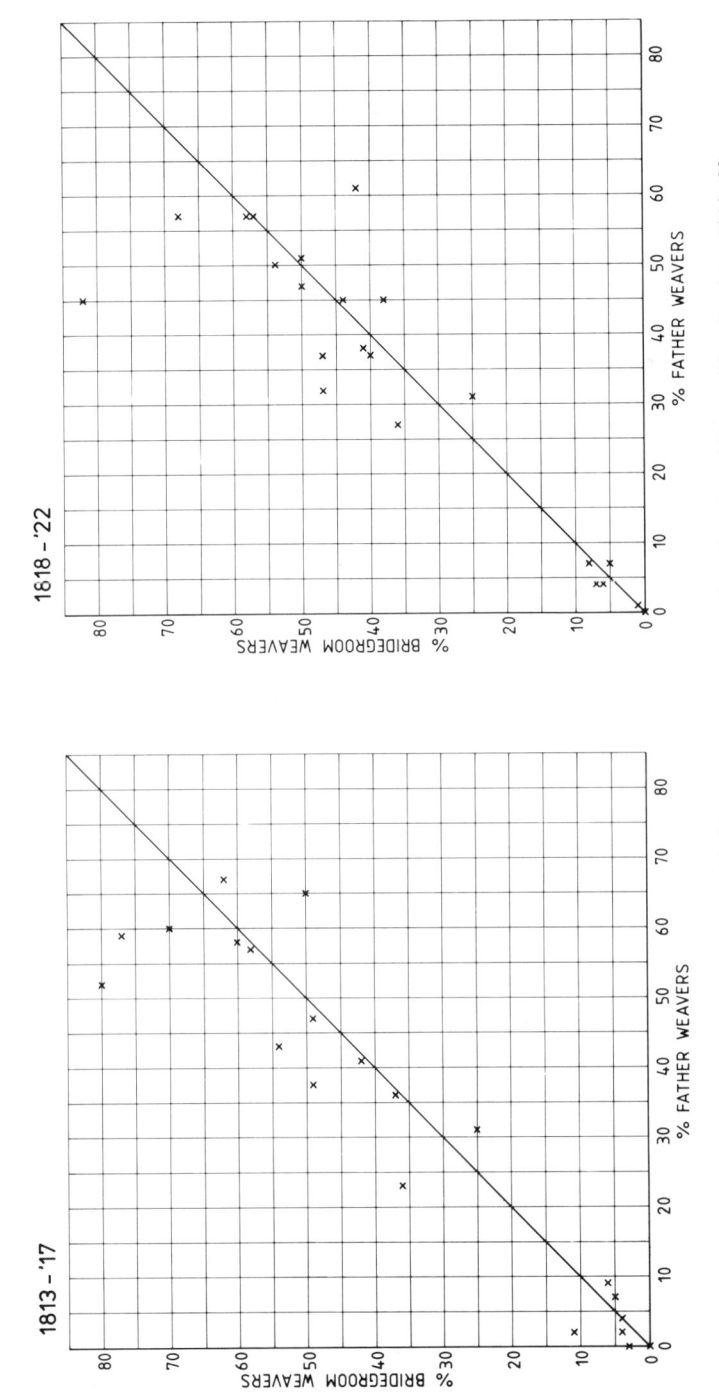

*Figure A1.2* Relationship of father and bridegroom weaver proportions in selected Lancashire districts, 1813–22

Table A1.5 *Rankings of bridegroom weaver proportions in Lancashire parishes, groups of parishes and parish districts, 1813–17*

| | Parish, parish district or parish group | Bridegroom weaver proportion | | Parish, parish district or parish group | Bridegroom weaver proportion |
|---|---|---|---|---|---|
| 1. | Newchurch-in-Pendle | 80 | 27. | Wigan Parish* | 32 |
| 2. | Colne | 78 | 28. | North Meols Parish* | 30 |
| 3. | Leigh Parish | 62 | 29. | Accrington* | 30 |
| 4. | Blackburn Parish | 61 | 30. | East Bolton | 29 |
| 5. | Flixton Parish* | 60 | 31. | West Central Lancashire | 25 |
| 6. | Haslingden | 60 | 32. | Altham* | 23 |
| 7. | Penwortham Parish | 58 | 33. | Manchester Parish+ | 22 |
| 8. | Church* | 57 | 34. | Preston Parish* | 20 |
| 9. | Oldham | 54 | 35. | St Michael's-on Wyre Parish* | 20 |
| 10. | Prestwich* | 50 | 36. | Clitheroe* | 17 |
| 11. | Middleton Parish | 50 | 37. | Warrington Parish* | 15 |
| 12. | Bolton Parish | 49 | 38. | Tarleton Parish | 10 |
| 13. | Central Lancashire | 49 | 39. | Ormskirk* | 8 |
| 14. | Padiham* | 48 | 40. | Prescot Parish | 8 |
| 15. | Eccles Parish* | 47 | 41. | West Fylde | 6 |
| 16. | Newchurch-in-Rossendale* | 47 | 42. | North Fylde | 4 |
| 17. | Whalley* | 47 | 43. | West Lancashire Coast | 4 |
| 18. | Ribchester Parish | 44 | 44. | Aughton Parish* | 3 |
| 19. | Bury Parish | 42 | 45. | Garstang Parish* | 3 |
| 20. | Winwick Parish* | 37 | 46. | Lancaster Area | 3 |
| 21. | Downham* | 37 | 47. | Lune Valley | 3 |
| 22. | Walton-le-Dale | 37 | 48. | Merseyside | 3 |
| 23. | Burnley | 36 | 49. | Rufford Parish* | 3 |
| 24. | Ashton-under-Lyne Parish* | 32 | 50. | Central Liverpool+ | 1 |
| 25. | Kirkham Parish* | 32 | 51. | Heysham Parish* | 1 |
| 26. | Standish Parish* | 32 | 52. | Huyton Parish* | 1 |
| | | | 53. | Toxteth Park | 0 |

\* Indicates estimates based on baptism register data
+ The Central Liverpool figure is derived by summing the Liverpool totals listed in Table A1.1 and that of Manchester by summing the Central and West Manchester figures.

For the most part, the figures reveal a clear contrast between the western part of the county, where ratios of Anglican to non-Anglican church sittings were relatively high, and the eastern part, where they were relatively low. Given the extent to which hand weaving was localised in east Lancashire, it may seem that hand weavers did favour Nonconformity, as Gilbert suggests. Caveats must be made, however. In the first place, the relationship does not always hold. Thus, in the handloom weaving stronghold of Leigh, one of the highest

Table A1.6  *Anglican and non-Anglican church sittings in Lancashire, 1851 (thousands)*

| Enumeration district | (a) Anglican sittings | (b) Non-Anglican sittings | Ratio of (a) to (b) |
|---|---|---|---|
| Liverpool | 14.7 | 16.1 | 0.9 |
| West Derby | 22.1 | 15.9 | 1.4 |
| Prescot | 25.6 | 17.0 | 1.5 |
| Ormskirk | 27.5 | 19.8 | 1.4 |
| Wigan | 16.0 | 16.7 | 1.0 |
| Warrington | 27.2 | 21.5 | 1.3 |
| Leigh | 20.7 | 18.6 | 1.1 |
| Bolton | 17.4 | 20.4 | 0.9 |
| Bury | 18.5 | 25.2 | 0.7 |
| Barton-Upon-Irwell | 22.2 | 27.0 | 0.8 |
| Chorlton | 12.7 | 19.2 | 0.7 |
| Salford | 12.7 | 18.9 | 0.7 |
| Manchester | 14.5 | 18.5 | 0.8 |
| Ashton-Under-Lyne | 17.5 | 21.1 | 0.8 |
| Oldham | 14.6 | 18.3 | 0.8 |
| Rochdale | 14.4 | 29.2 | 0.5 |
| Haslingden | 19.4 | 37.7 | 0.5 |
| Burnley | 22.6 | 34.2 | 0.7 |
| Clitheroe | 39.4 | 51.8 | 0.8 |
| Blackburn | 21.8 | 25.0 | 0.9 |
| Chorley | 26.1 | 23.3 | 1.1 |
| Preston | 21.6 | 19.3 | 1.1 |
| Fylde | 40.1 | 25.9 | 1.5 |
| Lancaster | 14.8 | 6.0 | 2.5 |
| Garstang | 8.4 | 3.8 | 2.2 |

ratios of Anglican to non-Anglican sittings was recorded. Secondly, the districts in which Nonconformity was strong were sometimes those where hand weaving was once important, but had declined appreciably by the mid-nineteenth century. Haslingden and Oldham provide examples.[32] Lastly, variation between eastern and western district figures may be as much a function of the degree of urbanisation as of the relative importance of hand weaving. Here again, though, the relationship is not clear-cut, with Preston and perhaps Wigan — both of which were districts with a major urban centre — having rather higher ratios than might have been anticipated.

Despite these objections, the figures still suggest there was a tendency for handloom weavers to embrace Nonconformity. If anything, therefore, the figures of weaver proportions derived from Anglican registers will understate actuality and this must be allowed for in estimating overall weaver numbers.

The next stage is to calculate, parish by parish, the proportion of males within the 20–39 age group. Here the 1821 census returns are helpful, since, for each enumeration district, the adult population is divided into standard ten-year age groups.[33] Because groups of these districts can be aggregated into parishes, it is a straightforward matter to calculate the totals. Each parish total, or group of parish totals, can then be multiplied by the appropriate weaver proportion figure derived from the baptism entry counts. The results of this procedure are given in Table A1.7. Taking the county as a whole, it is estimated that some 36,000 male hand weavers in their twenties and thirties would have been found in 1821.

The union between the two sets of data would be more satisfactory if the census year (1821) coincided with the central year of the parish register counts (1820). However, had 1821 been chosen as the central year for the register figures, the quinquennial averages would differ little from those obtained for the slightly earlier period. Comparison of the annual percentages within particular parishes sometimes reveals quite substantial variations, even in the more populous parishes, but often there is high consistency. Thus, whereas the range of weaver proportions between 1818 and 1822 is from 42 per cent to 54 per cent at Blackburn and from 23 per cent to 30 per cent at Bury, it varies only from 33 per cent to 36 per cent at Bolton and from 34 per cent to 37 per cent at Wigan. But even where the differences are fairly large as at Blackburn or Bury, substituting the 1823 figure for that of 1818 is unlikely to alter the five-year average to any significant degree.

There is also another concern with the procedure. It relates to the completeness of the 1821 census data. The general returns note that the population of Lancashire was enumerated at 1,052,859, whereas the people whose ages were returned amounted to only 839,461, a shortfall of some 15 per cent. Only 11 out of 484 enumerations were involved, but, disturbingly, they included the major towns of Salford and Manchester.[34]

One way around the problem was devised by contemporaries who compiled more detailed breakdowns of the 1821 age structure. They gave figures for each township and chapelry, estimating the missing totals by reference to the age structure of neighbouring settlements, where the population was 'nearly the same amount' and was 'employed in nearly similar Pursuits'. Salford and Manchester townships, for example, were deemed to have had the same proportions of people in each age group as Great Bolton. An obvious

Table A1.7  *Male weavers in Lancashire, 1821*

| Parish, parish district or group | Males aged 20–39 | Male weavers aged 20–39 |
|---|---|---|
| Accrington & Altham | 1,067 | 213 |
| Ashton-under-Lyne | 3,476 | 1,042 |
| Aughton | 177 | 5 |
| Blackburn | 5,685 | 3,127 |
| Bolton | 6,596 | 3,100 |
| Burnley | 1,897 | 683 |
| Bury | 4,560 | 1,824 |
| Central Lancashire | 2,664 | 1,172 |
| Church | 931 | 400 |

Table A1.7  (cont.)

| Parish, parish district or group | Males aged 20–39 | Male weavers aged 20–39 |
|---|---|---|
| Clitheroe | 705 | 84 |
| Colne | 2,228 | 1,515 |
| Deane | 2,415 | 918 |
| Downham | 149 | 57 |
| East Bolton | 501 | 180 |
| Eccles | 3,263 | 1,403 |
| Flixton | 272 | 147 |
| Garstang | 704 | 35 |
| Haslingden | 1,083 | 531 |
| Heysham | 54 | 1 |
| Huyton | 386 | 4 |
| Kirkham | 1,488 | 417 |
| Lancaster Area | 2,547 | 127 |
| Leigh | 2,295 | 1,308 |
| Lune Valley | 920 | 18 |
| Manchester | 24,497 | 4,409 |
| Middleton | 1,271 | 534 |
| Newchurch-in-Pendle | 311 | 255 |
| Newchurch-in-Rossendale | 1,436 | 531 |
| North Fylde | 754 | 60 |
| North Meols | 333 | 77 |
| Oldham | 5,172 | 2,431 |
| Ormskirk | 1,415 | 142 |
| Padiham | 747 | 314 |
| Penwortham | 603 | 350 |
| Prescot | 2,770 | 139 |
| Preston | 3,606 | 829 |
| Prestwich | 1,619 | 890 |
| Ribchester | 510 | 209 |
| Rochdale | 4,541 | 2,270 |
| St Michael's-on-Wyre | 612 | 98 |
| Standish | 959 | 326 |
| Tarleton | 209 | 29 |
| Walton-le-Dale | 652 | 267 |
| Warrington | 1,949 | 292 |
| West Central Lancashire | 974 | 244 |
| West Fylde | 792 | 55 |
| West Lancashire Coast | 1,170 | 12 |
| Whalley | 262 | 87 |
| Wigan | 4,668 | 1,494 |
| Winwick | 1,964 | 845 |

concern about this approach is that the populations of the towns selected for comparison may have had abnormal age structures. As far as Great Bolton is concerned, however, this was not the case. Males aged 20–39 in the town constituted 13.2 per cent of the population, a figure of the order commonly occurring in contemporary Lancashire towns.[35] Since there is no reason to suppose that the age structure of the Salford and Manchester populations departed radically from the norm, the estimates given in the 1821 census returns are probably reasonably accurate.

An appropriate method of finding the proportion that each group of male weavers in their twenties and thirties formed of the total weavers in their district is now required. Such calculations can be readily made from the mid-nineteenth century census schedules, though they obviously relate to a later period when the hand weaving trade had declined appreciably. Accordingly, to use census data for the purpose may lead to further distortion in the analysis, since a declining trade would be characterised by an aging labour force; the proportions obtained from the census might be far too low. However, as demonstrated in Chapter 5, there were still areas in Lancashire where handloom weaving had probably declined very little by mid-century and where powerloom weaving, or, for that matter, other types of factory industry, had made little or no progress. In these areas, the trade absorbed high proportions of the working population — perhaps a third or a half — and its age structure was biased towards younger workers, features that would have been expected of the hand weaving labour force during the early nineteenth century before long-term decline became evident. By working out the proportions of male weavers aged 20–39 in these districts, therefore, a suitable figure, or set of figures can be obtained to apply to the early nineteenth century data. Altogether, twenty-one enumeration districts can be used, yielding a total hand weaver population of 4,471, and they can be separated into five groups, each from a different part of the county. The groups are shown in Table A1.8, along with the proportions of male weavers aged 20–39 which they contained.

Whilst there is variation in weaver proportions between the groups, the range is not particularly wide, varying from 18.4 per cent to 23.3 per cent. The mean is 21.2 per cent. Which of the figures can be best applied to the parish register data is uncertain, though the use of the lowest might be misleading. This is because, with the exception of the Flixton area, the greatest weaver proportions occurred in areas which had experienced the least decline in population during the third quarter of the nineteenth century. The Lowton area population, for example, had fallen by 14 per cent compared with its peak, whereas the corresponding figure for the Samlesbury area was 22 per cent. It is possible, therefore, that, in 1851 some areas had comparatively low proportions of male hand weavers in their twenties and thirties because of rather higher migration rates amongst young men than occurred elsewhere, or because they could offer greater numbers of alternative jobs for young men in non-factory jobs. To an extent, this may have been linked with the type of fabric woven, since, except in the Croston area, the districts remaining with cotton rather than switching to silk or mixtures, record the lowest proportions of young male weavers. Where cloths other than the plainer and coarser cottons were being woven, opportunities for young people in domestic weaving may still have remained good well into the mid-Victorian period.

Summation of the absolute numbers of male hand weavers given in Table A1.7 gives a countywide total of 35,500. By applying the mean weaver proportion figure to this total, it is estimated that 167,453 hand weavers would have been found in Lancashire during 1821. Using the proportion figures from either end of the range, alternative totals of 152,361 and

Table A1.8  *Handloom weavers recorded in selected census enumerations*

| Area | Total | Males aged 20–39 | % Males aged 20–39 |
|---|---|---|---|
| Samlesbury | 264 | 46 | 17.4 |
| Balderstone | 197 | 33 | 16.7 |
| Osbaldeston | 125 | 24 | 19.2 |
| Clayton-le-Dale | 150 | 31 | 20.6 |
| Ramsgreave | 155 | 29 | 18.7 |
| Salesbury | 180 | 31 | 17.2 |
| Wilpshire/Dinckley | 144 | 30 | 20.8 |
| Total | 1,215 | 224 | 18.4 |
| Flixton | 319 | 62 | 19.4 |
| Urmston | 189 | 33 | 17.5 |
| Total | 508 | 95 | 18.7 |
| Croston | 311 | 89 | 28.6 |
| Ulnes Walton | 91 | 16 | 17.6 |
| Bretherton | 133 | 31 | 23.3 |
| Hoole | 214 | 48 | 22.4 |
| Longton | 387 | 79 | 20.4 |
| Hutton | 66 | 16 | 24.2 |
| Howick | 18 | 5 | 27.8 |
| Total | 1,220 | 284 | 23.3 |
| Kenyon | 50 | 11 | 22.0 |
| Lowton | 755 | 177 | 23.4 |
| Croft-with-Southworth | 318 | 67 | 21.1 |
| Total | 1,123 | 255 | 22.7 |
| Foulridge | 405 | 90 | 22.2 |

192,935 are obtained. Since there is concern about accepting the lowest of the three proportion figures, it is unlikely that the actual number of hand weavers in 1821 would have attained the highest figure. Nor is it probable that the lowest figure would have occurred, since in only one district (Croston) did the proportion of young male weavers exceed the mean figure to any marked degree. The indications are that the Croston figure was exceptional and that, in general, the proportions of male weavers aged 20–39 would have been less than the 23.3 figure at the upper end of the range. Probably, therefore, the mean figure is the most appropriate, especially if the proportions of young male weavers varied from district to district during the early 1820s, as was the case at mid-century.

## The last shift

One further consideration remains. It is noted earlier that weaver proportions derived from Anglican baptism registers may be on the low side because hand weavers may have been drawn strongly towards Nonconformity. Consequently, the range within which the number of hand weavers falls may be higher than that suggested. In trying to determine how much higher, parishes are sought in which both Anglican and Nonconformist registers give father occupations, so that comparisons can be made. Unfortunately, the results prove inconclusive. The main problem is that the Nonconformist registers do not record fathers' occupations frequently enough. At Bury, for example, four out of six registers do so between 1818–22, but at Bolton the figure is only two from seven.[36] Furthermore, the results are inconsistent. Thus, the Bury Nonconformist registers give a weaver proportion of 26 per cent for the period 1818–22, compared with the Anglican proportion of 40 per cent. At Bolton, by contrast, the Anglican figure is rather lower than the Nonconformist, 47 per cent compared with some 53 per cent.[37] It is unclear from such results whether any adjustments should be made to the overall weaver totals, let alone in which direction they should lie.

It would be unwarranted to claim too high a precision for estimates of handloom weaver numbers derived from parish register counts, especially at local level. Yet it is plain that if new estimates are to be attempted, some contemporary statistical source must be used. Parish registers, despite their inadequacies, are the only source available for the purpose. Inevitably, the procedures involved in using them require judgements to be made and evidence to support some of the steps involved is limited. At least, though, they enable an independent assessment to be made of the size of the hand weaving labour force when the trade was at, or near to, its peak.

### Notes

1  E. Baines, *History, Directory and Gazetteer of the County Palatine of Lancaster*, II (1825), p. 739.
2  The detail he gives is generally fuller for urban areas than for rural.
3  W. Farrer and J. Brownbill, *A History of the County of Lancaster* (1908), vols 3–8.
4  *PP*, 1822 (502) XV, p. 61.
5  LRO., Middleton Wesleyan Chapel Registers, MF.81.
6  J. Richardson, *The Local Historian's Encyclopedia* (1974), p. 73.
7  D. J. Steel, *National Index of Parish Registers* (1976) vol. 1, p. 61.
8  E. A. Wrigley and R. S. Schofield, *The Population History of England, 1541–1871* (1981), p. 89.
9  J. C. Cox, *The Parish Registers of England* (1910), p. 70.
10  Wrigley and Schofield, *op. cit.*, p. 25.
11  Such declarations appear in the transcripts.
12  The first appreciable wave of investment in powerlooms took place in the mid-1820s. See D. Bythell, *The Handloom Weavers* (1969), p. 53.
13  They are all kept in the LRO. The total is close to that of the 107 sets of Anglican marriage registers given in the PRAs for 1812 (*Abstract of the Answers and Returns to ... the Population Act, 51 Geo. III*, 1811, pp. 73 and 76).
14  The numbers involved are small.
15  The map is prepared from those for individual parishes given in Farrer and Brownbill, *op. cit.*, vols 3–8.

16   For marriage seasonality, see, for example, Wrigley and Schofield, *op. cit.*, pp. 298–305 and the essays in *LPS* by L. Bradley, W. J. Edwards and M. Massey. They are reprinted in M. Drake (ed.), *Population Studies from Parish Registers* (1982), pp. 1–21.

17   They were from Formby; Rivington; Altcar; Lancaster, St Mary; Tatham; and Liverpool, St George.

18   Each group includes at least 100 entries.

19   They are Burnley, Colne and Newchurch-in-Pendle.

20   See p. 200.

21   The approach follows that in R. Floud, *An Introduction to Quantitative Methods for Historians* (1973), ch. 7.

22   Recorded illegitimate births varied greatly from parish to parish. Thus, between 1813–17, they comprised 80 out of 610 baptisms in the Radcliffe Anglican registers (13 per cent), compared with only 27 out of 2,046 (1 per cent) at St Nicholas Church, Liverpool.

23   The mother church was several miles away.

24   A. D. Gilbert, *Religion and Society in Industrial England* (1976), pp. 112–13.

25   See, for example, D. Levine, *Family Formation in an Age of Nascent Capitalism* (1977), p. 58 *et seq*.

26   See p. 50.

27   See Farrer and Brownbill, *op. cit.*, vol. II, pp. 332–49.

28   See the piece rate figures in Bythell, *op. cit.*, pp. 275–6.

29   *PP*, 1852–3 (1690) LXXXIX, pp. 398–403.

30   There is a brief discussion of this issue in R. Dennis, *English Industrial Cities of the Nineteenth Century* (1984), pp. 29–30.

31   Catholic sittings were relatively unimportant. Only in Liverpool, West Derby, Manchester and Preston did they exceed 5,000.

32   See Table 5.2, p. 112.

33   *Abstract of the Returns . . . in the County of Lancaster in the Year 1821*, pp. 4–29.

34   *Ibid.*, pp. 30–1.

35   Examples include Burnley (13.5 per cent); Clitheroe (12.8 per cent); Colne (13 per cent); and Haslingden (13.2 per cent).

36   At Bury, those giving occupations are Bethel Independent; Union Street Methodists; Silver Street Presbyterian; and New Road Independent. At Bolton they are Duke's Alley Independent and Bridge Street Wesleyan (LRO, MF 67 and 68).

37   This assumes entries not giving occupations contained the same proportion of weavers as those that did.

# Appendix A2

# COMPUTING HAND WEAVER NUMBERS IN MID-VICTORIAN LANCASHIRE

Attempts to trace changes in hand weaver numbers during the 1830s and 1840s run into formidable problems with source material. Parish registers are of little help, since, beyond the mid-1820s, they record a growing and indeterminate number of power weavers. Nor are early census returns of much value. They give some occupational detail, but even the most explicit, those of 1831, provide only broad categorisations.[1] As a result, it is not possible to extract hand weaver numbers or, for that matter, numbers in any occupation.

In 1841, occupational detail obtainable from census returns improves appreciably when, for the first time, householders' schedules were introduced. Even so, it is incomplete, especially with regard to those other than household heads. Often, too, it lacks precision, a severe drawback as far as the weaving trade is concerned, since the distinction between hand and power weavers is seldom drawn. For example, of 1,015 weavers enumerated at Oswaldtwistle in 1841, as many as 999 were undifferentiated.[2] For this reason, the published occupational details from the 1841 census, which give an upper limit of around 35,000 hand weavers in Lancashire, massively understate reality.[3]

It is data from the 1851 census enumerators' schedules which provide the first satisfactory benchmark in assessing long-term changes in the importance of the Lancashire hand weaving trade. These data enable comparisons to be made with the peak years and form a base against which to judge the extent of further change during the mid-Victorian period.

In common with their predecessors, the mid-Victorian enumerators did not always distinguish between hand and power weavers, though they did so more frequently. Those of 1851 were the most diligent in this respect; many made only occasional lapses, so that quite precise numbers of hand weavers can be counted. But others made little or no attempt to differentiate and ways have to be found by which probable hand weaver numbers in their districts can be determined.

A second major concern with the mid-Victorian census schedules is the sheer volume of material available. By 1851, the population of Lancashire exceeded two million, growing to 2.4 million in 1861 and 2.8 million by 1871.[4] Of course, schedules from districts where hand weaving was absent or insignificant by mid-century, particularly Merseyside (including Prescot parish), north Lancashire and most of the Fylde, need not be searched.[5] And fewer areas have to be covered, or searched less intensively, at each successive census as hand weaving

## Computing hand weaver numbers in mid-Victorian Lancashire

gradually died out.[6] Even so, massive numbers of schedules must be examined and it is plain that sampling is necessary.

The first two sections of this appendix deal with the sampling techniques employed, especially the basis upon which the sampling fractions are determined. In the following section, the criteria for deciding whether undifferentiated weavers would have been hand or power weavers are discussed. Finally, the reliability of the evidence left by Lancashire's census enumerators is assessed.

### 1 Data extraction

It is probable that hand weaver proportions varied appreciably from parish to parish in mid-Victorian Lancashire, with a consequent effect on the size of sample required to locate them. Generally, the higher the anticipated proportion of weavers, the greater is the sample size needed, required confidence limits and degree of accuracy being given. Quite possibly, therefore, relatively high sampling fractions are necessary in order to estimate numbers of hand weavers in those districts where they were heavily concentrated, but in which the total population was comparatively small. Whether sampling is to be preferred to exhaustive analysis in such circumstances must be questioned.

A further consideration is whether to sample across entire parishes, or to sample only parts of parishes, especially the more populous urban areas. One difficulty is that, given the large size of many Lancashire parishes, and hence the likelihood that they would reveal wide variations in handloom weaver proportions from district to district, not least between rural and urban areas, optimum sample sizes can be difficult to calculate. Thus, the relatively small sample size required to analyse an urban population with comparatively few handloom weavers, would be inappropriate to assess weaver concentrations in surrounding rural areas, where numerous hand weavers could still be found. It should prove easier and more effective, therefore, to deal with urban and rural populations separately, perhaps using a combination of sampling and exhaustive techniques.

To assess more clearly the extent of these problems, a complete analysis of one parish in 1851 is undertaken. Blackburn is chosen, partly because it contained settlements of varying size, including one of Lancashire's major towns, and also because, judging from early nineteenth-century parish register statistics, it boasted one of the highest concentrations of handloom weavers in the county. Accordingly, guidance can be obtained regarding the maximum sample sizes required to analyse both rural and urban populations. The Blackburn counts are shown in Table A2.1. In most cases, maximum and minimum figures are given because enumerators failed to distinguish consistently between hand and power weavers.

As anticipated, the variation in hand weaver percentage was appreciable. In several cases, the figure exceeded 20 per cent of the total population, reaching as high as 50 per cent at Osbaldeston. However, in the more urbanised districts, notably Blackburn, Over Darwen and Walton-le-Dale, weaver percentages were uniformly low. This was also the case in enumeration districts containing substantial factory villages, including Lower Darwen, Great Harwood and Livesey. In fact, these findings reinforce the results of research previously undertaken to locate urban hand weavers' colonies in four of Lancashire's smaller towns.[7] In each case, hand weavers did not amount to more than a few per cent (Table A2.2).

For sampling purposes, therefore, likely proportions of urban handloom weavers lie within a narrow range, whilst those of rural weavers show wide variance. This raises the

Table A2.1  *Handloom weavers in Blackburn parish, 1851*

| District | Maximum number | Minimum number | Total population | Weaver % age |
|---|---|---|---|---|
| Balderstone | 201 | 201 | 660 | 30 |
| Billington | 227 | 121 | 882 | 14–26 |
| Blackburn | 4,257 | 986 | 46,536 | 2–9 |
| Clayton-le-Dale | 150 | 139 | 471 | 30–32 |
| Cuerdale | 10 | 9 | 80 | 11–13 |
| Darwen Lower | 380 | 137 | 3,521 | 4–11 |
| Darwen Over | 700 | 201 | 11,702 | 2–6 |
| Dinckley | 68 | 68 | 151 | 45 |
| Eccleshill | 76 | 76 | 598 | 13 |
| Great Harwood | 208 | 208 | 2,548 | 8 |
| Harwood Little | 51 | 51 | 316 | 16 |
| Livesey | 267 | 180 | 2,649 | 7–10 |
| Mellor | 706 | 371 | 1,668 | 22–42 |
| Osbaldeston | 125 | 123 | 250 | 49–50 |
| Pleasington | 64 | 61 | 428 | 14–15 |
| Ramsgreave | 155 | 155 | 438 | 35 |
| Rishton | 54 | 54 | 800 | 7 |
| Salesbury | 180 | 180 | 388 | 46 |
| Samlesbury | 269 | 264 | 1,435 | 18–19 |
| Tockholes | 223 | 219 | 939 | 23–24 |
| Walton-le-Dale | 596 | 506 | 6,855 | 7–9 |
| Wilpshire | 76 | 76 | 237 | 32 |
| Witton | 142 | 89 | 1,367 | 7–10 |

Table A2.2  *Handloom weavers in smaller Lancashire towns, 1851*

| Town | Maximum number | Minimum number | Total population | Weaver % age |
|---|---|---|---|---|
| Accrington | 234 | 50 | 10,374 | 0.5–2 |
| Bolton, Little | 1,154 | 261 | 20,468 | 1–6 |
| Chorley | 782 | 672 | 12,684 | 5–6 |
| Haslingden | 804 | 224 | 9,010 | 2–9 |

question as to whether satisfactory estimates of weaver proportions in rural areas can be made for sampling purposes.

That rural districts could support high concentrations of handloom weavers in 1851 also brings concern that relatively large samples are needed to achieve reasonably accurate and reliable estimates of weaver proportions. Thus, in a settlement with a population of 2,000 and a handloom weaver proportion of 20 per cent — a figure that might often have occurred if the Blackburn counts are any guide — a sample size of no less than 869 is needed to achieve a result accurate to ±2 per cent at the 95 per cent confidence limit. Even reducing the desired accuracy to ±3 per cent requires a sample size of 509. (Details of how these and subsequent sample sizes are determined is given in Appendix A3.) Clearly, to work at these levels of accuracy requires high sampling fractions (one in four at the ±3 per cent level) so that little, if anything, is gained in terms of efficiency.

The possibility remains, however, that adjacent enumeration districts in rural areas can be grouped together for sampling purposes. In this way, large enough population totals might be obtained to make sampling a more feasible proposition. In Blackburn parish, for example, the six districts situated to the south and west of the main town, comprising Eccleshill, Lower Darwen, Livesey, Tockholes, Pleasington and Samlesbury, might be taken as a single group, their collective populations in 1851 approaching 10,000.

This procedure is not always appropriate, however. One reason is that the mid-century population totals in a number of parishes attained only a few thousand. This was so in Leyland Hundred and in the sub-districts within Whalley parish, including Burnley, Padiham and Colne. A second reason is that rural populations in some parishes were equally limited. For instance, in Preston parish, under 4,000 people lived outside Preston township. In such cases, sampling brings no advantage.

In other parishes, though, including Bolton and Wigan, the total rural population numbered tens of thousands, so that the argument for sampling appears strong. Yet doubts remain. One is that sampling across groups of districts leads to a loss of potentially useful detail, not least concerning the extent to which family working groups remained a feature of the hand weaving trade. Nor is it certain that, with populations as low as, say, ten or fifteen thousand, sampling would be quicker than exhaustive analysis. This is especially so where concentrations of rural hand weavers were low, since little recording is then necessary and schedules could be worked through quickly. Also, time is saved by not having to count a regular sample interval. Lastly, the problem remains of how to calculate the optimum sample size for each rural district or group of rural districts, given that, as was the case in Blackburn parish, handloom weaver concentrations show marked differences both between and within enumeration districts. In fact, to ensure that the sample size is sufficiently large to pick up the overall proportion of handloom weavers in a group of enumeration districts, it would be necessary to err on the side of safety and use a larger sample size than, with more perfect knowledge, might be strictly required. On balance, therefore, it is more satisfactory to approach the rural census returns on an exhaustive basis.

If the case for sampling rural districts is less than convincing, that for sampling the major urban areas seems undoubted. This is most noticeably so with Manchester, where the population approached 200,000 in 1851, and with Preston, Salford, Oldham, Ashton-under-Lyne, and Hulme (Manchester parish), the populations of which were each in excess of 50,000. Other sizeable populations occurred at Great Bolton (almost 40,000); Chorlton-on-Medlock (about 35,000); at Wigan (approaching 32,000); and at Bury (over 25,000).

In sampling urban areas, it is again necessary to balance potential savings in time against losses in precision, a problem that is far from minimal given the low proportions of handloom weavers that were expected to have remained in Lancashire's major towns by 1851. Arguing in specific terms, to check within ±3 per cent whether 6 per cent of Bury's population in 1851 was hand weaving (1,500 people) requires a sample size of 240 at the 95 per cent confidence limit. The actual figure lies somewhere between 750 and 2,250 people — scarcely a very precise result. By raising the degree of accuracy required to ±2 per cent, the range within which the number lies can be narrowed to between 1,000 and 2,000, but only at the expense of increasing the sample size to 542. To compress the range to within ±1 per cent (1,250 to 1,750) requires a sample size in excess of 2,000. Evidently, then, it is not practicable to sample the more populous urban areas with a high degree of precision, though the alternative of complete analysis seems unmanageable.

In the light of these considerations, a decision has to be made on the degree of error within which to work. Plainly, much extra effort is entailed in return for a relatively small improvement in accuracy by working at the ±1 per cent level rather than at the ±2 per cent; to reduce by half the range within which the number of handloom weavers lies requires a four-fold increase in sample size. By contrast, to work at the ±2 per cent level rather than at the ±3 reduces the range by one-third and requires no more than a doubling in sample size. If the assumption is made that, at the most, 6 per cent of the people living in any of the larger urban areas were hand weavers, then a sample size of around 500 is required in each case, a number that does not seem excessive. Of course, should it prove possible to project a lower proportion of handloom weavers, the sample size can be reduced accordingly. It seems most appropriate to work to within ±2 per cent, therefore, even though this still leaves a comparatively wide range within which weaver numbers lie.

## 2 Urban samples and weaver proportions

Having decided on an acceptable degree of error, it is necessary to estimate as accurately as possible the likely proportion of handloom weavers in each of the urban populations chosen for sampling. The aim is to determine the most efficient sample size, large enough to ensure that the actual proportion of hand weavers can be confirmed within specified confidence limits and degrees of error, but small enough to prevent the collection of unnecessary data. For the most part, reliance has to be made on contemporary surveys, though in the cases of Preston, Oldham and Bury, useful evidence is available from recent studies based on census schedule samples.

Using a one in ten sample of Preston's population in 1851, Michael Anderson reports that 4 per cent of males aged ten and over were handloom weavers. Of males aged twenty and over, 5 per cent were handloom weavers and a further 3 per cent were unspecified weavers.[8] No details are given concerning the number of female hand weavers. However, at Blackburn and the other towns subjected to exhaustive analysis, female hand weavers were fewer in number than their male counterparts. Since there is no reason to suppose Preston did not conform to this pattern, 4 per cent seems an appropriate figure for sampling purposes.

For Bury, a one in fifty sample of the 1851 population is available, taken for purposes other than estimating the proportion of handloom weavers. The sample size is 508. Since the Manchester Statistical Society survey of the mid-1830s indicates that the proportion of hand weavers in the town was already extremely low — about 1 or 2 per cent — this sample is probably large enough to give an estimate well within a ±2 per cent error limit.[9]

The proportion of hand weavers at Oldham was also very low by the mid-nineteenth century. From a one in thirty sample of the 1841 census schedules, John Foster estimates that there were no more than 300 adult male hand weavers in the town.[10] Assuming there would have been roughly the same number of female as male hand weavers and, in a much-diminished trade, comparatively few juveniles, there may not have been more than 600 hand weavers altogether. They would have constituted little more than 1 per cent of the town's inhabitants.

Contemporary evidence is consistent with Foster's view. In 1835, Robert Gardiner, a cotton spinner and manufacturer, maintained that there were very few handloom weavers in the Oldham area, as well as at Ashton-under-Lyne, Hyde, Stockport, Dukinfield, Stalybridge, Hyde and Heywood.[11] Throughout this area, he thought, the powerloom prevailed. By 1841, Edwin Butterworth considered that the Oldham handloom weavers numbered only 200 and worked mostly with silk,[12] whilst in 1844, Samuel Bamford found that very few of them still remained in the township.[13] Before the decade ended, A. B. Reach, noted the 'very few old men' in Oldham, who, 'scattered in cellars or perched in garrets' still wove cotton at the handloom.[14] If these contemporaries are correct, hand weaving had all but disappeared in Oldham by the 1840s. Yet comparison of Foster's 1841 census figures with the estimate made by Butterworth in the same year strongly suggests that the latter gave too low a figure. Nor can the possibility be discounted that journalistic licence led Reach to err in the same direction. Certainly, he did not disclose his source of evidence. Faced with these uncertainties, it appears that a few hundred handloom weavers may still have remained at Oldham in 1851. The proportion they formed of the total population would have been extremely low, perhaps less than 1 per cent and almost certainly less than 2. For sampling purposes, it is safer to use the latter figure, which, to give a result accurate to ±2 per cent at the 95 per cent confidence interval, requires a sample of fewer than two hundred.

Other south Lancashire towns also showed small proportions of hand weavers by the mid-nineteenth century, as Robert Gardiner observed. To his evidence can be added that of the Manchester Statistical Society, relating to the period 1834–36. This shows only about 2 per cent of the total numbers examined at Manchester were handloom weavers, a similar figure to that at Ashton-under-Lyne; at Salford, the figure was as low as 1 per cent.[15] The incompleteness of this evidence, however, limits its use in computing overall numbers and proportions of hand weavers. It is impossible to know, for example, whether, in any of the towns covered by the survey, major colonies of hand weavers were overlooked. Yet it is probable that hand weaver proportions at Ashton, Manchester and Salford fell between the mid-1830s and the early 1850s, as their populations expanded appreciably and hand weaver numbers diminished. With regard to Ashton-under-Lyne, A. B. Reach went so far as to claim that, by 1849, there lingered on 'a handful of miserable old men the remnants of the cotton hand-loom weavers'. Younger people in the town, he declared, no longer considered entering the trade.[16]

There is nothing to show that the maximum proportion of hand weavers would have been higher at Manchester, Ashton and Salford than in other south Lancashire towns. Despite the inadequacies of the evidence, it may be supposed that, at the most, 2 per cent of the inhabitants in each town would still have woven by hand in 1851. Once more, therefore, this figure may be chosen for sampling purposes.

At Bolton, contemporary evidence suggests that a higher proportion of hand weavers survived in the mid-nineteenth century than in towns further south. It has been noted that contemporaries did not mention declining numbers of hand weavers in the town until the mid-1830s,[17] and that, according to Black's 1837 survey, some 5,500 were still at work there.[18] No doubt this number would have fallen somewhat by 1851, though if, say, 4,000 remained, they would have comprised virtually 7 per cent of the total population. At Little Bolton, however, where about one-third of the town's inhabitants lived, the proportion of hand weavers did not exceed about 6 per cent in 1851 (Table A2.2). Even so, Bolton's mid-Victorian hand weavers were likely to have been rather more numerous than those in other south Lancashire towns. With these considerations in mind, it is unwise to assume that fewer than 7 per cent of Bolton's population still wove by hand in 1851.

For Wigan, help in estimating hand weaver proportions comes from two surveys of cellar weaving shops. One, undertaken by a Mr Prichard in1849, reveals a total of 520, chiefly in the Scholes area.[19] The second, J. T. Jackson's analysis of contemporary maps, gives a figure of 567 for 1847.[20] Assuming, as is probable, four looms per cellar was usual, then around 2,000 hand weavers may have worked in the town at mid-century, about 6 per cent of the population.[21] However, it is not certain whether the recorded loomshops were all in use nor whether they were operating to full capacity. There is no reason to suppose, moreover, that Wigan would have maintained a higher proportion of handloom weavers at this time than the nearby towns of Bolton and Preston. For sampling, therefore, a figure of 4 per cent is taken.

As far as Chorlton and Hulme are concerned, evidence is lacking as to the strength of hand weaving and so rather arbitrary suggestions must be made. Yet it is improbable that these districts would have differed appreciably in terms of hand weaver proportions from those of neighbouring Manchester and Salford. Accordingly, a figure of 2 per cent is chosen in each case.

Summing the sample sizes for each major town reveals that no more than 2,500 entries must be extracted from a total population in 1851 of nearly 600,000. Also, over half the entries in the 1851 census schedules requiring analysis may be dealt with by sampling. Since districts with low weaver concentrations in 1851, including those in the Manchester area, are unlikely to require investigation in later census years, the task of searching census schedules to locate hand weavers is evidently manageable.

### 3 Computing weaver numbers

Mid-nineteenth century census enumerators distinguished inconsistently between hand and power weavers. Some made no attempt to do so, despite clear guidance being given that they should.[22] Others did so for some households but not for all, an indication, perhaps, that varying detail was provided by household heads. Whatever the reason for their lapses, ways have to be found of distinguishing between undifferentiated hand and power weavers if the extent to which hand weaving survived during the mid-Victorian years is to be adequately assessed.

One consideration is a possible contrast in the age structure of hand and power weavers. Some indication of this arises from statements of two contemporaries, William Rathbone Greg, the leading cotton spinner and manufacturer, and Richard Needham, a Bolton handloom weaver. The former maintained that the age range of powerloom weavers was between thirteen and forty-five and the latter that men were employed as powerloom weavers until they reached the age of forty.[23] To this testimony can be added the impression gained from the Blackburn pilot survey that whereas handloom weavers were well represented amongst all age groups in the labour force, powerloom weavers were nearly all young people, mainly in their teens and twenties. If this contrast was real, and if it occurred generally, an upper

Table A2.3  *Age distribution of powerloom weavers in selected districts, 1851 and 1871*

| Age group | 1851 weaver proportion | 1871 weaver proportion |
| --- | --- | --- |
| 10–19 | 45 | 45 |
| 20–29 | 39 | 34 |
| 30–39 | 11 | 14 |
| 40–49 | 4 | 4 |
| 50–59 | 1 | 3 |
| 60 and above | – | – |

age limit for the majority of powerloom weavers might be established. Undifferentiated weavers who exceeded this limit might then be counted amongst the hand workers.

The clearest guidance on the matter may be obtained from census schedules which distinguish consistently between hand and power weavers. These are quite numerous and a selection may be drawn to allow for geographical variation; for rural and urban differences; and for the possibility that the age range of powerloom weavers widened over time.[24] Data are presented on 1,180 individuals for 1851 and on 851 for 1871 (Table A2.3).[25]

In both 1851 and 1871, the vast majority of power weavers were under the age of thirty and only a small minority were forty or over; power weaving was mainly a young persons' occupation, relatively few remaining in the trade into middle age.[26] It is reasonable to assume, therefore, that undifferentiated weavers in their forties were far more likely to have been hand than power operatives and that those aged fifty or above were almost certain to have been. Exceptions inevitably occurred, but any underestimation of power weavers in the forty and above age groups would probably have been more than offset by underestimation of hand weavers in the below forty age groups, especially in 1851.

A second approach to identifying unspecified weavers is to consider the types of fabric used and the range of goods produced, details of which were frequently recorded by the census enumerators. The accepted view amongst historians is that weavers of silk or wool, and those producing fancy and fine goods, were more likely to have survived longer as hand workers than those who wove the plainer and coarser grades of cotton cloth.[27]

As far as silk weaving is concerned, useful evidence is provided by Angus Reach, following his tour of the Manchester textile districts in 1849. Writing about his visit to Macclesfield, in Cheshire, he observed:

'Very little silk, and that only of the coarsest kind, is woven by power. A small quantity of bandannas are thus turned out in Macclesfield; but in the production of the higher class of silk fabrics, and in all fancy goods, the delicacy and intelligence of human labour is requisite ...[28]

He noted that some silk weaving took place in mills equipped with the Jacquard loom, a machine which, at that time, was never 'beholden for its motion to the steam-engine'.

Details from factory inspectors' returns gives credence to Reach's views. In 1850, they counted only 1,977 silk powerlooms in use throughout Lancashire.[29] Furthermore, in those silk producing districts where hand workers are separated from power workers in the 1851 census schedules, the latter receive scant mention. This was also true in 1861, though less marked in later censuses. Nevertheless, it is quite certain that silk handloom weaving maintained its dominance well into the third quarter of the nineteenth century.

The situation was similar in the wool trade. In 1850, the factory inspectors returned fewer than 10,000 powerlooms used in wool manufacture and these probably gave employment to no more than a small minority of the labour force. During the mid-Victorian years, wool weaving by power gradually achieved dominance though, given the relative insignificance of the wool trade in Lancashire, failure to distinguish hand and power weavers in this sector does not bring serious difficulty in judging the overall importance of the hand weaving trades. Census evidence sheds little further light on the matter, except to show that in some woollen areas, the powerloom had gained ascendancy by 1851. This was so in parts of Spotland (Rochdale), for example.[30]

In cotton weaving, meanwhile, mechanisation proceeded space. Factory returns show that, by 1850, almost 250,000 cotton powerlooms had been installed in Britain and that, by 1870, the figure had reached 441,000.[31] At the start of this period there were already many more power weavers in the trade than hand weavers, so it is highly probable that the bulk of the undifferentiated cotton weavers recorded in the mid-nineteenth century censuses were using powerlooms.

Such considerations are complicated, however, by the wide variety of cotton goods produced. With all types of fabric, the powerloom made the swiftest inroads with plainer and coarser grades of cloth, as contemporaries disclose. In 1840, for example, Joseph Gillow of Preston remarked that powerlooms were

chiefly confined to coarse reeds and low counts of yarns, the finer reeds and yarns being much more difficult to manage; the finer the sorts the more inapplicable to their use.[32]

Moreover, such specialised cotton products as patterned counterpanes and quilts, much woven in the Bolton area, and mixed-fibre cloths, the most common of which was mousseline-de-laine, a worsted and cotton fabric, only gradually succumbed to the powerloom. Mention of power weavers in these trades is rare in the 1851 census schedules, though mousseline-de-laine was largely a powerloom product by 1861.[33] Also, the powerloom proved unsuccessful in weaving knotted counterpanes known as caddows.[34] In this trade, the number of hand weavers may actually have risen during the mid-nineteenth century, from 1,000 in 1833 to 1,700 in 1862.[35]

The demise of hand weaving in the production of fancier cotton goods, including counterpanes, was hastened by the invention of the dobby, a shedding mechanism which allowed the powerloom to be used for making patterned goods. The dobby was introduced into Lancashire around 1858, with an improved version, the Keighley Dobby, being developed in the late 1860s. The former wove patterned dhotis and the latter light fabrics. Both needed improvement, however, so that hand weaving may still have been usual in the fancy cotton trades during the early 1860s, if not beyond.[36] It seems, too, that the Jacquard loom, which was capable of making a far wider range of patterned goods than the dobby, was not harnessed to steam until 1860 and that its main use was in silk rather than cotton manufacture.[37]

From this discussion of fabric types, it may be concluded that, amongst the undifferentiated weavers listed in the 1851 census, those working with silks, mixtures and fancy cottons, including counterpanes and quilts, are far more likely to have been hand than power weavers. Accordingly, they are regarded as such in the census counts. Probably, too, the great majority of silk and fancy cotton weavers given in the 1861 census still used handlooms.

For the later census years, the position is more difficult to judge and so greater reliance has to be placed on alternative indicators, especially weavers' ages.

A third approach to identifying undifferentiated hand weavers is to consider the environment in which they worked. The Blackburn pilot survey indicates that hand weavers were most strongly concentrated in country districts and on town outskirts. Where rural textile factories were well established, however, concentrations of handloom weavers were often low. Indeed, their trade may have survived most strongly in areas where competition from mechanised textile production, and from other trades, was limited. Such areas can be identified partly from census evidence, but also from other sources, especially the mid-1840s six-inch to the mile O.S. maps.

To illustrate the approach, the census returns for Pilkington, near Bury may be selected. This township comprised the village of Whitefield and the surrounding rural settlements (Map 6). In 1851, the population was 12,863, of whom 693 were listed as hand weavers. There were also 549 undifferentiated weavers and several hundred power weavers. Most of the undifferentiated weavers were concentrated in one of thirteen enumeration districts, in which lay the settlements of Half Acre, Kirkham, Hardman's Green and Higher Lane, together with part of Besses o'th' Barn. As Map 6 reveals, these settlements did not contain factories in 1848, nor were there factories in the immediate vicinity. Situated away from the main village and consisting, in each case, of no more than a row or two of cottages, they displayed the characteristic settlement pattern of rural handloom weavers' colonies.[38]

However, whether all the weavers living in these colonies in 1851 still worked at the handloom is unclear. There were certainly some opportunities for factory work in Pilkington and in adjoining enumeration districts and these were perhaps extended by further factory building in the late 1840s and early 1850s. Yet the 1848 map shows that the nearest factories were in the north of the district, a mile or so from the settlements in question. Possibly some weavers were prepared to walk this distance to and from work each day; that the majority would have done so is unlikely. If anything, this line of argument is more compelling when applied to weaver colonists in the later census years, when the opportunity to remain at the handloom became much more limited. As far as the early 1850s is concerned, it seems that most of those who lived in fairly remote rural colonies and who were described only as weavers were, in fact, working at the handloom.

Two other means by which unspecified weavers can be separated into hand and power workers may be mentioned. One is to compare sets of enumerators' records from one census to the next. Thus, if an 1851 enumerator failed to distinguish hand and power weavers, his successor might. Where the successor still recorded appreciable numbers of hand weavers, it may be assumed that the unspecified weavers listed by his predecessor also worked in the trade. The number of occasions when this occurred, though, was extremely few, since the 1851 enumerators were generally the ones who made the most detailed record of occupations. The other way is to seek dates at which manufacturers in particular districts first began to use powerlooms. Again, however, few insights can be gained. Only occasionally is reference made to such developments either in primary or secondary sources and even then, the position is not always clear. For example, it is reported that a 'silk shed' was established at Brewery Lane, Leigh, in 1859,[39] and a cotton mill at Mellor, near Blackburn, in 1878.[40] No definite statement is made that either housed steam-looms, nor whether, at either place, earlier power weaving sheds had been built. Again, D. H. Langton does not state when powerlooms were introduced at Flixton, though a textile mill was built there in 1851.[41]

It is evident, then, that the problem of undifferentiated weavers can be tackled, if not

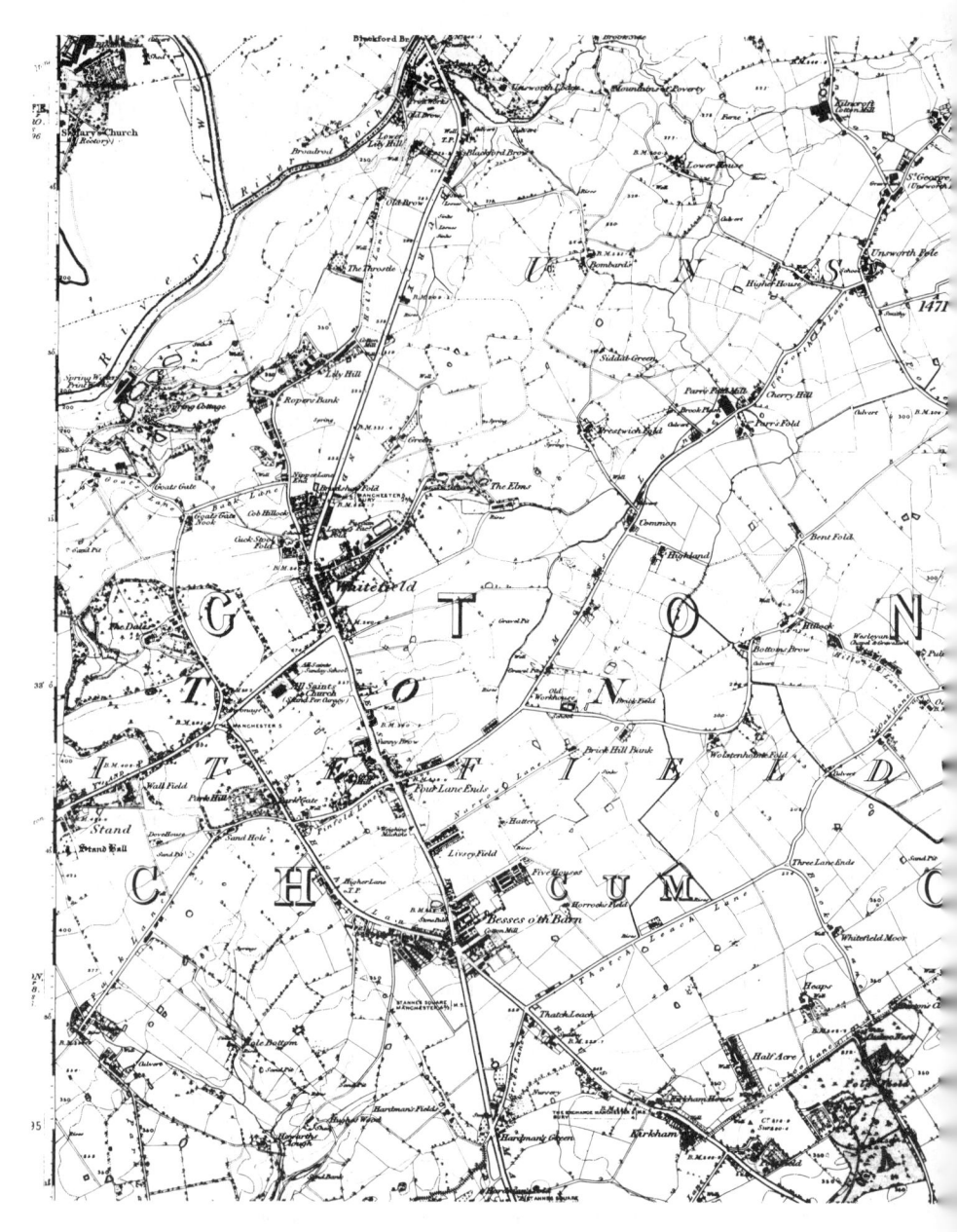

*Map 6* The Whitefield area in the mid-1840s

entirely resolved. In so doing, particular consideration has to be given to three criteria, namely the age of weavers; the sort of fabrics they wove; and the type of environment in which they lived. Admittedly, these criteria can be more convincingly applied in some instances than in others; elderly people living in remote country districts and described as silk weavers would more probably have been hand weavers than, say, middle-aged people recorded as cotton weavers who lived on the outskirts of a major town. Nevertheless, the use of the criteria enables quite accurate single-figure estimates of hand weavers to be obtained, despite the inadequacies of occupational recording. This is especially the case with regard to the 1851 census entries and to rural districts.

## 4 Reliability of occupational recording

Using mid-Victorian census schedules to determine hand weaver totals brings problems other than that of dealing with undifferentiated weavers. They arise because occupational entries are sometimes open to misinterpretation and from the possibility that details of occupation were not always correctly recorded by the enumerator, not least because of difficulties encountered in obtaining the required information.

The interpretative problems stem partly from the practice of recording jobs under the heading 'rank, profession or occupation'. One result is that enumerators listed not only individuals who actually were handloom weavers, but also others who appeared to have had only a tenuous association with the trade. They mainly comprise those given as 'handloom weaver's wife' and as 'formerly handloom weaver'; both descriptions apparently deal with status rather than occupation. Conceivably, the wives of hand weavers played some part in their husbands' work, if only on an irregular basis. They would plainly have been in a better position to do so than wives whose husbands worked in factories, say. Possibly, too, former hand weavers, nearly all of whom were elderly people in their seventies and eighties and whose regular working life was apparently over, may have continued to help out as occasion demanded. In terms of their overall contribution, however, the case for including either group in the hand weaving labour force does not appear strong and both are omitted from the census counts.

Another group to be excluded, though not a numerous one, comprises those given as 'pauper hand loom weaver'. Again, most were elderly, but no mention is made that they actually worked. Some were enumerated amongst the inmates of workhouses and may have been incapable of work. Others, though, lived at home and could have received out relief as an earnings supplement. This may have been the case at Tottington, near Bury, where, in the 1851 census, details were recorded of the weekly poor relief given to several hand weavers and to people in other occupations.[42] Most were elderly and the sums they received — mainly 1/6d per person — were modest. Whether such relief constituted the only source of income in such cases is uncertain, but since part of their income may have been earned, this group of paupers cannot be safely excluded from the hand weaving labour force.

Further uncertainty in interpreting occupational detail arises because enumerators were not required to enter every job entry in full. Instead, they frequently used the abbreviated form 'ditto' when recording apparently identical entries on successive lines.[43] In the great majority of cases their meaning is plain, because the abbreviation is written under each word, or group of words, given in the entry. Some enumerators, however, were lax in this respect. Thus, they might give the description 'Hand Loom Weaver Cotton' on one line followed by a single 'Do' — not always centrally placed — on the next. Whether this abbreviation refers to all four words is not entirely clear. The only indication that it probably does is found when the abbreviated entries reach the bottom of a page without being completed. The first entry on the following page is almost always written in full and is usually identical with that which gives rise to the abbreviation. Fortunately, the inconsistent manner in which abbreviations were used occur too infrequently to bring serious difficulties. If anything, it leads to the number of hand weavers being slightly overstated in the census counts.

One other interpretative problem, as P. M. Tillott points out, results from the failure amongst enumerators to state whether an occupation was followed full-time or part-time, or whether a person was unemployed.[44] Though it does not always apply, Tillott's point has especial relevance as far as hand weaving is concerned.[45] This is partly because the trade was largely domestic, thereby providing numerous opportunities for those who did not require full-time employment. Prominent amongst this group were married women with families. It is also because the census records of hand weavers were gathered when their trade was in long-term decline. Consequently, some of those listed as handloom weavers may have been redundant and would have given handloom weaving as the trade at which they last worked. Only those temporarily unemployed, perhaps through a short-term trade recession, would have remained part of the hand weaving labour force.

In deciding how many hand weavers who had permanently left the trade might still have been listed in the census entries, several considerations are important. One is the general level of economic activity. In each mid-Victorian census year, this was relatively high.[46] No doubt the hand weaving trades shared in the resulting prosperity and the workforce enjoyed quite full employment. Consequently, there would have been a limited number of unemployed hand weavers for the census enumerators to record. In fact, few instances of them doing so occur. One can be found at Croston in 1851, where, in the district concerned, only three unemployed hand weavers were given out of the 126 listed.[47] There is no way of knowing, of course, whether all unemployed hand weavers were included, or of how typical this situation was. Secondly, long-term unemployment in handloom weaving would not be expected to have occurred in those districts where appreciable numbers of young people continued to enter the trade. Yet, many such districts were to be found in mid-nineteenth century Lancashire, even though they became increasingly fewer during the 1850s and 1860s.[48] Thirdly, it seems that a high proportion of the census hand weavers produced either specialist cotton cloths, cloths composed of mixed yarns, or silk cloth.[49] In the production of these fabrics, the powerloom made slower progress than in the manufacture of plainer and coarser grades of cotton cloth. For this reason alone, there would still have been a substantial demand for handloom weavers during the middle decades of the nineteenth century, albeit a diminishing one as the powerloom gradually took over. The possibility that the census enumerators did list some redundant handloom weavers cannot be entirely discounted, but it does not seem probable that the numbers involved would have formed a high proportion of the whole.

As far as the accuracy of occupational recording is concerned, several points must be considered. Amongst them is that of deciding how far the enumerators themselves were guilty of error. Unfortunately, little evidence is available by which to judge. There is nothing to indicate, for instance, whether enumerators faced with listing large numbers of people — often well in excess of a thousand — made more mistakes than those who dealt with only a few hundred. Nor can it be shown whether rural enumerators achieved greater accuracy than their urban counterparts, despite, in general, having less to record and, perhaps, being better acquainted with families they surveyed.[50] Yet to assume that enumerators were faultless in recording occupations is to ignore realities. In the first place, they certainly made some mistakes through over-zealous use of the ditto abbreviation, leading, on occasions, to children as young as four or five years of age being given as hand weavers. Secondly, error could well have arisen when contending with omissions and suspected inaccuracies in householders' returns, as also with poor handwriting. As a rule, the enumerators of the returns studied remained silent on the nature and extent of such problems, but anxieties were occasionally voiced. For example, the 1861 enumerator at Rivington, near Chorley, encountered several setbacks in completing his schedules. He reported that one head of household, a woman aged seventy-four, forgot to give information about her son-in-law and her lodger. Again, people in another household in his district were away when he tried to deliver their schedule, though they had returned by census night. He observed, too, that of the sixty-eight schedules he collected, he had to fill up or amend half, presumably, as instructed, by questioning heads of household.[51] Rather more disconcerting was the experience of Francis Leary, one of the 1871 enumerators for Clayton-le-Moors, near Blackburn. To his dismay, not only were many of the schedules he delivered torn up, but others were burned by children! He also declared that he had found difficulty because some houses were 'oddly built' and without numbers and because many householders were out at work when he called. Undeterred by these difficulties, he made a second round of visits to seek the information he wanted. As a result, he 'omitted none nor lost any' of his schedules, he claimed.[52] No doubt the type of experiences recounted by these men were not uncommon. Whether every enumerator shared their apparent diligence in trying to ensure full and accurate schedule entries remains unknown, however.

In general, not much alteration of the enumerators' entries was undertaken by district registrars or superintendent registrars. This could indicate a high degree of accuracy amongst the enumerators; equally, it could show that the registrars were not usually in a position to make any appreciable amendments, beyond those arising through arithmetical error. Sometimes, though, they added useful detail. One example occurred in the returns for Ribchester, near Blackburn in 1851. For two districts, the letters 'HL' were inserted above entries concerning 'weavers of cotton'. Judging from the handwriting, the enumerator himself seems to have been responsible for the additions in one of the districts, but in the other they appear to have been made by the sub-registrar.

It is evident that the mid-Victorian census enumerators in Lancashire achieved much detailed and careful recording of occupations, even though their standards showed some variation. As far as weaving is concerned, their main shortcomings appear to have been through omission rather than through inaccuracy; all too often, they did not draw the distinction between hand and power weavers and they neglected to mention the type of fabric being woven. This is the more disappointing in view of the stress placed by the census authorities on creating not only a complete and accurate record of occupations, but also one based on a 'uniform plan'.[53] In this they patently failed, at least with regard to the weaving trades.[54]

### Notes

1   E. Higgs notes that much more extensive questions relating to occupations were asked in 1831 than previously, with seven economic categories being distinguished for males aged twenty and above (E. Higgs, *Making Sense of the Census*, 1989, p. 7).

*The last shift*

2   D. Hogg, *A History of Church and Oswaldtwistle*, 1760–1860 (1971), pp. 46–7.

3   *PP*, 1844 (587) XXVII, p. 174. Of this total, only about one-third were female. In the major hand weaving towns of Bolton and Blackburn, female hand weavers barely exceeded 500, compared with 4,450 males.

4   W. Farrer and J. Brownbill, *A History of the County of Lancaster* (1908), vol. 2, p. 332.

5   In 1851, only thirteen people were listed as cotton weavers at Prescot (J. A. Williams, 'A local population study at a college of education', *LPS*, 11, 1973, p. 36). At Poulton-le-Fylde, all hand weavers had disappeared by 1851 (D. Foster, 'Poulton-le-Fylde: a nineteenth century market town', *THSL&C*, 127, 1978, p. 91).

6   In the event, partial searches of the 1861 schedules for Manchester and several adjoining townships (Hulme, Salford, Chorlton-on-Medlock, Ardwick and Pendleton) were undertaken. This is because, in each case, searches soon revealed that weavers of any type were not numerous and of those that are recorded, relatively few were over the age of forty or wove cloth other than cotton. The indications are, therefore, that, at the most, a few hundred hand weavers would have remained in each of these districts. The total population of these towns and the size of the sample taken, given as a percentage, are as follows: Manchester 185,410 (7 per cent); Hulme 68,433 (17 per cent); Salford 71,002 (10 per cent); Chorlton-on-Medlock 44,796 (18 per cent); Ardwick 21,757 (33 per cent); and Pendleton 20,900 (25 per cent).

At Blackburn, Preston, Wigan, Chorley, Over Darwen and North Meols, only the areas where hand weaving was concentrated were searched in the 1871 schedules. This was also the case at Burnley in 1861. Some hand weavers, therefore, may have been missed, though numbers cannot have been large.

For the most part, districts where hand weaving had probably died out, or nearly died out, at the time of a census were excluded from subsequent counts. Several of these areas are shown in Table 5.1. They also include Heap (Bury) and Habergham Eaves (Burnley) from 1861 and Tottington (Bury) from 1871. In each of these areas, lack of differentiation makes it virtually impossible to identify surviving hand weavers. This is also true at Rochdale in 1861. Here, more cotton weavers aged forty and over (many in their forties) were recorded in 1861 than 1851, suggesting that hand weaver numbers had risen. More probably, though, the number of power weavers over forty years of age had become an increasing proportion of the whole. Accordingly, the 1861 cotton weavers were discounted. At Ormskirk, only about half of the 1871 schedules could be found.

7   For one example, see J. G. Timmins, 'Handloom weavers' cottages in central Lancashire', *Post-Medieval Archaeology*, 13 (1979), p. 257.

8   M. Anderson, *Family Structure in Nineteenth Century Lancashire* (1971), p. 26.

9   See p. 98.

10  J. Foster, *Class Structure and the Industrial Revolution* (1974), p. 294.

11  *PP*, 1835 (341) XIII, QQ.1, 741–4.

12  E. Butterworth, *A Statistical Sketch of the County Palatine of Lancaster* (1841), p. 99.

13  S. Bamford, *Walks in South Lancashire and Its Borders* (1972 reprint of 1844 edition), p. 64.

14  C. Aspin (ed.), *Manchester and the Textile Districts in 1849* (1972), p. 83.

15  Manchester Statistical Society, *Condition of the Working Classes, in an Extensive Manufacturing District in 1834, 1835 and 1836* (1838) see tables I and V.

16  Aspin, *op. cit.*, p. 73.

17  See pp. 99–100.

18  J. Black, *A Medico-topographical, Geographical and Statistical Sketch of Bolton and Its Neighbourhood* (1837), p. 53.
19  G. T. Clark, *Report to the General Board of Health ... of the Borough of Wigan* (1849), p. 8.
20  J. T. Jackson, *Housing and Social Structure in mid-Victorian Wigan and St Helens* (unpublished PhD thesis, University of Liverpool, 1977), pp. 57 and 61.
21  That four looms per domestic shop was common, see Timmins, *op. cit.*, pp. 266-7.
22  Examples are given in the instructions to enumerators, including 'Hand Loom Weaver (Silk)'. See *PP*, 1851 (1,339) XLIII, p. 6.
23  *PP*, 1833 (690) VI, QQ.11,341 and 11,837.
24  See p. 162.
25  Those of 1851 are from Todmorden (districts 4-6); Blackburn (1N and 1G); Burnley (6M and 6N); Leyland (4B-4F); Atherton (1C); and Walton-le-Dale (1A). Those of 1871 are from Chorley (11); Oswaldtwistle (13); Little Marsden (9); Farington (9); and Lower Darwen (28).
26  For evidence that this may have been the case generally with factory workers, see Anderson, *op. cit.*, pp. 26-7.
27  See, for example, J. H. Clapham, *An Economic History of Modern Britain*, 1 (1967 reprint of 1939 edition), p. 554 and J. Lown, *Women and Industrialisation; Gender at Work in Nineteenth Century England* (1990), p. 20.
28  Aspin, *op. cit.*, p. 92.
29  *PP*, 1850 (745) XLII, pp. 462-3.
30  In ED 1I, for example, fifty-one powerloom weavers of wool are given and just three wool weavers. However, cotton power weavers were more numerous than wool power weavers in mid-nineteenth century Rochdale.
31  B. R. Mitchell and P. Deane, *Abstract of British Historical Statistics* (1962), p. 185.
32  *PP*. 1840 (220) XXIV, p. 590.
33  It was not woven much by this date, however.
34  This was because the process involved raising loops in the warps, a technique which could not be mechanised. For further details, see W. P. Crankshaw, 'Famous Bolton cotton fabrics', in *Industrial Bolton: The Crompton Centenery Supplement to the Textile Manufacturer* (1927), p. 35.
35  *Ibid.*, p. 37.
36  W. Wilkinson, 'Powerloom Developments', *Journal of the Textile Institute* (Special Issue, 1927), pp. 136-8; T. W. Fox, *The Mechanism of Weaving* (1922), pp. 104-5; C. Singer, *et. al.*, (eds.) *A History of Technology*, V, (1958), p. 579; G. Greathead, *A Study of Handloom Weaving Decline in the mid-19th Century* (unpublished MA thesis, 1986), p. 34.
37  D. A. Farnie, *The English Cotton Industry and the World Market, 1815-1896* (1979), p. 282.
38  See J. G. Timmins, *Handloom Weavers' Cottages in Central Lancashire* (1977), pp. 48-56.
39  J. Lunn, *Leigh* (n.d.), p. 262.
40  T. Counsell, *Mellor in Blackburnshire* (1929), p. 141.
41  D. H. Longton, *A History of the Parish of Flixton* (1989), p. 122.
42  Tottington Lower End Census Returns, 1851, EDs 2E and 2F.
43  In this practice they were encouraged by the census authorities, if only for recording surnames (*PP*, 1851, 1339, XLIII, p. 36).

**44** P. M. Tillott, 'Sources of inaccuracy in the 1851 and 1861 censuses' in E. A. Wrigley (ed.), *Nineteenth Century Society* (1972), p. 117.

**45** Enumerators sometimes record unemployed people and, in later censuses, half-timers.

**46** In 1851, the cycle was moving from the trough of 1848 to the major peak of 1854 and in 1871 was approaching the next major peak of 1872. As for 1861, the peak had already occurred in 1860, but the trough was not reached until the following year. See D. H. Aldcroft and P. Fearon (eds), *British Economic Fluctuations* (1972), p. 97 *et seq.*

**47** Croston Census Returns, 1851, ED 4a.

**48** See p. 121.

**49** See pp. 135–42.

**50** Of course, the task of the rural enumerators was more onerous than that of their urban colleagues because of the time taken to distribute and collect schedules from scattered houses and farms.

**51** Rivington Census Returns, 1851, ED 2.

**52** Clayton-le-Moors Census Returns, 1871, ED 1.

**53** *PP*, 1851 (1339) XLIII, p. 36.

**54** Their failure has been attributed to inadequate guidance given to enumerators, the emphasis being on recording detail of landed and professional people and people outside the labour market. See W. A. Armstrong, 'The census enumerators' books: a commentary', in R. Lawton (ed.) *The Census and Social Structure* (London, 1978), p. 28.

# Appendix A3
# STATISTICAL TECHNIQUES

## 1 Sampling

Where infinite populations are concerned, the sample size or fraction (n) is calculated by means of the formula:

$$p(1-p)\left[\frac{1.96}{r}\right] \qquad (a)$$

where p is the proportion of a particular item in the total population and r is the stated degree of error within which the proportion lies. The formula gives a result at the 95 per cent confidence limit.

The formula may be restated to calculate the degree of error:

$$\pm 1.96\sqrt{\frac{p(1-p)}{n}} \qquad (b)$$

For finite populations, a correction factor is incorporated into the formula.

$$n = \frac{\left(\frac{1.96}{r}\right)p(1-p)N}{N-1+\left(\frac{1.96}{r}\right)p(1-p)} \qquad (c)$$

N equals the total population size. Restated to give the degree of error, the formula is:

$$r = 1.96\sqrt{\frac{P(1-p)}{n}\left(\frac{N-a}{N-1}\right)} \qquad (d)$$

### (a) Parish register samples

The average number of marriages recorded in the Manchester registers is 1,523 for the quinquennium 1813–17 and 1,869 for that of 1818–22. A pilot sample taken from the 1813

## The last shift

register suggests that the proportion of weavers amongst the total number of bridegrooms was around 25 per cent. Using (c), the formula for a finite population, the sample sizes required to check the accuracy of this estimate at several different levels of error may be calculated. Since the anticipated weaver proportion is quite high, the sample sizes needed to achieve any given degree of error are comparatively large. Thus, taking the 1813–17 population total of 7,615, to work at the 2 per cent error level requires a sample size of 1,456; at 3 per cent of 724; and 4 per cent of 425. At 2 per cent, therefore, nearly one in five of the 1813–17 entries must be sampled and the saving in time and effort compared with exhaustive analysis does not seem worthwhile. With a 3 per cent error level, however, a far more manageable sample of one in ten can be taken, which still gives a fairly high degree of accuracy.

Samples of 145 entries are taken for each year of the quinquennium (724 divided by 5). On this basis, the annual average proportion of bridegroom weavers works out at 24 per cent for 1813–17 and 20 per cent for 1818–22.

These figures may be fed into formula (d) in order to calculate the precise degree of error arising. For the 1813–17 data this works out at 3.0 per cent and for 1818–22 it is 2.8 per cent. For the first quinquennium, therefore, the number of bridegroom weavers is estimated to be 1,828 (±228) and for the second to be 1,819 (±261).

Because the parish register records were numbered more or less consecutively, it is possible to take random samples.

### (b) Census samples

Details of the samples taken from the 1851 and 1861 censuses are given below. Because infinite populations are involved, formulas (a) and (b) may be used.

At Ashton-under-Lyne only about 25 per cent of the 1851 census schedules have survived and at Manchester about 55 per cent. There is also a shortfall of about 10 per cent at Oldham. How far the results achieved at Ashton and Manchester are representative of the situation more generally in each town is impossible to know.

| Year | Town | Weaver percentage | | Total population | Sample size |
|---|---|---|---|---|---|
| | | (a) hand | (b) power | | |
| 1851 | Ashton-U-Lyne | – | 12.2 (±10) | 12,300 | 41 |
| 1851 | Oldham | 0.6 (±1.2) | 6.6 (±3.8) | 47,073 | 167 |
| 1851 | Bury | 1.2 (±0.9) | 10.0 (±2.6) | 25,484 | 508 |
| 1851 | Manchester | 1.5 (±1.5) | 3.8 (±2.3) | 105,579 | 264 |
| 1851 | Gt Bolton | 4.9 (±1.7) | 3.0 (±1.4) | 39,923 | 609 |
| 1861 | Bolton | 3.5 (±1.9) | 4.1 (±2.1) | 68,483 | 341 |
| 1851 | Wigan | 4.4 (±2.1) | 4.1 (±2.0) | 31,941 | 363 |
| 1861 | Wigan | 2.5 (±1.8) | 1.8 (±1.5) | 37,265 | 286 |
| 1851 | Preston | 4.1 (±2.0) | 12.4 (±3.4) | 69,542 | 370 |
| 1861 | Preston | 1.9 (±1.6) | 15.7 (±4.3) | 80,440 | 268 |
| 1861 | Blackburn | 1.8 (±1.6) | 16.8 (±4.4) | 62,552 | 279 |

## Statistical techniques

As explained in Appendix A2, the samples are worked at the 2 per cent level of error and at the 95 per cent confidence limit. They are also geared towards calculating proportions of handloom weavers rather than of powerloom weavers. This makes little difference when the proportions are similar, as at Wigan and Great Bolton. However, where they differ appreciably, the degree of error within which the power weaver proportions lie rises somewhat, as at Bury and Preston. In effect, the sample sizes are too small to find numbers of power weavers using this level of error.

Individuals in census enumerators' schedules are not separately numbered, so that systematic samples have to be used. The main problems arising in taking them are repetition of pages in microfilm copies; the inability of some enumerators and even registrars to sum page totals correctly; and coping with the occasional missing pages. Checks are frequently required to deal with the first two problems, whilst numbers recorded on missing pages are determined from the summaries at the front of each set of enumerators' schedules.

### 2  Regression analysis

Feeding the raw data on father and bridegroom weaver proportions for each quinquennium into Minitab, the following regression equations are obtained:

$$\begin{aligned} 1813\text{–}17 \quad & C1 = 1.68 + 0.851\ C2 \\ 1818\text{–}22 \quad & C3 = 3.66 + 0.809\ C4 \end{aligned}$$

C1 and C3 are father weaver proportions and C3 and C4 are bridegroom weaver proportions.

The standard deviation of the earlier data set is 3.3 and of the second 3.4. Only two sets of variables in each data set are distinguished as unusual variations, namely those from Newchurch-in-Pendle and Middleton. This may reflect the strength of local Nonconformity at Newchurch, where the marriage register recorded a far higher weaver proportion figure than the Anglican baptism register. The opposite may be true at Middleton, though the area was a major centre of handloom weaving and may, therefore, be expected to have contained a strong element of Nonconformists.

### 3  Parish register accuracy

Assuming a random distribution of marriages, the probability (Pr) with which a given number of marriages per month is likely to occur is given by the following formulas:

$$\text{Pr (0 in a month)} = e^{-\mu}$$
$$\text{Pr (1 in a month)} = \mu e^{-\mu}$$
$$\text{Pr (2 in a month)} = \frac{\mu^2 e^{-\mu}}{2!}$$
$$\text{Pr (3 in a month)} = \frac{\mu^3 e^{-\mu}}{3!}$$

where e is the exponential function and $\mu$ is the average number of marriages per month.

Estimates obtained by this means may be compared with the observed number of months in which particular numbers of marriages occur. Chi-squared tests may then be applied to assess the statistical significance of the comparisons.

## The last shift

To illustrate the approach, the data from Penwortham marriage registers may be used. Here, recorded marriages averaged 2.55 per month between 1813–22. Data for nine years (108) months is available.

|  |  |  | Expected no. of months | Actual no. of months |
|---|---|---|---|---|
| Pr (0 in a month) | = e | = 0.0781 | 9 | 11 |
| Pr (1 in a month) | = 2.55e | = 0.1992 | 22 | 33 |
| Pr (2 in a month) | $= \dfrac{2.55e}{2!}$ | = 0.2539 | 27 | 16 |
| Pr (3 in a month) | $= \dfrac{2.55e}{3!}$ | = 0.2158 | 23 | 14 |
| Pr (4 in a month) | $= \dfrac{2.55e}{4!}$ | = 0.1376 | 15 | 16 |
| Pr (5 or more in a month) | = by subtraction | = 0.1154 | 12 | 18 |

If the observed frequencies are denoted by 0 and the expected frequencies by E, the significance of the relationship between the two sets of figures may be assessed, making use of the Chi-squared tests.

$$= \frac{(O - E)}{E}$$

For the above data,

$$= \frac{(11 - 9)^2}{9} + \frac{(33 - 22)^2}{22} + \frac{(16 - 27)^2}{27} \cdots = 17.01$$

Using tables, the critical values are 9.49 at the 5 per cent level; 13.28 at the 1 per cent level; and 18.47 at 0.1 per cent level. Thus, there is a significant disagreement between the data sets at the 1 per cent level. This is also true of the data for Croston. It must be stressed that this does not necessarily indicate that these registers were inaccurately kept. The disagreement may result from a lack of randomness in the marriage register entries, a function of their seasonal nature.

Similar tests carried out with marriage entries from the registers at Prescot, Rainford, Christ Church, Liverpool and Newchurch-in-Pendle produced no significant disagreement between the observed and theoretical data. There is no reason to suppose, therefore, that these registers were inaccurately kept.

# INDEX

Abbot, John, cotton manufacturer, 155–6
Accrington, 37, 41–2, 44, 53, 109, 112
agriculture, 2, 3, 5, 25, 46–51, 71–8, 134, 135, 163
Aikin, John, 48, 71–2, 76, 79–81
Alston, John Anderton and John, 170, 175
Altham, near Accrington, 37, 44, 109, 112
Anderson, M., 165
Arkwright, Richard, 9, 71
Ashton, T. S., 7
Ashton-under-Lyne, 37, 80, 92, 98, 101, 108, 109, 111, 112, 116, 171
Ashworth, Henry and Edmund, cotton factory owners, 22, 92, 94–5, 170
Ashworth, James, woollen manufacturer, 100–1
Astley, near Leigh, 46
Atherton, 138
Aughton, 44

Babbage, Charles, 161
Bacup, 74, 171
Baines, Edward, 19, 25, 26, 80–2, 101–2, 118–19, 137
Balderstone, near Blackburn, 63, 133
Bamber Bridge, 96
Bamford, Samuel, 132, 158
bandannas, 139
Bannister and Eccles, cotton manufacturers, 63

Barber, Robert and Thomas, powerloom patentees, 19
Barrowford, 96, 99, 131, 132, 158
Bashall, William, powerloom manufacturer, 176
Bates, Jamieson & Co., Mexico, 178
Bedford, Leigh, 113
bed quilts, *see* quilt trade
Berg, M., 119, 156
Binns, J., agriculturalist, 77–8
Black, James, social researcher, 100, 141
Blackburn
 dandy looms, 160
 handloom manufacturers, 155–6, 171–2, 175
 handloom weavers, 26, 37, 41, 43–5, 75–6, 100, 109, 111, 112, 113, 116, 117, 133–4, 171
 handloom weavers' cottages, 39, 53, 55, 60, 63, 65, 82
 hand woven cloths, 79, 81, 92, 93, 102, 141
 powerloom weaving, 22, 101, 116, 155, 170
 road improvements, 58
 working capital provision, 59
Blackley, Manchester, 132
Blacko, near Colne, 87
Blaug, M., 29, 148

245

## Index

Bolton
  dandy looms, 159–60
  handloom manufacturers, 155, 170–3, 176–7
  handloom weavers, 26, 30, 37, 41, 42, 43–5, 102–3, 108, 109, 111, 112, 113, 116
  handloom weavers' cottages, 82, 86, 99–100
  hand woven cloths, 24, 29, 31, 75, 79–80, 81, 94, 96, 137, 141
  humidity levels, 51–2, 57
  poor relief, 165
  powerloom weaving, 22, 101, 116
  trade, 92, 94, 96
Bolton, Little, 134, 172
Bowland, Forest of, 31, 47, 50, 59
Brandwood, James, builder, 53–4, 56, 58, 82, 85
Brennan, James, hand weaver, 98
Bretherton, near Leyland, 114, 115
Brierley, James, cotton manufacturer, 59
Brigg, M., 49
Briggs, Edward, handloom manufacturer, 156
Brindle, near Chorley, 46, 82, 83, 114, 115, 133, 142, 162, 164
Brody, Hugh & Sons, handloom manufacturers, 172
building societies, 58–9
Burnley
  handloom manufacturers, 171
  handloom weavers, 26, 37, 44, 45, 72, 112
  handloom weavers' cottages, 53
  hand woven cloths, 79, 81
Bury
  agriculture, 46, 72
  handloom manufacturers, 170, 171
  handloom weavers, 37, 41, 44, 45, 98, 109, 112, 116, 117
  hand woven cloths, 80, 81
  powerlooms, 22, 101, 116
Butterworth, Edwin, local historian, 102, 137–8, 142

Butterworth, John, 72
Bythell, D., 7–8, 10, 21–2, 23, 25, 30–1, 41, 75, 78, 95, 96, 101, 107, 110, 118, 120, 123–4, 129, 137, 151, 152, 154, 155, 156, 157, 159–60, 163

caddow counterpanes, *see* quilt trade
Cairns, John, handloom manufacturer, 174–5
calico production, 40, 79, 81, 82, 92, 95, 96, 101–2, 140, 141, 159
Canada, 178
canals, 58
carding, 18, 131
Cartwright, Edmund, 19
Catling, H., 40
Catlow, Samuel, handloom manufacturer, 173
Chadderton, near Oldham, 138
Chadwick, Edwin, 92
Chadwick, John, silk handloom manufacturer, 173
Chapman, S. D., 32
Chapman, S. J., 10, 73, 107, 157
checks, 79, 131, 142, 176–7; *see also* ginghams
Cheshire, 101
Chorley
  handloom manufacturers, 171, 172, 173, 174–5
  handloom weavers, 26, 45, 111, 160
  handloom weavers' cottages, 63–4
  hand woven cloths, 81, 92, 96, 97
  powerlooms, 101, 102
Chorlton, 164
Church, near Accrington, 38, 44, 109, 112
Church, R., 8
Clapham, J. H., 6–7, 10, 29, 39, 74, 75, 118–19, 157
Clarkson, L. A., 48
Clayton-le-Woods, near Chorley, 114
Clitheroe, 38, 44, 82, 86, 109, 112, 161, 171
coal mining, 46, 134
Collison and Watson, cotton mill owners, 81

246

# Index

Colne
  handloom manufacturers, 171
  handloom weavers, 26, 38, 43, 44, 45, 92, 103, 109, 111, 112, 115–16, 122
  handloom weavers' cottages, 53
  hand woven cloths, 79, 81, 86, 139–40
  land inheritance, 49
  migrants, 50
  population, 41
colonies, handloom weavers', 36, 53, 59–60, 117, 185
Cope, Thomas, silk weaver, 137
corduroys, 80
cottages, handloom weavers', 39, 52–6, 58, 59–66, 72, 73–4, 76, 117, 185
cotton industry
  development of in Lancashire, 78–88
  fine and fancy branches, 11, 39, 51, 75, 92, 93, 94, 96, 101, 103, 128, 132, 140, 141–2, 146, 149–50, 151, 178, 186, 187
  impact of trade fluctuations, 92–7
  mechanisation, 18–23, 42, 147–50, 157–9
  plain branches, 24, 101, 159, 176
counterpanes, *see* quilt trade
Coventry, 175
Crafts, N. F. R., 1–2, 3, 5
Crankshaw, W. P., 24
Crawford, Robert, 99, 160
Critchley, Armstrong & Co., handloom manufacturers, 173
Croasdale, Benjamin, handloom improver, 160
Crompton, Samuel, mule inventor, 9
Crook, Henry, silk handloom manufacturer, 173
Croston, 47, 93, 114, 115, 119, 120, 140–1, 142
Crouzet, F., 2, 31
Cuerden, 114–15
Culcheth, near Warrington, 49, 138
Cunningham, H., 118

Dall, John W., cotton spinner and manufacturer, 174

dandy loom, 39, 152, 159–60, 187
Daniels, G. W., 73–4, 76
Darwen, 40, 77–8, 79, 81, 92, 133, 139, 171, 175
Darwen, Lower, 84, 85, 123
Deane, Bolton, 38, 44, 46, 109, 112
Deane, P., 2
Denton, near Manchester, 171
Dickinson, William, handloom manufacturer, 172
Dickson, R. W., 77–8
Didsbury, Manchester, 171
dimities, 79, 80, 81
Dinckley, near Blackburn, 63
dobby, 24, 150
Dodd, W., 132
Downham, near Clitheroe, 38, 44, 109, 112
dressing machinery, 19
Droylsden, Manchester, 138
Dukinfield, near Ashton-under-Lyne, 98, 101
Dutch loom, 18
Dutton, near Ribchester, 133

earnings, hand weavers, 129–35
East Bolton, 38, 44
Eccles, near Manchester, 38, 41, 43, 44, 108, 109, 111, 112
Eccleston, near Chorley, 114, 121
Eden, F. M., 72, 76
Edgworth, near Bolton, 58
Edwards, M. M., 59, 78–9
Egerton, near Bolton, 22, 92, 94, 170
Ellison, T., 27, 28, 29–30
Engels, Friedrich, 53, 132
English, W., 19
Entwistle, near Bolton, 142

factory industry
  design of premises, 184
  earnings of child workers, 130–1
  employment of former hand weavers, 161–2, 167
  employment of hand weavers' children, 133–4

## Index

hand weavers' objections, 169–70
reasons for development, 4
transfer of hand weaving firms, 155–6, 170–1, 173–5
Failsworth, near Oldham, 111, 138
Farington and Cuerden, near Preston, 114
Farnie, D. A., 24, 31, 51, 52, 149, 155
Feilden, William, cotton mill owner, 81, 155
Feinstein, C. H., 2–3
Fielden, John, factory owner, 161
finishing trades, 9, 40–1, 42, 57, 59, 131, 161
Fisher, James, cotton manufacturer, 175
flannel, 81, 97, 136
flax, 21
Fletcher, Joseph, hand weavers' commissioner, 163
Fletcher, T. W., 46
Flixton, near Manchester, 38, 43, 44, 47, 109, 112, 119, 142
fly shuttle, 18
footwear industry, 7, 8, 131
Foster, J. F., magistrate, 137
Foulridge, near Colne, 119
Freckleton, near Preston, 173
Freeman, T. W., H. B. Rodgers and R. H. Kinvig, 52
fustians, 13, 20, 25, 36, 71, 78, 79, 81, 88, 102, 136
Fylde area, 38, 43, 44, 47, 48, 80, 173

Gandy, G. N., 49
Gardner, Robert, cotton spinner and manufacturer, 92, 100, 102–3
Garstang, 38, 44, 82
Gaskell, Peter, surgeon, 72–6, 161, 162
Gatrell, V. A. C., 154, 155
Gibbs, H. S., 159
ginghams, 81, 96, 102, 129, 130, 142, 170, 174
Glossop, 159
Great Harwood, near Blackburn, 60, 63, 78
Greathead, G., 24

Gregs of Styal, cotton spinners and manufacturers, 22, 161, 162, 170, 174
Grime, James, handloom manufacturer, 175
Grimshaw, James cotton spinner and manufacturer, 25, 26, 27, 96, 99, 131, 158
Grimshaw Park, Blackburn, 75–6
Guest, Richard, 25, 26, 28, 39, 147
Gullickson, G. L., 48

Habakkuk, H. J., 3–4, 23, 150–1, 152
Hammonds, J. & B. L., 6–7
handkerchiefs, 81, 139, 177
Hargreaves, James, inventor, 9
Harling, William, handloom improver, 160
Harrison, J. F. C., 153
Harwood, Bolton, 122
Haslingden, 26, 38, 43, 44, 74, 79, 81, 82, 109, 112, 171
Henderson, Gilbert, poor law assistant commissioner, 99
Heskin, near Chorley, 114
Heywood, Robert, cloth finisher and handloom manufacturer, 155, 159, 176–7, 178
Heywood, near Bury, 101
Hickson, William, assistant handloom weavers' commissioner, 53, 72, 93, 103, 166, 168, 176
Higham, near Burnley, 72
High Crompton, near Oldham, 158
Higher Booths, Rossendale, 160
Hindley, near Wigan, 138
Hitchen, Jonathan, muslin and cotton manufacturer, 100, 172
Hoghton, near Preston, 114, 115, 119, 120, 133, 166
Holcombe, near Bury, 165
Hollins, W., and F. Hyde, powerloom patentees, 159
Hoole, near Preston, 47, 114, 142
Horn, P., 119
Horner, Leonard, factory inspector, 21, 132, 156

248

# Index

Horrocks & Co. of Preston, 64, 96, 129, 142, 173, 175
Horrocks, William, cotton manufacturer, 19
Horwich, near Bolton, 60, 61, 62
Hudson, P., 154
humidity, 36, 51–7, 82, 86
Hutton, near Preston, 173
Huyton, near Liverpool, 44
Hyde, near Manchester, 101
Hyde, F., *see* Hollins, W., and F. Hyde

Irish, in textile districts, 25, 163

Jacquard loom, 133, 139, *see also* dobby
jenny, spinning machine, 9, 18, 73, 99
Jones, S. R. H., 4–5, 139, 150
Joyce, P., 31

Kay, James Phillips, doctor, 95
Kay, John inventor, 18
Keighley, Yorkshire, 18
Kennedy, John, factory owner, 25, 26, 27, 39
Kenworthy and Bullough, powerloom improvers, 23, 96, 149, 157
King, W., 50
Kingan, John, muslin manufacturer, 169
Kirkham, near Preston, 38, 43, 44, 45, 46, 77, 80, 82, 109, 112, 160, 171, 173

Lancaster, 22, 38, 44, 45, 82, 101
Landes, D., 6
Leeds, Yorkshire, 161
Leeming, Richard, handloom manufacturer, 174
Leigh, 38, 41, 43, 44, 46, 47, 79, 81, 102, 109, 112, 137–8, 171
Lennon, John, handloom weaver, 99, 161, 163
Leyland, 47, 101, 114, 122, 142, 171, 173
linen, 25, 72, 78–9, 80, 81, 82, 136, 142, 161
Liverpool, 44, 45, 52
Livesey, Blackburn, 172
Livesey, Joseph, teetotal pioneer, 41, 76

Lloyd-Jones, R., 23, 40, 154
London, 7, 8, 59, 138, 176–7
Longridge, near Preston, 59, 173, 174
Longson, William, handloom weaver, 53, 99, 163
Lowton, near Leigh, 138
Lune Valley, 38, 44
Lyons, J. S., 6, 31, 75, 95, 96, 120, 122, 129, 133, 134, 142, 149, 151, 153, 155, 156, 157, 161, 173

Macclesfield, Cheshire, 133, 137, 139, 176, 177
McKenzie, Kenneth, fancy gingham manufacturer, 174
Makin, John, textile manufacturer, 99–100
Manchester
  child factory workers' earnings, 134–5
  cotton production, 79, 81, 101
  handloom weavers, 38, 41, 43, 44, 45, 47, 51, 73, 92, 93, 98, 102, 109, 111, 116
  handloom weavers' colonies, 63
  handloom weavers' earnings, 129, 130–1, 132
  linen production, 78
  powerloom weaving, 22, 101, 116
  silk hand weaving, 137–8
  size of cotton firms, 154
  visits by textile entrepreneurs, 58
  warehouses, 23, 173
Margerison, Martin, handloom manufacturer, 175
Marsden, R., 31, 149, 157–8, 178
Marsden, Richard, handloom weaver, 162
Marsden, William, cotton manufacturer, 174
Marshall, J. D., 50
Marshall, John, flax manufacturer, 161–2
Mawdesley, near Chorley, 93
Maymon, Ephriam, cotton manufacturer, 59
Mellor, near Blackburn, 60, 110, 140, 160, 177
Mellor, near Stockport, 72, 79
Mexico, 178

Middleton, 38, 43, 44, 71–2, 80, 81, 102, 109, 111, 112, 115–16, 132–3, 137, 138, 171, 173
Miles Platting, Manchester, 129
Miles, W. A., assistant handloom weavers' commissioner, 158–9
Milnrow, near Rochdale, 46
Mitchell, B. R. and P. Deane, 29
Mokyr, J., 5
Morgan, N., 63–4
mousseline-de-laine, 102, 132, 139–40, 170, 173, 177
Much Hoole, near Preston, 119, 120
Muggeridge, Richard, assistant handloom weavers' commissioner, 140, 161, 165, 168, 169, 177
mule, spinning machine, 9, 18, 40
Murray, N., 12, 39, 111, 118–19, 120
muslins, 24, 40, 79, 80, 81, 82, 100, 102, 113, 137–8, 141, 169, 170, 174–5, 178
Musson, A. E., 31

nankeens, 80, 81, 131, 170
Needham, Richard, handloom weaver, 26–7, 99, 100, 161, 162, 163
Newchurch-in-Pendle, 38, 43, 44, 109, 112
Newchurch-in-Rossendale, 38, 44, 74, 109, 112, 171
New Eagley, near Bolton, 22, 94
North Meols, 38, 43, 44, 46, 57, 77, 109, 112, 139
Nova Scotia, Blackburn, 75–6

O'Brien, P. and C. Keyder, 2, 3, 5
Ogden, W. H., 51–2, 56–7
Oldham
  cotton production, 81
  farmer/hand weavers, 72
  fustian weaving, 80, 102
  handloom weavers, 38, 41, 43, 44, 45, 92, 100, 109, 111, 112, 116, 117
  powerloom weaving, 101, 116
  silk weaving, 97
O'Neil, John, diarist and hand weaver, 158, 161

Ormskirk, 38, 44, 45, 80, 82, 109, 112, 139, 171, 173
Osbaldeston, 63, 123, 133

Padiham, near Burnley, 26, 27, 38, 44, 76, 100, 109, 112, 171
Parkinson, Robert, cotton manufacturer, 170, 175
Parkinson, William, handloom manufacturer, 172
Pearson, S., 46
Pemberton, James, cotton manufacturer, 155
Pendle area, 31, 46
Penwortham, 38, 43, 44, 47, 76, 109, 111, 112, 114, 122, 142
piecers, 131, 135
Pilkington, Bury, 117–18
Pilling, William, handloom weaver, 99, 100, 161, 162, 163
Pinchbeck, I., 122–3, 151, 152
pirn winding, 117
Pleasington, near Blackburn, 63
plush, silk, 139
Pollard, S., 31
Porter, J., 50
powerloom
  costs, 153–5
  early development, 18–20
  earnings from working, 130–2
  investment, 12, 17, 31, 35, 86, 93, 96, 111, 135, 173, 174, 175, 176, 185
  location, 21–3, 42, 98, 99, 100, 101–2, 108, 113, 114–17, 121–2, 138, 140, 141, 142, 174
  technical improvement, 19, 23, 146, 147–50, 157–60
  use in non-cotton production, 24, 27, 110, 178
Prescot, 38, 44, 45, 82
Prest, J., 175
Preston
  coach traffic, 58
  cotton production, 79, 81
  earnings of handloom weavers, 129, 165
  fancy trades, 92

250

## Index

handloom manufacturers, 171, 173, 175
handloom weavers, 38, 41, 44, 45, 99, 101, 109, 111, 112, 116, 177
handloom weavers' colonies, 63–4
handloom weavers' cottages, 39
powerloom weaving, 96, 116, 142
Prestwich, near Manchester, 38, 43, 44, 109, 112
printing trade, cotton, 40, 79, 81, 92, 161
proto-industrialisation, 12, 35–6, 46–51

quiltings, Marseilles, 80
quilt trade, 24, 31, 81, 92, 96, 100, 129, 131, 141, 155, 156–7, 159, 170, 176, 177, 178

Radcliffe, near Bolton, 171
Radcliffe, William, 18–19, 72, 73, 79
railways, 94
Ramsbottom, 171
Ramsbottom, Jonathan & George, cotton manufacturers, 160
Ramsgreave, near Blackburn, 63
Reach, Angus Bethune, journalist, 133, 134–5, 137, 138, 139, 176, 177
Ribble Valley, 22, 31, 43, 110, 111, 121–3, 133, 134, 141
ribbons, *see* smallwares
Ribchester, near Blackburn, 38, 43, 44, 60, 109, 110, 111, 112, 171, 174, 175
Rishton, near Blackburn, 60, 63
road improvements, 58
Rochdale
  handloom manufacturers, 170, 171
  handloom weavers, 38, 41, 43, 44, 45, 100, 109, 111, 112, 116
  powerloom weavers, 116, 174
  types of hand woven cloth, 80, 81, 97
roller temple, 23, 149
Rose, M., 5
Rose, S., 5
Rossendale, 31, 46, 48, 50, 52, 58, 72, 74, 100–1, 160
Rostow, W. W., 7
Rufford, near Southport, 44
Rule, J., 31

Rumworth, near Bolton, 122
Russia, 157

sack cloth weaving, 173
sail cloth weaving, 25, 80, 82, 159, 173
St. Helens, 52
St. Michael's-on-Wyre, near Garstang, 38, 44, 109, 112
Salesbury, near Blackburn, 63, 119, 120, 121, 134
Salford, 98, 137
Samlesbury, near Preston, 63, 111, 114, 115, 119, 120, 121, 142, 174
Samuel, R., 4, 6
Sanderson, M., 152
sarcenets, 95, 96, 139
satin, 136, 139
Saul, S. B., 3
scavengers, 131
Schmiechen, J. A., 7, 8
Scotland, 12, 36, 39, 111, 118, 169
Scott, John, handloom weaver, 169
sheetings, 159, 176
shirtings, 24, 101, 159, 176
silk trade
  domestic loomshops, 86
  former cotton hand weavers, 11, 128, 185
  handloom weavers' earnings, 130, 132–3
  handloom weaving, 103, 110, 136, 137, 187
  location, 80, 92, 97, 102, 113, 173
  powerlooms, 20, 21, 150, 158–9
  products, 139, 140–1, 142, 177
slasher-sizing, 149
Smalley, John, cotton manufacturer, 59
smallwares, 18, 101
Smelser, N., 29
Smith, George, cotton spinner and manufacturer, 25, 26, 27, 30, 39, 163
Smith & Wiseman, handloom manufacturers, 132
Southport, 43, 51, 56, 57; *see also* North Meols
spinning trades
  capital, 101

251

*Index*

domestic production, 25, 72, 74, 99
earnings, 130
firms, 22, 81, 154, 170, 174
growth, 23, 184
productivity, 40–1
technical development, 9, 18, 73
water-powered mills, 57
Spitalfields, London, 138
Stalybridge, 80, 81, 98, 101
Standish, near Wigan, 38, 44, 109, 112
steam-power, 1, 2, 4, 6, 7, 94, 147, 148, 149, 162, 164, 166, 174
Stockport, 19, 72, 73, 79, 99, 101, 103
stripes, 176–7
Styal, Cheshire, 22, 170, 174
Swain, J., 49

tapes, *see* smallwares
Tarleton, near Southport, 38, 44, 109, 112
Taylor, A. J., 22, 29, 30, 101, 164
Taylor, W. C., 101
thicksets, cotton, 80
Thomas, James, calico printer, 86, 161
Thompson, E. P., 151, 153
Tockholes, near Blackburn, 46, 63, 133
Todmorden, 26, 101, 161
Tootal, Broadhurst & Lee, handloom manufacturers, 173
Tottington, near Bury, 46
Toxteth Park, near Liverpool, 44
Toynbee, A., 7
Trawden, near Colne, 140
Tufnell, E. C., 174
Tunzelmann, G. N. von, 3, 148–9, 152
Tupling, G. H., 46, 48, 49, 50, 74
Turner, John, handloom weaver, 129
Turton, near Bolton, 53, 54
Twiss, Travers, political economist, 168
Tyldesley, near Bolton, 80, 171

Ulnes, Walton, 114, 115
United States of America, 3, 4, 93, 97, 148, 178
Ure, A., 161

Valentine, Foster & Haworth, 158

velvets, 80, 82

Wadsworth, A. P. and J. de Lacy Mann, 49, 74–5, 78
waistcoats, 177
Walton, J. K., 49, 50
Walton-le-Dale, near Preston, 38, 41, 43, 44, 76, 109, 111, 112
warehouses, 23, 58, 117, 160, 173
warpers, 172
warping, powered, 49
Warrington, 38, 43, 44, 45, 46, 52, 57, 80, 82, 101, 109, 112
water power, 18, 22, 57, 164, 174, 184
Watson & Co., cotton spinners, manufacturers and printers, 79
weft stop motion, 23
welts, 177
Westhoughton, near Bolton, 46, 138, 173
West Riding, 2, 53, 154
Whalley, near Blackburn, 38, 44, 109, 112, 171
Wheelton, near Chorley, 119, 120, 122
White, G., 159, 160
Whittaker, Joseph, handloom manufacturer, 175
Wigan
  cellar loomshops, 63
  dandy looms, 160
  early cotton mills, 79
  handloom manufacturers, 171
  handloom weavers, 26, 38, 41, 44, 45, 93, 100, 109, 112, 116, 122, 134
  powerlooms, 101, 116
  types of cloth produced, 81
Wild, M. T., 11
Williamson, J. G., 3
Williamson, O. E., 4
Wilpshire, near Blackburn, 63
Winstanley, David, schoolmaster, 118
Winwick, 38, 44, 109
Wood, G. H., 28 29, 111, 132, 148
wool trade
  handloom manufacturers, 170
  handloom weaving, 25, 100, 136
  location, 78, 79, 80, 81, 86, 88, 97

*Index*

powerloom weaving, 20, 21, 24, 154, 158–9
Worsley, near Manchester, 171
worsted goods, 20, 79, 86, 136, 140, 154, 155, 159

Wrigley, A. E., 11
Wuerdale and Wardle, Rochdale, 174

Yorkshire, 21, 155; *see also* Keighley, Leeds, West Riding